DOG COMPANY

COMPANY

A True Story of American Soldiers Abandoned by Their High Command

LYNN VINCENT
AND
CAPTAIN ROGER HILL

CENTER
STREET

New York Nashville

Center Street
Hachette Book Group
1290 Avenue of the Americas, New York, NY 10104
centerstreet.com
twitter.com/centerstreet

First published in hardcover and ebook in April 2017.
First Trade Paperback Edition: May 2018.

Center Street is a division of Hachette Book Group, Inc. The Center Street name
and logo are trademarks of Hachette Book Group, Inc.

The publisher is not responsible for websites (or their content) that are not owned
by the publisher.

The Hachette Speakers Bureau provides a wide range of authors for speaking events.
To find out more, go to www.HachetteSpeakersBureau.com or call (866) 376-6591.

Library of Congress Cataloging-in-Publication Data has been applied for.

ISBNs: 978-1-4555-1623-0 (trade paperback), 978-1-4555-1625-4 (ebook)

Printed in the United States of America

LSC-C

10 9 8 7 6 5 4 3

To our fallen

CONTENTS

FOREWORD

I first had the honor of meeting Captain Roger Hill in April of 2016, when the hardcover edition of *Dog Company* was released. Tall, commanding, and yet soft spoken, Roger exuded a humble confidence that I could tell made him a great leader.

I remember sitting in my radio studio completely stunned and outraged by what Roger was telling me: He learned that spies were working at Forward Operating Base Airborne, his combat post in Wardak, Afghanistan. Roger's higher command ignored his repeated warnings about these infiltrators. Finally, upon learning of an imminent attack on Airborne, Roger and his first sergeant, Tommy Scott, took matters into their own hands. What happened next will shock you, anger you, and inspire you.

The actions taken by Roger, Tommy, and the men of Dog Company undoubtedly exemplify the Army's Warrior Ethos:

I will always place the mission first.
I will never accept defeat.
I will never quit.
I will never leave a fallen comrade.

And yet—somehow—their own leadership failed to recognize this. As a result, these leaders subjected Roger and his men to a type of persecution that has become all too common: young soldiers put through hell in the military justice system while the enemy goes free.

Dog Company is a clarion call to our nation's military leaders and federal bureaucrats. The United States needs to focus less on winning "hearts and minds" and more on winning wars. This book is a powerful reminder that if we are committing our brave men and women to war, we must commit them with the intention of actually *winning* the war. The United States cannot send our warfighters to bleed and die for our country if we are not willing to support them in the life-and-death calls they make while fighting an enemy that neither wears a uniform nor adheres to the law of armed conflict.

Under the leadership of President Donald Trump and Defense Secretary James Mattis, the rules of engagement are beginning to change. But this new culture will last only as long as the current administration unless it is made permanent with formal legislation. Today, Roger and his coauthor, Navy veteran Lynn Vincent, are focused on fighting for that legislation. As Roger and Lynn advocate for troops already wrongfully accused of war crimes or rules of engagement violations, they hope to team with U.S. lawmakers to create permanent legal protections for future generations of American warriors.

I'm humbled to have had the opportunity to get to know Roger and Lynn over this past year, and I'm honored to recommend this book to anyone seeking the truth about the legal abuse of soldiers and Marines. I'd like to thank these authors for fighting to tell the truth, no matter the cost.

Sean Hannity
New York City
March 2017

AUTHORS' NOTE

What you hold in your hands is a book the government does not want you to read.

We know this because the Department of Defense spent a year throwing spike strips in our path to publication.

The Pentagon does not want you to read about its catch-and-release detention system that allows the same enemy fighters to ambush, bomb, and shoot at America's sons and daughters over and over again.

The Pentagon does not want you to read about unworkable rules of engagement that tie our troops' hands behind their backs while sending them to fight against an enemy that has no such rules.

The Pentagon does not want you to read about a system in which young soldiers are court-martialed, kicked out of the service, or even imprisoned, while enemy spies who kill Americans are set free.

Dog Company tells the story of one Army unit's tragic experience with all those evils. But Dog Company, a unit of the famed 101st Airborne, is not alone. Her story is being replayed again and again in a lawyered-up war in which, the enemy leverages our rules of engagement by blending into the local population while our warriors, operating in a combat environment, are held not just to the laws of armed conflict but to unprecedented standards of *criminal* law. Senior civilian and uniformed leaders allow our soldiers and Marines to be tried and convicted for war crimes when, in bygone eras, their actions, motivated by the desire to protect their mates, would have been viewed as collateral damage in the fog of war.

The military prison at Fort Leavenworth, Kansas, is the next assignment for these young Americans, whose battlefield judgment is second-guessed by lawyers who have never been under fire, and a military-diplomatic mind-set that elevates enemy lives over American lives.

As you read this, one young officer is serving a nineteen-year sentence at Leavenworth. His crime? He ordered his soldiers to fire on three riders who were speeding toward his platoon on a single motorcycle. The officer was convicted of murder and attempted murder, though it later came to light that the assailants were registered in U.S. databases as known enemy fighters—a fact the prosecution failed to disclose. The case is now on appeal.

Dog Company exposes such systematic persecution of America's soldiers and Marines, nearly powerless against a system bent on labeling them for the rest of their lives, all in the name of placating enemy actors who have sworn to eradicate the United States in the name of tribe and jihad.

That's the story the military doesn't want you to read.

We, the authors, used to work for the Department of Defense (DoD). Roger Hill served more than ten years in the Army. Lynn Vincent served eight years in the Navy. Lynn held a Secret security clearance while on active duty; Roger held a Top Secret clearance.

Today, we are veterans and patriots. That is why, throughout the writing of this book, we were careful to omit or "write around" any material that might be considered classified or a threat to national security.

But that was not enough for the Pentagon.

In March 2015, we submitted the manuscript to the DoD's Office of Security Review (OSR)—a condition of the nondisclosure agreement Roger signed in connection with receiving his Top Secret clearance. The OSR website says that a security review—that is, screening a manuscript for material that is classified or represents a threat to national security or troops in-theater—takes about thirty days. Our book was a bit long, OSR said, so we could expect to receive it back in two months.

Four months later, the manuscript you now hold came zinging back via email—*riddled* with censored material, under the dark black bars known as "redactions."

Two things surprised us. First, the sheer number of times the Army had blacked out information. There were scores of redactions, and if you count items redacted multiple times, hundreds.

Second, we were surprised at the type of information the Army censored from public view.

While we could concede that a handful of items that we had not considered problematic could be construed as sensitive, we believed—and could prove—that more than 90 percent of what the Army redacted was not only already public information, *but information already made public by the government itself.*

Okay, we thought. This is all probably just a mistake—bureaucratic bungling, or maybe an overzealous second lieutenant armed with a Sharpie.

We decided to remove without question those sensitive items the Army identified. For redactions that were already public information, we prepared a detailed appeal, itemizing the sources of our data.

To evaluate our conclusions, we retained attorneys specializing in military intelligence and information security, as well as a former Army intelligence officer who now works in the private sector as a military security expert.

In September 2015, we sent our appeal—with confidence. Surely when Pentagon reviewers saw that the information they redacted was already available on multiple federal websites and in print publications, they'd agree to reverse those redactions.

This time, we waited five months.

On January 19, 2016, we received our answer from Michael Rhodes, director of the Office of the Deputy Chief Management Officer at the Pentagon:

"The DoD conducted a thorough review of the authors' supporting documentation and proposed rewrite of the pages identified in the appeal letter. The amendments identified during the initial review of the manuscript are affirmed in their entirety. The DoD does not approve the rewrite or any of the submitted alternative language in the appeal submission."

Translation: "We reject your appeal. All of it."

Minds. Blown.

Why on earth would the Pentagon forbid us from publishing material that it had already made public? Why would the government not concede even a single redaction, such as those blacking out common military weapons and operations, or terms used in the news media every day?

In retrospect, perhaps we should not have been surprised. In December 2008, officers of the 101st Airborne tried to shield the case at the center of this book from FOIA—the Freedom of Information Act. They didn't want anyone to learn about this story at all, and they tried to prevent the American public from its rightful access to documents at the heart of the case.

Fast-forward seven years: The FOIA dodge didn't work, so the Army tried to gut the book. In case that sounds like hyperbole, consider this: In two of three cases, the government censored events in the manuscript that expose the catch-and-release, revolving-door system of prisoner detention that puts American soldiers and Marines at constant, unnecessary risk of injury and death.

While the Pentagon's spike-strip review process delayed this book by two years—and nearly derailed it altogether— here it is, *Dog Company: A True Story of American Soldiers Abandoned by Their High Command*.

To get the book to press, we left the redactions in. We trust that you, the American reader who cares about our men and women in arms, will be able to fill in the data the government hoped would remain shrouded in black.

Because many of the men in this story are now out of the Army, they are able to speak freely. But other soldiers and Marines face similar persecution, often under gag orders from their higher commands, as they fight a military justice system in which the deck is stacked against defendants.

Supreme Court Justice Louis Brandeis said that sunshine is the best disinfectant. We hope that *Dog Company* sheds light on an unintended consequence of the Terror War: the sacrifice of the American soldier on the altars of careerism and enemy appeasement.

> Lynn Vincent and Roger Hill
> San Diego, California, and Atlanta, Georgia
> November 2016

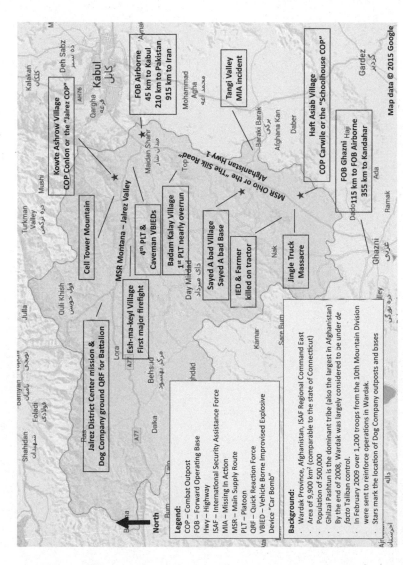

Action in Wardak Province, Afghanistan, 2008

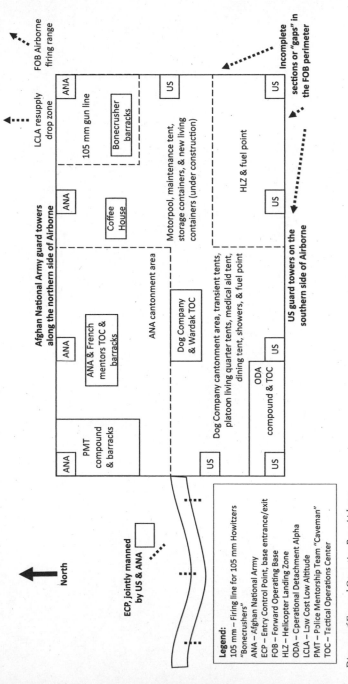

North

Afghan National Army guard towers along the northern side of Airborne

FOB Airborne firing range

LCLA resupply drop zone

ANA

105 mm gun line

Bonecrusher barracks

US

ANA

Coffee House

Motorpool, maintenance tent, storage containers, & new living containers (under construction)

US

HLZ & fuel point

US

Incomplete sections or "gaps" in the FOB perimeter

ANA cantonment area

ANA

ANA & French mentors TOC & barracks

Dog Company & Wardak TOC

Dog Company cantonment area, transient tents, platoon living quarter tents, medical aid tent, dining tent, showers, & fuel point

ODA compound & TOC

US

US

US guard towers on the southern side of Airborne

PMT compound & barracks

ANA

US

US

ECP, jointly manned by US & ANA

Legend:
105 mm – Firing line for 105 mm Howitzers "Bonecrushers"
ANA – Afghan National Army
ECP – Entry Control Point, base entrance/exit
FOB – Forward Operating Base
HLZ – Helicopter Landing Zone
ODA – Operational Detachment Alpha
LCLA – Low Cost Low Altitude
PMT – Police Mentorship Team "Caveman"
TOC – Tactical Operations Center

Diagram of Forward Operating Base Airborne

BOOK I

Insider Threat

Boy, the enemy is inside your wire.

U.S. Army Colonel Dave Brostrom,
speaking to his son, Lieutenant Jonathan Brostrom, May 2008

CHAPTER I

14 August 2008
Forward Operating Base (FOB) Airborne
Wardak Province, Afghanistan

THE PHONE CALL was one Lieutenant Larry Kay would always remember, not for its content but for its consequence. Sergeant Raul Lopez, the platoon sergeant at Sayed Abad Base, coming through his cell: "The CLP didn't bring any food and water with them this time, sir."

The CLP—Combat Logistics Patrol.

Lopez paused for emphasis, then said: "Sir, I am *black* on food and water."

An epithet shot through Kay's mind. Black on food and water? How could soldiers in the most powerful fighting force ever to march on the face of the earth not have food and water?

But Kay kept these thoughts to himself. Most of the time, being Delta Company's executive officer (XO) was great; other times, being an enlisted Marine had been better. At least then, he could vent aloud about this kind of insanity. Something along the lines of *Those CLP guys are a waste of the entire macroevolutionary process.* That would have been perfect.

Instead, he said to Lopez, "Okay, I'll get some supplies down to you ASAP. Is there anything in particular you want?"

"Yeah. Hot dogs and some of those blueberry sausage-stick things we eat for breakfast."

"Not a problem. I'll try and be down there tomorrow."

"Okay, sir. Thanks a lot."

Kay didn't hang up the phone but thumbed the Talk button, waited for a fresh dial tone, and punched in the number for Forward Support Company at 1st Battalion headquarters in Ghazni Province, about three hours south. As the ringtone whined in his ear, the red heat of righteous anger crept up his neck.

Stocky and barrel-chested with huge arms, Kay, twenty-three, fit the dumb-jock mold from a distance. But as soon as he opened his mouth, you found out a couple of things right away: One, he had a razor-sharp intellect and an astonishing knowledge of politics, religion, and culture. And two, he was utterly incapable of bullshit. If Kay perceived dead weight in his own ranks, he would unapologetically say so. The way he saw it, his men would literally die if they didn't get proper logistics support, and he had zero tolerance for sectors of the Army that weren't working twenty-hour days to support the tip of the spear.

Finally, a voice came through the telephone line. "Forward Support Company, Lieutenant Taylor."

Kay unloaded. "What the hell is going on over there, Josh? My guys at Sayed Abad are black on food and water! How can the CLP forget to bring food and water?"

But Taylor knew nothing. It wasn't his fault, but it still pissed Kay off. It wasn't the first or even the dozenth time Delta Company—call sign "Dog Company"—had been shorted on supplies. But this screwup wasn't over sleeping cots or spare vehicle parts. It was over basic essentials for staying alive.

At the daily synchronization meeting that evening, Dog Company commanding officer Captain (CPT) Roger Hill folded his six-foot-three frame into a plastic chair at the end of a conference table, picked up a pen, and set his ears on *listen*. There was a lot to discuss. Since Dog Company took over Forward Operating Base (FOB, pronounced "fob") Airborne in Wardak Province, Afghanistan, Taliban aggression had heated from a simmer to a rolling boil. That had been six months ago, in March 2008. Since then, fully one-third of Hill's men had been wounded in action. Suicide bombers had hit a 4th Platoon gun truck just a few days before. Mercifully, the bomb failed to detonate on impact.

Dog Company had suffered no fatalities yet. But Hill's vehicles were in shambles, repair parts, ammo, and batteries were in short supply, and the number of replacement soldiers he'd received from Battalion was exactly zero. Hill's heavy weapons platoons—1st through 4th, just over sixty men—were now spread across four static outposts. His platoon sergeants, veterans with multiple combat tours and more than fifteen years' service each, said they had never seen a company stretched so thin.

Now in the synch meeting, Kay, the platoon leaders and platoon sergeants weighed in on a series of briefing items: Intel updates, upcoming missions, personnel status, base security, and progress in developing the provincial government. Logistical issues such as vehicle readiness, weapons, fuel, ammo, food, and water were also covered.

Hill, thirty, a West Point grad with a degree in environmental engineering, was an organized man. At the beginning of the Wardak deployment, he'd run each of these daily meetings personally, using a printed, bullet-point agenda. But as his men learned what was expected, Hill had let Kay take over as master of ceremonies while he listened and jotted notes.

Near the end of the meeting, Kay brought up the Sayed Abad supply snafu, winding up with, "Lopez and his guys are black on food and water."

"Battalion didn't bring *food and water*? What the hell?" said Lieutenant (LT) Donnie Carwile, 3rd's platoon leader. Formerly enlisted, Carwile, twenty-nine, had put himself through college while working as a policeman in Oxford, Mississippi, then returned to the Army as an officer.

Similar incredulous curses sizzled around the conference table like sparks on a fuse. Hill glanced up at his mission board. He tried to keep it meticulously current, but with the spiraling operational tempo, it stayed stubbornly out of date. He was glad it was dry-erase.

"We're about two weeks past due for some vehicle and equipment checks at Sayed Abad," Hill said. "If we have to go down there with food and water, we may as well knock those out, too."

He tapped 3rd Platoon for the job.

15 August 2008, 0600 Hours

The next morning dawned a scorcher, and Sergeant First Class (SFC) Shon Haskins cursed the heat. It would be 110 degrees in full kit by lunch. Haskins, thirty-six, a wily 260-pound bruiser out of Mattawa, Washington, was platoon sergeant for Dog Company's 3rd Platoon. He marshaled his men and checked his Humvees. Haskins would ride in the lead truck, call sign 3-1, with Specialist (SPC) Joel Ochoa in the gun turret. (The call signs for Humvees in a heavy weapons platoon begin with the platoon number; the second number varies according to mission and personnel.) Also in 3-1:

Khan, a young Afghan interpreter who reminded Haskins of a college kid from the '80s, all polo shirts and skinny jeans. Once, when he was a boy, the Taliban caught Khan listening to "infidel" tunes and sentenced him to walk his village wearing a sign around his neck that proclaimed his shame.

Haskins's best friend and platoon leader, LT Donnie Carwile, would ride in 3-2, second in the order of movement, with SPC Paul Conlon as gunner and SPC Joseph Coe driving. Back in June, Conlon, twenty-one, of Mashpee, Massachusetts, had taken heavy shrapnel wounds during a vicious firefight. This trip to Sayed Abad was his first chance to get back into the field with his platoon brothers, and he was pumped.

Coe, twenty-four, and Sergeant Todd Parsons, a forward observer, were sitting in 3-2, engine running, when an officer they'd never met approached. "Hey, I'm Captain LeMaire, Alpha Company. I'm going to be riding with you guys."

"Okay, sir," Coe said. "Hop in."

At noon, the patrol rolled out. Four Humvees rumbled through the FOB gate, the lead truck towing a trailer stacked with cartons of food and bottled water for the guys at Sayed Abad.

In 3-2, Carwile rode TC, or truck commander, sitting in the front passenger seat with an ever-present wad of dip in his lip. "Hey, anybody got a spit bottle?"

"Hold on a second," Coe said. Driving with his left hand, he whirled the cap off a bottle of Cool Blue Gatorade with his right, downed the whole thing, and handed the bottle to Carwile. "There you go, sir."

"Thanks, brother."

Coe steered the Humvee past the village of Maidan Shar, Wardak's provincial capital, which lay just outside FOB Airborne's gate. Then he bumped the truck from dirt to pavement and turned south on Highway 1. The road was a main transportation artery linking the city of Kandahar in the south with Kabul, Afghanistan's capital city, an hour north of FOB Airborne.

On Google Maps, this slice of east-central Afghanistan looked like a crumpled brown paper sack with handfuls of moss sprinkled on it for relief. Up close, it didn't look much different, at least along this stretch of Highway 1. Dusky green scrub dotted thirsty plains that marched away to mountains the color of dust.

Riding third in the order of movement in HQ-6 (Headquarters Six), LT Larry Kay could see August heat shimmering on the highway, arguably the infrastructural centerpiece of the U.S.-led counterinsurgency. The security of Highway 1 was Dog Company's primary mission. Were the road to fall to the Taliban, the loss would cripple the Afghan government, cutting off the supply of food, oil, and gas.

Two years earlier, in 2006, NATO had made history, assuming control of the International Security Assistance Force (ISAF) in Afghanistan. It was NATO's first-ever operational commitment outside Europe. That same year, ISAF took over command of international military forces from the Americans. At a NATO summit, Secretary General Jaap de Hoop Scheffer set for Afghanistan a target date of 2008 for "a more stable political architecture... with a strong interface between NATO and the civilian agencies, and effective, trusted Afghan security forces gradually taking control."

Now it was late summer of 2008, President Hamid Karzai was in charge of the country, and Kay didn't think Scheffer was going to make his goal. What he had seen on the ground—corruption, infighting, and a general lack of will to win—did not match the shiny oratory emanating on the global stage.

The patrol moved into a long, flat-floored valley veined with wadis, natural tear ducts in the earth that channeled down rainwater from the mountains. Where the wadis intersected the highway, culverts burrowed underneath. Kay thought "highway" was a pretty glorious name for the piebald patchwork of third world wannabe asphalt cobbled together in haphazard shapes of black, brown, gray. The irony was that American taxpayers paid millions to have Afghan contractors pave the road, then paid millions more to have it repaired after Afghan fighters blew it up, killing U.S. soldiers with pressure-plate IEDs (improvised explosive devices.) Worse: U.S. soldiers had to provide security for the Afghan contractors to repair the road so that Afghan fighters could turn around and blow it up again.

Another insane calculus of the counterinsurgency, Kay thought, right up there with forgetting to bring his soldiers food and water. Kay kept an eye on his Blue Force Tracker, a GPS-enabled display that provides battlefield and personnel data. Friendly forces appear as blue icons, hostile forces as red.

When the patrol had moved about twelve kilometers south of Airborne, Kay's driver, Specialist Eric Westerhaus, guided HQ-6 toward a dust-swept Afghan National Police (ANP) station. When Kay noticed that there were no ANP guarding either the station's perimeter or their assigned stretch of the bomb-cratered road, he cursed. Not ten days earlier, he, CPT Hill, and their first sergeant, Tommy Scott, had driven down this same road and found the exact same lapse in security.

The ANP were supposed to guard this and other stretches of the highway to prevent Taliban ambushes and the emplacement of IEDs, the leading cause of death among Coalition troops. The ANP's absence had infuriated First Sergeant (1SG) Scott, who leapt from the Humvee, stormed into the station, and made his displeasure known as only a battle-crusted, ex–drill instructor can. Scott's ass chewings were so thorough that he didn't even need an interpreter.

Kay glanced down at the ███████████████ and noticed that the Airborne Tactical Operations Center (TOC, pronounced "tock") had just issued a warning:

> Be on the lookout for a small arms ambush in the vicinity of Haft Asiab Village.

The village was on the way to the convoy's destination, Sayed Abad. These little nuggets of intel usually trickled in from sources U.S. forces had established among the Afghan population. Since Dog Company landed in Afghanistan, a steady stream of rockets, IEDs, and full-blown firefights had established a kind of intel algorithm: eight out of ten times, the sources were right.

Kay keyed up the net and passed the data to his gunner, Sergeant (SGT) Andrew Doyle, and the rest of the crew, and knew that each of the other TCs was doing the same. The convoy's gunners were already locked on, but the update made them cradle their heavy weapons a little tighter.

The patrol rolled past the ANP shack, and Kay thought the Afghan police inside were lucky SOBs: If Tommy Scott had been in the truck, he would've demanded the convoy stop so he could get out and enlighten the guys inside with another vintage Army ass chewing on the topic of abandoning one's post. This pleasant image had just finished playing in Kay's head when, up ahead, the road underneath Carwile's Humvee erupted.

CHAPTER 2

KAY SAW THE blast before he heard it: The earth vomited up a massive volcano of dirt and asphalt, and all of the colors of the world disappeared in a veil of dust.

From the gun, Doyle screamed: "IED! IED!"

The explosion sucked the air from around the patrol then slammed it back down in a blast wave of sound that crashed in at the same instant Westerhaus slammed on the brakes. Kay watched in sick disbelief as Specialist Paul Conlon rocketed like a human missile from 3-2's turret, reached an apex three stories high, and plummeted back to the pavement.

Westerhaus skidded the Humvee to a halt a hundred meters from the edge of the blast crater. The smells of burning rubber and asphalt choked the air. A thousand thoughts ticker-taped through Kay's mind: *Conlon is dead. What about Donnie and the others? How many? How many KIAs?*[1]

Small arms fire peppered in from both sides of Highway 1. Doyle and SPC Joel Ochoa answered in a series of staccato bursts. Shon Haskins jumped from the lead truck and ran back toward 3-2. Weapon in hand, Kay started to join him, but the cord to his radio headset yanked him back, reminding him it was first his job to report the contact to higher.

Fingers flying, he dialed up Airborne on the TacSat, a satellite communications link.

"Wardak TOC, Dog 5! Wardak TOC, Dog 5!" As Kay yelled into his mic, he caught a glimpse of Haskins leaping into the blast crater. It was an image he would remember forever: Haskins's huge form midair, body

_____
1. KIA: killed in action.

armor flying up around his ears, exposing his belly as he jumped into the pit to aid his brothers.

The choir of American guns blasted away at ambushers on both sides of the road. Kay transmitted: "This is Dog 5! We hit an IED at Highway 1 and Durani Village! Request immediate air MedEvac, QRF,[2] and air support!"

Kay yelled the message over and over, but he was broadcasting in the blind and couldn't tell if other equipment was jamming his transmissions. His heart tried to pull his feet toward the bomb crater, but he willed himself to stand fast as his mind clicked over options for calling in essential support. He had no way of knowing whether or not his satellite comms had been received, and the convoy was currently out of range for line-of-sight transmission—

Cell phone.

Kay yanked his cell from his vest pocket. Just then, Wardak TOC came back over the net: "Dog 5, this is Dog 6. Dog 5, Dog 6, over."

In the Airborne TOC, CPT Roger Hill's heart dropped into his belly. He heard an urgency in Kay's voice that he hadn't heard since they landed in Afghanistan. He knew the worst had happened, just not who or how many.

Hill keyed his mic and kept his voice calm. "Dog 5, tell me what you got."

Kay's transmission scratched across the frequency in tight bursts: "Sir, we've got one KIA. We might have more. At least three to four wounded. Still working on that."

"Got it," Hill transmitted. "The TOC's going to work on getting the MedEvac, and I'm on my way with the QRF."

"Roger, sir."

"Dog 6 out."

As if Kay's grim report were somehow telepathic, the TOC had already drawn a crowd. The artillery platoon commander and his men rushed to draw up target reference points for enemy exfiltration routes near the patrol's location. Already kitted up, Hill grabbed fresh batteries for his field radio. Kay's words squirmed in his mind like worms: *At least one KIA...*

He snapped his chinstrap and chambered a round in his M4. "Dog 6 is moving!" he yelled over his shoulder and headed toward the TOC door.

"Sir, you're still within 105 range down there," the artillery officer, Charlie Weaver, called to Hill. Weaver pronounced it "one-oh-five," as in "105 mm artillery." Hill acknowledged with a nod then turned to see his first

---

2. QRF: Quick Reaction Force.

sergeant, Tommy Scott, filling the TOC door with his defensive-back frame. The two men locked eyes.

Usually controlled, Scott could not hide his anguished rage. "Sir, I just need to grab a radio and I'll be ready to go with you."

Hill knew Scott wanted to go after the bastards that had blown up his boys, and it killed Hill to say what he had to say next. "Tommy, you've got to stay here." He emphasized his next words gently: "The most important thing now is the MedEvac. Right now, the MedEvac is more important than getting the guys who did this."

Scott was silent. His jaw muscles clenched. Then he nodded, a quick, shallow movement. Professional. By this point in the deployment, Scott had handled MedEvacs for more than forty wounded, but no KIAs. They both knew this one had to be right.

"Dog 6 out."

As Kay registered Hill's last transmission, a fresh storm of bullets kicked up dirt around his feet. He let go the radio mic and dialed Sergeant Lopez at Sayed Abad on his cell.

"*I need you right now!*" Kay yelled. "*I got guys dead!*"

Instantly, through the phone, Kay heard Lopez yelling orders, Humvee engines roaring to life. Kay snapped his cell shut and sprinted toward the blast crater. He'd only gone thirty meters when he saw Paul Conlon lying faceup, spread-eagled, body armor blown off. His camo pants hung around his legs in tatters like a castaway's. The side of his head appeared road-rashed and dented in, but his expression was peaceful. Grief sucked the air from Kay's lungs and for an instant the rattling guns, burning truck, and shouts from the crater faded into a surreal bubble of silence.

He was only twenty-one . . .

Kay tried to blink away the image of the young man's broken body, but it would remain forever, burned into his retinas like a brand.

"Contact, left, three hundred meters!"

Doyle's warning shout yanked Kay back into the moment. He heard a bubble-wrap *snap* as a round zinged past his head, then the *smack-smack-smack* of an M240B machine gun from the trail vehicle in the patrol. To his left, giant rings of dirt blossomed near the wadis as Doyle served up MK19 grenades.

Kay raced back to his vehicle for cover as two men on a single moped broke cover and raced west, away from the highway.

Taliban spotters, Kay thought. *Fuckers probably detonated the IED with a cell-phone trigger.*

As Kay took aim across the Humvee hood and snapped off shots with his M4, an incongruent thought shot through his mind: *I've got to get home and see my wife.*

He kept firing until a Dog Company gunner's 40-millimeter grenade burst dead-on in front of the scooter, killing the spotters. Kay safed his weapon and turned his attention to the burning gun truck. He dispatched Westerhaus to aid CPT LeMaire, who was hanging out of the driver-side door murmuring incoherently like a heat stroke victim. Kay then sprinted to Carwile. Haskins had already dragged the lieutenant out of his seat onto the ground. Doc Scott, an enlisted medic, had cut away Carwile's body armor and uniform. Blood streamed from the lieutenant's right ear, and a mixture of blood and clear liquid streamed from his nose and mouth. Battery acid dripped down over his arms and torso, leaving a trail of chemical burns.

Specialists Daniel Siler and Andrew Huston knelt close as Ochoa, crying openly, cradled Carwile's head in his lap.

Khan, the Afghan interpreter, was on his knees near Carwile, screaming, arms thrust at the sky.

Doc knelt in front of Carwile and got six inches from his face. "Lieutenant! Hey, Lieutenant Carwile! Look at me, Lieutenant...I need you to look at me!"

Carwile tried. His eyes were open, but they seemed to Kay to drift in their sockets like lost ships.

"Don't close your eyes, sir!" Huston pleaded. "Just push through it...just stay with us!"

Carwile's color drained fast as shock dropped over him like a lead curtain. He coughed—a gruesome, bubbling sound—and a gout of blood spilled down his chin.

"Collapsed lung," Doc said crisply. He threaded out a spool of plastic tubing, preparing to intubate.

Carwile's body began to jerk and twitch as if attached to electrodes. Kay forced himself to look into Carwile's eyes, and was surprised when an image of Carwile's wife, Jennifer, and the couple's two little girls, flashed into his mind. He had seen them back in the States while on midtour leave. Jennifer wore a pink blouse. The girls wore matching pink dresses. Kay and his wife, Jill, visiting Jennifer in her kitchen. So normal.

Carwile's body shivered and bucked. Ochoa laid him on the ground and began mouth-to-mouth. He blew in a breath, then spit out blood, blew in a breath, spit out blood.

"It's not working, man!" Huston cried. "Let me try—"

They traded places for a few moments, then traded back again, Ochoa now bending to the task between sobs, tears streaming down over his blood-smeared chin.

Khan had collapsed on the dirt hardpack and was descending into shock. Haskins saw him, hoisted him back to his knees, and tried to soothe him. "It's going to be okay, Khan. Conlon's okay. Lieutenant Carwile's going to be okay."

Haskins then rose, grabbed Doc Scott, and whispered fiercely in his ear. "Khan's going into shock. Go over there and tell him everything's okay. I don't care if you have to lie your ass off!"

CPT Hill and Dog Company's QRF roared up in a swirl of sand and fine debris. Hill surveyed the scene and registered the damage: a massive blast crater. A knot of soldiers on the ground, working to save someone. Larry Kay walking toward him through gun smoke and the shimmer of burning fuel.

The enemy had already begun to exfil the ambush using the maze of deep wadis. Hill's driver pulled his vehicle up to the blast site as 1st and 4th Platoons' vehicle crews peeled off to form a perimeter. Sporadic small arms fire crackled in as Hill jumped down from his truck and went to meet Kay.

"Hey, sir," Kay began, but his eyes welled up and he stopped. He stanched his tears by sheer force of will.

Hill kept his voice soft. "Hey, buddy, what's going on? What do you need from me right now?" He labored to keep his eyes and attention fixed on Kay and not on the devastation all around.

Kay swallowed, steeled himself, and rattled off a complete sitrep (situation report): status on the enemy, number and type of casualties, how first aid was being rendered. A detailed triage on the injured had not yet been feasible, because the blast had thrown soldiers in so many different directions relative to the vehicle. Paul Conlon was dead, and Doc Scott was working furiously to save Donnie Carwile.

"Haskins is organizing a casualty collection point, and we need security," Kay finished. "Most of the guys are helping with CPR."

Behind Kay, Hill could see SPC Joseph Coe's lanky form lying on the other side of the Humvee. Someone had already wrapped his head in a bandage, and his dark hair poked from underneath. Ochoa was hunched over Donnie Carwile administering CPR, with Khan in hysterics nearby. In his grief, Ochoa had begun to punctuate his CPR breaths by screaming at the sky.

Hill clenched his jaws as if he could cut off the horror with his teeth. He dragged his eyes from Ochoa. "Okay, here's what we're going to do," he told Kay. "Mo and Hulburt are taking up positions on both sides of the road." Sergeant First Class Grant Hulburt was platoon sergeant for 1st Platoon, and Sergeant First Class Tim "Mo" Moriarty was acting platoon sergeant for 4th.

"MedEvac birds and CAS[3] should be here soon," Hill continued. "Let's start consolidating everybody on the LZ. Where do you want the birds to come in at?"

Kay pointed to a flat stretch of desert floor just east of the highway where Haskins was now setting up security. That would be the LZ, or landing zone.

"Got it," Hill said. "Keep doing what you were doing. I'll send this up to higher and check on our air and MedEvac."

Kay nodded and started to turn back toward the blast crater when Hill grabbed his shoulder. "Larry, you did a good job. You did a good job today."

Kay's eyes welled again and he turned away.

Hill started toward his truck then caught sight of Paul Conlon lying faceup, as though gazing at the sky. Hill flashed to a snapshot of Conlon and Carwile mugging for someone's iPhone camera: Carwile in a gray ARMY T-shirt, his arm draped around Conlon, flashing a peace sign; Conlon rocking a fake mustache, head thrown back, ripping his T-shirt apart at the neck to show off some fake chest hair he'd drawn on with a Sharpie.

Looking at Conlon now lying dead in the road was like looking at a bright light gone out forever. A phantom garrote closed Hill's throat.

Hill ran back to his truck, called in the sitrep, then sprinted to the crater to lend a hand with the casualties. Haskins had moved to get Coe and others clear of unexploded ordnance surrounding the burning Humvee. SFC Tim Moriarty—"Mo"—a buzz-cut bear of a man, was on the ground, bending to breathe life into Carwile. Now an infantryman, Mo had been a medic in the '80s and '90s. He let another soldier take over compressions on Carwile, and moved to triage the wounded.

Conlon's head wound declared he was beyond help. Mo directed some soldiers to pull Carwile near him, away from Coe, Parsons, and LeMaire. During Desert Storm, Mo had pulled dead American boys from under the tracks of Bradley Fighting Vehicles, and tended a young corporal killed by

---

3. CAS: close air support, pronounced "kass."

a mine blast to the head. He'd learned then that it was best to separate the living from the dying and the dead.

Mo knelt near Conlon and Carwile, and laid a hand on each man's head. Other soldiers saw what he was doing, gathered in a hushed circle, knelt and bowed their heads. As the first MedEvac helo thumped over the horizon, Mo began to pray: "Dear Lord, please take these fallen warriors and keep them. Be with their families now as they are about to face the most difficult times of their lives..."

One night during the initial invasion of Iraq, Mo's unit lost three men. The mother of one soldier later grieved in a blog post that her son had died alone. In a dark, lonely place with no one to pray for him. Since that day, Mo prayed for the fallen whenever he could. But he believed that mother's boy had not been alone; that God was everywhere, even in the hell of a battlefield, and that He could be seen in the actions of men.

CHAPTER 3

15 August 2008, 1400 Hours
Bagram Airfield
Parwan Province, Afghanistan

JUST OVER TWO hundred kilometers northeast of FOB Airborne, SPC Allan Moser was on his way back from chow. He wound through the rigid ranks of olive-drab tents that formed the Bagram Airfield bivouac area for transient troops. In the near distance, the mountains of the Hindu Kush raced skyward, their razored peaks smudged pink by a dusty haze.

Moser, twenty, of Post Falls, Idaho, was a squad leader in Dog Company's 2nd Platoon, the Jolly Rogers. The platoon had spent the previous six months fighting farther east, in Kapisa Province, and was transitioning back to Wardak to rejoin Dog Company on FOB Airborne. In Kapisa, Moser had taken over as a squad leader in charge of roughly half the thirteen-man platoon. This though he was only a specialist, or E-4.

A squad leader is normally a sergeant (E-5), but the Jolly Rogers were short on sergeants. To fill the gap, one had been detailed from another unit. The guy meant well and had the book smarts, but his people skills were lacking, and the job was suddenly open again. Moser got the nod and, after just eighteen months in the Army, was leading a team of 101st Airborne soldiers in combat. He couldn't have written the script any better if he'd tried.

A church youth-group kid from a refreshingly ordinary childhood, Moser had always dreamed of being a soldier. Inspired by the HBO series *Band of Brothers*, Moser wore his prized 101st Airborne T-shirt for years before he learned toward the end of boot camp that he'd received orders to the famed unit. But LT Dick Winters and his boys weren't the first to spark Moser's dream of serving in the infantry. That honor went to the Duke. Moser's mom—a cheerful, neighborhood den mother type—raised her son on John Wayne movies. Moser's favorite was *The Longest Day*, in which the Duke played Lieutenant Colonel Benjamin Vandervoort.

"You can't give the enemy a break," Vandervoort tells troops as they embark on the D-Day invasion of Normandy: "Send him to hell."

Moser joined the Army immediately after high school. During basic, when the drill instructors screamed in his face, he loved it. He loved the eye-pleasing orderliness of the barracks, the camaraderie, the drilling, even the skanky chow hall food. He missed his tight-knit family badly and hated getting "smoked" all the time with extra running and push-ups, but by the time he finished boot camp, Moser had dropped almost forty pounds: *Hell, yeah!* Then, upon graduation, he received orders to the 101st Airborne, 506th Parachute Infantry Regiment, the dream team: Double *Hell, yeah!*

Under the umbrella of the 506th, Moser was assigned to Dog Company, 1st Battalion. Now, eighteen months later, he'd been recommended twice for Soldier of the Month and was up for early promotion to sergeant. He was looking forward to rejoining Dog Company, though he would miss the amenities at Bagram. He'd had three hot meals a day since arriving—including the cheeseburger he'd just packed down at the chow hall—as well as daily hot showers. At Firebase Pathfinder in Kapisa, there had been one hot per day and a cold shower whenever he could squeeze it in.

The bivouac area was in sight of the airfield and a C-17 cargo jet landed, its turbine engines screaming as Moser threaded through the tents to the Jolly Rogers' temporary quarters. SFC David Anderson, his platoon sergeant, met him at the door.

"Get your guys," Anderson said. "I need our whole platoon here. Right now."

"Roger that, Sergeant," Moser said.

It was something bad. He knew it from Anderson's face. A few minutes later, Moser and the other squad leader had rounded up the Jolly Rogers, and they huddled in the tent around Anderson and their platoon leader, LT Mason Ward.

"I'm letting you guys know that D Co got hit," Ward said. "We don't know what platoon it was. We just know there are two KIAs, and there are three other guys who were wounded pretty bad."

A dark hush settled over the men. They looked at each other and then at the floor. Moser clasped his hands together and stared at them, his rising dread pulled along in a slipstream of names: *Was it Kamp? Or Steinle? Gibson? Or Conlon or Coe or Wilson?*...

As the faces of his eighty-nine platoon brothers ticked through his brain, Moser realized it didn't matter who it was, because he didn't want it to be anybody. While he liked some better than others, he loved every one of them, down to the last man.

15 August 2008, 1500 Hours

CPT Roger Hill sat in the TOC staring at his computer, a pall of grief encasing his body like a toxic cloud. The brotherhood Dog Company shared surpassed every expectation he'd ever had for an infantry company, stretching back to his years at West Point. Even before his arrival in the unit, its leaders had nurtured genuine concern for one another. It was a brotherhood beyond blood.

And he had failed them.

Donnie Carwile had made it onto the MedEvac bird alive but died en route to the aid station. Hill thought of Jennifer Carwile, Donnie's wife, and their girls, Reece and Avery Claire, their heartbreak. Jennifer and Hill's own wife, Lauren, had become best friends during Dog Company's garrison time at Fort Campbell, Kentucky. Both women were new to Army life and far from home, Lauren from Atlanta and Jennifer a nurse from Oxford, Mississippi. When they met, Jennifer's southern cadences had sounded to Lauren as welcoming as sweet tea.

Hill had called Lauren from Highway 1. As head of the Dog Company Family Readiness Group, she would be a key person providing aid and comfort to the Carwiles and Conlons. As he told her what he could, he sensed shock and dread coalescing in her mind. Like waking from a nightmare, but in reverse.

In some ways, it had seemed only a matter of time before she received that call. Since March, Lauren had carried a special cell phone and company call-down roster everywhere, had walked out of the classroom where she taught special needs kids; out of dinners with friends; once out of a wedding shower, to take emergency notification calls. Lauren had already passed news on more than two dozen of Hill's soldiers who were WIA, wounded in action. It had been like carrying the war in her handbag.

Now, the worst had happened.

Sitting at his desk, Hill found that his grief seemed to have actual weight, made it difficult to raise his hands to his keyboard. Willing himself forward, he opened an email from his intel sergeant, Luis Tamariz, "Taz" for short. Fourth Platoon (the Shockers) had been hit by suicide bombers a week and a half earlier. According to Taz, human intelligence sources said there were more suicide bombers coming out of the Jalrez Valley, the Taliban stronghold near FOB Airborne. A warlord named Abdul Razak, along with a man named Noor Sayed, supported by Pakistani jihadists, maintained iron-fisted control of the valley.

Hill considered where the suicide bombers might be headed. Kabul? Airborne? Or maybe another Coalition base in Wardak Province, like Sayed Abad, which sat like a catcher's mitt on the outskirts of its namesake town. He pondered how to track this new intel, especially with a key clearing operation called Nomad less than a week away.

This assignment, as a combat commander in the 1-506th (1st Battalion, 506th Parachute Infantry Regiment) had been Hill's dream. During more than ten years' service, his Army career had marched him through West Point, Korea, and the prestigious Old Guard. After a 2006 tour in Iraq, Hill had talked with Lauren about leaving the Army for a civilian career. Eight years would be a tipping point—if he was going to make a change that was the time. But when a chance arose to serve in the 506th, Hill changed his mind.

These were the Currahees—a Cherokee word that means "Stands Alone"—a unit name taken from the mountain near Camp Toccoa, Georgia, where the 101st Airborne began. This was the unit where Dick Winters and the Army's first airborne unit had made history, seizing high ground behind the Normandy beaches at the cusp of the D-Day invasion. They liberated Eindhoven during a daring daylight drop into Holland known as Operation Market Garden. In one of the most brutal winters on record and lacking cold-weather gear, medical supplies, and ammunition, they drove back a massive German panzer attack on the strategically critical city of Bastogne. The 506th had been among the first Allied units to storm Hitler's Eagle's Nest, and her commander, Colonel Robert F. Sink, accepted the surrender of the German 82nd Corps at Gestein. For its heroism in Normandy, twenty-five members of the 506th received the Distinguished Service Cross.

These soldiers past inspired soldiers present, showing personal courage so great that it became the standard by which every infantryman measures himself. Hill's men, the men of Dog Company, had measured up. Now, six months into deployment with a third of his company stricken by injury and now death, and a province to hold that equaled the size of Connecticut, it was becoming difficult to make mission. And Hill didn't have near the optimum combat power to contribute to a key operation like Nomad.

He sighed and turned his attention to the memorial service for Donnie Carwile and Paul Conlon. Normally, a company's first sergeant—in this case, Tommy Scott—would handle every detail. But Hill's experience in the Old Guard, a regiment that conducts memorials for the fallen, drove him to help in planning the service more than most commanders might have. He wanted it to be perfect. He wanted one last time to show Donnie and Paul how much they meant to him, to show their families. It crushed him that he hadn't taken the time to tell them when they were alive.

Chaplain Steve Moser had sent Hill some PowerPoint templates for memorial service bulletins. Each bulletin would include an order of service, along with bios and photos of Carwile and Conlon. Hill began to work on the bios immediately, thinking the task would keep him busy, move him forward. But as he wrote, he found himself having to refer to both men in the past tense. He stopped typing, unable to process the idea that they were never coming back—

Stop. Hill arrested his thoughts. *Focus,* he told himself. *Keep moving forward. Change tasks.*

His patrol calendar was supposed to project out at least ten days' worth of missions. With all the QRFs, patchwork manning, and last-minute patrols, it had been a week since he'd updated it. Hill walked into the empty conference room, picked up an eraser and, beginning at the top, began wiping the board clean. Then he saw it: The last entry on the board was today's disastrous mission. Hill's arm froze, and an illogical notion swept over him: To erase the mission would be like erasing Donnie and Paul.

Guilt crashed in like an avalanche. He had failed. He had not been able to protect them. He had not been able to bring them home to their families.

CHAPTER 4

15 August 2008, 1700 Hours

A CHINOOK HELICOPTER touched down in the moondust outside FOB Airborne, dispensed a dozen counterintelligence (CI) agents and support staff, then chugged away into the northern sky. The CI team leader, known only as "Dave," grabbed his duffle and led the way to the FOB gate. For the millionth time, he braced himself for the reaction of the gate guards to his unconventional-looking crew.

Dave himself sported shaggy hair, a scruffy beard, and utility civilian clothes. Every time he stood in a lineup of awardees, his staff intel officer said he looked like an air conditioner repairman. It was a perfect look for counterintel: Be forgettable or, better yet, invisible. A relatively junior agent, Dave had been perceived to color outside the lines of good order and discipline. His fondness for using the F word in government email rankled his major, for example. But he had laser-like analytic skills and did his job strictly by the book, which earned him the respect of his bosses, as well as a pass on gentlemanly manners.

A soldier driving a Gator met Dave and his team at the gate, casting a skeptical eye on their appearance, all plainclothed and anonymous looking. But they had the proper ID, so the soldier pointed the way to the TOC. Dave left his guys with stacks of tuff boxes containing their gear, and walked past plywood huts and olive-drab tents looking for the base commander, CPT Roger Hill.

Dave had studied Wardak, along with the rest of Regional Command (RC) East. The east-central Afghanistan province was 3,800 square miles and home to half a million souls. Some called it "the south gate of Kabul" because of its proximity to Afghanistan's capital city. As he headed toward the TOC, he noted the FOB's topography. The base sloped down toward Highway 1, which lay about half a click away. Beyond the highway, a gradual incline led toward the Jalrez Valley, a Taliban nesting ground.

The RC East deputy commanding general had planned a large-scale clearing operation in Jalrez dubbed Nomad. The general hoped to disrupt Taliban operations in the valley, capture enemy fighters, and net actionable intel. In the process, a participating Special Forces team hoped to certify an Afghan National Army (ANA) special ops battalion as ready to ditch their training wheels.

Dave's interest in Wardak had begun months earlier at Bagram when he learned of suspect signals in the province that fit in with another set of intel variables he'd been working on. The proximity of these signals to Jalrez Valley and Operation Nomad was serious enough that the general had sent Dave and his team to lock it down.

Dave reached the TOC, knocked on the door, and poked his head in. Whether it was a palace or a shack, his tour of the Afghanistan badlands had taught him never to walk into a commander's office uninvited.

"Come in," said a young lieutenant whose face was set in grim lines. The name "Kay" was embroidered on the lieutenant's desert-camouflage uniform. Across the room, Dave saw a captain he knew to be Roger Hill—tall, dark hair, a vaguely Asian cast around the eyes. A black soldier built like an NFL defensive back stood at Hill's shoulder. Dave glanced at his rank insignia and name: First Sergeant (1SG) Scott. From the look of it, Hill and Scott were in the middle of something serious. The first sergeant glanced up briefly, then looked away.

"I'm Dave with the Division counterintel cell," he said to the lieutenant. "We just landed. Is it possible to have a minute with your commander?"

Larry Kay's voice was flat, emotionless. "It's not really a good time. Come back tomorrow. Or the next day."

Dave remembered the general's final words to him—"Don't let my op get compromised. Hear me?"—and felt his blood pressure tick upward. In his pocket, Dave had a FRAGO, a fragmentary operations order, requiring Hill's full cooperation. But he didn't want to play that card if he didn't have to, so he struck a note between cordial and firm.

"Sir, I really don't have that kind of time," Dave said.

Kay tried not to look annoyed. "What is it then?"

"My team and I just arrived. We're here to help you with some security issues, screen some Afghan employees, that kind of stuff. Where can we put ourselves?"

Kay relented. "Look, stop back in later. We'll figure something out. There's an ODA across the FOB. Stop in there and talk to Captain B."

Works for me, Dave thought.

The ODA (Operational Detachment Alpha) Kay referred to was a Special Forces team that operated out of FOB Airborne. Dave bowed out of the TOC, crossed the FOB, and tracked down the team leader, "CPT B," who showed the CI guys a couple of plywood B-huts where they could bunk down.

When the counterintel team had settled in, CPT B pulled Dave aside. "Listen, Dog Company got hit this morning. A couple of guys got blown up just down the road a ways. A lieutenant and a specialist. Not a good day. Figured you might want to know."

Now Dave understood the cold reception at the TOC. Hill was busy dealing with casualties, and here he was with his merry band of misfits trying to get his foot in the door. He was glad he hadn't come in hot with the FRAGO.

Over his time in Afghanistan, Dave had learned that when he stepped off a bird at a combat base, he was on the commander's sovereign territory. There were entire bases in Afghanistan from which counterintel agents were banned because one of them had gotten into a chest-thumping match with a combat commander like Hill. Or worse, had gone all spooky and said something like "Sorry, sir, I can't tell you who I'm with...but you can call me Bob."

Dave's first meeting with CPT Hill and 1SG Scott hadn't gone as expected. But he and his guys could still set up shop and start working. He'd loop Hill in when it seemed appropriate.

When Dave left the TOC, LT Larry Kay was glad. He had not wanted to spare the emotional bandwidth to deal with whatever this new guy was selling. Now he returned his attention to his computer screen and checked the status on Carwile and Conlon. The bodies of both men were being flown to Bagram Airbase for their final transit home.

After the QRF cleared the rest of the wounded from the IED blast site, Hill had dispatched patrols, including a section of 1st Platoon—the Dirty First—into the nearby village of Andar to knock on doors looking for the bombers who had killed their brothers. Hill and Kay had known it might look like retaliation. But the reality was that these bastards attacked Americans then melted into the local population.

The patrol's emotion had been well beyond rage. In Andar, Grant Hulburt, 1st Platoon's platoon sergeant, teamed with SGT Jason Dudley and busted down a dozen doors without compunction. In 2006, the two men fought together at the dawn of the Surge in Ramadi, Iraq. Had cleared whole buildings—just the two of them, alone. By comparison, Andar was a nothing little village, and they moved from house to house with fluid aggression.

Five foot ten and wiry, Hulburt, thirty-seven, was old-school crusty, a dedicated chain-smoker, "motherfucker" every other word out of his mouth. He gave the impression that he had possibly never been a child but had arrived on some secret Pentagon loading dock packed in a clear case bearing a sign that read IN CASE OF WAR, BREAK GLASS.

Dudley, twenty-eight, of Plano, Texas, had earned a psychology degree before enlisting. He could have joined the Army as an officer, but he did not feel that a college degree gave him the right to lead men. That, he felt, had to be earned.

At each mud-brick *qalat* in Andar, householder males squatted with fearful women and children, and the answer was always the same: "We saw no one! No Taliban!"

By the thirteenth *qalat*, Dudley had had enough of that answer. When an Afghan male in his thirties claimed ignorance, Dudley whipped his combat knife from its sheath and began tapping its gleaming tip against his thigh. The Afghan's eyes grew wide and his story changed: "We heard the explosion," he said through Hulburt's interpreter. "We saw two men ride off on a motorcycle."

"Which way?" Hulburt said through clenched teeth.

The man pointed northwest. "Badam Kalay."

It was the village where the Dirty First had been nearly overrun by Taliban fighters a few weeks before. But further patrols to the area did not yield Carwile's and Conlon's killers.

Word of their deaths spread quickly throughout the AO (Area of Operations). Now Kay sat at his desk reading the messages of condolence that poured in. He read a note from his former company commander, CPT Spencer Wallace of Bravo Company. He opened another from Major Christopher Faber, an engineer who had served with Dog Company as operations officer from April to mid-July. Faber had been with Paul Conlon during the firefight in the Jalrez Valley that took Conlon out of the fight for a while. Conlon had earned a Purple Heart that day.

Faber's sympathy note was earnest and touching, remembering how

Conlon had been the one to care for the stray puppy Dog Company had adopted and how the Afghans had loved Carwile with his easy southern manner.

Among the messages of sympathy, however, Kay noted a glaring absence: There was nothing from Lieutenant Colonel (LTC) Anthony DeMartino, Hill and Kay's battalion commander.

Dog Company was one of five in 1st Battalion, 506th Parachute Infantry.[4] Alpha, Bravo, and Charlie were infantry "line" companies, 120 to 130 soldiers each. Line companies are the proverbial "boots on the ground." Echo was the Forward Support Company that handled supplies and logistics. Delta Company—call sign "Dog Company"—which Hill commanded, was a heavy weapons unit, about ninety men at full strength.

As 1-506th Battalion commander, Lieutenant Colonel DeMartino was Hill's immediate superior. Kay was astonished that he had thus far not acknowledged the loss of his men, especially LT Donnie Carwile, one of his officers. Kay felt DeMartino should have been first in line.

A hand grasped the top of Kay's laptop screen and he looked up. It was the chaplain, Steve Moser, an Army major.

"Larry, if you ever want to talk, let me know," Moser said.

"Thank you, sir. I will," Kay said.

Kay wasn't ready to talk to anyone just yet, perhaps most particularly not a chaplain. Some soldiers carried those little camouflage-covered Bibles in the sleeve pockets of their uniforms. Kay carried a copy of the Constitution. He lived in a tangible world, focusing his energy and intellect on what was in front of him, what could be done, and what resources he, personally, could bring to bear to make that happen. Or, in this case, how to keep what had happened from ever happening again.

---

4. 1st Battalion, 506th Parachute Infantry Regiment. This is written "1-506th" and pronounced "first of the five-oh-sixth."

CHAPTER 5

15 August 2008
Bagram Airfield

AT BAGRAM AIRFIELD, the sun slid low, casting the mountains in a glow like dying embers. Since learning that two Dog Company soldiers had been killed in action, SPC Allan Moser hadn't been able to think of anything else. He sat brooding in the transient tent, names from the company roster tripping through his mind. Finally, LT Ward broke the news: It was 3rd Platoon that had been hit. The KIAs were Donnie Carwile and Paul Conlon.

Sorrow flooded Moser's brain: LT Carwile? He was such a great L.T., not a tight ass like some. He had two little girls...how could he be gone? And Conlon? He was only twenty-one. He hadn't even been in the Army for a year.

Then anger rocketed in. Moser found himself wondering, *Did they get the motherfuckers who did this?*

All three of the wounded—Joseph Coe, Todd Parsons, and Al LeMaire— had been MedEvaced to Bagram, and the Jolly Rogers had trooped over to the hospital to see them. LeMaire was sequestered in intensive care.

Hours later, the platoon learned that Carwile's and Conlon's bodies had arrived at Bagram. They would be flown home on a C-17, an Air Force transport plane. There was to be a "ramp ceremony," the solemn rite of loading the men on their final flight. Asked if they wanted to be the ones to bear Carwile's and Conlon's caskets, the Jolly Rogers responded, "There's no 'if' we want to. We *are*."

Late that evening, the platoon formed up at the airfield under a glittering midnight sky. Nearby, a cavernous cargo plane hulked on the tarmac. An Army chaplain was there, along with about a hundred other soldiers, arrayed in silent ranks. Meanwhile, along Bagram's main thoroughfare, Disney Drive, soldiers, sailors, Marines, airmen, and civilians streamed out from their work spaces and lined the street.

Hundreds came. Military from every service. Men and women. Soldiers and airmen from other nations. Some had just come off double-digit shifts, gone back to their barracks, put on their cleanest uniforms, and returned. Few, if any, knew Carwile or Conlon. They were there out of respect. Athletes and movie stars often touched down at Bagram to boost troop morale, but none of them drew as large a crowd as a single soldier going home in a coffin.[5]

On the airfield, Moser and the Jolly Rogers waited in formation. SGT Brandon Vega, one of Carwile's 3rd Platoon soldiers, had been at Bagram for an appointment when the IED hit. A Jolly Roger gave up his spot in the ceremony so that Vega could help carry his platoon leader on his journey home.

Near midnight, a procession crawled down Disney Drive, including a pair of A2 series Humvees configured with beds like pickup trucks. Each cradled a casket draped with an American flag. Along the street, those in uniform saluted as the trucks rolled past.

The procession turned onto the tarmac, rolled slowly to the waiting plane, and stopped. Moser listened as the chaplain intoned a brief sermon under a chapel of a billion stars. On signal, a bagpipe sounded, and the plaintive notes of "Amazing Grace" floated across the night. Beneath the strains, Moser could hear men crying.

The men of 2nd Platoon marched to the Humvees, eight to a truck, and lifted their fallen brothers down. As they marched slowly toward the C-17, the weight of Donnie Carwile's body rested on Moser's shoulder like the sands of all the ages. Grief swelled up in his chest, broke up through his throat. As he trudged up the aircraft ramp, the first tears spilled from his eyes. The men set the caskets down and slid them home.

All sixteen men marched down the ramp. As the plane's massive cargo door closed, a bugle note cut the clear night like a blade, and "Taps" began to play. Those who knew the century-old lyrics recited them inwardly:

---

5. Michael Holmes, "CNN Reporter witnesses solemn 'ramp ceremony,'" *Afghanistan Crossroads* (blog), CNN, April 23, 2010. Available at http://afghanistan.blogs.cnn.com /2010/04/23/cnn-reporter-witnesses-rare-ramp-ceremony/. Accessed January 29, 2015.

Day is done, gone the sun
From the lakes, from the hills, from the sky
All is well, safely rest
God is nigh.

Fading light dims the sight
And a star gems the sky, gleaming bright
From afar, drawing near
Falls the night.

Thanks and praise for our days
Neath the sun, neath the stars, neath the sky
As we go, this we know
God is nigh.

16 August 2008

In war, death leaves no room for rest. The day after the IED claimed Carwile and Conlon, CPT Roger Hill had to make time for an in-brief with Dave, the counterintelligence agent. The two men settled at the long table in the TOC conference room.

Dave launched into his brief Army-style, bottom line up front: "Sir, you're looking at one or more insider threats."

At first, Hill was taken aback. One or more threats from inside his own organization? Then he felt the click of resolution in his mind, like a puzzle piece sliding into place. Hill picked up his pen. "Go on."

"I work in the Division counterintel shop at Bagram. A few months back, I noticed a trend in the intel reports."

There had been a repeated pattern, Dave explained. It ranged from low-level Afghan workers selling scraps of data to the Taliban to actual attacks— on both Coalition bases and personnel—perpetrated by people thought to be allies. With his commander's blessing, Dave had spent a couple of months visiting small, exposed bases. His tour revealed a startling discovery: U.S. forces had somehow missed flourishing networks of infiltrators.

"I asked myself, 'How had that happened?'" Dave said as Hill scribbled notes. "Were Coalition forces not reporting what they saw? Or were they reporting it, and counterintel simply wasn't seeing it?"

He ran down the answers, which were yes and yes. The reporting was available, but not easily accessible. And there weren't enough counterintel personnel in-theater to circulate the battlefield on a regular basis. Plus, with literally thousands of intel reports streaming in from 130 bases in RC East alone, the twenty-five CI personnel at Bagram had a workload akin to drinking from a fire hose. Insider threat reports were easily lost in the shuffle.

Still, Dave knew the problem had to be wrestled down, and his OIC (officer in charge) agreed. "I spent a month combing through a twelve-month pile of intel reports," Dave said.

What funneled out at the end was daunting: four hundred reports of infiltrators and spies working on Coalition bases in eastern Afghanistan alone.

Hill was stunned. "Four *hundred?*"

Dave nodded. Some reports included Afghan allies on U.S. bases working specifically to get American and Coalition forces killed. In January in Waygul, they might have succeeded: An Afghan National Army soldier had leapt from a bunker, shot and killed 1SG Matthew Kahler, twenty-nine, and run. Investigators called it an accident, but Kahler's soldiers witnessed the shooting and swore the Afghan killed Kahler intentionally.

Dave's OIC authorized small, ad hoc teams to visit RC East bases to try to get out in front of what appeared to be a rampant problem. At one base, Dave and his guys busted a particularly nasty crew of local national infiltrators. The base commander was livid and fired them all. Soon afterward, the base received accurate indirect fire—rockets and mortars—for the first time in months. The attack became a briefing point for future commanders dealing with insider threats: If you let spies go, expect a retaliatory attack.

Months passed. While his OIC focused on gathering resources to scrub the data gathered thus far, Dave zeroed in on learning more about advanced-threat areas like Khost, Logar, Paktika—and Wardak.

Hill's pen froze. He could hear the rumble of Humvees outside, rolling on and off the FOB as the glimmer of a red flag waved in his mind. It was beginning to sound like Divison intel had been tracking a threat on his base for some time.

Dave didn't skip a beat. He ticked off questions he'd been running down for weeks: How were enemy infiltrators getting on base? What systemic issues allowed them to elude U.S. screening protocols and gain employment? And who were the bad guys working off base and directing the bad guys working on base?

Hill thought of the local national workers on Airborne. Each man, from the bulldozer operator to his own interpreter, had undergone a vetting process ultimately overseen by ISAF, the International Security Assistance Force, NATO's arm in Afghanistan. Hill's mission in Wardak fell under ISAF, an authority with its own set of rules.

Dave continued. "Just like any army, terrorist networks rely on logistics, recruitment, training, financing, and intel, as well as communication between commanders and foot soldiers," he said. "When I started dissecting the main networks, I immediately saw trends."

For example, main Coalition logistics lines weren't being attacked by local criminals, as a recent national-level assessment had concluded, but by organized insurgent support structures. This had not been a popular discovery, but Dave backed it up with data from thousands of intel reports stretching back several years. Then, at a morning briefing in Bagram, he learned of suspect signals emanating from FOB Airborne, Dog Company's base in Wardak. After a series of briefs up the task force intel chain of command, the commanding general made a decision: bust the insider threat so that it didn't compromise Operation Nomad.

"And now," Dave said, "here I am."

Hill sat back in his chair, astonished. How could Division know about, or even suspect, an enemy on his base—*inside his wire*—and he, the base commander, not be privy to that information? By Hill's accounting, counterintel assets at Bagram had been tracking the threat for at least six weeks.

If Hill had known, maybe Donnie and Paul...?

But his mind couldn't go down that road.

Dave slid Hill the FRAGO, or fragmentary order, that had brought him and his team to Airborne. Hill scanned the document. It was dated 12 August 2008 and came straight from the Division commander. According to the order, the CI team's sole purpose at Airborne was to protect the operational security of Nomad, the clearing operation in Jalrez, the Taliban stronghold that lay in view of the FOB. Dave's team was to provide counterintel support to units executing the op, and thereby prevent the operation from being compromised by intel leaks.

But there was a twist, and for Hill it was a big one: Because of the combination of units involved in the operation, Nomad was to be conducted under Operating Enduring Freedom (OEF) rules of engagement, *not* ISAF rules. For Hill and Dog Company, this was a huge advantage. ISAF's rules of engagement were highly restrictive, particularly its rules on taking and holding prisoners.

Under ISAF, all prisoners enjoyed something called the 96-Hour Rule. Under the rule, every prisoner captured had to be transferred either to

Afghan custody, or to the next-higher level of U.S. detention, within ninety-six hours—or they were set free. And not only set free, but given a few bucks to see them on their way.

In Dog Company's case, the next echelon of detention meant Battalion headquarters at FOB Ghazni, where Hill's boss, LTC DeMartino, was in command. But for six months, the problem had been this: Every time Dog Company sent captured enemy fighters to Ghazni, Battalion let them go. Without exception.

This had been true whether the fighter was caught with bomb-making materials or in the act of firing on American soldiers. Hill and his men found the pattern bizarre, as though they were engaged in some kind of catch-and-release trophy-fishing contest instead of locked in lethal combat with Osama bin Laden's deadly acolytes.

Now, Hill stared at the FRAGO as if it held a miracle: Operation Enduring Freedom rules of engagement did *not* include arbitrary detention time lines. If there were spies on his base, capturing them under OEF rules meant D Co might actually get them off the battlefield. No threat of the ISAF revolving door. It meant Hill would be able to make his men safer. In the long run, Operation Nomad might weaken the enemy's intel apparatus in the province, possibly even lead to the dismantling of the warlord Razak's entire Jalrez cell.

This wasn't the first time Hill had had to purge his base of an insider threat. In April, D Co had busted a dirty interpreter, or "terp." They also caught a local national worker "walking in" rounds—providing azimuth and range information to enemy fighters firing rockets and mortars into the FOB. After Dog Company rolled those guys up, a Brigade-sourced counter-intel team was requested and sent to screen all local nationals working on Airborne. They pronounced the base clean.

Still, Taliban attacks had grown increasingly accurate, cutting into Hill's unit by attrition as the number of wounded mounted. In view of Dave's brief, he was beginning to understand why.

An incident earlier that summer now seemed darkly comic. To shore up D Co's manning shortage, the Army had sent thirty-two privately contracted Afghan security guards to help protect the FOB. When they showed up without uniforms, weapons, bullets, or food, and asked that their families be housed on base, 1SG Scott smelled a rat. He decided to run the contract guards' names through the ███████████. Twelve of the thirty-two popped up with ties to the Taliban, including eight so hot they were to be detained on sight.

Hill called the procurement officer on Bagram who had approved the Afghan guards. How was it that the Army could send Taliban-linked contractors to staff his base, he wanted to know?

The procurement officer told Hill that only one of the thirty-two men who presented themselves at Airborne had been personally interviewed. "It's standard protocol," he said, no apology in his tone.

Standard protocol to send arrest-on-sight Afghans to pull security on an American base?

Hill blew a gasket, dialed Battalion at Ghazni, and unloaded over the phone. How could they sign off on a system that carried so much potential for harm? And when he asked what to do with the detain-on-sight prisoners, he was told: Let them go.

Now Hill laid the FRAGO on the conference table and looked at Dave. "Okay. What's your plan?"

"Well, ███████████████ indicates one or more threats on your FOB. My team will conduct a comprehensive screening of every one of your Afghan workers. How many do you have?"

"About fifty."

"Okay. ██████████████████████████████████
████████" Also, the CI team planned to employ the ██████, Dave said.
██
██████████

"Sounds good," Hill said. "I'll have First Sergeant Scott and the FOB mayor help you with the LNs." Local nationals.

Hill's tone was even and confident, but it masked a new urgency. Dave's brief had switched on in him a ticking clock. It hadn't been proven yet, but it was very likely that the spy or spies conspiring on Hill's base had cost Carwile and Conlon their lives. His platoons were still operating outside the wire, running missions every day. How long would it be until the insider threat struck again?

CHAPTER 6

In the TOC, Larry Kay's phone rang. It was a battle NCO—a noncommissioned officer—calling from Battalion at FOB Ghazni.

"Hey, Lieutenant," the NCO said. "You guys need to go back out to the IED site. That crater is pretty big and it needs to be filled. We've gotten a lot of complaints from the Afghans."

Kay's anger was instant and white-hot. "I'll tell you what, you can fuck off. I don't give a *shit* what the Afghans think. In fact, if they want it filled, they can go out there and fill it themselves."

Kay hung up, steaming. He knew there was a contractor in Wardak available to repair roads. Dog Company damn well didn't need to fill what amounted to a freshly dug grave for her own men. But Kay had been in no mood to explain that to the NCO. He predicted the number of minutes until the phone rang again. In about the time it would take for the NCO to notify his XO, it did.

"FOB Airborne, Lieutenant Kay speaking."

"Larry, did you just tell one of my NCOs to fuck off?" It was the 1-506th XO, Major Rob Smith.

"Yes, sir, I did. We are not going to fill holes less than twelve hours after some of our boys got killed. Especially not *that* hole."

Smith's voice turned sympathetic. "Listen, Larry, I've lost men in combat, too. But you have to pick yourself up and move on, continue the mission."

"Sir," Kay replied calmly, "Dog Company will not fill that hole."

Dave and the CI team set up shop in an empty green tent. From what he'd gathered so far, it appeared that were more advanced problems on Airborne than he'd thought. Hill had already fired two local nationals, the dirty terp and the guy walking in rounds. In the old days, Dave imagined Hill and his men would simply have lined them up against a wall and shot them.

In the new Army, however, commanders' options were limited mainly to kicking suspect locals off their bases, even if caught red-handed. Booted workers often got a new national ID card with a slightly different spelling of their name, hiked down the road, and got hired at another base. Then maybe a couple of years later they'd get caught again. From a counterintel standpoint, it was maddening.

Dave's plan to interview every local national on the FOB would establish baseline data on them all. These initial interviews were critical, but the approach casual. Kind of a "Hey guys, let's work together to keep the Taliban from blowing us all up." No need to trigger tight tribal loyalties that might result in Afghans calling their coworkers and telling them it might be a good idea to call in sick for a few days.

One by one, the local nationals streamed through the tent, where they were engaged in friendly ten-minute chats with the CI team, a bunch of guys who looked nothing like soldiers. Dave and his team kept the questions basic and benign: name, base access info, cell number, what part of the province they were from. It was a good drill, Dave felt, as his next interviewee, Aziz Dalmar, took a seat.

Dave put on his friendliest Gullible American face and said, "We really appreciate the work you do here. We're just concerned about terrorists working on our bases."

Dalmar and his brother, Malik, ran the little coffeehouse at the top of the FOB. "Yes, of course," Dalmar said. "Whatever we can do to help."

Dave noticed that he spoke excellent English.

"If you know of any terrorists working on Airborne, you can tell us now and we will protect your identity," Dave said. "We just don't want anyone to smuggle a bomb onto the FOB. It's happened at other bases and we don't want that to happen here."

His tone said, *Rah-rah, we're all on the same team*; his pen jotted cryptic notes.

"I understand," Dalmar said. "I don't know of anyone like that, but I will stay alert."

"Thank you," Dave said. *Next*, he thought.

All told, the first round of interviews took a couple of hours. Dave collated the data then fired it over to a Bagram colleague, "Ben Travlin," a veteran of special operations combat deployments who was generally an

amiable pain in the ass if he had not recently convalesced on some Carib-
bean island somewhere. Dave allowed a couple of hours for Ben Travlin to
walk the intel through existing databases then dialed him at Bagram.

"Ben Travlin, brother, what's up, man? You decided to finally come to
work?"

"Whatever, dude," Ben Travlin snorted. Then he lowered his voice,
almost whispering. "We've got some good shit for you, man. You'll be proud.
We just have to find a way to get it to you."

He meant an instantly secure way, Dave knew, and he wished for the
thousandth time he had a Bat Phone, or at least a portable cone of silence.
"Well shit, son, email it to me pronto. I've got shit to deal with here that
can't wait."

"Okay, I'll get on it. What's it like down there?"

"Same ole. Moondust, FOB smells like diesel and shit, and everybody's
tired of dying and bad guys."

"Yeah man, pretty much the same up here except for everything you just
said. The chow hall served lobster last night. Not bad, either."

Dave laughed, but knew that the disparity between the luxuries of
Bagram and Spartan conditions at outlying FOBs were a sore spot for grunts
in the field. "Drink a near beer for me, man. When should I expect to see
something from you?"

"I'm attaching a dumbed-down version now. Check your secure email in
an hour or so."

"Hey thanks, buddy. Later."

An hour later, Ben Travlin's analysis arrived via encrypted email. Dave
saw a couple of knocks on some highly placed local national workers. But
nothing firm, really. Just shadows and smoke.

17 August 2008

Hill had received some good news: There was an Operation Enduring
Freedom (OEF) Special Forces team participating in Nomad along with
CPT B's team. The team had agreed to come to Airborne after the op and
take custody of any spies rolled up during Dave's CI hunt. Hill was elated.
The catch-and-release detention pattern with Battalion that had plagued
the company for months seemed to be crumbling in the face of the deputy
commanding general's FRAGO.

Now, though, there was a task Hill had been putting off: calling LTC

DeMartino, his Battalion commander. He was disappointed that DeMartino had not been among those who'd sent messages of condolence after Carwile and Conlon died. Through Larry Kay, DeMartino had requested Hill call *him.*

Hill grabbed Kay and 1SG Scott, and the three went into Hill's TOC office. At this juncture, he wanted his leadership in the loop. Scott dialed and put the call on speaker.

Without preface, DeMartino said, "I'm thinking about bringing Second Lieutenant Zach Morris up there to take over 3rd Platoon."

Hill glanced at Scott and Kay, who both shook their heads.

"Sir, I'd appreciate it if you could hold off on that," Hill said. "I don't think it would be good for the soldiers to have a new platoon leader so soon after—"

He couldn't finish. Hill's throat closed and he walked out of the room, and out of the TOC. *Air,* was all he could think. *I need some air.*

Outside, the wreckage of Carwile and Conlon's IED-blasted gun truck sat near the FOB gate. A recovery crew had been forced to heave it onto a flatbed and deposit it back on Airborne, where it hulked like a grim monument, scorched and broken.

Hill paced the dirt nearby, searching his brain for the benefit of the doubt. Maybe DeMartino didn't handle loss well. Maybe he was one of those people who felt uncomfortable in times of high emotion and therefore went straight to dotting i's and crossing t's.

It was not urgent that 3rd Platoon get an instant replacement for Donnie Carwile. Months earlier, Hill had reassigned the Shockers' platoon leader to Battalion's logistics shop. The platoon sergeant, Sergeant First Class Kris Wilson, had run the Shockers for weeks before DeMartino sent a replacement. You could still count the time since Donnie's death in days.

This wasn't the first time Hill had felt that DeMartino was tone-deaf when it came to his men. He just hoped his CO would have the respect and compassion to listen to him and not try to fill Donnie's shoes right away—at least not until after 3rd Platoon had some time to stand down at Bagram and grieve.

CHAPTER 7

18 August 2008

THE FIRST ROUND of CI interviews yielded the expected baseline data on a complete list of Afghan workers. Now it was time to learn whether any of them were working with the enemy. Most of Dave's team had administered the ████████████████████████████, at least a hundred times. The device wasn't designed as a single-source measure of credibility, but as one tool in the kit bag—one that was useful in narrowing a pool of suspects.

The CI team set up in the empty tent again. About fifty LNs submitted themselves to the screening. Most were cooperative. Some definitely had the shakes, which was duly noted.

About midway through the day, Hill's personal interpreter, "Sammy," entered the tent. Dave had already pegged the young Afghan as a supremely likable guy. Good-looking, easy smile, personality to match. He had established his position as the commander's go-to guy, and really had it all going for himself.

Sammy didn't match the physical type usually found among young Afghan males in the area. Most were thin bordering on gaunt, and narrow-faced with frazzled beards. Sammy, on the other hand, was fit and athletically built. He had a winning smile, which he flashed at Dave, beneath eyes that were large, dark, and arresting.

██
████████████████████████████████
██████████████████████████████████
████████████████████████████████████

When the screenings were complete, Dave rounded up some numbers and notes, crammed them in a cargo pocket, and walked over to the Special Forces compound to find CPT B. He wanted to talk a bit about Operation Nomad.

From an operational security standpoint, a joint operation like Nomad presented some issues. For one thing, the Afghan National Army (ANA) would join with Coalition Forces to secure an area while the Afghan National Police (ANP) actually entered houses. The problem was, both the ANA and ANP leaked like spaghetti strainers.

The ranks of both groups were stacked with young recruits who had direct ties to the Taliban, as well as old hands such as Wardak's provincial police chief, General Muzafarradin. The general had been a mujahideen leader in the Soviet-Afghanistan war, and you didn't stay alive as long as Muzafarradin had without connections. ██████████████████ ██████ said Muzafarradin had long-standing ties to both ex-mujahideen and Taliban commanders. Dave suspected he could be a major source of Hill's problems, as well as a major threat to Nomad.

Dave found CPT B. The Special Forces (SF) officer, a Muslim of Turkish descent, had olive skin and gem-bright eyes that gave him an appearance more Mediterranean than Middle Eastern.

"Hey, are you guys used to doing ████████████████?" Dave asked him.

"Like feints? Sure, as long as we can get it done without it looking like a feint."

A feint is a ruse that looks like a real op but is designed to divert the enemy or gather intel. It may include physical deception, false information leaks, even double agents. In World War II, the Allies famously employed Operation Fortitude, a two-phase deception op complete with fake ground armies fielded to deceive Adolf Hitler's high command in the run-up to D-Day.

Dave spent the next hour working up a less elaborate feint with CPT B's intel guy. The plan was to rally a combined force—ANA, ANP, and Coalition troops—and return to the ambush site where Carwile and Conlon were killed. ███████████████████████████████████

██

████████████████████████████████████ The process was delicate, though: If either the op or the intel felt phony, any spies on Airborne might get spooked and flee the FOB.

Dave showed the plan to CPT B, who pronounced it doable. The brief for Afghan forces would coincide with the Nomad leadership roundtable, set for August 19, the following day. The feint op itself was slated for August 20.

At Dave's recommendation, Hill reinstituted a policy requiring the FOB security detail to hold on to all local national phones and other personal electronics and allow for calls only at certain times of the day. People caught with banned electronics outside of designated times would be detained on the spot.

The trap set, Dave headed to the TOC, where he organized the ████████ results. Dozens of Afghans had passed; three had failed. Dave transmitted the names of the failures to Ben Travlin and settled down to wait for answers.

19 August 2008

Tommy Scott sat in his office, trying to finagle his numbers. No matter how many ways he tried to spread his soldiers across Dog Company's responsibilities, he kept coming up short. A vehicle-borne IED in early August had taken Shockers platoon sergeant SFC Kris Wilson out of the fight, along with three other soldiers from 4th. With the deaths of Carwile and Conlon, and with Coe and others recovering from their wounds, 3rd Platoon was down by a full truck.

Also, Haskins and the rest of 3rd's survivors were headed to Bagram Airfield to convalesce. That meant the Dirty First, led by LT Sean Allred and SFC Grant Hulburt, had been the only full-strength platoon left—until just days before, when the Jolly Rogers rejoined D Co in Wardak after their stint in Kapisa.

When Scott took over as Dog Company first sergeant in the spring of 2007, he had just completed a tour as a drill instructor, what some disparagingly called "the Trail." Dog Company, on the other hand, had just gotten back from Ramadi—the city *Time* magazine had dubbed the most dangerous place in Iraq—and the men's tolerance for inexperience was very low.

They didn't care that Scott had fought in Desert Storm, jumped through live fire into Panama in '89, and served at Khobar Towers in Saudi Arabia. That was ancient history. Besides, next to Al Qaeda, Manuel Noriega and his Panamanian Defense Forces were punks. The general consensus was that Battalion shouldn't be giving a first sergeant fresh off the Trail a company. They should be giving him a desk.

It didn't take long for Scott to change their minds. Across three combat tours, he had seen the maxim that an organization is only as strong as its weakest link play out in life-and-death scenarios. He knew that in Dog Company, he had been dealt a hand full of aces: In Ramadi, there were certain streets that American soldiers avoided, but Dog Company didn't avoid them. They went wherever the hell they wanted to go, and when the line companies got into trouble, D Co roared in and fished them out.

Scott noticed that every platoon had stellar NCOs: SFC Jason Bielsky and SFC Hulburt led the Dirty First. SFC David Anderson headed 2nd Platoon, the Jolly Rogers. SFC Haskins led 3rd Platoon, and the Shockers were in the care of SFC Kris Wilson. From their records, Scott knew his new men were battle hardened and fearless. In Ramadi, Haskins got into his first-ever firefight and earned a medal for valor. Wilson was wounded multiple times in Iraq but refused to claim his Purple Hearts, judging that others had been wounded worse, or killed.

But back at Fort Campbell, in garrison or "the rear," the Army was all about equipment inspections, drills, physical training (PT) scores, and paperwork. Those, Dog Company wasn't so good at. As a result, their reputation suffered. At a meeting of senior NCOs shortly after Scott took over, the other company first sergeants actually ridiculed D Co: They were the redheaded stepchildren, the lard-asses, the screwups. As the junior man at the meeting, Scott kept his mouth shut. But that night, Scott went home and told his wife, Cassandra, "I'm going to turn this company around."

And he did. Under Scott, there were surprise equipment inspections, surprise barracks inspections, surprise weigh-ins, and forced runs in which the men of Dog Company pounded up and down the rolling hills of southern Kentucky and northern Tennessee in full kit, humping their heavy weapons. At the top of a run, Scott would order the men to break their guns down to their smallest parts, reassemble them, set the weapons' timing, mount them on tripods, run machine-gun "crew drills"—then run back. He made them repeat these drills so many times that the more senior men could've taken down and rebuilt squad weapons in their sleep. Even the most junior soldiers knew how to disassemble and rebuild weapons they might never use.

Scott was right there with them. At forty-four, he could outperform any man in the company in any physical event. And where Dog Company's previous first sergeant had treated them like juvenile delinquents, Scott treated them like men. He checked up on their families. More, he genuinely loved them, and told them so.

With Hill's full endorsement, Scott fostered an environment that, had he posted a sign in the company spaces, it might have read, "You are men, not boys. We love you and want you to be your best, but we don't have time for bullshit."

The effect of Scott's leadership was as stark as rolling the stone from a mouth of a long-dark cave and watching sunshine pour in. Dog Company's PT scores shot from the basement to the highest in the battalion. Their marksmanship scores reached levels rarely achieved by regular line companies, and unheard of in a heavy weapons company. Soaring morale had a ripple effect: During the run-up to the Afghanistan deployment, Alpha, Bravo, and Charlie companies had numerous men chaptered out for drugs, alcohol, or domestic violence. Dog Company didn't have a single formal disciplinary incident.

The feeling had carried over to Afghanistan. Despite steady attrition and a punishing mission schedule, Scott had not heard any of the typical inter-platoon bickering or workload complaints.

Instead, Scott was the one complaining, but only to himself. He tossed his pen down on his manning roster and sighed. Dog Company had six months left in-country and was down to just over sixty bruised and battered men trying to secure a province the size of Connecticut. He and CPT Hill had been requesting replacement soldiers for months, but not a single new man had arrived.

The ones they had would bust their asses to make mission, though. Scott knew that.

20 August 2008

At 0200, CPT B's Special Forces team and "Caveman," a Police Mentorship Team out of Montana, conducted full rehearsals with the ANP for the fake op Dave and the SF intel guy had cooked up, just as though it were a real one. As the mission start time of 0300 approached, Caveman leaked the false intelligence to the ANP. Then the patrol rolled off Airborne and south on Highway 1.

Hill monitored the operation from the TOC. Within minutes, word came in from Dave's team: CI assets had detected multiple calls originating from inside Airborne. Their content matched the Caveman leak.

That's how easy it's been, Hill thought with dismay. *That's how easy it's been for them to set us up for an ambush or an IED.*

He flashed back to Dave's insider threat brief. Were the spies LNs working on Airborne? Or was it General Muzafarradin and the ANP?

The feint convoy received some small arms fire at their designated turn-around point but returned to base without casualties or damage. Unfortunately, the dirty source inside the FOB stayed a step ahead, and the CI team was unable to pinpoint the origin of the calls. They decided to zero in on the ANP commander, Muzafarradin.

That night, Hill and Scott sat in the TOC. Scott was working on the memorial service, Hill on the most difficult letters of his life.

"Paul was not afraid to be himself," Hill wrote to the Conlon family.

Paul was bursting with life. He was so intelligent and well spoken... Paul was one of those guys that could make or break a room. If he was there, then the room and everyone in it was at ease, but if Paul was not, then there just was not that same warmth we had grown to depend on. Paul had that rare and beautiful ability to make all feel unconditionally welcome. It really hurts all of us that he is gone. Part of us left with him.

Hill lifted his hands and they hovered over the keyboard. Between his time at West Point and the endless military correspondence and reports since, he calculated that he had written at least a million words on behalf of the Army. But these exacted a toll like none he'd ever penned. He rolled his neck first right then left. Paused midroll and stared at the ceiling. This building was one of the few reinforced with steel beams against mortars and rockets. Rows of bricks marched between the beams, blast-proof protection laid in, perhaps, by some of the same double agents who had likely killed his men. Who would go on trying to kill them.

Hill heard a knock on the door.

"Come in," Scott said.

Dave entered and gave an apologetic half smile. "Bet you're tired of seeing me by now."

"Absolutely not," Hill said. "You guys are doing incredible work." He pushed away from his desk, secretly glad for the interruption.

Scott rolled his chair across the floor to join them. Dave thought Scott seemed okay with him now, but the first day they met, Dave thought he'd detected a flicker of disapproval. Nothing anyone else would notice, just a thinning of the lips as if Scott had smelled something unpleasant. Dave was used to it. Scott was squared-away, tip-of-the-spear infantry. To him, Dave was a scruffy military intelligence puke. Scott was hard-core; Dave was a pussy. Scott didn't know Dave was former infantry, but if he had that would only make matters worse, Dave knew. Then he would not only have been a pussy, but a quitter.

Dave laid out what he had so far: "Five bad guys total. We've been sent some additional information on an LN named Kassiss."

Kassiss was a shop owner in the bazaar outside the gate. "He failed his ██████, and the data we're getting from Bagram is connecting him with some very scary characters. Same for the Dalmar brothers. Both are linked to terrorist networks in Iraq and Iran."

Unusual, Hill thought. The fighters Dog Company had rolled up, both on and off base, were mostly homegrown. Local boys. Since the revelation of insider threats on Airborne, Hill had wondered who the ringleader might be. Now he placed the Dalmars at the top of his list.

Both brothers failed their ██████ screenings, David said. "Also, your terp Sammy failed his ██████ on a question related to terrorism."

"Sammy?" Scott said. He was skeptical, but didn't show it.

Hill drew back his head and frowned, suddenly suspicious. Not of Sammy, but of Dave's approach and his team's methodology.

The young Afghan had been rock solid. He had served under several previous American commanders, and when Hill took over the FOB, officers from the outgoing 82nd Airborne told Hill personally that they trusted Sammy completely. Plus, after Hill kicked the other two LNs off his base, the Brigade-sourced CI team had screened all the terps, including Sammy, who came up clean.

"Dave, there's a mistake," he said. "Sammy's good. I know he is."

"Well, the ██████ isn't foolproof, and failing it doesn't necessarily mean he's a bad guy. It's only one indicator. I'll send all his stuff up to Division and get them working on his background. You'll be the first to know. Meanwhile, I recommend you minimize his visibility of ops, meetings, plans, et cetera. It may take us a few days to get to the bottom of it."

Hill had been in this situation before. Premature detainment of a valued team member could erase months, if not years, of trust and political capital. When the person in question was a local national, the distrust trickled down in varying degrees to every LN on the team. Hill had a special place in his heart for foreign nationals who risked their lives to stand beside U.S. troops. He realized that this fact, along with his fondness for Sammy, had reared up in the face of objective evidence.

It was a tough call. Hill felt confident of Sammy's allegiances. He would have to take some time and process Dave's input. Maybe there was a middle ground.

Dave moved on. "Also, sir, one of our guys found an Afghan talking on a cell phone inside a tent during this morning's op."

The CI team hadn't been able to link the forbidden call to the feint op, Dave said. Still, it was a serious violation. "On other bases, we've recommended a full sweep of Afghan employee work and living areas, tents, that sort of thing. We always find stuff of interest. It's time. We have a couple of days now before the Jalrez op. A search will give you a better idea of what you're dealing with."

Hill and Scott traded looks, and Scott left the TOC to make it happen.

CHAPTER 8

THE SWEEP TURNED up numerous banned digital devices, as well as weapons and ammunition that had been stashed in slits cut into mattresses. There was also a detailed map of the FOB marked with defensive capabilities and positions. For Hill, it was further proof that Dave had been right to target FOB Airborne.

Throughout the LN screenings, the CI agent and his men had gone to great lengths to put the Afghan workforce at ease. But there had been no way to completely mask the surprise inspection. Now, successive rounds of questioning, though necessary, increased the odds of spooking Airborne's spies out of play.

Hill ordered the Dalmar brothers and Kassiss, the shop owner, arrested. The move preempted any attempt to escape, and also reduced the chances of a leak on Operation Nomad. Still, it was a risk: Hill was banking on the Division FRAGO and Operation Enduring Freedom's rules of engagement, with their less restrictive rules on detention.

If all went according to plan, the OEF Special Forces guys would swing by after Nomad, take custody of the prisoners, and Hill could get back to the business of securing Wardak. But if Nomad leaked and was canceled, then the ISAF stopwatch on the prisoners' detention would have just begun. That meant Hill would have just ninety-six hours to either transfer the insider threats to Battalion or let them go. Hill desperately did not want the latter. The feint op had opened his eyes to how easy it was to target his men.

21 August 2008

"Hey, where does 3rd Platoon stay at so I can go put my shit down?"

Larry Kay looked up from his desk to see the speaker: Second Lieutenant Zachary Morris, Donnie Carwile's replacement. A hundred curses ricocheted through Kay's mind. It had not even been a week since Donnie died. Kay was astonished that LTC DeMartino had ignored CPT Hill's request that he give 3rd Platoon a little time to grieve.

Kay eyed Morris, a square-jawed strawberry blond with puppy-dog eyes and cheeks still round with youth. Two sides of Kay's brain warred. One side said it wasn't Morris's fault; he was just doing what he was told. The other side said he might have introduced himself with a little more respect for the dead. The second side won, and Kay restrained an urge to Frisbee off Morris's head with his laptop like Oddjob with his bowler hat in *Goldfinger*.

"Come outside with me for a minute," Kay said tightly.

Under a glaring summer sun, Kay rounded on the junior officer. "You don't need to worry about where 3rd Platoon stays. You will be staying in the transient tent for at least a week. You will not talk to 3rd Platoon for at least another week, and you will certainly not pretend that you are their platoon leader until you get your initial counseling from the company commander, or the platoon itself is ready for another leader. The commander and I asked Lieutenant Colonel D not to bring you here so quickly. If you value your role and position as an officer and a soon-to-be platoon leader, then you will not just walk into the platoon like it was Vietnam, when platoon leaders died within a matter of hours. Have some fucking respect."

"Yes, sir," Morris said.

The kid seemed a bit awkward, uncomfortable in his own skin, Kay thought. He throttled back. "Look, I know you want to be a hard charger, but this is certainly the wrong situation for that. If we were in the rear, I would say you had the right idea, but we are not in the rear. Do you have any questions?"

Morris kept his face neutral. "No, sir."

"Good. In the meantime, I suggest that you get with my armorer, SGT Doyle, and learn how to load, unload, reload, and shoot an MK19 and a .50-cal," Kay said. He knew that Morris had only a few weeks in-country; his first combat experience had been just two weeks before. "Just because you're an officer does not mean you will never find yourself behind one of those weapons laying scunion on the enemy. When you're done with

that, learn how to use ███████████████████████████
██████

"Yes, sir," Morris said.

Kay walked back into his office, still royally pissed.

SFC Kris Wilson grabbed his M4 rifle and walked out of his hooch into the August heat. Moondust hung in the air, an ever-present cloud over the FOB. The memorial service for Carwile and Conlon was scheduled for the next day and rehearsals were underway. 1SG Scott had tapped Wilson to lead the rifle detail, the traditional twenty-one-gun salute. The company had only enough blank rounds on hand for a couple of practices. A proper rifle salute features three distinct *cracks*. At yesterday's practice, Wilson had heard more like seven or eight.

Wilson, thirty-one, of Bakersfield, California, waited for the rest of the rifle detail near memorial stands that had been erected for the fallen. Each was composed of an M4, its bayonet stabbed into a sandbag, along with combat boots and dog tags. Each man's stand also held a photograph. The guys had already begun leaving mementos: unit patches, expended brass from particular firefights, even their own dog tags.

Wilson gazed at Donnie Carwile's photo. During rare downtimes, Carwile and Shon Haskins had liked to sit in their hooch, drink near beer, and play *NCAA Basketball* on Xbox. Wilson played, too, and Carwile always bagged on him: "I tell you what, son, you *suck* at this game!"

Then he'd laugh his country laugh and polish off half a near beer in a single gulp. Now Wilson pictured Carwile in his younger days, sitting on his pickup tailgate drinking real beer by a Mississippi lake. His throat tightened. It was so fucking unfair.

The rifle team showed up, and Wilson ran them through their paces. They'd improved, but the gun reports were still staggered. Nearby, Shon Haskins, 3rd Platoon's platoon sergeant, and other soldiers with active parts in the memorial service also gathered in front of the TOC.

Haskins walked to the place where a podium would be and rehearsed the eulogy he had written for his best friend. Carwile's death clawed at Haskins's soul. Each morning since the day of the blast, the loss crushed him all over again the instant he opened his eyes. He managed to breathe in and out, but couldn't seem to get any oxygen. When people other than his platoon brothers spoke to him, it was as though their voices came from a great distance, finding their way down to the end of a long, dark tunnel where he sat alone, staring at the pieces of his shredded heart.

Soon the rehearsal was over. Fifteen minutes later, a young officer walked up and introduced himself. "Hi, Sergeant Haskins. I'm Lieutenant Morris. I'm going to be 3rd Platoon's new PL."

PL—platoon leader.

Haskins eyed Morris warily. "Hi, sir. What's up?"

"I'd really like to get a chance to meet the boys," the lieutenant said.

Haskins looked at Morris, who appeared to him as green as a gecko. Couldn't have been more than twenty-two, twenty-three years old. Donnie Carwile had not only been Haskins's best friend, but also a father and a husband, a man with some life under his belt. An infantry peer and role model in every way. They had fought together, survived rockets, bombs, and ambushes, bandaged bleeding brothers. Bitched, moaned, joked, and dreamed in between. And this kid, Morris, thought he was going to barge in and take Donnie's place? The thought made Haskins's stomach roll.

In his heart, he knew Morris was just following orders. What else was he supposed to do? But the loss of Donnie and Paul was still raw, as bloody as butchered game, and Haskins couldn't help his resentment. His parents, salt-of-the-earth farming folk, had brought Haskins up to know his place. But God had made him a passionate man, and he had to work to control his temper.

Haskins measured out his next words as if they were the last patient ones he might ever speak. "I'm sorry, sir, but you're not meeting them right now. You and I can talk policies and procedures and that kind of thing at a later date, but not right now."

Then he turned and walked away.

CHAPTER 9

22 August 2008

AN HOUR BEFORE the memorial service, Hill found himself outside the TOC hovering near the memorial stands, looking at Donnie Carwile's picture. Desert camouflage uniform, Oakley shades, looking off to the right. A serious Donnie. But he had actually laughed a lot; Hill wished they could have found a photo showing that.

He tipped his face skyward and breathed deep. Though it was still morning, a dry heat pressed in. He pulled written remarks from his chest pocket, unfolded and scanned the pages. There were only two. He had tried hard to keep it short, but tender and sincere. The remarks weren't the problem, though. For a couple of days, twin curtains of tears had hung just behind Hill's eyes, sometimes spilling over. The families would see today's videotaped memorial. Out of respect, he wanted to maintain his composure.

By noon, Dog Company had formed up for the service. CPT B and his Special Forces team joined the formation. Often bearded and in plain clothes to resemble their Afghan counterparts, they had shaved, gotten haircuts, and put on uniforms. Hill, Scott, and Kay walked up and down the ceremony area, making sure all was in order before the official party arrived—Colonel (COL) John "Pete" Johnson, Command Sergeant Major Vincent Camacho, LTC DeMartino, and Battalion Sergeant Major Charles Judd. Judd had been on Airborne for a couple of days now, checking on the troops, lending an ear to the men where he could.

Mo paced the edges of the formation with a camera in his hand. It was a practice he'd begun in Iraq, during Operation Iraqi Freedom. Memorial services were usually videotaped, but he wanted the families to get the whole picture: the rifle-and-boots stands, fellow soldiers paying their respects.

Over his twenty-year career, Mo had watched many soldiers process the deaths of their battle brothers. The immediate reaction was almost always rage, accompanied by a seething desire to lay waste to the enemy. Then came deep, solemn reflection punctuated by convulsing guilt, and days or even weeks when a laugh or a joke seemed so inappropriate as to be grotesque. If the lost soldier had been a close friend, grief burrowed in deep—an insidious monster that stacked weights on a man, like lead plates on his chest, making it difficult to drag himself from his bunk, lift his weapon, or even breathe.

Kris Wilson stood with the rifle detail to the rear and right of the main body. The last memorial he'd attended was for SFC Greg Rogers in Ramadi, Iraq. Rogers was Wilson's platoon sergeant and mentor then, and had been grooming him to take over a platoon himself. Then Rogers was killed by an IED in April 2006, and Wilson replaced him as platoon sergeant. It was the shittiest way on earth to get a promotion.

At Rogers's memorial service, Wilson's overriding hope had been that he would never have to attend such a service again. But now, here he was.

Larry Kay took his place next to Second Lieutenant (2LT) Pat Curran, Dog Company's fire support officer, behind 3rd Platoon, which was centered on the rifle-and-boots stands. Dave and the CI team joined the ceremony, careful to stay on the periphery where their unorthodox appearance wouldn't detract from the rite's order and solemnity. Dave surveyed the traditional monuments then gazed past them to the FOB gate, the Afghan bazaar outside, and the near-distant mountains that marked the entrance to the Jalrez Valley beyond. Even now insurgents were likely scoping these soldiers in formation, trying to scramble a mortar team.

He thought about the local nationals who'd both failed the ▮▮▮▮▮ and popped up in intel reports. He had no doubt that Dog Company's insider threat had killed these two men.

The official party filed in and took their places. Then Hill walked to a wooden podium and began his remarks, directly addressing the families of the fallen as if they were right down front.

"I'll never forget Paul's smile and humor," Hill began. "His humor and laughter were contagious. He was kind and had a natural instinct to care for things or others that were weaker than himself."

Hill stopped. Actual pain pierced his chest, as though an unseen hand were sawing his heart in two with a bayonet. He took a breath, then switched from addressing the families and spoke directly to the assembled men.

"Paul's mother, Maria, and brother, Daniel, wanted me to share with all of you not to feel badly for Paul because he believed in that for which he died... Paul's mother also wanted the men of Delta Company to know that the best way for us to honor Paul would be to ensure that the rest of us made it back to our families safely."

In the formation, Larry Kay heard a sound beside him. Curran, a proud, introverted New Yorker, was openly crying. Kay put his arm around Curran's shoulders as Hill began to speak about Carwile.

"Donnie, brother, your friendship and leadership will be missed. I remember telling Shon Haskins what an awesome job you were doing just a couple of nights before you left us. I should have told you face-to-face."

Hill felt a hitch in his voice. He paused and collected himself. "I should have told you how much I appreciated you more often, but I know you are listening even now."

The service continued with remarks from Haskins. Staff Sergeant Anthony Dominguez shared a funny Conlon story to lift the somber mood. Then it was Tommy Scott's task to perform the roll call, a time-honored way to remember that a soldier has not just been taken, but taken from among his brothers.

Scott walked to the podium and called the company to attention.

"Specialist Siler!" he began.

Siler had been among those pounding on Carwile's chest, trying to revive him.

"Sergeant Eisinger!"

"Here, First Sergeant!"

"Lieutenant Carwile."

Silence.

"First Lieutenant Carwile!" Scott said, then paused. "First Lieutenant Donald Carwile!"

Silence.

"Specialist Ochoa!"

"Here, First Sergeant!"

"Private Conlon."

A ticking quiet.

"Private First Class Conlon!" Scott's voice became dry and hoarse. "Private First Class Paul Conlon!"

Where men had let silent tears stream before, the sounds of grief now echoed up into the glaring sky.

"Specialist Coe!"

Coe had been driving the truck that day. His forehead was bandaged above his nose where shrapnel had zinged in and dug a divot from his skin. But he was alive while his brothers were dead. He answered Scott's call— "Here, First Sergeant!"—and guilt flowed like acid through his veins.

Scott finished the roll call. Then a bugle sounded the plaintive notes of "Taps." Behind the formation, Wilson commanded the rifle detail.

"Ready...Aim...Fire!"

"Ready...Aim...Fire!"

"Ready...Aim...Fire!"

Seven rifles, one report, three times. Twenty-one bullets piercing a merciless blue sky.

CHAPTER 10

23 August 2008

ONLY TWO DAYS remained until Nomad, the Jalrez Valley clearing operation. After the memorial service, Hill and his command team had met with LTC DeMartino, his immediate boss, and COL Johnson, the Brigade commander, to update them on preparations for the op. Hill also looped them in on the evolving insider threat situation on Airborne, including the initial detentions.

1SG Tommy Scott made a key suggestion and Hill implemented it: D Co temporarily transferred Kassiss and the Dalmar brothers to the National Directorate of Security (NDS), an Afghan government version of the CIA. Prisoners required guards. Scott reasoned that the move would reduce Dog Company's manpower requirements while preventing knowledge of Kassiss's and the Dalmars' detention from spreading to the other LNs. It wasn't the best-case scenario. The NDS was known by human rights groups to torture prisoners and extort their families for money. But Hill felt the local NDS had good oversight, and they maintained a detention facility less than a mile from Airborne.

Next, Hill moved to improve operational security for Nomad, asking all Afghan workers to remain on the FOB overnight. The LNs didn't like it, but with the number of D Co soldiers wounded in action or reassigned without replacement, Airborne had plenty of tents, cots, and floor space to accommodate them comfortably.

The CI hunt continued, and each LN underwent screening at three separate stations. ███████████████████████████████████████

██████████████████████████████ Again, Dave marshaled the data and fired it over to Ben Travlin at Bagram.

He also spent significant time considering Sammy.

Did Dave *know* the young Afghan was a spy? Not for sure. Failing the ████████ wasn't completely damning in and of itself. Still, Sammy was the CO's terp. He would be privy to mission planning and rehearsal sessions. Also, if there *were* bad guys on the base, he would likely know something about it. Perhaps he was the leader, a willing participant, Dave thought. Or maybe he was being threatened. "Keep quiet or we'll hurt your family," that kind of thing. It wouldn't be the first time Dave and his team had seen either of those scenarios.

Meanwhile, rehearsals for Nomad continued with various units running through their individual missions: The Afghan National Army commando element, trained by U.S. Special Forces, would air-assault into the western end of Jalrez Valley within range of Airborne's 105 mm artillery. The ground element—CPT B's Special Forces (SF) team, the Caveman Police Mentorship Team, and three Dog Company platoons—would focus on objectives in an eastern subvalley closer to Airborne. This ground element would attempt to herd the Taliban from east to west, with the air assault element serving as a backstop for fleeing fighters. The ANP were read into the plan, but again, generically. They would not be told the location of the mission's objective.

Hill had considered Dave's warning about Sammy. He tried to balance it with his firsthand, daily observations of the terp, and the fact that he had already passed the earlier ██ screening. Hill was certain Sammy would again come up clean. Still, he was keeping the terp away from command-level meetings about Operation Nomad.

LT Mason Ward and 2nd Platoon had arrived at Airborne the day after the ramp ceremony for Carwile and Conlon at Bagram. Operation Nomad would be the Jolly Rogers' first trip into the Jalrez Valley since rejoining Dog Company. Hill decided to send Sammy, an experienced hand, into the valley with them. It seemed to be that middle ground Hill was seeking—a way to partition Sammy from the data that would flow through the TOC during Nomad without shaming a friend who had not yet been proven guilty. Plus, as short as Dog Company was on manning, every friendly Hill could send into Jalrez would count.

On 23 August, Dave's team began to focus on intercepting enemy reports prior to the mission start time of 0100, one hour past midnight on 24 August.

The Dirty First, the Jolly Rogers, and the Shockers got busy resetting their trucks and checking their weapons. Day waned into twilight. Soldiers wandered in and out of the chow hall and their hooches, snatching rest where they could.

With five hours to go until launch, CPT B found Hill in the TOC. "Bad news," he said. "Nomad leaked."

Hill was stunned. "How could that be? We've got every worker locked down here on the FOB. We've got all their cell phones."

"Someone must have snuck in another phone or had one hidden on the base," CPT B said. "Here's the worst part: Our sources in Jalrez say that enemy leaders in the valley are starting to bug out."

"You've got to be kidding me."

"Nope. We also have reports that insurgents are planting IEDs along Route Montana in preparation for our movement into Jalrez. The general has delayed the op twenty-four hours to give us time to come up with a plan for clearing our routes."

CPT B paused, then added, "Roger, there's more."

Hill braced himself.

"I just got word from the OEF Special Forces command. The team that was going to take custody of the prisoners isn't coming."

It was bad timing, CPT B explained: The SF team would participate in Nomad, but would then immediately transition to another high-priority op. The general's twenty-four-hour delay had crowded the prisoner-pickup plan out.

Hill went silent. This was worse than canceling Nomad. At least then there might have been a chance that the OEF guys would still swing down and pick up Airborne's detainees. Without an OEF unit to receive the detainees under OEF rules, Airborne's spies had just defaulted to ISAF rules of engagement.

That meant the ninety-six-hour clock on Kassiss and the Dalmar brothers was already forty-eight hours old.

██████ reports streamed in from sources in Maidan Shar and Jalrez Valley, so many calls that CPT B and Taz, Hill's intel sergeant, often had to put one source on hold to speak to another. Again, the news was bad. Word of the operation was completely out. Sources reported multiple IED emplacements along the only road into Jalrez. Also, a new wrinkle: A couple of sources mentioned a possible eighty-man attack on a U.S. base in Wardak Province, but did not say which one.

In the TOC, a live drone feed showed the enemy digging into fighting positions and planting explosives. All Hill and CPT B could do was watch.

By the morning of August 24, insurrection was brewing among the sequestered Afghan workers. Some began demanding their phones. Others threatened to quit their jobs. Indignance broke out: They had not been officially detained, and yet were being "watched" by armed guards. Several attempted to leave Airborne against instructions.

Dave continued administering ██████████████ while Ben Travlin pushed back assessments as quickly as the Bagram analysts could turn them around. Airborne's list of suspects was growing, as was tension on the base. In addition to Kassiss and the Dalmars, CI had identified several more suspects. The situation was beginning to spiral. Dog Company needed a new plan.

Hill called an all-hands meeting. A contingent of Dog Company and SF leadership assembled in the Airborne conference room. Hill updated the group and briefed a plan for arresting emerging suspects. Dog Company's Headquarters Platoon, led by Kay and Scott, would handle these detentions. The rest of the company and the Special Forces team needed to finalize preparations for Nomad.

Scott reminded Hill that the situation could be volatile since the workers were on the verge of mutiny.

"Do what you have to do," Hill said. "We don't have time to fuck around."

One of the suspects CI had identified was the FOB fuel truck driver, "Kader." As XO in charge of coordinating logistics, Kay knew the FOB fuel point well. He volunteered to detain Kader. Another lieutenant volunteered to go with him. Kay directed a soldier to covertly check to see whether Kader was in his little hut, then went to his desk to ensure that his sidearm was loaded. He also grabbed spare magazines.

The soldier returned from the fuel point. "Yes, sir. He's there."

"Thank you," Kay said. He thought about the terrain in the area, where diesel was stored in "blivets," bladders made from heavy, rubberized nylon. Berms protected the blivets on three sides to mitigate fires and the chance of perforation by shrapnel from incoming artillery or rocket fire.

If I were Kader and looking to escape, Kay thought, *how would I do it?*

He decided he should approach from a direction that backed Kader into the berms in the event he tried to run.

Kay took off his desert camouflage blouse. He would look less formal wearing only his sand-colored T-shirt. He reholstered his weapon and, with the other lieutenant, walked out of the TOC to the fuel point. Diesel fumes hung thick in the area, and Kay hoped he would not have to fire his weapon.

The two officers scanned for any other local nationals who might come to Kader's aid. Seeing none, they stood before a small hut with walls of corrugated aluminum. Kay rapped on the metal—*tap-tap-tap*—as if dropping by for a visit. With the other officer at his shoulder, he stood at the doorway and looked in. Kader was inside, lying on a pallet covered with a thin mattress, his head on a pillow. He was wearing a blue head wrap and a *dishdasha*, the traditional ankle-length white tunic. Both were stained with diesel and grease.

Kader sat up, and Kay saw that the Afghan had kept his hand under his pillow.

Kay left his 9 mm Beretta holstered. He did not want the situation to escalate. As he now did not trust any Afghan on the FOB, he had not brought an interpreter, so he said in English, "Come outside." Kay gestured with his left hand.

Kader met Kay's gaze with a blend of surprise and defiance. But he remained still, his hand hidden.

Kay raised his voice. *"Come outside."*

In one fluid motion, the Afghan stood, pulling a small blade from beneath the pillow. Instantly, Kay and the lieutenant drew their sidearms and burst into the tiny room. "Get on the ground! Get on the ground *now!*"

Kay motioned with his arm—*Get down!*—and a thought arrowed through his mind: *If he moves toward me, should I shoot?*

"Get on the ground *now!*" Kay yelled again.

But Kader did not move. Tense moments ticked by as all three men stood freeze-frame still, Kay and the lieutenant with guns drawn, aimed at Kader, who stood rigid with his knife hand at his side.

To break the stalemate, Kay reached up with his left hand and racked the slide on his pistol. The weapon ejected an unspent round, inserting another into the chamber.

Kay's message needed no interpreter: *I. Will. Shoot. You.*

Kader tossed down his knife and lowered himself to the floor, belly down. The lieutenant took an angled stance, holding his weapon on the Afghan as Kay zip-tied his hands behind his back and cinched them tight. A search revealed no more weapons on Kader's person. Kay kicked over the pillow on the Afghan's pallet. Underneath was a cache of contraband: a cell phone, a couple of SIM cards, and two more knives.

CHAPTER 11

25 August 2008

SIX HELOS ROARED into the Jalrez valley: two lifts of two Chinooks each, with each lift escorted by two Apaches, the terror of the Taliban. Nomad was underway.

The Chinooks touched down near the village of Esh-ma-keyl, depositing a phalanx of ANA soldiers and their Special Forces trainers.

The intel that Taliban leadership had already bugged out turned out to be true. Ground commanders encountered little resistance apart from *qalats* festooned with "welcome" banners written in Pashto:

DEATH TO AMERICA!
GO HOME, U.S.A.!

Only two IEDs and sporadic small arms fire greeted the advancing ground patrol, halfhearted attacks mounted by low-level insurgents who likely had fields to tend between firefights.

Upon commencement of the op, Scott and the FOB mayor had supervised a mass exodus of angry Afghan workers. Many vowed never to return. About fifteen LNs were asked to stay, pending further CI screening results. The ██████ exams, ████████████████████████████████ produced a steady churn of data between Bagram and Airborne. Dave sent periodic info blasts to Division CI analysts, who scrubbed and sifted the data then boomeranged waves of feedback.

*   *   *

Among Dog Company's Nomad targets was a foothill they called Cell Tower Mountain. For a couple of months, the Shockers had manned a COP (Combat Outpost, pronounced "cop") in the Jalrez Valley. From there, they had seen lights flashing atop the mountain. The pattern resembled Morse code and seemed to coincide with the movement of Airborne's troops. Lack of manpower had prevented Hill from exploring the cell tower before. Now, though, the entire valley teemed with Coalition Forces and Hill exploited the opportunity.

Grant Hulburt, Jason Dudley, and the Dirty First pulled security on the road up to the mountain while the Shockers and Hill, with HQ Platoon, crept up toward the tower, clinging to the mountainside on the hairiest dirt road any of them had ever seen.

Washboarded and potholed, the road was missing entire sections.

As the patrol strained up the mountain, Hill locked his eyes on the road, which seemed to sheer away from under his truck. From the TC seat, it appeared that the Humvee was suspended out over the gorge. Hill's gut roiled.

Westerhaus stole a glance from the driver's seat. "Hey sir, are you feeling all right?"

In the rear seat, Doyle chuckled. "Yeah, sir, you look kinda green."

"No, I'd say it's more of a pale beige," Westerhaus said.

Hill smiled wanly. "All right, no talking! Everyone quiet."

The whole truck laughed.

Farther back, the Shockers' trucks struggled up the steep ascent. In 4-1, Staff Sergeant (SSG) Ray Davis's entire crew had to focus its attention on navigating the road. Davis's gunner, SPC Carlos Lugo, stood in the turret and called out warnings while the driver scraped his door along the mountainside to keep the passenger-side wheels from slipping over the edge.

Finally, the patrol reached the mountaintop and a small shack surrounded by a crumbling wall of stone. Inside the hut, the Shockers discovered three men. Mo looked them over. One, who claimed he was there to do repairs, wore decent clothes. A second was much older than the other two. The third appeared to be very poor, wearing tattered clothes and half a flip-flop on one foot.

The men were separated for questioning while Davis and a group of soldiers fanned out to search the hilltop. Through his terp, Habibi, Wilson began to grill the younger, more well-dressed Afghan about the light signals from the tower. After three squirrelly answers, Wilson lost patience and began yelling his questions in English. He realized even as he yelled that the guy had no idea what he was saying.

Davis reappeared in the hut. He held in his hand several cell phones his team had found stashed in the compound wall, in hidey-holes covered with rocks.

"What are these for?" Davis asked the Afghan, whose eyes grew wide. "Why are you hiding them?"

Then one of the phones began to ring in Davis's hand.

Wilson nodded at Habibi, who grabbed the ringing phone from Davis and answered it with a one-word greeting in Pashto. Muffling his voice and keeping his answers short, Habibi engaged the caller in conversation. Suddenly, the Afghan Wilson had been questioning started yelling, apparently at the caller on the other end of the phone.

"What's he saying?" Wilson asked Habibi.

"He is saying, 'Don't talk! The Americans know! The Americans know!'"

26 August 2008

Operation Nomad was neither a jackpot nor a bust. The ANP, the Afghan commandos, and their U.S. Special Forces trainers netted a dozen predetermined enemy targets by day's end. Coalition Forces also captured and neutralized several weapons caches. Before leaving the valley, the Jolly Rogers leveled one of Razak's homes, destroying a small IED manufacturing facility in the process.

Hill and the Shockers detained all three men on Cell Tower Mountain. Once back at Airborne, Hill pulled CPT B and Kay in for further instructions.

"We need to start shaking the bushes for help on these detainees." Hill said. "I know we are zero for twelve on prisoners staying in the system, but we have to continue to push for these guys to stay in custody. Larry, keep pinging Battalion about the issue. Including the call I made with you, how many times have you called them so far?"

Kay scowled. "At least three."

"Okay, let's make it four here in the next few minutes. I'm going to see if we can broker a deal with Afghan National Security Forces to take the entire group. I believe they're our best bet for at least stopping the clock until higher coordinates for transport, or someone under OEF rules wakes up and circles back for these guys."

CPT B spoke up. He would continue to work his channels, trying to revive the Kabul Special Forces team's cooperation.

"All right, let's synch up later this evening," Hill said, and like a football team dispersing after a huddle, Airborne's primary leadership team broke.

Kay headed straight for the TOC to call Battalion. The battle captain answered.

"We've already had these guys for a couple of days," Kay said, then explained the ISAF 96-Hour Rule. "We've busted these guys as insider threats, and we don't want to have to let them go."

"Don't worry, sir. We're working on a solution over here. Also, sir, check with Lieutenant Scheppler. He should be able to give you guidance."

Steve Scheppler, the Battalion OIC for detainee operations, was currently on Airborne. Kay tracked him down and brought him up to speed on the prisoners.

"Would you be able to help us prepare the evidence packets sufficient for U.S. Forces to maintain legal custody of them?" Kay asked.

"I'll do what I can," Scheppler said. "But I'm here to help Able Company assume this battlespace. That's where I have to focus."

Able, another 1st Battalion company, was slated to take over FOB Airborne from Dog Company, which was scheduled to move farther east. CPT Al LeMaire had just taken over as Able's commander when he was seriously wounded in the IED blast that killed Carwile and Conlon.

"I understand," Kay said. "Whatever help you can give us, we'd appreciate it."

Kay left Scheppler and walked to his hooch, wondering how many times their "allies" had tried to kill them.

The pool of insider threat suspects narrowed to twelve—nine identified by Dave and his CI crew, and the three taken off Cell Tower Mountain. Based on the Shockers' account of events, Hill had reason to believe that the cell phone call Habibi intercepted had originated on Airborne.

Hill first ordered the suspects brought to the TOC conference room one at a time for questioning. Scott then escorted those under arrest to the coffeehouse at the top of the FOB. He assigned the head terp, "K.J.," a wizened man in his forties, to translate during detention operations. K.J. had sailed through the ▮▮▮▮▮ and all of Dave's database queries and come up clean.

The coffeehouse was a single room with mismatched tables and chairs and a makeshift counter off to one side, banged together from plywood. It separated the main part of the room from a bare-bones food prep area.

A metal cashbox sat on the counter. Until three days earlier, the Dalmar brothers had stood behind it, whipping up cappuccinos and chai tea, joking with the Americans, taking their money. Now the Dalmars sat facing the wall opposite the counter, prisoners in their own concession.

Seven other detainees were distributed along the left and rear walls. Some sat erect and others reclined, all on Army-issue blankets. Though all wore flex-cuffs and blindfolds, the atmosphere was low-key. Hip to American culture, the Dalmars had always run tapes of American music videos on a wall-mounted TV. Now, Britney Spears hiccuped in the background.

Dave worked through the night refining "link analyses"—charts showing which LNs were dirty and how they were connected to other bad guys. By dawn, he had built out an organization chart for each suspected spy, including the names and phone numbers of everyone in their respective networks. Most disturbing were the Dalmar brothers. Among their contacts were confirmed Taliban insurgents, and confirmed IED facilitators, including a known facilitator of a particularly vicious type of IED known as an EFP (Explosively Formed Projectile).

Designed to deform a metal plate into an aerodynamic, armor-piercing slug on detonation and accelerate it toward its target, EFP devices had been deployed against Americans in Iraq with savage results. Equally alarming was this detail: The facilitator with whom the Dalmars were linked had known connections to advanced IED and bomb-making trainers in Iran.

Later that night, Dave checked his secure email. Finally, he had results. He jotted down the initials of a few names and went to find Hill. He found him the conference room. Dave reeled off what he had: Division's counter-intel analysis confirmed that the insider threat aboard Hill's base met the formal definition of espionage: intent, capability, and demonstrated success. Bagram analysts had also refined their picture of the Dalmar brothers. Aziz Dalmar's contacts included an Afghanistan provincial council member in Herat, a province bordering Iran. ███████████████████████

███
███
███
███████████████████████

Malik Dalmar's list of contacts included highly placed Afghan officials. An employee of the Dalmars, Roohulla Hamadi, had contacts that included Taliban insurgents *and* officials in Afghanistan's ministries of industry and defense, as well as an Afghan general and a provincial intelligence chief.

The question became: Why did the owners of a crappy little FOB coffee shop and their lowly barista have contacts like these?

Hill was astonished. How could enemy infiltrators of this caliber have been allowed to infect his base, passing through an ISAF-sanctioned process for screening and hiring local national workers? He knew that employee database systems stayed out of date, often due to a lack of support needed to repair or replace broken equipment provided by big defense contractors whose service reps never graced the likes of FOBs Ghazni or Airborne and their outlying outposts.

In light of Dog Company's situation and Dave's brief about four hundred insider threats in Regional Command East alone, it appeared that these security gaps enabled spies and Taliban sympathizers to move at will among American installations simply by changing the spellings of their names.

According to Dave, it had taken only a short query by the CI team at Division to established that Aziz Dalmar was among the most lethally con-nected of the group. How was this possible? Hill wondered. Why wasn't this basic capability accessible by units on the front lines?

Dave continued with his brief: The ██████████████████ revealed that "Issa," who operated a grader on the FOB, had also been in contact with insurgents, as had Kader, the FOB fuel truck driver. Airborne's nine sus-pects also included a man named "Morcos," the supervisor of all LNs work-ing on the FOB.

Even that, though, was not the worst news Dave had for Hill. "I know this isn't going to be easy to hear, sir, but my suspicions of Sammy were correct."

Hill's face fell. "That can't be true."

"Sir, he's the worst of the bunch."

Sammy's list of contacts included the Iranian Embassy in Kabul and the Islamic Revolutionary Guard Corps, Iran's most powerful military and security arm.

Hill felt the gut punch of betrayal. He thought of late-night discussions with Sammy about America while out on missions, Sammy's dreamy-eyed fascination with the ideas of freedom and democracy, his youthful dreams for a better Afghanistan.

A *lie*, Hill thought. *It was all a lie.*

CHAPTER 12

WHEN HILL TOLD Dave it was "a mistake" suspecting Sammy as a spy, he didn't mean, *It's a mistake because I don't want to believe it.*

He meant it wasn't true. Period. End of story.

He had been wrong. Now he sat in the TOC conference room waiting for his terp. He had taken two chairs from the long table and placed them in an open area, facing each other.

Kassiss and the Dalmars were still in detention up at the coffeehouse. The only reason they weren't free to run to their enemy handlers was the brief stay at NDS that had stopped the ninety-six-hour clock. In less than forty-eight hours, Hill would be forced to let them go. But first he wanted to see if Sammy could provide intel that would keep that from happening.

Two armed guards arrived with the terp in tow.

"Just bring him in here and sit him down," Hill said.

Obediently, Sammy let himself be led to a chair across from Hill. He raised his eyes, which appeared to Hill guarded yet full of sorrow. The guards left.

"Sammy, do you know why you are here with me?"

"Sir, I did not do anything, I swear by Allah."

Hill leaned forward, elbows on his knees, and studied the Afghan. He could see the fresh crop of razor stubble that rose on the young man's face each afternoon. It added a decade to his face in the space of a day. In the morning, after a fresh shave, he was a fresh-faced boy again. Handsome, accommodating, easy to like. All these qualities had once seemed to Hill the agreeable traits of a good man trying to make the best of the situation that had befallen his country. Now they seemed perfectly suited for a spy.

I've got to get Sammy to talk.

Hill sat up and let his eyes bore into the younger man's. "Sammy, we know everything. We know who you've been calling. We know you've been giving the Taliban information about us. Sammy, we know."

"I swear by Allah! I swear by Allah! I swear by Allah!" Sammy chanted, as if repetition would vindicate him.

The captain held up a pair of cell phone SIM cards. During a search of Sammy's quarters, Mo had found them in slits that had been carefully cut into Sammy's mattress. "If you're telling me the truth, then why did you lie about these? You aren't supposed to have a phone other than the one we give you. And we asked you, all of you, to give us your cell phones and SIM cards for inspection two days ago, didn't we?"

Sammy hung his head. Abruptly, Hill stood and his chair flew back, skittering across the floor. "Sammy, answer me! We know you've been lying to us this whole fucking time!"

The terp folded his arms across his chest and began to rock in his chair. "Sir, I would never hurt you! I swear I would never hurt you!" He began to cry.

Hill walked around behind Sammy, leaned down near his ear, kept his voice soft. "You've already been caught. You can help yourself by giving us more information."

His words were not bait, entirely. Sammy became a target the day he signed up to work for the Americans. The Taliban were notorious for holding family members of Coalition allies, leveraging their safety for information. Maybe Sammy's family was in danger. Maybe that was how they'd gotten to him. Part of Hill deeply wanted to believe Sammy had not committed these offenses of his own free will.

"Sammy, if it's your family, we can work something out. Just talk to me."

"Sir, I would never hurt your men. I swear by Allah!"

Inwardly, Hill cursed. He was at his legal limit for questioning a detainee, and he felt trapped. ████████████████████████████████████ ██ Everyone from Division on down had the intel on the prisoners, knew how dangerous they were, and had offered no help. Every time Dog Company had captured prisoners, they were released. His men had been pushed to the brink—shorted ammo, batteries, food, water, even *walls* for their fucking FOB. Meanwhile, this traitor, this spy, and all the ones up in the coffeehouse, could kill and maim his men, and all he could do was stand here and be lied to.

Hill circled to face Sammy, pulled his arm back in full and swung it down, slapping the terp hard across the face. It was a solid blow and it knocked Sammy from his chair to his knees. ████████████████████

██

████ At that moment, Hill was a man at his limit who had just put his toe across the line.

When he stepped back, he saw a drop of blood thread down from Sammy's nose. "Dammit, Sammy, just tell me what you know!"

"Sir, I don't do nothing!" Sammy's perfect English faltered. A long stream of spit dripped from his chin and he began rocking on his knees like a penitent at prayer.

"Tell me!"

"No! It's not me!"

Hill knew he had been played, stabbed in the back, and he felt like a fool. And now it was pretty clear that everyone from Battalion on up had washed their hands of this situation and intended to let these prisoners go, just like all the rest. The difference was, *this* prisoner had almost certainly killed Hill's brothers—

Why don't I just drive him out to the desert and kill him?

The thought flashed into Hill's brain from nowhere, surprising him. But after it arrived, he let it marinate. He would take Sammy to the desert, shoot him, and bury him. He'd use a confiscated enemy weapon. He would get away with it, too, there was no doubt about that. He'd just say Sammy stopped showing up for work. Local nationals did that all the time.

As he stared at the terp, Hill saw Paul Conlon lying dead on Highway 1...soldiers hustling Donnie's bloody form onto the MedEvac helo...the mutilated body of an American soldier D Co found in the Tangi Valley...

An eye for an eye, Hill thought. The idea of retribution warmed him—

What am I doing? The thought was like ice water in Hill's face. *Am I really sitting here thinking about executing this person?*

Abruptly, he stood. He rolled his neck to loosen it, his eyes coming to rest again on Sammy. Dark notions aside, Hill knew he wasn't going to kill him. That just wasn't who he was.

Crossing the room, he opened the door and told one of the guards to go get Mo and Hulburt. Within three minutes, they arrived. Hill took them inside to an adjacent room and brought them up to speed. "The last dozen guys we sent up to higher were released. Under ISAF rules, Sammy and the rest of these spies will eventually walk free. We have intel on an eighty-man attack planned against an American base. We need to get some answers out of Sammy so that we can at least know who and what we're up against."

Hill continued, thinking on the fly. "You guys should go in and try to reason with him. Be the good cops."

He surprised himself. It all sounded so Hollywood, like one of those cheesy detective shows he'd watched growing up. He was sure he played a terrible bad cop. Scott had once told him that it was a good thing he was an officer, because he was terrible at yelling.

"Let him know how disappointed I am," Hill said. "Tell him I was just a little angry back there, maybe a little unreasonable. He can fix it just by telling us what he knows."

Tommy Scott sat at his desk, the smell of day-old coffee worming into his nose. He stood and crossed the room to a stained coffeemaker, drew himself a nasty cup, and thought of Sammy. When Dave had first suggested Sammy might be a traitor, Scott had wanted to laugh out loud. Sammy? No way. Now, though, Scott cast a fresh eye on incidents that had once seemed innocent. He had often seen Sammy go over and eat with the Afghan soldiers, buddy-buddy, laughing it up. At the time, he thought the terp had been building rapport, acting as a kind of ambassador from the American side of the FOB.

What if he had been conspiring instead? It wasn't like the Afghans were reliable foxhole allies, anyway. A couple of times during firefights, instead of fighting alongside the Americans, the ANP had crawled around behind them, collecting brass shell casings they could sell later for cash. ANA soldiers had also been caught stealing sensitive, high-end equipment and laptop computers from the U.S. side of the FOB. They'd carted it all off base, dug a hole, and cached it there.

But what if the problem ran even deeper? What if Sammy and the other detainees were in league with the Afghan soldiers who lived on the FOB? What if their capture triggered a revolt—two hundred Afghan soldiers *plus* the Taliban against Dog Company? The ANA had turned on Dog Company before.

On May 28, an ANA patrol escorting an Afghan fuel truck convoy through Wardak into Ghazni was attacked near Sayed Abad. CPT Hill, on a routine patrol nearby with the Dirty First, had launched Hulburt and LT Sean Allred's crew as QRF to support the Afghan Army. By the time 1st Platoon arrived, the ANA were mopping up after a solo victory, which was good, a mark of progress. They had some Taliban fighters hog-tied and piled in the back of their trucks. Five were alive and several were dead. After being whittled down by successive enemy attacks, this was a major win for the ANA.

The Dirty First pulled up in four trucks, and a couple of soldiers dismounted. Allred located the ANA commander, congratulated him, and explained that his platoon was there to help with the detainees. Per standard procedure, Allred explained, his men would like to enter data on each of the captured or killed Taliban into the ███████████████████████████

Without warning, the ANA commander bristled and barked an order. The entire Afghan company charged their weapons and leveled them at 1st Platoon, whose gunners immediately returned the favor.

Allred and the Afghan commander froze, standing toe-to-toe in the middle of Highway 1, their soldiers squared off behind them, weapons ready.

Tense seconds passed, the players still as a frieze. Inside the American trucks, a Dirty First gunner keyed the platoon's internal radio net. "We could kill them all," he said quietly. "But it would be messy."

Then, wisely, Allred stepped back. He gave way to the ANA commander. The Afghans rolled proudly away. The Americans avoided a headline on CNN.

Those, Scott thought, *were our Afghan "allies."*

Scott himself had walked the perimeter with Sammy a hundred times, checking in with the American and Afghan guard towers, inspecting the holes in the perimeter, the result of a mandated FOB expansion. He thought of the evenings when he and the young terp had stood together in the darkness, jawing. All the times he'd trusted Sammy, considered him not only an ally but a friend.

How many times had Sammy observed gaping security holes on the ANA side of the FOB? Or Afghan soldiers who were supposed to be pulling guard but were up in their towers sleeping or smoking hashish? Or that they arrived for guard duty with no weapons? Or that they had failed to come at all, leaving the entire northern half of the FOB open to attack?

Sammy knows, Scott thought. *Sammy knows everything.*

CHAPTER 13

SPECIALIST ALLAN MOSER was sitting in a personnel tent prepping for a promotion board. After only two years in the Army, his performance had been so solid that he was up for early advancement to sergeant, or E-5. The board was in a couple of weeks, but he was already studying: He wanted to knock it out of the park.

The tent flap rippled and Sergeant Andrew Doyle appeared in the doorway.

"First Sergeant needs a couple of guys," he said.

Moser sprang to his feet. "I'll go."

He didn't need to know what for. He and 1SG Scott had bonded long before, when Scott saw Moser twisting up guys in hand-to-hand combat drills back at Fort Campbell.

"That's my *son*, right there!" Scott had said, which cracked everybody up since Scott was as black as midnight and a guy couldn't get much whiter than Moser.

Doyle, Moser, and another young soldier, PFC Curtis Frey, trooped off and found Scott, who dispatched all three men up to the coffeehouse.

Doyle, Dog Company's armorer, was one of those guys with a knack for fixing things. He wore a mustache that his boyish face hadn't quite grown into. Quiet and mild-tempered, he was a fantastic shot and could walk a 40-millimeter grenade through a mud-frame window from a thousand meters out.

"What's at the coffeehouse?" Moser asked him as the three trudged uphill.

"The detainees are up there," Doyle said. "The spies."

Moser felt blood rush hot to his ears. *The spies who killed Paul and Lieutenant Carwile...*

Moser had known the spies were in custody, but not where. Now, he felt a certain satisfaction that for once he would be able to lay eyes on his enemy. In Kapisa Province, from which 2nd Platoon had just returned, the Taliban had seemed virtually invisible. As small arms fire showered in, bullets seemed to dart from the air itself, attackers melting like phantoms into the mountain brush.

In Moser's second firefight, the first in which he'd fired his weapon, he hammered back so hard with his SAW[6] that SSG Mike Anzalone had to pound on Moser's leg from the TC seat, yelling, "Slow your rate of fire! Slow your rate of fire!"

But Moser had already shot away half a tree. A raft of branches crashed to earth, revealing a Taliban gunner literally hanging among those that remained, weapon still in hand. Moser fired again and sent his enemy to hell. (He later told his dad and grandpa, a World War II vet, about this kill, but not his mother. There were some things, he decided, that you just don't tell Mom.)

Actually spotting a Taliban fighter was so rare that Moser had felt at times he was fighting ghosts. Now, tramping with Doyle and Frey up the dusty grade, Moser thought, *Hell yeah! I want to* see *these motherfuckers!*

At the top of the FOB, Doyle opened the coffeehouse and the two stepped inside. Moser let his eyes sweep the room, until they landed on Sammy.

What. The. Fuck?

Rage surged through Moser's body. He could actually hear blood humming in his ears. Sammy had been with 2nd Platoon during Nomad, clearing houses in Jalrez. Acting like he was looking for bad guys, scanning for IEDs. And come to find out he's a double agent? A piece-of-shit spy?

No wonder they'd taken two dozen wounded and now two KIA since landing in-country, Moser thought: *This fucker and his fucking friends.*

Moser flashed back to Bagram Airfield, a hundred grown men crying unashamed, the cavernous C-17 and the gentle thump of LT Carwile's casket coming to rest in the belly of the plane—a horrible, final sound. His guts twisted in the grip of betrayal, buffered only by a slim satisfaction that Sammy and his friends had been caught. They were now EPWs, Enemy Prisoners of War.

---

6. SAW: Squad Automatic Weapon, a light machine gun.

Moser didn't know what would happen to them—some kind of prison, maybe, like Guantanamo. But at least they were off the battlefield. At least they would pay for what they'd done to his brothers. Still, like gunmetal clouds in a fast-moving storm, Moser's grief boiled into a black and visceral hatred. And the target of his hatred now had a face.

27 August 2008

Heads down and walking quickly, Hill and Scott crossed the dusty ground between the tactical operations center and their hooch, a one-room shoe box capped with a tin roof. The two men entered through one end of the shoe box and headed for their bunks at the back, where they sat opposite each other, faces grim. The lights were off, the room dim, but a relentless Afghan sun pried its way through seams in the walls, lighting up swarms of dust.

Hill closed his eyes, tilted his head back, and wiped both hands down across his face. Then he leaned forward, elbows on his knees, and locked eyes with Scott.

"Brother," he said, "I think we're fucked."

Scott waited.

"I think we're going to have to let these guys go," Hill said.

The ninety-six-hour clock was ticking down fast. Since the NDS returned Kassiss and the Dalmar brothers to Airborne, they had been in custody for more than eighty hours; the other prisoners were heading into their third day.

Hill saw emotions flicker through Scott's dark eyes. The first sergeant expelled a short, audible breath. A puff of disgust. "Larry try calling Battalion again?"

"Yeah."

"Why won't they take these assholes? We've shared the intel on them, the links to the Taliban, to Iran."

"If we let them go, we're gonna get hurt," Hill said.

"There's no doubt," Scott said. "Just like Wanat."

Four weeks earlier, a force of about two hundred Taliban fighters had overrun an American unit on a small OP near the east-central village of Wanat. Nine dead and twenty-seven wounded, the worst U.S. loss since the war began.

Hill combed his brain for options. Between meetings, he had pulled LT

Scheppler aside. He knew Kay had already approached Scheppler, but the Battalion's Detainee OIC was still Hill's best bet.

"Steve, we're in a tough spot here, you know?" Hill had said quietly.

"Yes, sir, I know."

"Dog Company has had every one of our detainees released by higher since we got here in the spring. All guys that we caught red-handed."

"I know, sir."

"What do you think will happen to these twelve—even if Battalion or Brigade comes to get them now?"

"They'll release them," Scheppler said.

Out of the horse's mouth, as it were. Hill had looked the lieutenant in the eye. "You know this meets the definition of insanity, don't you?"

"Yes, sir."

Though Scheppler represented Battalion, he was willing to shoot straight with Hill, a line company commander. Hill respected him for that.

In the dusky light of the hooch, Hill scuffed at the floor with his boot. He wondered how it was possible that he was having trouble getting these prisoners transferred. Evidence on Dog Company's previous captures had been solid; the evidence on these men was incontrovertible. Failed ▮▮▮▮▮ exams, link analyses showing each prisoner's network of contacts, their names coming up hot in databases tracked as high as the NSA.

What does it take to hold a prisoner in this war? Hill wondered.

The inertia was increasing the probability of one seriously bad option: releasing the infiltrators. Hill was beginning to realize that he might simply have to let them all walk out the front gate. And, according to ISAF's 96-Hour Rule, Dog Company would actually have to give the spies money to see them on their way.

He let that idea wash up against the tally of the deployment. Dozens of firefights, roadside bombs, suicide attacks. Rockets falling on the FOB as regular as tropical rain. He thought of the mutilated American soldiers he and his men recovered in the Tangi Valley. Of sifting through their charred remains, and how he learned later that the locals had been selling their amputated fingers in the market as souvenirs.

Third Platoon was grieving at Bagram. Fourth was still banged up from tangling with those vehicle-borne suicide bombers. Second Platoon had just rotated down from Kapisa and was still acclimating to Wardak. First was carrying a lot of the workload, and they were exhausted.

Meanwhile, Taz's ▮▮▮▮▮▮ sources were reporting whispers of the planned insurgent attack on a U.S. outpost, at least eighty fighters strong.

He remembered again the briefing point from Dave. Another commander who had busted infiltrators had simply fired them—and then his base had fallen under retaliatory attack.

If Hill just kicked the spies off the FOB, would that mean the Taliban no longer had a reason *not* to attack Airborne?

Hill knew his men were nowhere near empty. Their courage and commitment had never been an issue. But he also knew he had changed as a commander, had become more cynical and more conservative. He thought about Maria Conlon's message concerning Paul: The best way for Dog Company to honor him was to make sure the rest of the company made it home safe.

Hill raised his eyes to Scott's. "If these detainees get through that wire, they're going to come back with a vengeance. Can we live with that? Can we live with the outcome?"

The two men exchanged the answer with their eyes: No, they could not.

CHAPTER 14

HILL AND SCOTT emerged from the officers' hooch and trudged up the chalky hill in silence. Hill ticked through a mental bullet list of logic. The feint operation and counterintel sting had linked the IED that killed Carwile and Conlon to insider threats on his base. Now he had twelve men in custody. If he was going to have to release them, he was going to wring some information out of them first.

Two pieces of intel were crucial: Who the detainees' local conspirators were, especially those in Jalrez Valley, as well as every scrap of data about any impending attack.

Then there was the bonus round. U.S. detention channels had all but fallen through at this point. But if he and Scott could manage to get confessions, there might still be a chance to fatten the detainees' evidence packets enough so that the Afghan National Police or NDS would take custody of the spies if their own higher command would not. New intel might not prevent an attack, but if they could keep the prisoners in custody even a little while longer, it might disrupt the intelligence flow, put the enemy off their game plan, and buy some time.

If, just this one time, the detention process could proceed to a productive end, Hill thought—a *war-fighting* end instead of a public relations end—it could be a game changer. Not only could Dog Company prevent further attacks on civilians and Coalition Forces, they could seize the initiative, maybe even turn the tide in Wardak once and for all.

Hill and Scott entered the coffeehouse. The smoky bite of espresso hung in the air, mixed with the sharp tang of sweat. Britney Spears still shimmied on the television screen. Scott scowled. He was not a fan.

Hill glanced at the counter where one of the cell tower detainees sat with Mo, lifting forkfuls of ramen from a bowl. Moser, Doyle, Frey, and PFC Michael Peake, along with two sergeants, guarded the detainees.

Hill glanced at his watch. For Kassiss and the Dalmars, he had just over twelve hours left on the ninety-six-hour clock. Across the room, he saw Sammy against a wall. Mo and Hulburt had gotten nowhere with their good-cop routine. Now the young terp stared straight ahead, his face a cipher. The word that came to Hill was *professional*. He ground his teeth together and swallowed.

Leaving Scott in the middle of the room, Hill walked over to the guards and indicated that he needed to speak with them in private. The four men gathered near the counter and Hill spoke in a low tone, "Okay, we're at a point now where we know nobody's coming to pick these guys up. We've had some of them about eighty hours. The rules say that if we don't have formal charges pressed in ninety-six, we have to let them go."

Moser muttered a curse and made a face that looked like he wanted to spit. Hill continued. "I can't tell you guys everything I know about the detainees, but I know enough to tell you that they're really bad. With everything they know about us, if we release them, we're asking for retaliation."

Hill lowered his voice even further, and the guards leaned close. "We need to turn the heat up a little in this room. I need information. We're not going to hurt these guys, but we're going to make them think they're going to be hurt."

"Roger that, sir," Moser said. Doyle and Peake nodded their understanding.

Hill turned abruptly, belligerently. "All right, let's cut the shit! We know you guys have been spying for the enemy. I want answers and I'm fucking tired of waiting. You are going to start talking, one way or the other!"

Scott stood in the middle of the room, arms crossed, observing. Hill glanced at him, and a signal passed between the two men. Though they hadn't discussed it, Hill was sure Scott knew what was coming.

Hill pointed at Sammy. "Get him up!"

Moser and Peake walked over and hoisted the blindfolded terp to his feet. They pushed him toward Hill a little faster than necessary, purposely causing him to stumble on the way. Nothing shrinks a man's balls like helplessness.

Hill brought his face close enough to Sammy's to breathe on his lips. "You," Hill said, poking the interpreter in the chest, "are going to translate."

Hill could have used K.J. to translate, but Hill wanted to keep Sammy off balance. With K.J. in the room, Hill knew Sammy would have to translate accurately. God only knew what kind of crap he'd passed along before. He noted with satisfaction that Sammy's composure was cracking again, fear tugging at the corners of his mouth. Hill hoped to spread that emotion, stoke it until it filled the room like a choking gas.

"Somebody better start talking!" Hill yelled at the prisoners. "Right fucking *now*!"

Sammy interpreted quietly, rendering the curse word in its closest Pashto equivalent. Hill popped him in the shoulder. "Louder! You talk the way I talk! If I'm yelling, you yell!"

Sammy repeated Hill's command. His voice was louder, but it wavered. The detainees shuffled on their blankets, but there was only silence. Hill surveyed the room. The three spies with the most intel value were Sammy and the Dalmars. Those were the ones Hill wanted to crack. The rest needed to feel completely expendable unless they had something of value to offer.

Hill jabbed his finger toward the grader operator, Issa. Striding over, Doyle and Peake pulled the man to his feet and guided him, blindfolded and stumbling, to face Hill.

"Sit down!" Hill said.

Sammy duplicated in Pashto, but the prisoner did not move. When Doyle tried to push him down by his shoulders, Issa resisted.

"Get his ass on the floor!" Hill yelled.

With his right leg, Doyle swept Issa's legs from under him and he crashed onto his back. Using his flex-cuffed hands as a tripod, he struggled into a sitting position and sniffed the air like prey.

Hill bent on one knee and got three inches from the detainee's blindfold. "Who do you work for? What information are you passing?"

Sammy echoed the questions in Pashto. Issa swiveled his head back and forth like a radar dish. He flinched back as though expecting a blow, but he did not speak.

Hill raised his volume. "I said, who do you work for? Talk! Now!"

Silence.

Hill felt frustration creeping up his neck. He had read that in Vietnam, U.S. interrogators took Viet Cong fighters for helicopter rides and threatened to drop them from the sky if they didn't talk. This, however, was the best Hill could do.

He glanced at Scott, who lowered his chin and fixed Hill with a schoolteacher gaze: *I get what you're trying to do here, sir*, Scott's eyes said. *But you suck at this.*

Scott, the former drill instructor, did not suck at yelling. Again the two men traded signals with their eyes. Then, like a cage fighter, Scott waded in.

Hill turned toward the detainees. "Him," he said, pointing to Morcos, the FOB labor supervisor. The captain nodded to Doyle and another guard. Both slung their rifles, crossed the room, and hiked the prisoner up by his elbows.

"Why you do this?!" Morcos cried, as the guards dragged him toward Scott. "I don't do nothing! I promise you with my heart, I don't do nothing!"

He bucked and struggled, his legs scrabbling on the wooden floor. "No! I don't do nothing! This not human treatment!"

Daylight and shadow striped the room. Hill noticed that the other detainees were now on high alert, chins up, locked on, listening. He pressed the moment. "You heard me! Lay him down!"

"We'll have to cut the zip ties, sir," Doyle said.

"Do it."

Doyle whipped his blade from his kit and flicked it through the thin plastic strips that bound Morcos's arms. The other guard pushed the prisoner down on his back.

Immediately, Scott straddled him. "Talk, motherfucker! What do you know?" Scott then drew back his arm and struck the man, hard, across the mouth.

A collective gasp filled the room. Stunned, Morcos let his head drop to the floor—*thump*. His mouth hung open. Sammy stammered out a translation, stumbling on "motherfucker." Along the walls, the prisoners shifted and squirmed on their blankets, exchanging a hushed buzz of Pashto and Dari.

CHAPTER 15

Across the FOB, Dave tallied the results of his mission, and of Operation Nomad, as he packed his gear. While it was true that most of the enemy in Jalrez had opted for escape over ambush, the Coalition had still inserted more than 750 troops into a Taliban sanctuary without taking a single casualty. Also, Dave and the CI team had narrowed the gap for CPT Hill, identifying nine insider threats.

Counterintel-wise, the net gain was a little spooky considering a remark his OIC had made just before Dave's team left Bagram for Wardak less than two weeks before.

"Go catch some spies," he'd said.

It was hyperbole, Dave knew. He had actually laughed.

"No, seriously, moron," the OIC said. "You're gonna catch some spies this time, so get to work."

Dave had laughed again and walked out of the building. His OIC had never given him such an obvious and direct order. The fact that he had in this case was strange since nine spies were now in custody.

Dave had suspected that he'd find a leak on Airborne. Instead he had found a flood.

It did not surprise him that the commander's terp was dirty. The best spies were usually the go-to people—the most useful, and frequently the most entertaining. These were necessary traits, since a spy with crappy people skills or a poor work ethic would simply be replaced, and therefore lose their access to whatever sensitive information the enemy wished to capture.

Now, though, Dave's team had orders to pack up and move out. There were pressing issues elsewhere.

* * *

In the coffeehouse, a fresh bar of white sunlight broke through a high window, lighting up squadrons of dust. Poised over Morcos, Tommy Scott raised his arm again. "You think we don't know you're connected to the Taliban in Jalrez?" he roared, letting spit fleck the prisoner's face. "We *know*! But you better tell us exactly who. If you don't, you're gonna pay the price. You better trust me on that!"

"I don't do nothing!" the prisoner yelled, struggling to free his arms from beneath Scott's knees. "I talk to no one!"

Scott's hand cracked Morcos's face again.

And again.

And again.

A minute passed as Scott struck the Afghan over and over.

"Who are your contacts?" Scott yelled. *Crack!* "Who do you know in Jalrez?!"

Morcos began to cry. Actual tears, Hill saw. Useless fucking tears.

Just then SGT Jared Allen walked into the coffee shop. Allen was a part of Able Company. What he saw as he walked into the coffee shop likely stunned him, Hill thought, since he had not been read in on the ruse. But Hill didn't have time to explain.

Allen spotted Scott on the floor and called his name.

"What?" Scott said.

"We need you down at the ECP, First Sergeant." The ECP: entry control point—the FOB main gate.

"Can't this wait?"

"No, I think we need you down there."

Scott looked over at Hill. "Sir?"

"Go ahead, First Sergeant, we've got this."

Scott stood and dusted off his pants.

"All right, I'll be right back." Scott and Allen headed out the door and down the hill toward the ECP.

As Morcos caught his breath, Hill paced the floor.

We need intel, he thought.

We need confessions.

And we need them now.

He looked at his watch again. Time seemed to be draining faster now, the way the last sand falls more quickly through an hourglass. Hill felt frustration crawl up his collar. Again, he wondered how he'd reached this point. He felt surrounded, unprotected, powerless.

These fuckers knew the 96-Hour Rule as well as he did, knew how many times the sun had risen and set. All they had to do was keep their mouths shut for a few more hours. Then they could get back to the lucrative business of killing American soldiers while collecting American paychecks.

"Okay, that's it," Hill said suddenly, looking directly at Sammy. "I'm taking care of this right now. Guess what, motherfuckers?" Hill drew his sidearm, a Beretta 9 mm, and racked the slide. "Some of you are going to take a walk outside."

Sammy's voice quavered as he rendered Hill's words in Pashto.

Around the room, blindfolded heads swiveled, waiting for the sound of approaching boots.

Hill pointed to Issa, the grader operator. "That guy, get his ass outside."

A guard crossed the room and grabbed Issa, hoisting him by one arm. "Let's go."

Panic spiked among the Afghans, who began chattering wildly in their native tongues. Issa, a handsome man in his early thirties, went limp and began to moan in Pashto. His shoulder-length hair draped forward, hiding his face. Sammy translated his words: "Please, no . . . *please*, no!"

Moser ran over to help the other guard, and the two soldiers dragged Issa, the tops of his bare feet sliding across the wooden floor. Doyle opened the coffeehouse door, and light spilled into the room. The prisoner's feet bumped over the threshold as the guards pulled him outside into the dirt.

Doyle turned to see Hill kneeling beside Morcos. The captain pulled down the blindfold, stared into the Afghan's eyes, and said in a low, even tone, "Do you want to die? I'll make that happen."

Tears streamed down Morcos's face, but he remained silent. Hill stared down at him. He did not think about the future. He felt no fear.

"Fine," he said. "Fuck it."

He stood, the Beretta in his right hand. Took a final glance around the coffeehouse. Morcos was sitting up now, cringing away. Doyle stood near the other prisoners, who sat erect against the walls, still flex-cuffed, yelling out in erratic bursts.

"I'm going to take care of your friend outside," Hill said to the room.

He waited for Sammy to translate, then walked out the door. One minute later, every man in the coffeehouse heard a gunshot. Then they saw Hill reappear in the doorway, backlit by the Afghan sun.

BOOK 2

Brothers in Arms

The only redemptive feature of war is the brotherhood which it forges.

Max Hastings

Whether fighting its way out of 5:1 odds after being ambushed during a humanitarian assistance food drop in or giving way to the Afghan Army to prevent an international incident when their ANA "allies" turned their weapons on them during joint operations; the Dirty First epitomized the aggression, agility, and intelligence intrinsic to all Dog Company Platoons.(L to R) SFC Jason Bielski; SFC Grant Hulburt; PFC Daniel Rogers; SPC James Doyle; 1SG Tommy Scott; SPC Trevor Carlin; SPC Trent Crane; SGT Jason Dudley; PFC Justin Downie, and PFC Nickolas Williams.

Longhorn Conference Room
FOB Salerno, Afghanistan
LT ZACHARY L. MORRIS, Alpha Company, 1st Battalion, 506th Infantry Regiment, Combined Task Force Currahee, was called as a witness, was sworn, and testified, in substance, as follows:

Prosecutor, CPT Stephen Latino: Do you swear and affirm that the testimony that you will give in the case now and in this hearing shall be the truth, the whole truth, and nothing but the truth, so help you God?

Morris: I do.

Latino: How are you doing today?

Morris: Good, sir.

Latino: Do you know Captain Hill?

Morris: Yes, sir.

Latino: And you know First Sergeant Scott?

Morris: Yes, sir.

Latino: Are you a member of Delta Company?

Morris: Yes, sir. I'm the third platoon leader...

Latino: Do you remember being in a meeting where something was mentioned about detainee abuse?

Morris: Yes, sir...Basically CPT Hill came in and said that there is a chance that we will be investigated for detainee abuse or fake murders or murders...Also, that we need to be more careful, and that if Battalion or Brigade come to investigate to tell them nothing, or that you saw anything.

First Sergeant Scott said, "They aren't here or a part of Delta Company, and don't understand what is going on or what it's like over here...They either believe us or fuck them."

Latino: What was your reaction when you heard this?

Morris: My jaw hit the floor...The next morning I saw [LT Anthony Dey] and asked him, did you hear anything about detainee abuse? He's like, yeah, I heard about it, and my guys came and talked to me, and said, "Hey, we saw some stuff that shouldn't have happened." So I was like, okay, I'm not completely off...something bad happened. I was like, all right, I'm going to go call Major Smith, our battalion XO...I ended up calling on the speakerphone with Major Smith, and Colonel DeMartino. I was like, hey, I really think there is detainee abuse or something going on that shouldn't be, and that day Major Smith showed up to start the investigation.

Latino: When you arrived at FOB Airborne what was your overall impression of both Alpha Company and Delta Company?

Morris: Very, very poor command climate, lack of discipline on the little things, and tension with the Battalion. I guess there was a huge focus on taking care of soldiers, which I appreciated. But the biggest thing was...the lack of discipline...

Prosecutor, CPT Devon Runyan: When you say lack of discipline what do you mean?

Morris: I think just blaming everybody else for all of the problems. Lack of support, this, that, and the other...Soldiers walking around the FOB wearing flip-flops and T-shirts and just whatever else. You just got an attitude of okay, we're in Delta and we hate everybody else and we're going to do our own thing.

CHAPTER I

September 2007
SEVEN MONTHS BEFORE
THE AFGHANISTAN DEPLOYMENT
Fort Campbell, Kentucky

CPT ROGER HILL, twenty-nine, steered his gray Toyota Tundra pickup across Fort Campbell, Kentucky, past towering pines and wide lawns of neatly clipped grass. He pulled into a parking lot in front of the redbrick complex that housed the 1-506th. Paint-stenciled letters marked the parking stalls, and he scanned until he found his new spot: COMMANDING OFFICER, DELTA COMPANY.

It was Hill's first time in command. Seeing it in print was kind of cool.

Hill threw the truck in park, got out, and grabbed from the truck bed a couple of boxes filled with file folders, manuals, and personal items, including a photo of him with Lauren and their dogs, Buddy and Daisy. As he made his way to his new office, his mind buzzed with a first-day agenda.

First, get organized. That was key. Then he would have a series of sit-downs with the platoon leaders and platoon sergeants, along with his new first sergeant, Tommy Scott. Hill wasn't flashy, the type of guy to come in hot, barking orders, making sure soldiers knew he was now in charge. He had never believed that rank merits personal deference or respect. Respect as a formality, yes, but not personal respect and certainly not trust.

Hill wound through the corridors until he found his new office. It was a basic company-grade space: ten-by-twelve cube, blank walls, with a military-issue desk and gray metal file cabinet, equally worn. He set his boxes on the desk, extracted an armload of file folders, and headed straight for the file cabinet. He could think just fine amid a moving-day mess, but he preferred things labeled, ordered, and current.

He pulled open the top file drawer, expecting it to be empty. But amid the drab green hanging files, he spotted an unmarked manila folder about half an inch thick. Old files from the previous commander, no doubt. Hill pulled it out, flipped it open.

The first sheet of paper was a recommendation for a Bronze Star. The Army can award a Bronze Star for meritorious service of different kinds; this one carried a V for valor. Hill glanced at the soldier's name on Form 2823, the Department of the Army's form for sworn statements. Given under oath, soldiers use these statements to document various events, including the actions of their comrades under fire. Hill scanned the densely typed text and got the gist: battlefield heroics in Ramadi. He skipped down to the signature line, where the battalion commander would approve the award.

It was blank. Odd.

Quickly, he paged through the folder. It contained recommendations for combat awards, some of them Purple Hearts, all of them unsigned. A puzzling find. Maybe these were just drafts, or award packets previously rejected, as often happens, because of substandard writing or strength of justification. Maybe the final awards had already been conferred on these soldiers. Hill drifted to the chair behind his new desk, laid the folder out in front of him, and skimmed through a couple of the statements, eyewitness accounts of battlefield action in Ramadi the previous year, 2006. He had been there, too, fighting in the Mulaab District, just a mile or so from the 1-506th.

Hill had only meant to get a handle on the file, figure out who to hand it off to. But the sworn accounts detailed blazing firefights. Devastating war wounds. Men risking their own lives to save their brothers. Valor beyond most men's imaginations. Stories about the men of whom he had just this morning assumed command.

Hill, who ran his life on schedule and on plan, suddenly found himself reading a story he couldn't put down...

8 April 2006
Route Michigan, Ramadi, Iraq

SPC Andrew Doyle sat low on the gun. Low because it was broad daylight. Low because his Humvee was parked just off the bloodiest street in Ramadi.

Low because in this city, there was always a sniper waiting for you to stick your head up just one more time.

Tucked in behind a .50-cal in 4-2, Doyle scanned his sector, a slice of Main Supply Route Michigan. He remembered a previous run down the MSR. Just as his driver had careened into a right turn off Michigan onto Front Door Alley, three masked insurgents with AK-47s opened fire on Doyle's truck from a rooftop. Doyle swiveled his weapon, a MK19 that day, and kicked out three grenades—Thunk! Thunk! Thunk! Every round splashed down at a bad guy's feet and blew him out of his shoes.

Below him, the radio in Doyle's truck had gone hot. "Holy shit, 4-2! Your gunner can shoot!"

Doyle's marksmanship and short stature earned him a nom de guerre: Battle Troll.

Now Doyle was on Route Michigan again, and despite his previous success, it was always an ass-puckering experience. The road was the principle highway between Iraq and Syria, but where it shot through Ramadi, it was a minefield of IEDs. First Battalion's Bravo Company, the Outlaws, "owned" the MSR; the route was their AO, or area of operations. Their job was to kill or capture anyone caught planting a bomb.

The Death Dealers (then the call sign for 1st Battalion's heavy weapons company) didn't have an AO. Instead battalion commander Ron Clark had turned the Dealers into a specialty unit. Many battalion commanders, having grown up in line companies, lacked Clark's vision in effectively employing their Delta companies. In combat, they put them under the operational command of line units. During field problems, some actually cast their heavy weapons guys as enemy fighters, having them fight against their own guys as OPFOR, the opposing force.

Most battalion commanders staffed their Delta Companies with "low speed" guys, the ones without Ranger tabs, the fat boys, the problem children. Conventional wisdom went like this: Why waste your best, most athletic infantrymen on a company that doesn't march into battle, but instead rolls in, mounted behind massive firepower. But Clark took a different approach. He staffed the Death Dealers with his most experienced lieutenants and senior sergeants, men who had seen combat before. Then, instead of limiting his heaviest firepower to a single area, Clark turned the Dealers into a roving sledgehammer. Their job was to augment the line companies—Alpha, Bravo, and Charlie—and when the shit storms hit, bring the thunder. Clark's thinking was bold, out of the box. Now, midway through the Ramadi deployment, it had paid off: Everyone knew they could trust the Death Dealers to fish them out of trouble.

Clark had increased the number of observation posts, and tasked the Dealers with rotating through the OP at the T-bone intersection of Michigan and Highway 1. Four-two was parked on the southeast corner, facing the top of the T, backed in at an angle so that Doyle, up high on the gun, could see a few hundred meters west without getting sniped. 1SG Greg Rogers, Doyle's platoon sergeant, was dismounted, his M4 at low ready. Rogers stood behind a ten-foot steel-reinforced concrete barrier meant to ward off insurgent potshots. Inside 4-2, Doyle's squad leader and another soldier kept watch to the east.

Doyle noted the bright blue day: Spring had dawned in Iraq. He felt grateful temperatures hadn't yet reached the molten hell he'd heard was in store for summer. Then he heard a low rumble from the west.

Rogers heard it, too, and called up from behind the barrier. "Doyle, what do you got?"

"Marines!" Doyle shouted down. "Pretty big convoy."

The rumble grew louder, and a convoy of American vehicles came into view. It was a Marine Corps engineering unit, filling IED holes with concrete so that insurgents couldn't resow them with more explosives.

The squad leader's voice blew up through 4-2's turret like smoke through a factory stack. "It's the middle of the day! Why are they filling potholes in the middle of the fucking day?"

Other than overwatch positions, such as those along Route Michigan, 1st Battalion tried to restrict movement to the cover of darkness, when they had the advantage of night vision devices. That was because every building, every rooftop, every window in the city, was a potential hide for snipers. Especially along the MSR. It was rumored that a Chechen husband-wife sniper team operated in the area.

The convoy crept closer. Every so often, Doyle saw the trucks stop. A couple of Marines would dismount, toil over the road momentarily, then get back in their vehicles. After ten or fifteen minutes of this, the convoy was passing 4-2's position. Humvees, a wrecker, a Buffalo, more Humvees.

About half the convoy had rumbled past when a Humvee stopped in the middle of the intersection, less than ten meters from Doyle. Two Marines got out, one of them female. The pair walked around to the back of their truck and opened the door. Doyle saw what looked like coolers and inflatable mattresses begin to tumble out, and wondered if some of the Marines were medics.

"Corporal!" Rogers called out from behind the barrier.

The woman turned her head, and Rogers saw that she wasn't much older than his oldest daughter, who had just started college. "You need to take cover!

This AO is crawling with snipers! You guys shouldn't be doing this during daylight hours in the first place!"

The other Marine got back in the truck, but the woman kept standing there. Alone in the intersection, her back angled toward 4-2.

Doyle gripped his .50-cal tighter. Move! *he thought, silently willing her to get back in her truck.* There's a reason my platoon sergeant is standing behind a concrete barrier!

A gunshot cracked the afternoon. Doyle saw a pink mist erupt in front of the woman's head and her sunglasses slingshot away. She fell like a blade, her back smashing pavement.

"Holy shit!" Rogers yelled. "Doyle, light 'em up!"

Doyle opened up on the .50, firing diagonally across the intersection, in the direction of the rifle report, the big rounds blowing chunks out of the building across the street.

The convoy disgorged dozens of enraged Marines who charged toward the sniper's hide. Rogers called out fire-sector data as he snapped off M4 rounds over the barrier. The intersection popped and boiled with gunfire and the acrid smell of cordite, the sound of Doyle's gun jackhammering over it all.

Within moments, Marines began crossing Doyle's sector, and he was forced to stop shooting. He released his butterfly trigger and glanced down at the female Marine. A crimson pool was spreading around her head.

I hate this fucking place, *he thought.*

CHAPTER 2

As HILL READ, the shadows in the room grew longer. All the awards in the abandoned folder bore the names of young soldiers, squad level and below. And all were already highly decorated. These weren't guys who just happened to fall into a firefight and emerge with glory. They were guys who had done this day after day and had the medals to prove it.

How many more in this company are like these? Hill wondered.

He turned another page and another. He read until the lowering sun painted his office gold. When he finally closed the awards folder, Hill knew that he was confronted with a leadership challenge. It wasn't that these men would be hard to lead. The challenge would be getting them to respect him. In some ways, it was a cool problem to have, wondering whether he could harness and employ their talent. But it was also outright intimidating.

Like the men he would be leading, Hill had fought in Ramadi, but not in the same way as the 1-506th. After serving on a Military Transition Team in northern Iraq, he led a small contingent of Iraqi soldiers into combat in a Ramadi district called the Mulaab. The Iraqi unit had begun with eight hundred men. The area outside of Mosul where they joined their nation's new army was relatively safe. It had been a good spot for these green fighters to get some practice. But later, it became apparent that American decision makers reversed the logic: The area was safe, they decided, because this Iraqi battalion was so good.

At some point, this theory had to be put to the test, a condition made necessary by the Bush administration's decision to dismantle the Iraqi military and start over. The choice, based on the question of loyalty to Saddam Hussein, seemed sensible at the time: Any officer in the Iraqi military was presumed to be a Baathist, period. The Bush administration did not relish the idea of combing the Iraqi ranks for Saddam loyalists, or leaving in place born-again Iraqi troops who preached democracy but turned out to be moles and traitors. The short-term effect of scrapping Iraq's army was to rip out the nation's security backbone and, along with it, all military expertise and discipline. The long-term effect was a long-term war, as the Americans tried not only to hold territory but also to grow an entirely new army from scratch.

Not that there weren't some badass Iraqi soldiers. "Haziq," the commander of the Army battalion that Hill's team advised, began the war as a low-ranking soldier. After the U.S. invasion, Haziq came out of the pro-democracy closet and made a name for himself, going balls-out in firefights, tying dead Al Qaeda fighters to the back of his truck and dragging their bodies through the streets. He even looked like a badass: six-three or six-four, aviator shades at all times. Barrel-chested, poured into a crisply pressed uniform covered with honorary ribbons and badges conferred on him by departing American units.

When word came down that the battalion was headed for Ramadi, he mustered the unit, all eight hundred men, on a sprawling dirt field used for training. Summer had raised its ugly head, and the morning already simmered.

"Gather round! Gather round!" Haziq boomed in Arabic from a small platform. A translator repeated his words in English for the American advisors as the Iraqi formation collapsed into a huddle around their local war hero.

"You have proven yourselves worthy to go into combat!" Haziq proclaimed, his aviator shades reflecting the faces of soldiers crowded in close. "In two weeks' time, we will take the battle to the enemy in Ramadi, where we will fight proudly alongside our American brothers and drive Al Qaeda from our sovereign nation!"

The battalion cheered. Iraqi soldiers pumped their fists in the air and draped their arms around each other in a show of esprit de corps.

And the next day, six hundred of them did not show up for work.

Hill and the other American trainers had suspected that the announcement they were going to wade into the bloodiest area since Fallujah might trigger fear, even a few desertions. But they were stunned when *three-quarters* of the battalion packed their gear and left. Actually took their American-supplied weapons and uniforms and went home.

This just when U.S. trainers were on the verge of certifying the battalion at "Level 1" readiness, meaning they were ready to take off the training wheels and go on their own. The Ramadi announcement stripped away the bravado and revealed the truth: The unit might have been ready to rock in Beverly Hills, but not in Compton.

Several weeks into what would later be called the Surge, Hill and about two dozen soldiers from the Iraqi remnant were ordered to join a SEAL team on a routine patrol based out of COP Falcon, about two miles from Camp Corregidor. As they pushed deep into the Mulaab district, a no-man's-land held by Al Qaeda, the element came into heavy contact. An Iraqi fighter maneuvering just a step ahead of Hill caught a sniper's bullet through the forehead. The wound left his brains leaking into the street.

In succeeding missions, Iraqi casualties mounted. Then one day, several Iraqis threw down their weapons, sat down in the street in the middle of a known sniper zone, and refused to fight. It was then that Hill wondered if instead of disbanding Saddam's entire army, it might have been better to have chopped off the head of the snake and helped it grow a new one. Years later, he would watch as the new Iraqi Army's weakness of will came back to terrorize the region—and the world—in the form of ISIS, the Islamic State.

Now, Hill considered what to do with the orphaned awards, still marveling at the courage of these young American soldiers. He himself had dreamed of serving in the infantry since he was six years old. His father, Larry Hill, was an NCO with an infantry unit in Weisbaden, Germany. Hill, his mom, and his younger sister were allowed to attend a nighttime maneuver exercise. Hill remembered the crisp German night, huddling in the bleachers as armored personnel carriers and dismounted troops moved across the battlefield. Flares speared the darkness. Star clusters burst and shimmered down. Machine-gun fire rattled in Hill's chest. For a young boy, it was glorious.

Hill fingered the edge of the awards file. The write-ups seemed solid; it appeared that they'd simply never been processed. But bringing that up probably wouldn't be a popular move. Hill knew that Battalion had already made a big deal with outgoing commanders about getting all their paperwork processed so that they didn't leave a pile of crap in the incoming's lap.

Well, he was the incoming. It wouldn't be the first pile of crap he'd dealt with. Hill glanced up at the schoolhouse clock on the wall. It was 1700— 5:00 p.m. Rolling a problem into his higher's office might not be the best way to end his first day. Hill closed the folder and tucked it in his backpack. He'd go home and sleep on it, then decide what to do.

CHAPTER 3

1SG TOMMY SCOTT was at his desk by 7 a.m. He'd already PT'd (physical training) with the company and most of the men were back in the barracks showering up, getting ready for the rest of the workday.

Scott sipped his coffee and chuckled. Earlier that morning, when he joined his guys for PT, he'd caught two of them dozing.

"Wake your asses up!" Scott had snapped in the predawn darkness. He turned to another soldier and demanded, "How long were they asleep?"

"Just a couple of minutes, First Sergeant."

Scott turned back to the snoozers. "All right, I want you to take your asses to finance and tell them you want two minutes deducted out of your damn pay because you're on the clock right now!"

Everybody cracked up laughing, but Scott doubted he'd find anyone sleeping again anytime soon. Sometimes, a light touch was all it took.

When Scott arrived at Dog Company's work space, he'd noticed that his new commander, CPT Roger Hill, was already in his office. He was a West Pointer, Scott knew. That was a strike against. A lot of academy grads Scott had worked for seemed to have sticks permanently wedged up their asses. And Hill had that recruit-poster, college-quarterback look to him, too. Young, tall, fit. West Point *and* poster boy. Probably not good.

On the other hand, Hill seemed squared away, Scott thought. Had a quiet way about him. Not weak or tentative, just...low-key, not ready to bust into the company and start throwing his rank around.

Scott set his mug down and tried to form a one-word impression of Hill. *Careful* was the word that came to mind. Time would tell.

Scott reached down and squeezed his left knee, then his right. After more than seventy parachute jumps from Long Range Surveillance teams to the 82nd Airborne, both knees were shot. Doctors told him that running was like driving on flat tires; his bones were riding on rims. He agreed, could feel it every day.

Scott blamed it on Nick Kanus. Growing up in Tarpon Springs, Florida, Scott got his first job at age fourteen, gophering at a restaurant called Chicken King. The owner, Mr. Kanus, regaled Scott with tales of his own Army service during Vietnam—the strict physical regimen, parachuting into live fire, secret missions behind enemy lines. By contrast, everyone Scott knew in Tarpon Springs stayed in Tarpon Springs. Got into drugs, racked up two or three baby mamas, scraped by day to day. Scott imagined a life for himself beyond the metro-Tampa hood. A life serving his country, becoming a warrior like Mr. Kanus.

When he was nineteen, Scott signed on the dotted line and took to soldiery with athletic zeal. He blew the top out of the Army's PT regimen, earned his jump wings, completed the elite Recondo school. After serving a few years, Scott went home for a visit. He had learned a lot about combat operations by then, and a lot about Vietnam, the nation's most recent war at the time. And, well...some of Mr. Kanus's stories just didn't add up.

After hugs and a few war stories, Scott sat at the restaurant counter sipping an icy Coke. "So, Nick, tell me again what exactly it was you did in the Army."

Nick wiped his hands on his apron and grinned. "I was a cook."

Scott laughed out loud. "All those stories you told me and you were a damn *cook?*"

"Yeah, you dumbass, I was a cook."

Scott was smiling at the memory when Captain Hill appeared in his doorway.

"First Sergeant."

Scott stood. "Sir?"

"I've got something I need you to take a look at."

Hill vanished from the doorway, and Scott trailed him to his office, where the captain handed him a manila folder. "Have you ever seen these?"

Scott thumbed through the folder as though flipping through the pages of a magazine. Awards. Awards his guys had earned and never received. He felt his jaw muscles clench. *Son...of...a...bitch...*

"No, sir," Scott said aloud. "I've never seen these. These haven't been submitted yet."

Hill grabbed his cover off his desk. "Let's find out what's going on."

The two men headed over to the S-3 shop, or operations office, a little maze of desks in 1st Battalion headquarters. Scott stood at Hill's shoulder through a series of conversations that turned into an on-the-spot investigation.

Why weren't these submitted? the S-3, Major Rob Smith, wanted to know. *Where did you find them?*

So they were never passed up from the previous chain of command?

Hill and Scott watched as Smith pulled up personnel rolls on his computer. Some of the soldiers named in the awards packets were already out of the Army.

"Who else knows about these?" Smith said.

"Nobody," Hill said. "Just me and First Sergeant Scott."

"Well, what do you want to do?"

Hill stood quietly for a moment, thinking. Even bringing up the awards was like putting a boulder at the top of a hill and letting it roll. Hill didn't know where it would land.

First, how would Battalion track down the guys who were already out to confer their awards? Second, the signature line on the awards belonged to 1st Battalion's previous commander. That meant LTC DeMartino would have to sign off on the awards, acts of valor and battlefield wounds over which he had not commanded, then forward the awards to the Brigade commander, COL Pete Johnson. This would make it obvious that somebody in D Co had screwed up, which meant that the 1-506th had screwed up, which meant much weeping and gnashing of teeth, along with a great big fucking paper chase. Because, if heads are going to roll in the Army, there must an accompanying paper trail.

It didn't matter. Hill had made up his mind. "I think we need to submit these and get them processed so these guys can get their awards."

From across the room, another major chimed in: "I don't know whether you want to do that...Heads are gonna roll."

Laughter rippled across the room. Scott felt his jaw go again.

Hill stood quietly for a beat, then said, "Sir, these are Delta Company awards and I'm Delta Company commander. We're going to process these whether some of these guys are out of the Army or not. They deserve to get what they earned."

Major Smith nodded. "All right. Let's do it. But the boss is going to be hot, and his boss, even hotter."

Scott looked sideways at Hill and suppressed a smile. Maybe he would be okay.

CHAPTER 4

INDIAN SUMMER HAD settled across Kentucky and Lieutenant Larry Kay's running shoes pounded the pavement on Market Garden Road. Humidity leeched from the air, soaking the back of his gray Army T-shirt with sweat. Kay was one of the few men keeping pace with the run leader, a very young platoon sergeant. This was a six-mile company run and the platoon sergeant, a six-foot-five tower of muscle, was as usual intentionally running his soldiers into the ground.

Nothing wrong with tough training, Kay thought. But he didn't care for the way the sergeant mocked the men who fell out of the run. Kay ran past a young corporal puking; an NCO with shrapnel wounds who'd stopped to stretch his injured leg; and Shon Haskins, a senior NCO who had just returned from Ramadi with a medal for valor.

Kay was a platoon leader, or PL, his first time in the post. As a former enlisted man, he knew the protocol: The platoon sergeant, not the PL, takes care of things like physical training. On the other hand, it was the PL's job to make sure his soldiers were being developed.

Right now, the platoon sergeant is the only one being developed, Kay thought. *And he's developing into an asshole.*

One by one, Kay ran past the roadside casualties until he jogged up beside the run leader. "Hey, Sergeant, I think it's okay if the sergeant back there doesn't run. I can see his leg bleeding where the shrapnel wounds are."

The sergeant just pumped his arms, kept running. After a pause, he said, "Whatever, sir."

In the infantry culture, a leader who falls out of a company run might as well not consider himself or herself a leader anymore. But Kay saw another side of the issue: People who had been in the Army for fifteen or eighteen years and been blown up half a dozen times—sometimes the value of their expertise and experience began to overtake their physical abilities. And while it was good to have a healthy serving of lithe, agile soldiers in your unit, Kay also saw the value in senior NCOs like Haskins and SFC Tim "Mo" Moriarty, whose legs had been spiderwebbed with stress fractures even before he went to Ramadi. Men who would stand tall in a firefight, handle themselves on the radio, and say to their soldiers, "Good job."

Later, in the platoon office, Kay tried another tack. "Sergeant, I don't think there's any purpose in running like you do because everyone eventually falls out anyway. There's no point to it. The platoon's not even there with you."

"Hey, Lieutenant, I've *got* this," the platoon sergeant shot back. "You're the PL, but I'm going to run this platoon the way I want to run it. And when you go to combat *then* you can tell me how to run PT."

Kay carefully leveled his gaze. He did not raise his voice. "Sergeant, I'll go to combat when I go to combat. Until then, you will run this platoon in a manner that develops soldiers, not in a way that degrades them. Any questions?"

The sergeant spun on his heel and stormed out.

A month later, Kay was standing near Market Garden Road stretching out for another run. The weather had turned the corner toward fall and he was wearing full sweats. Haskins had been transferred to Dog Company to become a platoon sergeant, and Mo, too. Too bad. He liked both men.

At twenty-two, Kay was on the fast track. After earning a boatload of college credits while still in high school, he graduated from the University of Florida in only two and a half years with a degree in Asian studies and a fluent command of Japanese and Mandarin Chinese. He would've finished school more quickly, but he fell in love with a blue-eyed microbiology major named Jill and slowed down to marry her before she could get away.

Kay was nearly finished stretching when the Battalion commander, LTC Anthony DeMartino, walked up and joined him. DeMartino bent to stretch his hamstrings as though he planned to run with the group.

"I'm thinking of making you XO of Delta Company," DeMartino said. "What do you think?"

"Well, sir, to be honest, I'd really like to remain a platoon leader. But I'll do whatever you ask me to do."

"Great," DeMartino said. He stopped stretching and walked away.

Kay was disappointed. Being named executive officer was a privilege, he knew. It meant that officers higher in the Battalion had confidence in him. On the downside, a big part of being an XO was tracking logistics, supplies, and equipment—making sure the company had plenty of so-called beans and bullets. Kay hadn't signed up after 9/11 for that. He wanted to lead a platoon in combat.

He stood still for a moment and peered up into a cobalt Kentucky sky, letting inevitability sink in. He'd probably have to *really* screw up, he thought, like get arrested for DUI or something, to change this destiny. Kay sighed and took off running.

CHAPTER 5

DURING HIS FIRST months in command, Hill marveled at the dedication of his first sergeant, Tommy Scott. Doctrinally, officers and NCOs are taught that mission comes first and soldiers come second. Hill got that—the whole is greater than the sum of its parts. In the heat of battle, though, with bullets snapping at their heads, when rockets sear across their backs, when men throw themselves on top of live grenades, when they carry bleeding brothers through live fire, most are not doing it for the mission, for democracy, or even for their country. They are doing it for each other.

An infantryman fights for the man next to him who fights for the man next to *him*. Which was why Hill and Scott emphasized soldiers first. Both had found that if they took care of soldiers well enough, soldiers would take care of the mission.

Hill and Scott absolutely saw eye to eye on this, which was why both had been so concerned about the missing Ramadi awards and were pleased when soldiers began receiving them.

MAJ Smith seemed pleased, too. One day, he pulled Hill aside and told him he liked the fact that Hill had pressed for those awards in the face of almost certain static. Then the major said, "When I was a young officer, senior leaders took the time to mentor me, and I'd like to do the same for you."

"Sir, I really appreciate that," Hill said. "I'd be honored."

Smith's offer seemed to validate Hill's decision to stay in the Army, where he had spent his life since since he was a teenager. At eighteen, Hill was accepted to West Point, and the military academy's storied history shone for a moment on his northeast Alabama hometown. One Sunday at church, just before he was to report, a prominent citizen tapped him on the shoulder. "Roger, we love you, and we're proud of you."

"Thank you, sir."

"Listen, if it gets too hard up there, there's no shame in coming home." The man then slipped a couple of hundred-dollar bills into Hill's shirt pocket.

"Yes, sir," Hill said. "Thank you."

And it *was* hard. In high school, Hill had been an athlete and honor student, but small-town academics had not prepared him for the rigors of West Point, and he struggled every semester. He wanted to quit, but his heritage wouldn't let him.

His father, retired Army. His Korean-born mother, an honest-to-god Tiger Mom. His paternal grandfather, a Depression-era farmer who slept under a wagon each night until the crop was in. Hill's Korean uncles had immigrated to America, each with little more than twenty dollars and the clothes they were wearing. For twenty years, they worked their way up in construction until each owned his own firm.

Twenty bucks and twenty years. Hill wasn't going to quit. It wasn't in his DNA.

In this, he felt instant kinship with Tommy Scott. At forty-four, Scott was there with his men doing everything he asked them to do. During company runs, his knees swelled up and he had to grit his teeth until the endorphins and synovial fluids kicked in. But Scott never failed to show up, and he never complained. The only place Hill noticed was in his jaw muscles. Just a tightening, never a grimace. In fact, when the two ran together, Scott usually had to slow down for Hill.

Army docs said he needed surgery—both knees. Hill and Scott talked it around one day over lunch.

"It's more important that you be able to play with your grandkids than that you go on this deployment," Hill said.

Scott's son, Jaylen, was only nine, but Hill knew Scott hoped his retirement included spending time with a big, extended family.

"Stay here," Hill said. "Get the work done on your knees."

Tommy took a bite of his Chick-fil-A and shook his head. "No," he said. "I'm not going to do that."

Hill pressed: "Okay, get the surgery first then join us in-theater."

"No," Scott repeated. "I'm not leaving my boys."

Longhorn Conference Room
FOB Salerno, Afghanistan
LT ZACHARY L. MORRIS continued testifying, in substance, as follows:

Defense Attorney Neal Puckett: Good morning, Lieutenant Morris.

Morris: How you doing, sir?

Puckett: Good. How are you today?

Morris: Very good, sir.

Puckett: My name is Neal Puckett. I am a retired Marine lieutenant colonel. I'm a civilian attorney and I represent Captain Hill. You and I haven't spoken before?

Morris: No, sir.

Puckett: I'm going to read a little bit about your background. Did you graduate from West Point?

Morris: Yes, sir.

Puckett: What year did you graduate?

Morris: 2007, sir.

Puckett: Was that in June?

Morris: May.

Puckett: Where did you go after that?

Morris: After West Point, I took thirty days' leave then went to Fort Benning for Officer Basic Course, Ranger school, and Airborne school. I arrived Fort Campbell April 14th of 2008, spent a couple of months getting ready to come over here. Got to Battalion on July 1st.

Puckett: July 1st, so you got to Battalion on July 1st. When did you report to Delta Company?

Morris: Middle of August, late August.

Puckett: Can you give me a date?

Morris: Right around August 20th, I'd say.

Puckett: How long had your company been there?

Morris: I think about five months.

Puckett: So how long had you been with the company at FOB Airborne when you went to this meeting with Captain Hill where you heard something about detainee abuse?

Morris: About a week.

Puckett: Had you been out and been shot at prior to that?

Morris: Yes, sir. I had been on a couple of missions with the Scouts.

Puckett: With *this* company? What patrols with this company?

Morris: A couple operations with 1st and 2nd Platoon.

Puckett: Combat with the company?

Morris: Get shot at with the company? No. We were doing patrols but we didn't get shot at.

Puckett: So you come in, and in six days you evaluate this company, and you don't like what you see?

Morris: I didn't like the climate I saw.

Puckett: You don't like what you see? Isn't that right? You don't like what you see?

Morris: That's not what I said, sir. I thought it was a poor climate, soldiers not in proper uniform.

Puckett: Is a poor climate a good thing?

Morris: Negative.

Puckett: Do you like a poor climate?

Morris: No, sir.

Puckett: You didn't like what you saw, did you?

Morris: I thought it could be done better, sir.

Puckett: And these guys who had been in combat since the spring, including patrols around the clock since April, who were sometimes wearing flip-flops and sometimes weren't in perfect Army uniforms, that disturbed you, didn't it?

Morris: It didn't disturb me, sir, so much as it was a sign of possible lack of discipline and other issues.

Puckett: Yet, this is a problem, isn't it, if soldiers aren't in proper uniform all the time, right? It's a sign of bad discipline?

Morris: It can be, sir.

Puckett: I'll bet you learned that at West Point, didn't you?

Morris: In the Army, sir.

CHAPTER 6

January 2008
Fort Campbell, Kentucky

THE DEPLOYMENT TO Afghanistan was less than sixty days away. Hill and Scott sat with Hill's new XO, LT Larry Kay, in a conference room slightly dimmed for a PowerPoint presentation. Kay had transferred in from Bravo Company, along with Tim Moriarty and Shon Haskins. Haskins, who was senior, took over as 3rd Platoon sergeant. Mo went to 4th, the Shockers, where he would work just under SFC Kris Wilson.

Hill and Kay had bonded quickly. Kay appreciated serving under a more senior captain, someone who'd already seen combat, and who had spent time teaching the basic infantry officer's course, or as Kay thought of it, *teaching guys like me how not to screw up.*

Hill, meanwhile, couldn't believe he'd drawn such a sharp, unusual young officer as XO. Hill was astonished to learn that Kay spoke four languages, including Japanese. The young lieutenant had maybe one flaw: He called things exactly as he saw them and without filter. Hill knew he would need to file off the rough edges, teach Kay a bit of verbal discretion. But he'd rather have a plainspoken XO than a born politician.

Now, an officer stood at the front of the room, preparing to deliver the assignments brief for the 1-506th. In the hierarchy of an infantry command, Battalion falls one level below Brigade, which sits one level below Division, in this case, the 101st Airborne Division. First Battalion was one of three in the Brigade, and was parent command to six companies, Headquarters (HQ), plus Alpha through Echo.

Headquarters Company consisted of the Battalion commander—LTC Anthony DeMartino and his staff—as well as specialty platoons, such as communications, mortars, and Scouts. A Battalion commander's staff is divided into six departments: personnel, intelligence, operations, logistics, civil military operations, and communications. These departments are known as the "S-shops," S-1 through S-6.

The assignments brief was a big deal. Though company commanders like Hill had known for a couple of weeks which province they'd be covering in Afghanistan, the information was largely confidential. In a closed-door meeting with DeMartino, Hill had learned that he and his men would be relieving the 82nd Airborne, Scott's old unit, at FOB Airborne in Wardak. The province was one of Afghanistan's poorest, Hill had since learned. It had no industry and very few commercial activities. Apart from marble and gypsum mines, Wardak had only whatever produce its people could coax from its stingy, arid soil.

The provincial governor, Abdul Jabbar Naeemi, an early supporter of Afghan President Hamid Karzai, had set out to change that. To boost the literacy rate, he built schools and libraries in Maidan Shar, the village just outside Airborne's gate. He worked with the Coalition to increase development. As IED attacks and random shootings fell off, the village economy began to perk up. In the process, Wardak grew so peaceful that Karzai had declared it a "model province."

The briefing officer at the front of the room called the men to order and began. First, an overview of Afghanistan. On the screen, a provincial map of the whole country appeared, followed by zoom graphics on the provinces of Ghazni, Kapisa, and Wardak.

The officer clicked a remote, and the province graphics morphed into a photograph of gray desert circling a bustling city center. "This is where FOB Ghazni is located; both the Battalion headquarters and Bravo Company will be located here."

"Pretty nice," Kay said aside to Hill, who nodded as he scribbled notes.

Next to the FOB photo, bullet points listed amenities that included a gym in a hardened building, a motor pool with civilian maintenance support, and hardened structures for most everyone's quarters.

The briefing officer reviewed the list for the group then clicked again. FOB Warrior, Charlie Company's assignment, was located in the Nawa District of Ghazni Province. Kay noted that the base had a few hard structures, along with tents for quarters, and a fleet of military vehicles.

Again, the briefing officer went over the FOB's amenities then clicked to a new slide.

"This is Dog Company's area..." And he clicked again. "FOB Airborne, Wardak Province."

The slide flashed by so briefly that Kay barely had a chance to take in the grainy black-and-white photo. But what he did see was essentially a shanty town. A warren of tents surrounded by a perimeter wall with gaping holes in it. Wide spaces where protection from rockets, bullets, and even, say, pedestrians, was simply...missing.

He shook his head and uttered an ironic laugh. "Hell yeah!" he whispered mostly to himself. "This is *awesome!*"

Scott smiled. Over his twenty-two-year career, his wartime experiences had ranged from parachuting into Panama and rescuing a wounded American behind enemy lines, to the first Gulf War, Desert Storm, which for Scott was really less a war and more a camping trip. Wherever his unit, the 82nd Airborne, showed up, the Iraqis surrendered. Often they were already dead. Scott remembered seeing scores of burned-out tanks and five-ton trucks, some with bomb-crisped men still inside, limbs missing, mouths seared open in protest. His most bizarre memory, though, was seeing hundreds of shoes, charred and tattered, littering the red desert sand—the sartorial confetti of bombing runs on Iraqi columns. Coalition jets had blown Saddam's soldiers out of their shoes.

Scott looked again at the rudimentary FOB pictured on the PowerPoint slide. Hell, if he could could march across Iraq, or find his way out of Panama in the dark, he could handle this. And he knew his boys could handle it, too.

The photo of FOB Airborne did not surprise Hill. After the discussion with DeMartino, he had chosen Wardak. It was a little farther from "the flagpole," or Battalion, than the other choice. The self-containment had seemed to Hill to offer a greater leadership challenge.

The briefing officer clicked his remote and a list of Wardak facts appeared on-screen. Capital village: Maidan Shar, just outside the FOB gates. Significant regions: Sayed Abad, Nerkh, Tangi, Jalrez.

That last name triggered a memory for Hill. He gazed at the slide, let his mind work on it.

Jalrez.

In a couple of moments, he had it. During a rotation at the Joint Readiness Training Center (JRTC), Hill and a group from the 1-506th had received a state-of-the-war, lessons-learned brief on a punishing firefight in the Jalrez Valley. A platoon from the 82nd Airborne, had been traveling near the village of Esh-ma-keyl when a fierce Taliban ambush wounded every man in the platoon. Some seriously.

By any measure, the ambush had been a huge Taliban victory. That didn't fit well with the "model province" Hill had been told to expect.

Nerves stirred at the back of his neck. Suddenly, he felt behind the data curve. He lifted his pen from his pad and leaned over to Kay. "Get on email with the XO over at Airborne. We need to get smart on this place. Seriously."

CHAPTER 7

SFC Grant Hulburt and SGT Jason Dudley sat in the 1st Platoon offices finishing up Hulburt's least favorite thing: paperwork. But he had found a way to redeem the time. A loose line of young soldiers stood queued up at the door. One by one, Hulburt called them in and peppered them with questions.

"Give me a nine-line MedEvac," Hulburt would say. The young men tried to spit back the nine required lines for calling in a medical evacuation: pickup location, radio frequency, number of patients, and other pertinent data.

Or, "Tell me how to call in CAS." Close air support, usually A-10 Thunderbolts or Apache gunships to fire on the enemy in support of troops on the ground.

Or, "Run through the call-for-fire procedures." How to call in an air strike or artillery fire.

In many platoons, this was a skill handled mainly by sergeants and above. But Hulburt wanted the Dirty First—to the extent possible, given wide gaps in age and combat experience—to be uniformly skilled, no matter what they wore on their sleeves. He had no patience for units whose leaders believed otherwise. Once, during a training exercise, a platoon from another company needed to call for artillery fire, but not a single man on the ground knew how. Hulburt could have called it in himself. Instead, he rolled his eyes and had one of his most junior guys do it, just to prove a point.

Eighteen years of service, including the bloodbath months in Ramadi, had given Grant Hulburt's thirty-seven-year-old face the look of worn leather. If there are living antonyms, he was the opposite of politically correct. An avid hunter and self-taught survivalist, if Hulburt were to live through a nuke, he could have, no joke, lived off the land Native American style. A crack tactician, Hulburt was very hands-on with teaching and coaching his men. He had a brand-new lieutenant, Sean Allred, and a bunch of kids on their first deployment. He was tough on them in garrison, but no one could mistake his toughness for a lack of love.

Hulburt and Dudley, both Ramadi veterans, made a ritual of drilling their guys on combat procedures before they could go home. They knew they were taking several cherry privates, including PFC Trevor Carlin, to their very first war.

One night soon after the 1-506th returned from Ramadi, there was a party. Not yet twenty-one, but newly liberated from the moral straits of Utah, Carlin got ecstatically drunk. He and a buddy had decided to drive to Nashville and party on, but Dudley got wind of it and caught up to Carlin in a barracks hallway.

"Where do you think you're going?" Dudley said.

Carlin executed a wobbly about-face and tried to focus his eyes. "Nowhere, Sergeant," he said. It came out *Nowhere, sharshent.*

Dudley wasn't buying it. Carlin was all dressed up—and grunts don't get dressed up unless they're hoping to get laid.

Dudley's gaze hardened. "Don't be stupid, man. You just got here, and you want to get chaptered out for a DUI?"

"I'm okay, I swear." *I shware.*

"You should probably know," Dudley said, "that I'll do whatever it takes to protect you. Even from yourself."

Carlin widened his stance and stuck his chin out, ready for a bear-hug trip back to his room, or maybe a body slam. But Dudley didn't move. Instead a twinkle appeared in his eyes. "Are you really gonna make me do this?"

"Do what?"

With ninja speed, Dudley snatched Carlin's cell phone from his hand, and grinned at him. "Call your mom."

"Call my *mom?*" Carlin said. "Are you kidding me?"

"Nope." Dudley smiled.

Carlin uttered a skeptical puff. "You're not really gonna call my mom..."

Dudley thumbed the cell a couple of times, and Carlin saw his address book pop up on the screen. The sergeant scrolled down to the Ms.

"Shit. Oh, come *on...*"

But the phone was already ringing in Utah. Smiling at Carlin, Dudley spoke amiably into the phone to Mrs. Carlin about her son's intention to drive to Nashville drunk.

He nodded. "Mm-hmm...yes, ma'am." Nodded again. "Okay, ma'am, no problem at all. Nice talking to you, too, ma'am. Here he is."

Dudley held out the cell, still grinning. "She wants to talk to you."

Carlin grimaced. "Oh, man, I can't *believe* this!" He took the phone, put it up to his ear, and got an earful from four states away. When he hung up, he handed over his spare keys to Dudley. "I can't believe you told my mom on me, man!"

Dudley just shook his head and laughed. Carlin went back to his room. The next day, a freezing March morning, a 1st Platoon NCO marched Carlin out to the Fort Campbell baseball field and smoked him 'til he puked. From that point on, Carlin set out to prove his worth.

Now, as Dog Company prepared to ship out to Wardak, Dudley and Hulburt continued their ruthless preparation. Hulburt continued calling soldiers into the platoon office, one by one. If a man answered correctly, he got to go home for the night. If not, he went to the back of the line, over and over, until he got it right.

CHAPTER 8

It was nearly evening, about a month before Dog Company's date with Wardak, and Corporal Joseph Coe sat downstairs in the company spaces. His uniform was recruit-poster perfect, which made sense, since he was reporting from recruiting duty.

Coe studied the sparse space. A big conference table surrounded with plastic chairs. Clipboards with required reading tacked across the wall in precision ranks. In-country photos of platoon-sized groups of men in desert ACUs,[7] weapons brandished, astride and front of Humvees. Ramadi pictures, Coe guessed.

He wasn't nervous... but he was nervous. He knew the company was deploying to combat again in just a month. Coe looked down, straightened his tie. Another corporal—a short, stocky guy in charge of in-processing—walked up and pointed at Coe's uniform. "They're not gonna like that."

Coe glanced down. The corporal's index finger was aimed at his recruiter badge.

"Okay," Coe said. He reached up, ripped off the badge, and put it in his pocket.

"And they're *definitely* not gonna like that."

Now he was pointing to Coe's corporal patch, the insignia designating him as an E-4. After recruiting school, he had been automatically promoted to corporal—it was part of the deal. Better to have a little more flash on your uniform when you're trying to get America's best and brightest to sign on the dotted line, raise their right hands, and swear to defend the Constitution so help them God.

---

7. ACUs: Army Combat Uniform.

But Coe knew what the other corporal was saying: *I've looked at your service jacket. You've been in for four years, you've got an infantry MOS,*[8] *but you've never been in the real infantry. You may as well be a brand-new private.*

The corporal moved away. Without hesitation, Coe ripped the stripes off his sleeves. Now he looked like an E-1. And, with his baby face, probably like he was just out of high school.

When ordered, Coe appeared in the doorway of 3rd Platoon's office and braced himself for a heavy dose of *Omigod, a useless cherry private.*

"Private Joseph Coe, reports as ordered," he said.

SFC Shon Haskins was sitting at a desk, his back to the right-hand wall, the desk facing out into the room. The room had no windows, but Haskins had had someone draw a window on the wall with chalk, complete with blue curtains and scenery "outside." He had grown up on a six-acre farm in central Washington and wanted a view.

LT Donnie Carwile was half seated on the front corner of Haskins's desk, right boot on the floor, left swinging casually. Fit and handsome, Carwile was both a former cop and prior enlisted. That made him an older lieutenant, and he seemed to Coe to emit a laid-back vibe.

Haskins looked up at Carwile, eyebrows raised. "Joe Coe? Sir, did we seriously just get a private named Joe Coe?"

"Sounds like we did, Sergeant." Carwile regarded Coe genially. "Do push-ups," he said.

Coe assumed the position and began flexing his arms. Up, down, up, down. Carwile: "Where you from, Joe Coe?"

"Kind of all over, sir." Up, down. "Grew up part-time in Ohio and part-time in North Carolina, sir."

Carwile could relate to that. A Mississippi native, his parents had divorced before he was six, each remarrying after just a year. For six years, Donnie shuttled back and forth between his real mom and her new husband, and his real dad and his new wife.

Coe was still banging out push-ups. "Okay, you can get up," Haskins said.

Coe unfolded himself and stood at attention. For the first time, he noticed that both the lieutenant and the sergeant had wads of tobacco tucked in their lips.

Carwile raised a Gatorade bottle to his mouth and spit. "At ease, Coe. Brand-new private?"

"No, sir."

---

8. MOS: Military Occupational Specialty.

"What was your last assignment?"

"Recruiting duty, sir."

"*Recruiting?*" Haskin said in mock disbelief. "Oh my God! Get back down, Coe!"

Carwile laughed. Coe dropped and resumed the push-ups.

"How long you been in the Army, son?" Carwile said.

"Four years, sir."

"What did you do before recruiting?"

"Tested new weapons systems at the 1-29th, Fort Benning."

Up, down, up, down. Coe's PT scores had always been off the charts, so he wasn't winded. Perhaps this impressed Haskins, because the sergeant let him up.

"Well, L.T., what are we gonna do with young Private Coe here?"

"Your call, Sergeant," Carwile said.

"Why don't we make him a driver? I just moved Ochoa to gunner. It'd be cool to have a driver named Joe Coe."

Without prompting, Coe dropped to the floor and started pumping out push-ups on his own, this time even faster.

Surprised, Carwile laughed again. "You do know how to drive, don't you, Coe?"

"Yes, sir!" Up, down, up, down. "But my driver's license is suspended."

Once again, Carwile burst out laughing. "Holy shit, Sergeant! A weapons-testing recruiter with no combat experience and a suspended license! He'll fit right in!"

The next day, Carwile, the former cop, telephoned the North Carolina jurisdiction where Coe had been nabbed for—seriously—doing 30 in a 25. Given that his driver's license was needed in service to his country, North Carolina was willing to let it go. Haskins also "promoted" Coe back to E-4, and he was wearing a specialist insignia—instead of corporal—by his first full day with 3rd Platoon.

SPC Paul Conlon reclined on his barracks bunk, a laptop propped on his legs, updating a document he's been working on for some time. He called it *Synopsis*. Conlon leaned back and stared at the ceiling for a moment, then refocused on the computer screen and let his fingers go to work.

I don't know if I am making the right choices, but I would like to think that I am. So much is happening to me, both big and small. My life's happening. It's moving at the slowest rate, somewhere

along the rate of continents. I know that in time I'll be able to see
the progress I made, but sometimes I wish I could fast-forward to
the middle of my life.

There had been a time in his late teens when Conlon had been sure he
wasn't making good choices. A brief and tumultuous marriage that didn't
work out. A stint in Marine Corps boot camp cut short because of an injury.
After that, he cast about for some direction in life. He applied to Franklin
Pierce College and was awarded a scholarship for writing. He'd written
all his life, loved art and music, taught himself to play guitar. Studying on
a writing scholarship seemed like a natural fit, but somehow it didn't *feel*
natural.

When Conlon received the acceptance letter and scholarship, he had sat
down with his mom, Maria, a tiny, tough New Englander who had raised
two sons alone. "Is this really what you want to do?" she said.

"No," he told her. "I was doing it for you."

That had been just a few months ago. Conlon had joined the Army in
the fall of 2007, gone to boot camp at Fort Benning, and landed at Fort
Campbell, assigned to the famed 101st Airborne. His unit was set to deploy
in just a few weeks, but he wanted to see his family one more time before
he went. He'd been playing with the idea of sneaking up to Cape Cod and
buying his mom a gift, something really special. He'd have to talk to his
aunt Victoria about it, get her to help him. Conlon looked at the computer
again, thought some, tapped the keys.

I want to know who I'm going to be when I'm almost thirty.

Am I going to have earned medals? Am I going to be remarried?
Am I going to have children that look up to me? Will I have even
made anything of myself?

He looked hard at the screen, decided the answer was yes, and typed
some more:

Give me five to ten years and I promise to have made something
of myself. Somebody will have taken note.

CHAPTER 9

TIM "MO" MORIARTY waded into an emerald lake of kudzu that spilled down through a gulley on Fort Campbell's "back forty," a verdant slice of northern Tennessee used by the Army for training. Behind him, SPC Carlos Colonruiz, twenty-seven, trudged along, head down, followed by Private Ryan Haffner, nineteen, and a couple of other junior soldiers from 4th Platoon, the Shockers.

The patrol had been walking for hours through undergrowth that was rain-forest wet and alive with spiders. Sunlight poured down through an oak-pine canopy, dappling the ground with silver coins of light. Some of 4th Platoon's Ramadi vets—Mo, SSG Ray Davis, and SPC Mike Judd—had set up this training exercise. Davis and Judd were playing the role of the OPFOR, or opposing force, occupying some "caves" that were actually a string of empty concrete ammo bunkers located several clicks into the Fort Campbell wilderness. The objective for Mo's men was to clear the bunkers and capture the OPFOR.

Mo himself had a different objective: SPC Carlos Colonruiz.

Colonruiz (the Shockers always called him Colon—pronounced "KOE-LONE"—for short) had been in Ramadi, but only briefly. He reminded the guys of a Puerto Rican Schwarzenegger—ripped to shreds from bodybuilding, speaking barely passable English instead of German.

Since Mo came over from Bravo Company, he had observed Colon, watched him racing up and down the barracks stairwell wearing full body armor and a fifty-pound ruck. No one had told him to do it; he did it for himself. Colon was a little older than the other junior guys, and married with two kids. It was as if, because he was further down the road in life, he didn't have time to screw around. As a result, he wasn't willing to be led simply because another man had more stripes on his sleeve. With Colon, trust had to be earned. It was a trust Mo coveted, because he saw in Colon a strong-minded, valuable ally.

For that reason, Mo had receded into the role of observer at the beginning of this training patrol. He let Colon lead the other soldiers against Judd and Davis, who proceeded to kick the young Shockers' asses. The OPFOR crept through the kudzu and ambushed the patrol again and again. Each time, Mo conducted a brief after-action review on terrain and tactics. Finally, he stepped into the role of instructor and pulled out a map.

"They're going to expect us to approach from this area," he said, tapping the map with his index finger. "But we're not going to do that. We're going to take the worst terrain out here"—he pointed to a grid that looked so remote as to be traveled only by bears—"and approach from over here."

That had been three hours earlier. Now, the patrol descended the gulley slope until it ended at the edge of the Cumberland River, which flows generally west from Appalachia through Tennessee and into Kentucky. The Shockers sloshed into the river, fording its breadth in a waist-high current. On the far bank, Colon climbed out, his ACU pants streaming river water into his boots, and walked straight into a chest-high spiderweb.

"Shit!" he said. He scraped the sticky silk off his ACUs and flicked his hands to shake it loose. But the web clung like double-sided tape. "*Shit!*"

Tramping upslope under a stand of towering pines, Mo smiled to himself. "Hey, Colon," he called over his shoulder. "Seems like we're just walking all damn day, don't it?"

Colon's tone was surly. "Yeah, Sergeant Mo."

"And you're wondering why we're walking through all this nasty shit when all we had to do on this exercise was clear out four bunkers and take out the enemy?"

"Yeah, so...?"

"So, just wait 'til we get there. Then you'll see why we went the hard way."

Mo, thirty-six, was accustomed to doing things the hard way. His mother had preferred soldiers as husbands, though she tended not to stay married for long. In his childhood memory bank, he had a video clip from around age six: his mother and him hitching a ride away from a marriage she had discarded in Fort Knox, Kentucky. Seeing the big Army tanks flanking the roads as they hitched a ride out of town.

Ironic, he thought, and pressed through an oak copse. The patrol continued for another hour until it reached the crest of a low hill. Mo raised his arm and made a fist: *Stop*. Behind him, Colon, Haffner, and the others froze.

Mo motioned Colon forward and pointed down into the shallow valley. Mike Judd and Ray Davis were sitting in front of a concrete bunker built into the opposite hillside, their M4's at rest. At intervals, three more bunkers punched into the hillside, each fronted with a huge steel door. Between Mo's position and the bunker, Judd and Davis were keeping an eye on Mo's likely avenue of approach—roughly opposite the direction from where Mo's patrol stood now. Their casual posture telegraphed their thoughts: Mo's patrol had probably given up and gone back to base.

Quickly, Mo divided his men into two assault teams and briefed a plan. One team maneuvered down the hill and cleared two bunkers in utter silence, while the second team held the high ground and kept watch on Judd and Davis. With the first two bunkers cleared, the maneuver team sprinted full speed at the OPFOR guards, "shooting" both dead before they had time to resist. After an all-day march, Mo's team seized its objective in less than five minutes.

Later, Colon pulled Mo aside and admitted he thought Mo had been throwing his seniority around, dragging the patrol through the woods all day.

"I was pissed," Colon said. "But from now on, I'll do whatever you tell me."

Mo clapped him on the shoulder and smiled. Mission accomplished.

The United States of America
v.
CPT Roger T. Hill and 1SG Tommy L. Scott
1 December 2008

SPECIALIST ALLAN J. MOSER, Delta Company, 1st Battalion, 506th Infantry Regiment, Combined Task Force Currahee, was called as a witness, was sworn, and testified, in substance, as follows:

Prosecutor Stephen Latino: You are Private Allan Moser?

Moser: Yes, sir...

Latino: Do you swear the testimony you are about to give to be the truth, the whole truth, and nothing but the truth, so help you God?

Moser: I do.

Latino: How are you doing today?

Moser: Pretty good, sir.

Latino: Do you know that the commanding general has given you immunity to testify?

Moser: Yes, sir.

Latino: Who was at the coffee shop? Who did you see there?

Moser: First Sergeant Scott was there. The CO was there. I was there. Specialist Peake was there. Sergeant Doyle was there. I saw Sergeant Davis there, saw Sergeant Moriarty there.

Latino: Now when you say the CO and First Sergeant, are you talking about Captain Hill?

Moser: Captain Hill and First Sergeant Scott.

Latino: What was happening to the detainees in the coffee shop?

Moser: First Sergeant was questioning the detainees.

Latino: How was he questioning the detainees?

Moser: He had them mounted and was asking them questions.

Latino: Describe "mounted."

Moser: Um, you know when in martial arts you have a mount, with the guy sitting on the other guy's chest with his knees up in his armpits?

Latino: Was he talking to the detainee at this point?

Moser: Yes, he was asking him questions, sir.

Latino: What exactly was First Sergeant saying?

Moser: Asking them the names of Taliban leaders, who they were working for, stuff like that, sir.

Latino: Did you ever see First Sergeant strike the detainee?

Moser: Yes, sir, a couple of times.

Latino: Right hand, left hand?

Moser: Right hand, sir.

Latino: How many different detainees did you see him do this to?

Moser: Three or four, sir...

Latino: What happened after the first sergeant was striking the detainees?

Moser: They were telling them to tell the truth and quit lying to them. Then he would slap them...

Latino: Now, did you strike any detainees?

Moser: I did strike them. I was putting a gag in a detainee's mouth and he bit my finger, so I hit him four or five times.

Prosecutor Devon Runyan: Why did you hit the guy who bit you multiple times?

Moser: What would you do if a Taliban guy bit you in the hand?

CHAPTER 10

February 2008
FOB Airborne, Wardak Province, Afghanistan

IN LATE FEBRUARY, LT Larry Kay stood by the FOB Airborne landing zone, his desert camouflage uniform rippling in the rotor wash of a landing Chinook. The helo dispensed Haskins, Hulburt, and large chunks of 1st and 3rd Platoons, about two dozen men. The first thing Hulburt noticed was that the guys from the outgoing 82nd couldn't wait to leave. Relief-in-place operations were supposed to span two to two-and-a-half weeks, but as Dog Company soldiers jumped off arriving birds, equal numbers of 82nd soldiers climbed aboard and took their seats. The pattern would continue as Chinooks and Blackhawks vacuumed up the outgoing 82nd in what seemed to D Co record time.

Kay had deployed early to Wardak, leading a small advance team to prepare the way for the larger company. Now, he led the senior NCOs on a tour of FOB Airborne. What hit Haskins immediately was the same thing Kay had noticed back at the assignments brief: The FOB perimeter was incomplete. Huge gaps broke the exterior walls, creating a series of virtual welcome mats for suicide bombers wearing explosive vests. And if the Taliban wasn't particularly motivated—or even, say, ambulatory—they could shoot rockets straight into the base.

"Great spot for a FOB," one of the sergeants muttered. "For the Taliban."

He was right: Airborne was an eight-acre open shoe box. The long sides of the "box" stretched east and west. The FOB rested on a slope, with one short end of the shoe box at the top of the hill, and the other at the bottom.

At that lower end was the main gate, or entry control point (ECP.) Just beyond the ECP lay the village of Maidan Shar, and beyond that a ridgeline that ran left to right as viewed from the FOB. Airborne's position on the slope tipped it toward Maidan Shar and the ridgeline, offering a generous view of its inner workings to anyone who cared to look.

Standing at the top of the FOB, Haskins and Hulburt peered downslope. Kay pointed out the perforated row of HESCO barriers (portable, earth-filled barricades) that split the base into symmetric rectangles. The northern rectangle contained the Afghan National Army perimeter and barracks. It was a base inside a base—a doctrinal strategy for working with foreign defense forces—with a crumbling Soviet-era building squatting at its center. The ANA contingent, about half a *kandak*, or battalion, would conduct independent missions, as well as joint training missions with Hill and his men.

The U.S.-populated rectangle on the south end of the FOB contained the TOC, well constructed from stone and concrete. From the TOC and adjoining offices, Headquarters Platoon would manage tactical operations, as well as company administrative and logistical functions. HQ Platoon would include Hill, Kay, Scott, and a small crew of NCOs.

Next, Kay briefed Haskins and Hulburt on a number of specialty units that would be working with Dog Company, and pointed out their locations on the FOB: an artillery platoon (call sign Bonecrusher); a Police Mentorship Team out of Montana (call sign Caveman); and the Special Forces unit led by CPT B. Neither the specialty units nor the Afghan *kandak* would serve technically under Hill, but he would have the last word. As "op com," or operational commander, Wardak was his battlespace and Airborne his base.

In addition to military personnel, as many as fifty local national laborers were on Airborne's U.S. payroll. Their numbers varied according to construction projects underway. One constant were the interpreters who would work under Tommy Scott. Haskins had also seen a little bazaar just outside the gate where some Afghans were selling DVDs, gum, and foreign cigarettes. Inside the gates, dozens of LNs were building hard structures.

Probably also stealing, Haskins thought. He had never trusted LNs. He hadn't in Iraq and he wouldn't here.

"This place is huge," he told Hulburt when Kay finished the tour. Too big for a Delta company, they agreed.

CHAPTER II

IN EARLY MARCH, the balance of Dog Company streamed into Afghanistan via Bagram Airfield, Manas Air Base in Kyrgyzstan, and FOB Sharana in Paktika Province. Hill and another Dog Company element were transitioning through Bagram, sleeping in a tent next door to some soldiers from the 82nd who had just flown out of Wardak. One evening, Hill, Mo, and a couple of other soldiers wanted to get the lowdown on Airborne, so they visited the next tent.

"We were running the FOB on a skeleton crew," a sergeant said to the D Co delegation, who sat on cots around him. "The ANP in Maidan Shar are dirty. That's the best-case scenario—that all they do is take bribes and shit. The worst-case scenario is that they're working with the Taliban."

Several times the 82nd had run missions that were supposed to include the ANP, the sergeant said. The ANP wouldn't show up, but the Taliban would be there, lying in wait. The worst was that firefight in October in Jalrez, when the Taliban shredded an 82nd platoon using small arms and armor-piercing RPGs.[9] It was the firefight Hill had heard about at the October rotation at JRTC.

"After that, we didn't go in there," the sergeant said, his face grim. "Into the valley, I mean."

Hill had been listening quietly. Part of him was anxious to leave the tent and get back to work. He had business to attend to: inventories, even training. Air Force Major Dave Rayman and some A-10 pilots on the other side of Bagram had agreed to talk Hill's men through some CAS drills from

---

9. RPG: rocket propelled grenades.

their perspective. Hill was eager to capitalize on this rare opportunity for his soldiers to interact with the pilots who might someday come to their rescue. Still, what the sergeant said concerned him.

Before he took command of D Co, LTC DeMartino had briefed him on what to expect. He told Hill that one reason he'd selected him to take command of Dog Company was his counterinsurgency experience while serving in Iraq. Hill's successful tour there had led to a follow-on assignment at Fort Benning, where he rewrote the counterinsurgency module for the Infantry Officers Basic Course.

Ramadi had been about destroying the enemy, DeMartino said. Afghanistan was about winning the confidence of the people. Ramadi had been about body bags. Afghanistan was about hearts and minds. The entire battalion needed to be "reprogrammed," DeMartino said, Hill's Delta Company most of all.

Although he had not seen it in writing, Hill had heard that D Co had had the most kills of any company in Ramadi. In Wardak, though, they would be working primarily to build schools and improve on the already peaceful security situation in the province—a completely different mission.

"More than any other company commander," DeMartino told him, "you've got a tough bunch of guys to reprogram for hearts and minds."

Hill had developed a respect for his CO by then. Looking at DeMartino's career, it seemed as though he'd checked all the right boxes, been in all the right billets. Platoon leader, Desert Storm; Multinational Force and Observers, Sinai, Egypt; Battalion operations officer, and later assistant chief of staff in the 82nd Airborne. DeMartino had also served in the office of the deputy secretary of defense. And to be placed in command of a battalion in a storied regiment like the 506th was no small accomplishment.

His insight about the temperament of Dog Company seemed to prove true at the October 2007 JRTC rotation. At JRTC, exercise scenarios simulate conditions units will face in actual combat. Units under training are deployed to "the Box," where they face realistic battles against the OPFOR. Usually, the OPFOR kills everybody in the training unit—just lays absolute waste.

SFC Kris Wilson had gotten some advance intel about the October operational order, or official scenario script for culminating the exercise.

"All right, listen up," Wilson said after rounding up his guys. "This isn't official, but I heard we're supposed to go out to some crappy little FOB on Peason Ridge, where the OPFOR is supposed to overrun us so that Charlie Company can air-assault in and save our sorry asses."

The room erupted in laughter.

"Sounds like a good time," Mike Judd said.

Wilson had lost count of the number of times he'd been blown up, a fact he avoided sharing with his wife. In Ramadi, he'd been winged in the head with flying hunks of asphalt, peppered with scalding shrapnel, and had his legs nearly crushed between two Humvees. The latter resulted in his only stay at an aid station. But Ramadi was a boiling hell, and he had known he needed to get back to his men. After a couple of days, Wilson faked being able to walk. An Army doc eyed Wilson's painful stagger with a wry smile but released him.

After all that, Wilson didn't really feel like being overrun in a *training* scenario, no matter what the exercise observers had planned. Neither did the rest of Dog Company. And so, within twenty-four hours of the Box going hot for the final scenario, D Co had either killed or captured all the OPFOR in their sector, grabbed valuable intel that disrupted further attacks, and gone to the aid of one of their sister companies during a critical juncture in the operation.

That had been Hill's first chance to watch his future company in action. Two months later, the 1-506th returned to JRTC, this time with Hill in command of Dog Company. Once again, the unit excelled. Near the end of the rotation, Hill was leaving a briefing at a large complex of tents when LTC DeMartino walked up and tapped him on the shoulder. "Roger, let's go for a walk."

"Yes, sir." Hill zipped his jacket against the chill and followed him outside. The two walked into a wide field ringed with old-growth trees stripped bare by winter. A low overcast dulled the sky.

"What do you think of First Sergeant Scott?" DeMartino said. His words made puffs of white that slipped into his wake as he walked.

"I think he's great," Hill said, puzzled by the question.

"Well, I'm not sure about him. He doesn't seem to command the respect that we need him to, and I'm not sure if he's that strong a leader." DeMartino paused. "And he doesn't have his tab."

His Ranger tab, Hill thought. Tommy hadn't been to Ranger school. Hill wanted to say, *No, but he's been in combat in three different countries.*

The Ranger obsession was beginning to frustrate him. It wasn't that Ranger school wasn't important—it was, especially as a soldier ascends in the Army's hierarchy. There's a camaraderie and level of understanding that passes unspoken between men who have marched and starved and sweated and bled through the school's punishing weeks.

But one thing Hill had learned from Dog Company, beginning with reading those awards packets from the file cabinet, and continuing through both JRTC rotations, was that Ranger school did not necessarily determine how a man will perform in combat. It's certainly a true test of a man's mettle, of what he's willing to endure on behalf of other soldiers. But this company of all companies, this battalion of all battalions, had already been tested. Hill knew that tab or no tab, that special blend of competence, experience, and heart was what mattered most. And he saw that in Scott.

Even apart from combat or tabs, Hill wanted to ask DeMartino if he'd noticed the difference in the company since Tommy took over. Their PT scores. Their rifle scores. Their morale. The fact that disciplinary problems had utterly vanished.

But Hill didn't ask. DeMartino was his commander, and Hill wasn't going to question his judgment. They continued striding across the field, weeds crunching under their feet. Ahead, a flock of crows scattered.

DeMartino glanced his way. "I've got somebody in mind as a replacement for Scott. He's another first sergeant I'd like to have come to our brigade. If you're interested in switching Scott out, we can probably make that happen."

It wasn't the first time that DeMartino had tried to swap out Hill's men. About a month before, he'd tried to replace Larry Kay, referring to him as "a box of rocks." Hill had refused.

Now he walked a few more steps before speaking. Then Hill said, "Sir, I appreciate that, but I'm really happy with First Sergeant Scott. I think he's a fantastic leader and, more importantly, the guys really respect him. I don't think there could be a better fit for the company than Tommy Scott."

And so Hill had held on to Scott as first sergeant. Now, in the tent at Bagram, Hill measured DeMartino's hearts and minds speech against what this sergeant from the 82nd Airborne was saying—that in Wardak, his unit had been up to its eyeballs in Taliban.

The sergeant's assessment aligned closely with the Intelligence Preparation of the Battlefield (IPB) that Larry Kay had put together since landing in Afghanistan. At the northeastern end of the Jalrez Valley, insurgents under the command of the warlord Razak were using "rat lines," little-traveled routes through the mountains, to rally at the outskirts of Kabul and plan attacks on the city.

East of Highway 1, in the district of Sayed Abad, were the Taliban's less ideological players. These criminal types were not so much into IEDs as robbing Afghan supply convoys and selling the spoils.

South of Jalrez was Nerkh, another valley run by higher-level Taliban who were essentially interchangeable with Razak and the Jalrez crew. Moving south to Route Georgia was the Tangi Valley, run by a different Taliban cell. The key feature of the Tangi was its sheer roadside cliffs and general self-containment. The terrain put the bad guys in a position not to be messed with, while allowing them to mess with anyone who encroached on their turf.

The 82nd, Kay had learned, suspected that Taliban fighters were stealing police cars, taking them back to a chop shop in Jalrez, and converting them into Trojan horse VBIEDs intended for Kabul. Kay's IPB reports dovetailed with open-source intel that Hill had tasked his platoon leaders with gathering. In tandem, the open-source and IPB intel planted red flags all over the rosy "model province" picture coming out of the 1-506th intel shop.

Before leaving Fort Campbell, Hill had approached the 1-506th intel officer with this information, but was told flatly, "Kabul is not your focus."

Hill argued that since the Taliban had to drive their suicide bombs right past FOB Airborne's gates to detonate them in Kabul, it should be. Not only that, but the IED makers working in Jalrez directly affected the security of Highway 1, the crown jewel of the RC East counterinsurgency, and that was Dog Company's *primary* focus.

The intel officer downplayed Hill's argument, as well as the IPB Kay had built. His basic message, as Hill took it, was: *Don't try to make this assignment a bigger deal than it is.*

Now, Hill sat in the tent at Bagram wishing he had pressed harder. He did not comment on the sergeant's revelations, just thanked him and walked out of the tent. He had things to do. Still, he let the NCO's assessment simmer on the back burner of his mind.

DeMartino had implied that Dog Company would be handing out bouquets of number two pencils. Instead, it seemed to Hill that they were walking into a knife fight.

CHAPTER 12

THE FOB AIR horn sounded and a now familiar cry sounded across the base:

"INCOMING!"

A rocket whistled in and boomed to earth, echoing down the valley. Smoke and dust mushroomed into the late afternoon sky, like the fallout of a mine collapse.

Dog Company sprinted to fighting positions or took cover in bunkers or up-armored Humvees. Hill, Scott, and Kay rushed to the TOC as another rocket exploded just outside the FOB's northern wall.

Hill stopped at a HESCO barrier and braced for impact before bounding up the stairs. In quick succession, more rockets smashed down around the base, sending up towers of smoke and debris. Forward Observers (FOs) ran to their towers. Each carried a GPS-enabled laser range finder, a radio, binoculars, a compass, and a map.

Hill had counted five, maybe six rocket impacts by the time he stepped inside the TOC. Already, the count was higher than any previous attack— and this one had just begun.

In the TOC, Bonecrusher commander Charlie Weaver and Sergeant Dan Schonberg were coordinating for a fire mission. Schonberg, a cool-headed junior NCO with combat experience in Ramadi, had earned the job of D Co night battle captain. He swapped data with the FOs, who worked with D Co tower guards to pinpoint the rockets' point of origin.

On a map board, Weaver tracked fire missions—target selection, azimuth, and range—scratching out calculations by hand. He and his fire direction chief punched them into a computer that would transmit detailed firing instructions to the Bonecrusher gun line. When the guns were ready and Battalion granted permission, Bonecrusher would launch a battery of steel back onto the enemy.

Outside, PFC Bradford Bitting hunkered low in a plywood guard tower. The sun was melting behind the ridgeline and he could see the rocket flashes more clearly against the darkening sky. Everyone called Bitting "McLovin" after the nerd-turned-badass in the movie *Superbad*.

He radioed the TOC: "Two-four-five degrees, eighteen hundred meters! The village just to the right—*hey, get down!*" A rocket rattled the earth, scissoring Bitting's transmission. "I say again! The village just to the right of Baby Razorback!" He rattled off grid coordinates. "How copy, over?"

Another rocket sailed long and crashed into the mountainside beyond the FOB's eastern wall.

In the TOC, Kay was on the phone with Battalion, trying to get permission to fire the 105s. He looked over at Hill. "They won't approve fire. They're afraid of collateral damage."

Hill shook his head. "Not again."

During D Co's first weeks in-country, Battalion had already laid down a pattern: lengthy discussions at FOB Ghazni while Dog Company weathered heavy attack in Wardak, three hours away. Hill would give the command to fire if things got worse, but he preferred that Battalion would do the right thing and provide him top cover. With Weaver, he surveyed the map board and had a quick discussion: Where could Bonecrusher place their first rounds so that they could "walk" the shells onto a target while minimizing damage to surrounding buildings? Weaver adjusted his calculations.

Meanwhile Kay snatched up a mic and radioed Donnie Carwile. Third Platoon was QRF.

"Dog 3-6, that point of origin should be within .50-cal range."

Carwile responded instantly. "Dog 5, 3-6, already on it."

Mo's voice came next on the net. "Dog 5, this is 4-3, we're gonna reposition our vehicles just outside the gate to get a better angle."

Kay looked over at Hill, who nodded in agreement.

"Roger," Kay said. "As soon as you acquire a target, you are cleared to fire."

Humvees from 3rd and 4th rolled toward the FOB's barrier wall. With an infrared laser, Carwile's gunner "painted" a house at the outskirts of the village. At the same instant, a flash erupted from the house, signaling another inbound rocket.

"*INCOMING!*" Mo yelled on the net.

Third Platoon's gunners engaged the house. In the plywood guard towers, Bitting and the FOs crouched with D Co guards and braced for impact below waist-high sandbag barriers. The rocket whistled overhead and slammed into the back of the ANA perimeter wall.

Underneath the maelstrom, Schonberg had relieved Kay and was now on the horn with Battalion still awaiting clearance to return fire. Hill glanced at Schonberg, who shrugged: *Same shit.*

Then, suddenly, Schonberg got clearance to shoot. Hill thought that maybe whoever was on the other end of the phone heard that last impact and gave in. Weaver issued the command and something like sheet lightning flashed over the FOB; 105-millimeter artillery shells boomed from the cannon, arced over the rocket house, and smashed into the desert floor just beyond.

From a couple of ridgelines to the right, a pair of rockets seared up into the night sky. From his truck at the barrier wall, Haskins watched them burn over the ANA compound toward Airborne's cannons.

Good tactics, Haskins thought. *Bastards.*

The Taliban were sighting Airborne's cannon flash and using it to walk rounds toward the artillery battery.

The FOs radioed a small adjustment. Eight more rounds thundered from the FOB cannons, splashing like steel rain into the first point-of-origin site. Fourth platoon fired a cascade of .50-cal, and tracer rounds stitched the night.

Third Platoon had a TOW, an antiarmor missile system, and Carwile readied his men to use it.

"Acquire target," he transmitted to the gunner.

The gunner trained the ███ optic on the second origin site. "Target acquired."

"Prepare to fire!"

"Ready!"

"Fire!"

The gunner pulled the trigger, heard a *pop-whiz* and a searing sound like brakes on a semi. Felt the whoosh of the four-foot missile leaving the tube. Saw the air in its flight path twist and relax as the missile nicked the sound barrier, propelling a five-inch warhead at a thousand feet per second.

The missile burst on target, a bloom of orange fire hitting 3rd Platoon's eyes before the blast hit their ears. Bonecrusher fired one more volley, sending shock waves throughout the FOB.

And suddenly, it was over. After the one-two punch of the TOW and 105s, the Taliban checked out for the night.

A dozen rockets landed on or around the FOB that night, making the attack the most aggressive of the deployment so far. But Dog Company and the rest of the FOB had weathered two-thirds of the attack before receiving permission to defend themselves. The delay dismayed Hill. He knew Battalion officers at FOB Ghazni were looking at the same map he was. But as they weighed each round's kill radius against possible collateral damage to civilian lives and property, they were more risk averse.

They could afford to be, Hill thought, since the rockets were landing on FOB Airborne and not FOB Ghazni.

On the issue of collateral damage, he had little sympathy for civilians who watched insurgents set up fighting positions clearly aimed at Coalition troops, but who did not warn the Coalition. Hill wanted to set a simple precedent: *If you shoot at us, we will shoot back.*

Once the noncombatants of Wardak received that message, Hill believed, they could either make that warning phone call or get the hell out of the way.

CHAPTER 13

SEVERAL DAYS LATER, CPT B found Hill at the chow shack dining on his usual breakfast of sausage and biscuit with a smear of mustard. When Hill and the rest of D Co landed in Wardak, the pace of operations had resembled a runaway mine cart on a downhill rail. First through 4th Platoons patrolled constantly. Headquarters Platoon—Hill and a handful of his men, plus other soldiers rotated in and out by battalion—split time between combat patrols, QRFs, and the seemingly futile task of making America's allied Afghan partners play nice.

The relentless patrols seemed to be reducing insurgent activity in Wardak. First Platoon had air-assaulted into the Jalrez Valley in support of a Special Forces team on the hunt for the warlord Abdul Razak. The SF team had so narrowly missed capturing Razak that they found his bed warm and his tea hot, steaming bedside in a little cup.

CPT B seemed more urgent than usual, and Hill gave him his undivided attention. The SF team commander kept his voice low. "The Chief and I attended an intel brief that our group hosts every month. We don't always get to go, but we were able to make this one. Well, after the roll call, a Norwegian intel officer from Task Force 51 pulled me aside and told me that he had something for me concerning FOB Airborne."

Hill was locked on, listening. CPT B continued. "He said that his team was informed of an insider threat on Airborne, an interpreter actually, as they were prepping for a recent op in Jalrez. The Norwegian also told me that the intel came from the 101st J2."

"Are you fucking kidding me?" Hill said. He set his breakfast aside. His own division's intel officer had told the Norwegians? Why wasn't he getting this intel from his own chain of command?

CPT B leaned closer. "Task Force 51 was tracking a top-tier target when he made a reference to having access to a terp on Airborne for information on troop movements. I've already started to ping my chain of command for info. I thought you might want to do the same."

"I will," Hill said. "Thanks for the heads-up."

Within the hour, Hill fired off an email to Battalion regarding this new intel. He restrained the urge to bitch about the fact that he'd had to get it not only from another command but from another country. The next day,

███
███
███
███

████████████████ Hill and CPT B decided to track him for a few days to see if he might lead to bigger fish.

The discovery of this dirty terp, Abdul Sabur, was the second domino in a sequence of three that began with the twelve-rocket attack. Next, a Bone-crusher NCO caught an Afghan bazaar shopkeeper pacing off the distance to Airborne's 105 mm cannons. As Hill ordered a detainee packet prepared on the shopkeeper, he stopped in his tracks: What if the shopkeeper and the terp were working together?

Hill gave Tommy Scott the order to detain Sabur immediately. Search teams were formed and the FOB split into quadrants. A few minutes later, Scott drove up to the TOC in a gator with another LN in the back.

"Guess what I caught him doing?" Scott said to Hill and Kay. "He had this and was using it."

It was a cheap cosmetic mirror, the kind American women carry in their purses. A sliver of murky data crystallized: While out on patrol, several Dog Company soldiers, including Hill, had observed what they thought might be signal flashes between the FOB and a mosque in Maidan Shar. The signals were randomly timed and there had been no way to track them down. Now it made sense.

Hill dialed Battalion and handed the phone to Kay. "Find out what we need to do to transport these guys to Ghazni for processing. I'm going to fire off a summary to the boss and the Battalion intel officer."

"Yes, sir," Kay said. He got Lieutenant Scheppler on the line, Battalion's officer in charge of detainee processing. The terp, Sabur, and Signal Mirror Guy were now sitting at the conference room table, eyes cast at the floor.

Scott stood over them squeezing a rubber stress ball, trying to drain some of his anger into it.

Kay gave Scheppler the short version. "We've secured their cell phones and personal belongings. What else do you need from us?"

"That should be good enough right there," Scheppler said.

"What do you guys plan on doing with them?"

"What do you want us to do?"

"We want you guys to take them because we think they've been collecting intel on us for a while now."

"That should be all right," Scheppler said. "When are you going to bring them down here?"

"ASAP," Kay said.

By afternoon, LT Sean Allred and the Dirty First had packaged up the prisoners and rolled out to deliver them to Battalion custody at FOB Ghazni. Later that evening, Kay sat in the TOC shooting the breeze with Scott about a sacred topic: college football. Scott, a Florida native, and Kay, a University of Florida alum, had declared the Gators the official team of Airborne, with only one serious dissenter. Moore, the FOB cook, was a diehard Crimson Tide fan.

The conversation had rolled around to Tim Tebow when Allred walked in, visibly pissed off. He and his platoon had just returned from Ghazni, where they'd attempted to drop off Signal Mirror Guy and the dirty terp.

"What's up?" Kay said.

"They didn't take the detainees," Allred spat.

"What are you talking about? Who didn't take the detainees? Battalion?"

"The intel guys said our paperwork wasn't good enough, that we didn't have any 'proof.'"

Proof? Kay thought. *How about cell phone records matching the Norwegian intel? How about catching these guys in the fucking act?*

Allred was hot. "We risked our lives to drive down to Ghazni through a Tier 1 IED threat area. Then we have to drive all the way back and drop these assholes off in Haft Asiab?"

The lieutenant summed up the entire evolution in three words—"This is bullshit!"—then spun on his boot heel and walked out the door.

The United States of America
v.
CPT Roger T. Hill and 1SG Tommy L. Scott
1 December 2008

SPECIALIST ALLAN J. MOSER continued testifying, in substance, as follows:

Prosecutor Latino: Do you remember First Sergeant Scott making a statement, words to the effect of "Do you want to die like your friend?"

Moser: I think so, sir.

Prosecutor Runyan: And what do you think he meant by that?

Moser: Just to scare him.

Runyan: Was that before he sent him outside?

Moser: I believe so, ma'am.

Runyan: Around the same time you heard gunshots?

Moser: Yes, ma'am.

Runyan: And where was Captain Hill during this?

Moser: I believe outside, ma'am.

Runyan: Do you think those gunshots were from the range?

Moser: Could have been, ma'am.

Defense Attorney Neal Puckett: After the detainee bit you and you struck him five or six times, who witnessed that?

Moser: I think Captain Hill, but I'm not sure…

Puckett: Did Captain Hill say anything to you?

Moser: Yes, he told me not to do it.

Puckett: Did either Captain Hill or First Sergeant Scott order you to punch this guy after he bit you?

Moser: No, sir.

Puckett: It was just something you did?

Moser: Yes, sir.

Puckett: In fact, didn't First Sergeant dress you down afterwards for maybe going overboard?

Moser: Yes, sir.

Puckett: It's his job to correct the mistakes of juniors?

Moser: Correct, sir.

Puckett: None of us were there. None of us were in your shoes, experiencing what you were experiencing. Would it be fair to say that you still had the memories of the deaths of Lieutenant Carwile and Specialist Conlon in your mind?

Moser: Yes, sir.

Puckett: You were still pretty upset about that?

Moser: Yes. When I saw those guys, I saw the guys who killed my brothers.

Puckett: You had information that these guys were bad guys, right? Basically traitors, right?

Moser: Yes, sir.

Puckett: Given the threat that existed, and given the fact that these guys were found to have betrayed you even though they worked on the FOB, did you think the measures that they took to segregate them and blindfold them and also flex-cuff them were appropriate?

Moser: Yes, sir. They had a lot of information on us, sir.

Puckett: Right. So did you see them as a real, immediate threat?

Moser: Yes, sir.

Puckett: Do you believe that the measures that you saw being taken with these detainees were inappropriate?

Moser: No, sir.

Puckett: Why not?

Moser: Because they were Taliban, and if it was the opposite, where the Taliban captured us, they would've cut our heads off and videotaped it for our families to see.

CHAPTER 14

ON MAY 2, 2008, three clicks west of the village of Kowte Ashrow, Kris Wilson, Mo, and the Shockers were pulling security near a squat mud hut called a *qalat*. The hut was once the property of the Jalrez warlord Razak. He had abandoned it the night that Special Forces team nearly caught him drinking his tea.

Now, chattering children crowded around the Shockers' trucks, led by a lanky-faced boy who lobbied the soldiers for candy and gum.

"People in my village are hungry," the boy said to Mo. The kid didn't look hungry, but Mo pulled out an MRE and gave it to him anyway. They were well inside the eastern end of the Jalrez Valley. If Mo lived in this place, he thought, he'd flag down everyone he saw and take anything he could get.

Wilson surveyed the terrain: Dusky fields and apple orchards embraced in a ring of low mountains. Two of the peaks, Razorback and Baby Razorback, were east of their position, back toward Airborne. They formed the valley entrance and were prominent terrain features visible from the FOB. While relieving the 82nd, several soldiers had warned him: "Do *not* go between those two mountains."

But the thirty-vehicle convoy *had* gone between the mountains. It included D Co's 4th and HQ Platoons, a French mentorship team and their ANA mentees, and LTC DeMartino and his Battalion PSD (Personal Security Detachment).

Mentally, Wilson ran through his roster. He thought about his new soldiers: PFC Michael Peake, twenty-one, of Columbia, South Carolina. PFC Tyler Steinle, twenty-five, of Nevada City, California. PFC Ryan Haffner,

nineteen, of Nashville, Tennessee. Their training was solid. They were surrounded by veterans. Mo, Davis, and Colon had all been in Ramadi, along
with SPC Randle Henderson. None of the cherries had been in a serious
firefight yet, but he thought they'd be fine.

A few meters away, Hill and Sammy stood with DeMartino and the Battalion leadership. A pair of Apache Longbow helos circled overhead, the
convoy's CAS. A plan was underway to establish a new COP, or combat
outpost, in Jalrez. The group was finishing recon on Razak's abandoned
qalat, one of two proposed sites.

A couple of weeks earlier, Hill had briefed DeMartino and the Battalion staff on the Taliban threat in Jalrez. An SF team had been working sources in the valley for several months. Intel said Razak could easily
raise a force of two hundred fighters—more than double the size of Dog
Company—including a platoon of Pakistani jihadists. His compound in
the valley's Gindi Khil region was a sort of third world military-industrial
complex, producing IEDs, vehicle-borne suicide bombers, and guns. The
area had a long history of war. During the Soviet invasion of Afghanistan,
Wardak's protected flanks and proximity to Kabul made it a meeting hub
for the Afghan resistance fighters known as mujahideen. The dominant
mujahideen faction in the province was then the Hizb-e-Islami, whose
famous commanders included GEN Muzafarradin, the current ANP chief
in Wardak.

The SF team had learned that insurgents' recent hands-off policy toward
the province was not a sign that they'd been driven out. Instead, the presence in Jalrez of Razak's insurgent cell and its bomb-building enterprise
was the primary reason for the relative peace. It wasn't so much that Wardak
was a "model province." It was that the Taliban had simply decided it best to
not piss in its own front yard.

Based on the SF commander's assessment, Hill had proposed to DeMartino that D Co establish the new COP. A presence was necessary, he said,
to secure Wardak, support Governor Naeemi's development plan, and sta-
bilize Kabul. DeMartino agreed.

Hill made it clear that his company was too small to provide a consistent
presence in the valley without reinforcements. He left the meeting with a
verbal agreement by DeMartino that reinforcements for a new Jalrez COP
would be provided by higher headquarters.

Naeemi, Wardak's provincial governor, was in full agreement with 1st
Battalion's decision to put an outpost in Jalrez Valley. He wanted to expand
the region's budding commercial enterprises, including exporting the

produce of the valley's flourishing apple orchards. If the people could get their apples to market, economic prosperity—or at least something a notch or two above subsistence farming—might follow. If that happened, the locals might start their own resistance to the Taliban. Classic counterinsurgency.

Now, Hill stood beside DeMartino surveying Razak's abandoned *qalat*. It would be nice, they agreed, to poke a finger in the warlord's eye by turning it into an American outpost. But another proposed site in the village of Kowte Ashrow ("KOE-tee Ash-ROE") had several advantages. The biggest would be the increased potential to partner with the ANP at their station there. Also, the Taliban had shut down the local school and terrorized anyone who tried to resurrect education in the village. The school site was across the street from the ANP station. With Dog Company providing security, the village children might be able to return to their classrooms.

The issue was settled: The new COP would be built in Kowte Ashrow. Hill was ready to order the convoy to begin movement back to Airborne when DeMartino surprised him.

"We're going to conduct a movement to contact," he said.

The order knocked Hill back for a moment. "Movement to contact" means an element moves until it encounters enemy resistance. Another way to put it: *Let's go pick a fight.*

Certainly we can make it happen, Hill thought. But with so large a convoy, the enemy had to be well aware that the Americans had been in the valley all day. Every minute of early warning ceded to the Taliban could mean lives lost. Plus, if Jalrez was rich enough in guns and IEDs for Battalion to establish an entire outpost there, what was the point of mounting a seat-of-the-pants operation?

Carefully, Hill formed his objection. "We're going to be outside our 105 range. And we only have CAS for about another twenty minutes."

But DeMartino had already begun walking away. He snapped his chinstrap and called over his shoulder, "Then I guess you better find us some more air."

CHAPTER 15

FOR A SURREAL moment, Hill followed DeMartino. "Sir? . . . Sir? . . . *Sir!*—" DeMartino kept walking.

"What's the turnaround point?" Hill called out, now really half to himself. Up ahead, DeMartino and his battalion sergeant major, a twenty-five-year veteran named Judd, were already leaned close in conversation.

Hill turned back to his Humvee and sent out a net call to his platoon leaders.

"Guidons, Guidons, Guidons, this is Dog 6. I need all platoon leaders at the hood of my truck, time now. Acknowledge receipt. Over." He glanced at his watch, thought about the clock ticking down on their CAS.

"And let's make it quick," he added. "I've got a FRAGO."

A series of responses by platoon leaders dominoed over the net, and soon the PLs were making their way toward Hill. As they came, two memories flashed through his mind: the JRTC brief about the shredded platoon in Jalrez and the warnings from the 82nd Airborne sergeant back at Bagram.

Hill glanced again at his watch. He had the Apache Longbow attack helos on-station for only about twenty more minutes. With the patrol now spread out about four hundred meters along the road, it would take at least five to seven minutes to brief a plan. He gave the hand-arm signal for "double time," and the PLs broke into a jog.

Hill checked in with the Longbows circling above.

"Bearcat One-Six, Bearcat One-Six, this is Dog 6."

The Longbow flight leader's voice scratched over the radio. "Dog 6, this is Bearcat. I've got you Lima Charlie." Loud and clear.

"Roger, Bearcat. Hey, we need you for one last mission. We're about to push due west, an extension of our recon. Can you check out our route before you are bingo on fuel and head back to base?"

"That's affirmative. We'll let you know what we see. Bearcat One-Six out."

Hill pulled out the three-by-two whiteboard he carried everywhere and drew up a quick CONOP (Concept of the Operation), sketching out three phase lines dissecting a trio of prominent villages along the route. The third would be the turnaround point.

Hill briefed the PLs. Fifteen minutes later, Dog Company rolled out. The French mentorship team and their pupils, the ANA, led the way, grinding away from Razak's neighborhood. The Shockers followed and Hill's HQ platoon fell in behind them, with DeMartino's trucks in trail.

As the patrol headed deeper into Jalrez, Hill radioed the Wardak TOC and passed Kay the details of the plan.

The element trekked west on Jalrez's only road, and Hill saw the village of Esh-ma-keyl on the Blue Force Tracker just two and a half clicks away. Esh-ma-keyl was the Taliban's line in the sand, the village where that 82nd platoon had been so badly hit. Dog Company was better armed and better trained than the enemy, but the Taliban had the advantage of surprise and terrain. In just over six weeks' time, Hill and his men had developed a respect for these fighters. They were tenacious and resourceful and, on the whole, a cut above the insurgents in Iraq.

As the French and ANA vehicles rumbled ahead and radio chatter poured into Hill's ear, he thought about DeMartino's order, a movement to contact. DeMartino could easily have requested more air himself. Putting that last-minute responsibility on Hill seemed odd. And though he would never second-guess his commander in front of the men, doubt warred in his mind.

He understood the psychological currency earned by taking it to the enemy. Of saying, *We're here, we're in your face, what are you going to do about it?*

Hill got that. But with all their advantages in firepower and tactics, wouldn't it be better to make their first ground thrust into a known Taliban stronghold a slam dunk with a little rehearsal and planning? After all, Jalrez was practically out Airborne's front gate. Dog Company could do this op any day—every day, in fact. Only later would Hill realize that while Dog Company could, DeMartino himself could not. And that might have been the whole point.

Approaching the village, Hill could see that the narrow dirt road curved to the right; on the left, it fell away, revealing an unexpectedly lush valley.

Apple orchards extended as far as Hill could see. Out the passenger-side window, he saw a steep, rocky incline and ahead, a klatch of *qalats* built into the bank. His truck rounded the curve and heavy machine-gun fire exploded.

The platoon net erupted. *"Contact! Twelve o'clock!"*

Enfilade fire pounded the lead truck, Taliban gunners firing directly into the windshield. Hill could see the truck shuddering, rocking on its tires under a tidal wave of lead. The ANA tumbled out of the vehicle and ran past Hill's Humvee. Directly in front of him, 4th Platoon's gunners were already engaged. Wilson's drivers were trying to move forward toward the fight, but the ANA truck was shot to hell and it blocked the narrow road, trapping the convoy.

RPG rounds scorched overhead, slamming into ditches, rocks, banks, each a near miss. The enemy was now engaging the convoy from three sides.

"Pull up! Pull up!" Wilson shouted orders on the net. His first section was already locked in battle directly at nine and twelve o'clock, due south and due west. "Rear two trucks orient to your three o'clock and engage!"

His order triggered a "mad minute": All gunners fire upon the enemy locations until that enemy shuts up. MK19 grenades and .50-cal rounds chopped into the trees and crumbled *qalat* walls.

The enfilade ambushers ceased fire, only to reposition. Then the high and low sides of the road erupted with AK and PKM crossfire.

An RPG seared up from the low side and slammed into the bank. Wilson ordered his gunners back to their original fire sectors and saw Peake and Steinle, his cherry gunners, hammering back at the enemy as if they'd been fighting all their lives.

Hill keyed his radio. "Wardak TOC, Wardak TOC. Troops in contact! Break. Front-line trace. Break. Route Montana and Esh-ma-keyl village. Taking heavy fire from due west and due north of our location. Break. Correction, taking fire from north, west, and south of our location—"

A rocket burned past Hill's truck and exploded into a berm behind him. "Requesting CAS at this time," he finished. "How copy, over?"

"Dog 6, Roger. Wardak TOC acknowledges all." It was Kay. "We'll get back to you with an ETA for CAS in a couple of mikes. And be advised, you guys are out of 105 range. Over."

"Roger," Hill replied. He was more than well aware.

The ANA bailed and the French pulled back. Then, enemy mortars rained on the road, launched from the heart of Esh-ma-keyl. A steady barrage of small-arms fire poured in from *qalats* higher on the ridgeline and from the orchards below. Twenty-one-year-old PFC Michael Peake, in his first firefight, aimed his MK19 into the trees. Consciously, he let adrenaline take over, pulled his trigger again and again. He fired on anything that moved in the orchard, but had the presence of mind not to shoot an ANA soldier whose bottle-green beret he saw at the last possible second.

The rest of the Shockers' gunners banged back in the crossfire, initially fighting alone at the front of the column. Wilson barked out fire-sector orders. Because of the abandoned ANA pickup trucks, the column was logjammed at an exposed bend in the road, certainly part of the enemy's plan. Something needed to break.

Mo and Wilson dismounted and moved down the column to find Hill. After a short discussion, it was agreed that Mo would advance on foot up the hillside and flank the *qalat* on the high ground to their north. Dog Company needed to control at least that piece of high ground in order to maneuver their vehicles. Wilson bounded back to the front of the column to fight his trucks while Mo continued toward the rear of the convoy in search of more dismounts.

As Mo approached the Battalion PSD trucks, he saw DeMartino, Sergeant Major Judd, and several officers.

"Hey, how you doin', Sergeant Major?" Mo said, as if the two were meeting at the mall. "We're gonna go up and take out that building, but I need some guys."

"I'll go," said Captain Al LeMaire, CO of Alpha Company. Another captain also volunteered, and the small patrol took off up the hill armed with M4's and grenades. Reaching a small compound, the team cleared a courtyard and a few rooms. Enemy fighters had already squirted out the back. Inside the courtyard fence, they found a hole in the ground, a weapons cache. Mo pulled a grenade from his vest, tossed it in, and blew the cache.

The ad hoc squad moved up to the compound rooftop. From that vantage point, they could see the convoy stretched east toward Airborne. Then they heard the thunder.

CHAPTER 16

THE AIR FORCE A-10's official model name is the Thunderbolt II, after the World War II P-47 Thunderbolt fighter. But flyers long ago dubbed the P-47's namesake the "Warthog" for its homely appearance. Twin turbines the size of industrial clothes dryers ride the skinny fuselage just forward of the A-10's boxy tail. The pilot sits in a "bathtub" of titanium armor, his cockpit roofed with a naked bubble canopy that juts from the airframe like an aftermarket part. The nose wheel is off center, the wings stubby and straight.

The Warthog may not look sexy, but its lethal fury has been known to trigger passion in American infantrymen from the Balkans to the Persian Gulf. Kris Wilson, a military weapons geek, revered the plane because it was the only one he knew of where engineers basically said, "Okay, here's a big-ass Gatling gun. Now build a plane around it."

Wherever there is an A-10 raining terror on the enemy, there are soldiers on the ground cheering, *"DIE, YOU BASTARDS!"*

On the road below Wilson's element, Hill was returning to his gun truck from the front of the column when a pair of Thunderbolts checked in.

"Dog 6, this is Hog 5-3." It was Major Dave Rayman, the A-10 pilot Hill's men had trained with at Bagram. "We'll be on-station in approximately three mikes."

"Hog 5-3, this is Dog 6, copy. It'll be hard to miss us. Our column is running from west to east on Route Montana, vicinity of Esh-ma-keyl village. Two tan pickup trucks will mark our front-line trace. We are taking heavy fire from the south, west, and north. How copy, over?"

"Dog 6, roger that. We'll be approaching from east to west, along Route Montana." Hill transmitted a refined front-line trace, a set of grid coordinates intersecting Montana. Rayman echoed back the numbers.

"That's a good copy, Hog 5-3. Dog 6 standing by for visual contact."

Hill switched to his man portable radio so that he could maintain comms with Rayman while he trooped the line. By now most of the enemy fire was streaming in from the slope-side village and the apple orchard to the south. Hill bounded to the front of the column again, doing his best to keep Dog Company Humvees between himself and incoming fire. He climbed onto the fender of a Shockers Humvee where the rookie Steinle was on the gun. Hill pointed at a mud house about six hundred meters up the slope and yelled over the rumbling firefight. "See that house with the blue door?"

Steinle nodded. "Yes, sir!"

"The A-10s are coming in! On my signal, I need you to put a couple of rounds right through that door so the pilots can see the impact and know where we're taking fire from!"

"Not a problem, sir!" Steinle wheeled his MK19 toward the *qalat* and held his fire.

There was no way in hell Steinle would hit that door, Hill thought, but its bright color made a brilliant target.

The A-10s, a flight of two, roared into the valley on a dry-run pass. "Dog 6, Hog 5-3 on station. Confirm you have visual on us."

"Hog 5-3, affirmative. I see your approach," Hill transmitted. "My gunner will paint the first target for you. You'll see rounds impact on a house six hundred meters northwest of our column up on a hillside. That will be your first target."

"Roger, we'll look for it."

Hill signaled Steinle, who aimed and fired a three-round burst. Grenades sailed up the hill, smashed directly through the blue door and... disappeared. No impact. No smoke.

Hill stared, amazed. Steinle grinned. The captain rolled his eyes and laughed. "All right, smart-ass. I need you to put one *on the wall of the house* so they can see the impact—we've got to paint the target for the A-10s."

"Roger that!" Steinle said, and fired again. Debris burst from the house wall, smoke spouting skyward.

"Dog 6, Hog 5-3, contact. We have eyes on your target."

"Roger, you are cleared to go hot."

The A-10s racetracked back and screamed in. Then a sound like a tractor trailer in radical downshift vibrated through the valley as their cannons rubbled the *qalat*.

Hill keyed his mic. "Hog 5-3, Dog 6, nice work. That should do it. Stand by for next target."

Hill dismounted and turned a half step to the right in time to see an RPG streaking toward him on a rope.

Arrowing across the top of the orchard, the rocket was on a line toward Hill's head. His eyes dilated. His brain clicked into slo-mo, recording each instant of the rocket's killing flight.

Then: *whooshBAM!* The RPG slammed into the soft hillside above Hill's head. Loose soil half-swallowed its muffled boom.

Hill whirled to see how close and caught SPC Randle Henderson glaring at him, furious. Rifle in one hand, mic in the other, the Ramadi veteran threw up his arms in disgust.

"*What the fuck, sir?!*" he yelled. "Would you just get back in your vehicle, please?"

This was a specialist talking to a captain. The put-upon look on Henderson's face said to Hill, *I've got all this shit to worry about, and now I have you running around out here!*

Hill turned away to hide a smile. His guys could be overprotective, guarding their commander at all costs. Sometimes they forgot he was a soldier, too.

Hill talked the Warthogs through two more passes, shredding lush orchards and enemy fighters in the valley below. Over the next few minutes, D Co gunners were able to slow their rate of fire. Most of the enemy had bugged out or been gunned down.

This was the first all-out firefight of the deployment, and Hill was pleased with how his men had performed. He continued to stride up and down the convoy, checking on his men and directing the order of movement for the convoy back to Airborne. On his last pass, he walked nearly back to the Battalion PSD trucks, where he did an actual double take.

LTC DeMartino was posing for pictures. Literally posing.

One with his arms crossed. One with his helmet off. Pulling in some staffers for a buddy shot, the smoking valley for a backdrop.

Hill cursed under his breath. Scant minutes before, that RPG had nearly taken his head off, and DeMartino's truck was just four or five back from his own. Again, Hill understood bravado. Communicating it to the troops. He loved the scene in *Black Hawk Down* where a major walks fearlessly through RPG and small arms fire, yelling into his radio, trying to rescue his wounded. Hill felt men deserved a leader who did not cower from risk, who transmitted the message, *I'm going to do what I have to do no matter the cost to myself.*

But what was DeMartino transmitting to his juniors, posing with his helmet off in the last throes of a firefight? For Hill the answer was plain: *He looks like a fucking tourist.*

CHAPTER 17

"GODDAMMIT!"

Kay lifted his gaze from an inventory spreadsheet and turned to see Tommy Scott slamming his laptop shut.

"One hundred hours!" Scott fumed. "We won the first Gulf War in one hundred hours and not one goddamn email was sent!"

Kay laughed. He had come up in the wired Army himself, but he had to agree with Scott, who was of the old school. Between the two of them, they spent so much time responding to trivial emails, it was a miracle they ever made mission.

Scott reached into a drawer, pulled an Otis Spunkmeyer blueberry muffin from the stash he kept in his desk, and took a bite to console himself.

"What is that, six of those you've eaten today, Tommy?" Kay said.

Scott took another giant bite and chewed around his grin. "Shut the fuck up, Larry," he said amiably. "Hey, you're not going to believe *this*..."

"What?" Kay said.

"You know that terp we busted, the one 1st Platoon took down to Ghazni and Battalion let him go?"

"Yeah?"

"That fucker called me this morning asking about his paycheck! Can you believe the nerve? He's a goddamn spy and I'm supposed to pay him!"

Kay shook his head. He wouldn't be at all surprised if someone up the chain actually ordered Dog Company to make that happen. The lieutenant turned back to his desk and dialed 2LT Miles Hidalgo, platoon leader for the Alpha Dawgs.

Hidalgo and his men were manning Sayed Abad Base, part of Dog

Company's AO, sixty kilometers south of Airborne. The platoon was originally part of the 1-506th's Alpha Company, whose AO was Kapisa Province. Prior to deployment and as a concession for Dog Company's manning limitations, DeMartino had agreed to send Hill's fourteen-man 2nd Platoon, the Jolly Rogers, up to Kapisa. In exchange, DeMartino sliced the Alpha Dawgs, a larger thirty-man line platoon, to D Co—enough soldiers to staff Sayed Abad.

It was already one of the toughest assignments in the Brigade, and now things were heating up on Highway 1. More ambushes, more IEDs. Hidalgo's men had just been in a firefight in which some of the Alpha Dawgs were incredibly heroic. Their platoon sergeant, Pablo Cadena, suffered significant leg injuries from RPG shrapnel and would not return to duty. Kay was following up with Hidalgo to coach him on recommending some of his men for awards, including multiple Purple Hearts, Bronze Stars for valor, even a Silver Star.

Hill placed a huge emphasis on awards. Not because he wanted his men to have bragging rights, but because awards were something tangible a command could do to formally recognize soldiers for their work, especially heroism under fire. Awards boosted morale, helped soldiers advance in rank, and shaped the perception of soldiers in their units and even in their families.

After the call, Kay opened an email screen. He had begun to blind-copy Major John Karagosian, the Battalion XO, on every email he sent to the S-shops, or Battalion support offices. Hopefully, Karagosian would realize that Dog Company's requests were not being made a priority. It was only their third month in-country and the company's vehicles were in shambles. In poor condition when CPT Hill signed for them, continuous patrols had turned them into rolling junkyards. At least three of D Co's twenty-one Humvees had become notoriously unreliable and sometimes wouldn't start at all. Third Platoon had a truck that could make only right turns. The tires jammed into the wheel well when the driver tried to turn left. Highly inconvenient in a firefight.

Kay's head mechanic, Staff Sergeant (SSG) Keveon Bass, had been making daily requests for parts to get the trucks in proper working order. Recently, a supply truck had pulled into the Airborne motor pool. As some E Co guys piled out and began unloading boxes with a forklift, Kay and Bass went outside to survey the cargo. Maybe for once, they were going to get what they asked for.

Kay peeled open a cardboard carton. "Oh, shit! Batteries!"

The men hadn't been able to get batteries to run their NODs (night vision devices) and had been writing home and asking their wives to send them.

"Oh, shit! Crunch 'n Munch!" Bass said.

Kay turned just as Bass retrieved a small box of kettle corn. He cradled it in his arms like Emmitt Smith protecting the rock on a touchdown run.

Kay laughed. "You like Crunch 'n Munch?"

"I fuckin' *love* Crunch 'n Munch!" Bass said, grinning.

Bass set his prize aside and poked his head and shoulders back into the carton. When he emerged, his joy had vanished. "Sir, I'm getting sick and tired of this! I did not order these parts." He glanced back in the box, then looked at Kay in dismay. "Half this shit is for a truck we don't have, and the other half is shit we don't need. Why would they send us this?"

Kay had no answer. Later that day, he heard that the police mentorship team, Caveman, was making a run to their headquarters in Bagram. He sent a D Co mechanic along, armed with a laundry list of vital vehicle parts. If the system wouldn't work, Kay thought, he'd have to work the system.

CHAPTER 18

TALIBAN FORCES CONTINUED to rocket Airborne at least weekly. Despite living mainly in tents and plywood shacks, Dog Company had sustained only a handful of minor injuries. But the enemy was growing more accurate with every attack.

Hill and his men analyzed the Taliban's firing patterns and began sending out patrols aimed at disruption. Wilson pitched the idea of setting up an OP on top of a building in downtown Maidan Shar. The building was really only a skeleton, unoccupied and still under construction. But it had a clear view of both "Razorbacks," the ridgeline opposite Airborne, where most of the rocket fire originated.

On May 8, the Shockers slipped off the FOB and into Maidan Shar. SPC Graydon Kamp, twenty-four, of Allentown, Pennsylvania, broke off with a squad to establish an overwatch position. Because the operation was taking place directly on Afghan National Police turf, Hill and Wilson agreed it would be wise to include them, but without advance notice so as not to compromise the mission.

On the way to the OP, Wilson stopped in at the ANP station and explained the operation to the captain, who rallied a contingent of men to accompany 4th Platoon. Wilson left SSG Ray Davis and a squad at the police station while the rest of the element, including their terp, Habibi, moved out on Maidan Shar's dirt main street.

The village lay mostly dark, an occasional window throwing a square of warm, yellow light onto the street. At first, the Shockers walked point. But Mo decided he didn't want the ANP's guns pointed at their backs, so the Americans slowed down to let the police walk ahead.

Late-night family sounds floated on the air, muffled by hut walls made of mud. The element reached the building, a concrete block structure that reached three stories into the night. A traditional Afghan courtyard stood behind an iron gate. The patrol stacked at the gate, then entered. The front door was not locked, but inside, the element found a different obstacle: The entire stairway was outlined in concrete construction forms. A kick board blocked each step.

SPC Carlos Colonruiz, Wilson's Puerto Rican Schwarzenegger, muscled the nearly seventy-pound MK19 up the stairs. PFC Michael Peake followed with the tripod.

Wilson and Mo brought up the rear. The objective was stealth, but with the weight of the weapons, the hinky stairwell, and the ANP's natural bluster, the ascent was a mash-up of whispered curses in English and Pashto, with Colon contributing curses in Spanglish.

There had been no end to the amount of shit Davis had given Colon in Ramadi over his crappy English. "What the *fuck* did you just say?" Davis would yell when Colon mangled a sentence. "Go back in the hooch and don't come out until you can speak English!"

This was a ritual of infantry bonding that some soldiers found rough at first. If a soldier had some deficiency—no neck, a woman's ass, whatever—it was his battle buddies' solemn duty to give him as much grief as possible. On the heavy side himself, Davis had been called everything from Hot Tub to Lunch Box. Soldiers learned to roll with the verbal hazing or lose the trust of their platoon. The way Davis saw it, if a man whined when he got called names, he sure as hell didn't want to stand next to him in a firefight.

Through the Ramadi deployment, Colon learned just enough infantry English to shotgun his own brand of insults. "Hey, Lunch Box, turn off that fucking cigarette! You know fat man not s'posed to smoke!"

The squad emerged onto the rooftop to find it covered in a layer of sheet metal. The ANP stomped aboard.

"*Jesus!*" Mo whispered. "Could they be any fucking louder?"

A wall about two feet high hemmed the roof. Wilson peered down into the small lot that surrounded the building. Below, on the west side, was a CONEX shipping container. Through the green haze of his NODs, he could make out some tools and construction equipment. Behind him, Colon and Peake assembled the MK19 in utter silence while Mo directed the rest of 4th and the ANP to take up positions at the roof's four corners. Mo set up on the corner facing west, toward the ridgeline. He could see Baby Razorback to the left. Ambient starlight silhouetted both mountains against the sky.

"*Sergeant Mo!*" It was Colon in a hushed whisper. He was huddled behind the rooftop wall a few feet away.

Mo turned toward Colon, who jerked his head toward the ANP. "Sergeant Mo, this guys getting on their cell phones!"

Mo saw that an ANP officer was not only trying to dial out, he was also scooting down into a prone position, as though to take cover.

Probably calling in the damn Talidizzle, Mo thought.

Staying low, he moved to where the Afghan held his cell to his ear, and held out his hand. "Give it to me."

The officer scooted backward, phone still to his ear. Mo followed, getting right in the man's face. "I *said*, give me the fucking phone. I'll give it back after the op."

Mo reached to grab the cell, and the Afghan, wide-eyed, fought him to keep it, prompting Mo to whack the guy on the side of his head. The phone clattered to the rooftop, and Mo scooped it up. "Like I said, I'll give it back after the op."

Returning to his position, Mo whispered to Wilson, "I knew we couldn't trust these sombitches."

The commotion had stirred the neighbors. Muffled Pashto fluttered down from nearby *qalats*. Wilson's soldiers scanned their sectors. The ANP fell silent. Maidan Shar nestled into a new quiet, and the Shockers settled in to watch the mountains for signs of a new attack.

Mo scanned the ridgeline using a CLU (Command Launch Unit, pronounced "clue") optic, part of the Javelin system, a portable antitank missile. The CLU sight had saved his life in Ramadi. An insurgent with an RPG had crept through a stand of reeds to within fifty meters of Mo's position before Mo picked him out of the darkness with the sight. Mo lit up the attacker with his night vision laser and fired on him with his rifle. His gunners followed his lead and finished the guy off.

Owing his life to the CLU, Mo rode Hill and Kay for weeks to get him one to use in Afghanistan. Then one day, CPT B's guys called him down to their TOC, where they surprised him with a brand-new CLU, still in the case. Special Forces got all the good toys.

Now on the rooftop, long, still minutes strung themselves into an hour, like beads on a string. Starlight frosted the night.

Mo hated the expectant hush of waiting for a fight. If he was going into battle, he wanted to close with the enemy and get it on. The concussion of mortars, the snap of near-miss bullets; every earth-jarring, bone-pulsing round that didn't hit him was both exultation and relief. There were times he felt he could make his home in a Wardak or a Ramadi. In combat, he felt at ease, relieved of the *threat* of violence he'd always lived with, instead meeting it head-on. Some ancient center in his brain powered up and became ascendant. He saw and heard and executed in high-def, with full assurance and zero hesitation. Something inside Mo, hardwired since childhood, made it easier to rejoice in life while tilting at death.

In a way, a counselor once told him, Mo had always been in combat. For a brief space while growing up, several months or a year maybe, he remembered being treated kindly by his mother's temporary husbands. He was around four when she connected with a decent guy. Too decent, Mo decided in retrospect, because she ditched him for a man who made the rest of Mo's childhood a nightmare, beating him from the time he was five until his early teens. Sometimes with a closed fist, sometimes a belt buckle. Once, he threw Mo through a wall.

Eventually, his mother met a man who showed him real love. But the flame of fear that burned inside young Tim Moriarty had already spread into a wildfire of rage. In school, he despised bullies and went out of his way to take them down. As he got older, Mo recognized this as a defect in his character. It was like looking into a mirror and seeing "them assholes," as he came to refer to the men who had abused him.

The flip side of this defect was a fierce loyalty to those who earned it. But he did not completely trust another man until he met Greg Rogers.

The two connected at Fort Campbell, where SFC Rogers had taken over as Delta Company platoon sergeant, with Kris Wilson as his right-hand man. Rogers embodied two things Mo had never found in a role model: He was simultaneously approachable and unbullshitable.

Slowly, Rogers became the mentor Mo never had. Rogers and his wife, Sandy, were only a few years older than Mo, but they became his adopted mom and dad.

As their friendship grew, Rogers was able to rein Mo in and harness his leadership qualities, the way an experienced rider brings out the best in a horse no one else can break. Backcountry syntax mangled Mo's speech; Rogers made him use proper grammar. Mo couldn't stomach technology; Rogers made him use a computer.

Neither man was supposed to go to Iraq. Mo's legs were laced with stress fractures from previous tours, and he was loping around on crutches. Then three months before the deployment, Sandy died. Complications from diabetes. Doctors had been able to revive her just long enough for Rogers to say good-bye.

Mo urged his friend to stay stateside and tend to his affairs, even though Mo himself wasn't willing to let his brothers go fight those Al Qaeda bastards without him. When medics refused to clear him off his crutches, he reported for deployment, leaving his crutches in the car. When Rogers found out Mo was headed for Ramadi, he said, "If you're going, I'm going."

It was one of those brief conversations on which a man's destiny turns.

One night, Rogers was slated to pull security for a route clearance mission in Ramadi's turbulent streets. He told Mo that he didn't think he was coming back.

"Man, don't even say that," Mo said. "That shit's not funny."

"It's all right," Rogers said. "I'd be cool with it. I could go be with Sandy."

Hours later, Rogers was killed by an IED, just as he'd predicted. That night, April 9, 2006, was the first time Mo cried openly about losing anyone in combat.

Rogers's premonition hadn't come from instinct, Mo was certain. That came from somewhere else, somewhere higher. In a way it was a mercy, he thought, a divine whisper preparing you for the next life.

Mo believed in God and knew Rogers had, too. It wasn't very politically correct, but Mo didn't want any soldier fighting next to him who didn't believe in Someone greater than himself. If a soldier didn't believe in life after death, Mo reasoned, it wasn't likely he'd give up his only life for another man.

Now on the Maidan Shar rooftop, grief stabbed Mo's heart. Resolutely, he pushed it away.

Near midnight, Wilson's earbud went hot. It was Kamp on the overwatch position. "Four-seven, we've got movement in the courtyard. Looks like two, maybe three pax. Armed, looks like AKs."

"ANP?"

"Can't tell."

Wilson stood and walked to the rooftop edge overlooking the gate. He flipped on the tac light mounted under the barrel of his M4, shot the beam down to the courtyard. Through his NODs, he saw three men, each armed with a rifle.

"Stop!" Wilson called out.

Wilson saw one man raise his hand. Some instinct caused Wilson to draw back his head a split second before a three-round AK burst reached his face. Two bullets snapped past his left ear, and the third smashed his NODs off his face. He pasted himself prone so quickly that Mo thought he was dead. But Wilson popped up almost instantly, NODs dangling from his helmet. He aimed his tac light again and saw the shooters running toward the CONEX. Wilson fired controlled pairs, allowing his men to get into firing positions.

"They're behind the CONEX!" Kamp called over the radio. "Stacked up on the other side!"

"Come out!" Mo yelled.

Wilson joined him. "Lay down your weapons and come out! We will not fire!"

Habibi translated for the ANP, who also began calling down surrender instructions in Pashto.

Silence.

"Four-two, what do you got?" Wilson said.

"They're still stacked," Kamp said.

"Do they still have their weapons?"

"Affirmative. Do you want us to take 'em out?"

"Negative, negative. I don't want fire coming toward our position."

During this radio traffic, Kamp's truck had been relaying sitreps back to the Airborne TOC. The word came back from Hill: Engage and destroy.

"I'm in grenade range," Mo said to Wilson, then gave the warning order—"Frag out!"—and tossed a grenade over the CONEX. The rooftop squad got low, prepped for the explosion . . .

. . . which did not come.

Crouching behind the wall, Mo looked at Wilson: *What?*

"Dude," Wilson said. "Did you pull the safety?"

Mo rolled his eyes. "Yes, Sergeant First Class Wilson, I did."

BOOM!

Mo and Wilson exchanged a look: *You can't make this shit up.*

Within thirty seconds, Colon and an assault team had flown down the staircase, rounded the CONEX, and found three Afghans on the ground, weapons flung away. Wilson followed and the postassault SOP began: weapons confiscated, pat-down search, first aid. The assault team triaged the men, now enemy prisoners of war (EPWs). Two were wounded, one seriously, with what the men would later call a Forrest Gump shot. Wilson had shot one of his assailants directly in the buttocks.

With his squad surrounding the EPWs, rifles aimed, Wilson examined the prisoners. All wore civilian clothes. Two of the three were filthy.

"*Talib,*" Habibi murmured. The men looked straight out of the mountain bush. Also, they reeked.

Via the terp, Wilson began tactical questioning. "Why did you shoot at us?"

"We are the governor's bodyguards," said the youngest of the three.

"Look, friend, I shined my light on you and told you to stop," Wilson said. "Why did you fire on us?"

"This is the governor's new house and we thought you were stealing."

"Okay, but the ANP commander knew we were here. Why did you shoot after hearing me? It's pretty clear I'm an American."

"We were coming here to take a generator..." The Afghan trailed off.

Wilson stopped. *Okay, first we were stealing, now you were stealing?*

He relayed a sitrep to the TOC via Kamp, who passed a message from the Airborne field grade, Major Christopher Faber: Do not return to base until you get sworn statements from the ANP about what they saw. Wilson got with Habibi and got it done.

CHAPTER 19

WHILE ROGER HILL sat in the TOC, tapping out an email to Battalion about the firefight in Maidan Shar, Larry Kay walked outside and looked up at the sky, taking a moment to soak in the alpine view. He listened to the stars and wondered when he would become a father. He thought about who the next president would be and sincerely hoped he would be one of the last men to have to take in Afghanistan's beauty through night vision goggles while carrying a hundred pounds of gear and wielding a weapon.

The Shockers were on their way back with the EPWs. Kay drew his sidearm, chambered a round, and reholstered it. He was a clear-eyed pragmatist. His longing for peace had zero bearing on the fact that his soldiers were returning to base carrying men with whom he was at war. Kay sat down on the steps and waited.

Moments later, one of 4th Platoon's beat-down Humvees rumbled through the gate and pulled up in front of the TOC. Davis jumped out of the TC seat, breathing fire. He pulled a blindfolded, flex-cuffed prisoner out of the truck, and steered him to Kay. "This piece of shit almost killed Sergeant Wilson!"

Ask an infantryman what his reaction is when someone shoots at his brothers and the answer will most always be "rage." It's an instinctive, familial fury. For Davis, it was as marrow-deep as if the prisoner had shot at his blood brother.

Just then, the prisoner tried to break free. Kay grabbed him by the shirt, lifted him, and jammed his back against the building. Ripping off the blindfold, he looked the prisoner in the eyes, inched him slightly higher, then let go. The enemy fighter slid to the ground. Kay pointed to his pistol then waved his finger in front of the prisoner's face in a no-no motion.

English or no English, the EPW got the message: *If you try to run again, you will be shot.* He did not move again.

The rest of 4th drove the other two Afghans onto the FOB, where both landed in the aid tent. The gaping wound in the first prisoner's buttocks was serious. Kay turned the uninjured prisoner over to SPC Joseph Coe, who escorted him to the TOC and kept him under guard.

For the next half hour, Hill sequestered himself in the conference room writing his report on the firefight. Then Kay poked his head through the door. The entry control point guards had called the TOC, he said. Airborne had visitors.

Hill glanced at the clock. Bizarre. It was the darkest watch of the night, well past midnight but nowhere near dawn.

"Who is it?" Hill said.

"It's Governor Naeemi's assistant, Hanif. COL Shah is with him, and some guards. Six of them."

Shah was head of Wardak's National Directorate of Security, NDS.

"Find out what they want," Hill said. "Take Chris. And Sammy."

This was MAJ Chris Faber's swim lane, dealing with local officials. A Las Vegas native and graduate of West Point and the Naval War College, Faber had been working farther south at FOB Salerno on COL Pete Johnson's staff, designing the brigade's counterinsurgency campaign plan. But each outlying FOB typically needed an operations staff headed by a field grade officer—a major or higher—who could nurture relations with local officials. So brigade had sent Faber to Wardak—minus a staff. Where the 82nd had run a seventeen-man ops staff, Faber was the lone guy.

Though senior to Hill, Faber, thirty-five, was not technically in Hill's chain of command. Still, Hill was finding in him a reliable foxhole ally, a sharp, levelheaded officer who could handle himself with Wardak's unruly cast of characters.

Kay grabbed Faber and Sammy, Hill's terp, and the three walked down to the gate. Kay looked the visitors over. Naeemi's assistant, Hanif, wore a navy blue windbreaker, Shah a sport coat over a light blue *dishdasha*.

After a round of traditional embraces, the whole group walked up to the TOC, where Hanif immediately broke into an urgent plea that ended in an action item: "We would like you to release the prisoners to us."

Kay and Faber glanced at each other, puzzled.

"You can take custody of the one who isn't wounded," Faber said. "But we are obliged to provide medical treatment to the other two."

"Thank you so much," Hanif said. "The governor would have been so upset if his security guards were put in jail."

"Wait! Hold on," Faber said. "You're going to transport these men to a detention facility, are you not? They opened fire on American soldiers."

Hanif and Shah seemed to draw themselves up a bit, make themselves taller. "No. We are taking them back to the governor's compound," Hanif said.

"Okay, look," Faber said. "When our soldiers spoke to those men in English, they opened fire."

Suddenly, Shah interjected loudly, speaking rapid-fire Pashto to Sammy, as Hanif continued to insist that the prisoners be set free.

Faber stood his ground. "Unless Governor Naeemi calls me right now and explains what's going on, we're not releasing those men. They shot at our soldiers. We're not going to just give them a pat on the head and send them on their way."

Hanif pulled out his phone and dialed, spoke a few words, then handed his phone to Faber, who listened and asked questions.

Kay knew Shah spoke English, and tried to lighten the mood. "Excuse me, Colonel," he said, nodding at Shah's sport coat/*dishdasha* combo. "Where can I get a suit like that?"

"Kabul," Shah said with a wry smile. "It's cheap. I will take you there."

Faber was still on the phone, talking to Naeemi. He considered the governor a good man, as honest as a politician can be in a country where being on the "wrong" side (i.e., cooperating with the Americans) could cost a man not just bad press or political fortunes, but his life. The Wardak governor had once showed Faber a portfolio of his accomplishments—articles with pictures of Naeemi with President Hamid Karzai, the two men rising together to power. Naeemi was clearly proud of the association.

Faber finished with Hanif's phone and pulled Kay aside. "The governor is insisting that those men are his private security guards. He wants us to let them go because he has to travel from Kabul tomorrow, and I agreed."

Kay stared at Faber. Growing up in Florida, he had once visited an alligator farm in the Everglades. That farm had smelled exactly like gator shit, and the prisoner Davis brought him smelled exactly like that farm. He wondered why someone in the private employ of the most powerful man in the province would smell like Taliban straight out of the bush. Also, Naeemi's security detail was always in uniform. This guy's clothes looked like he'd been living in a cave.

Still, Faber was the field grade, and he trusted Naeemi. Kay found Coe and ordered him to cut the flex-cuffs off the uninjured EPW. But just as Hanif and the NDS entourage were about to walk out the door with their prize, Wilson and Mo walked up with Hill in tow.

Wilson assessed the situation instantly. "Sir, that fucker almost killed me," he said to Hill. "He shot my night vision goggles off. I could have died, and we just let them go?"

"Wait a minute," Hill cut in. "What's going on with these guys?"

"The governor wants us to release them. They're part of his PSD," said Kay.

"I've already spoken to the governor and approved their release," Faber said.

Hill tensed. "Sir, can I speak with you for a moment?"

He walked with Faber back down the hall. Throughout the deployment, Faber and Hill had managed to minimize friction in their overlapping lanes of responsibility, and had done so with relative ease. Faber dealt with the provincial government officials on a day-to-day basis. Lots of necessary yet snail's-pace handholding of the government staff. That rapport was hard to develop and even harder to maintain. Hill, meanwhile, was the battlespace owner, the officer with overall command authority in Wardak.

Hill found himself a little taken aback by what had just transpired. He and Faber had always kept each other in the loop. Regardless, Hill had heard the Shockers' escalation-of-force procedures on the radio with his own ears. They were textbook. And even if he had not heard them for himself, he knew his men and respected their decision making. He wasn't about to question it, not like this.

When the two men reached Faber's office, they stepped in and Hill closed the door. "Sir, I'm not letting these guys go. Not yet. They are enemy fighters."

"Okay, Roger," Faber said, "but the governor is insisting that this is a case of mistaken identity, and that these men are a part of his security detail."

"But we just listened to the whole thing over FM comms," Hill said. "We know what happened."

We heard it, Hill thought, and what we heard matches the word of three seasoned combat veterans: Wilson, Mo, and Davis. To simply let these guys go was politics bleeding all over the mission, blurring its boundaries—and now, it seemed, altering the facts themselves.

How did we get to the point in a war, Hill wondered, where we are so afraid of political ramifications that we start to lie to ourselves and say, well maybe it didn't happen the way our guys say it happened? The way we *heard* it happen?

The buck had to stop somewhere, Hill decided. Someone had to trust senior, combat-hardened NCOs. Hill's men had to know that their leadership had their backs, that this shit was not going to fly.

"Sir, I hate to do this," he said to Faber, "but I'm not going to let the EPWs go free. Not until I know more."

Faber knew Hill's position as combat commander had to be respected regardless of rank. He nodded his assent and Hill returned to the foyer. Ignoring Hanif and Shah completely, he pointed at the enemy fighter and said to Coe, "Put his blindfold back on. Once Doc bandages up the others, they all go into the TOC conference room under guard."

"But sir, Major Faber just—" Coe began.

"Stop. I'm not going to repeat myself." Hill's eyes grazed the room, stopping on Kay. "These guys don't move unless I say so. Understood?"

"Roger that, sir."

Mo and Wilson helped Coe walk his detainee into the conference room. Faber began damage control with the Afghans. Hill continued into the TOC, where Kay was on the phone with the Battalion XO, Major John Karagosian.

Karagosian's voice was loud enough that the call might as well have been on speaker. "Larry, I heard your guys just shot up a bunch of Afghan National Security Force guys. What the hell happened up there? And what's this about someone throwing a grenade? Who threw a grenade and why?"

Hill gritted his teeth to keep from blurting, *Yeah, sometimes we do that sort of thing in combat.*

Kay muted the phone and offered it to Hill, who shook his head. He didn't have the energy.

Kay punched the Mute button again and spoke into the receiver. "I'm not entirely sure who threw it, sir, but it seemed like the best course of action at the time. From what I understand, it was an appropriate measure of force considering that the ANSF opened fire with automatic weapons."

"Yeah, okay," Karagosian said. "Make sure you guys write a detailed incident report. I can't wait for this to blow up tomorrow. All right? Out."

The United States of America
v.
CPT Roger T. Hill and 1SG Tommy L. Scott
1 December 2008

SPECIAL AGENT BRYAN McCOLLUM, Criminal Investigation Command, Bagram Airfield, Afghanistan, was called telephonically as a witness and testified, in substance, as follows:

Latino: Agent McCollum, can you hear me?

McCollum: Yes.

Latino: Sir, this is Captain Latino. I have Captain Runyan, for the government, and Lieutenant Colonel Byrd, the Investigating Officer, here. We also have Captain Hill and his defense counsel, Mr. Neal Puckett. We also have Captain Easterly and First Sergeant Scott. There are civilians in the room, so if you know that you are going to talk about something that is classified, just give us a heads-up so that we can clear out the room. And subject to any questions I will swear you in.

McCollum: Okay.

Latino: Please raise your right hand. Do you swear that the testimony that you are about to give in this case is the truth, the whole truth, and nothing but the truth, so help you God?

McCollum: I do.

Latino: How did you get involved in this case?

McCollum: Initially, we received a call from Major Mullins, and that's how I got involved.

Latino: Did you come down to FOB Airborne?

McCollum: Yes, I did.

Latino: What did you do once you were at FOB Airborne?

McCollum: My primary role while I was at FOB Airborne was the crime scene examination.

Latino: And when you say crime scene, what area of FOB Airborne are you talking about?

McCollum: The area known as the coffee shop...

Latino: On the inside of the coffee shop, what did you do?

McCollum: We brought Sergeant [Jared] Allen in, and actually before we brought him in, I went around the walls and you could actually see what appeared to be blood on the walls. Small amounts of it, but what I believed to be blood. And then I brought Sergeant Allen in and asked him where everyone was positioned in the coffee shop, and without telling him anything about what I had found or where I found it—and you'd have to look really close to find it. He was able to point out the same places where I found what I believed to be blood on the walls. He said that's where detainees were sitting.

Latino: Did you collect this blood, or what was the next step that you took?

McCollum: I swabbed the areas on the walls that appeared to contain blood.

Latino: Had there been an opportunity to compare that blood sample with any blood samples?

McCollum: No, there hadn't.

Latino: Why is that?

McCollum: The individuals involved in the detainee were released to NDS and then further released.

Latino: What about the floor of the coffee shop?

McCollum: We were informed that the flooring was removed and burned.

Prosecutor Runyan: Did you get the reason why?

McCollum: The reason why the flooring was removed and burned?

Runyan: Yes.

McCollum: They were going to turn the coffee shop into a place for soldiers to live, and that because of the dirt and grease and everything else on the floor, it was uninhabitable. So they removed the flooring and replaced it...

Investigating Officer Lieutenant Colonel Robert Byrd: This is Lieutenant Colonel Byrd. From the date you understood that this abuse occurred, this alleged abuse occurred, how soon did you arrive there?

McCollum: The 3rd of September.

Byrd: What date did you understand that the alleged abuse occurred?

McCollum: Sometime between the 26th and 28th of August.

Byrd: When did you understand that the floor had been taken out of the coffee shop and burned?

McCollum: I'm not sure if it was the same day that I arrived, which was on the 3rd, but it was during the interviews while we were there.

Byrd: Did that strike you as strange?

McCollum: Yes, it did.

Defense Attorney Puckett: Agent McCollum, was Captain Hill there during that time?

McCollum: When I got there, I believe he had already left the FOB.

Puckett: And he didn't return during the period of your stay, is that correct?

McCollum: No, he did not.

Puckett: You didn't recover any information that Captain Hill directed that the floor be removed and burned, did you?

McCollum: I don't believe so.

Puckett: Thanks.

CHAPTER 20

THE MORNING AFTER the Shockers' firefight in Maidan Shar, DeMartino called Hill and chewed him out over the incident. The EPWs were released the same day. It was the second catch-and-release incident in short succession. First, Signal Mirror guy and the dirty terp, now a group of armed men who had nearly killed Kris Wilson. What message was this sending to his men? Hill wondered. As important, what message was it sending to the enemy? That they could not only infiltrate Hill's base, but fire on his men at will and without consequence?

Hill remembered his counterinsurgency training, where he'd learned to study and understand the culture of the people he was trying to help. The culture of Afghanistan is tribalism, gamesmanship, survival of the cunning. In a land perpetually riven by war, it is the shrewd man, not the honest one, who saves himself and his family, and preserves his line. Honor, in the western sense, is an impractical virtue. Instead, the greatest leader is one who can delicately navigate internecine tribal pacts, alliances, and grudges, some of which have simmered for centuries.

Tribal elders practice the art of the deal, playing both ends against the middle, family over tribe, tribe over sect, sect over infidel. To lie convincingly in the service of those loyalties is not dishonesty but finesse, sagacity, the mark of a strong horse.

Hill had come to Afghanistan forced to operate under the American illusion that everyone wants to live under democracy and the rule of law. That Afghanistan's leaders would see the error of their ancient ways and cooperate in bringing their society into the twenty-first century.

Now, though, the looking glass had cracked, and seven years of war had produced an avalanche of data to the contrary—insider attacks, treachery among local and national leaders, and friendly attacks on American troops. But somehow that data had not entered the decision-making cycle. Somehow, facts on the ground were being reinterpreted to produce politically palatable results. In this particular case, the governor's men had simply made a mistake.

Hill had noticed a change in the color of MAJ Faber's daily reports. They contained more boldfaced, underlined phrases emphasizing unfulfilled requests for resources and support. Also, more summaries of TICs, or troops in contact. Three firefights off Highway 1. Four attacks on ANP stations around Wardak. Continuing rocket attacks on Airborne, with eleven rockets fired in one night, seven scoring direct hits.

Political instability was also on the rise. Governor Naeemi had warned that COL Shah and the National Directorate of Security could be trusted but that the Afghan National Police could not. Of particular concern was GEN Muzafarradin, the ANP's top man in Wardak. Muzafarradin was in near-daily contact with Faber and Dog Company, and was read in on many Coalition ops. If he was dirty, D Co was incredibly exposed.

As the next few days passed, Hill half-expected someone from Battalion to make some overture of support. Kind of a "Hey, we know it was a shitty deal. Politics, you know." Then, the attacker Wilson shot died. LTC DeMartino immediately launched an investigation to determine whether the Shockers were guilty of fratricide.

Hill was stunned. An investigation? To determine whether Wilson had committed a war crime by firing on a man who, after a warning shout, had tried to kill him?

Hill considered it an obscene violation of the covenant between the officer corps and NCO corps. Officers set direction and strategy, determined a desired end state, and led from the front when appropriate. NCOs, as much as possible, executed and took care of soldiers. Hill, for example, was a West Point grad who the Army had paid to receive a fancy education. But he had only eight years of active duty. His NCOs, meanwhile, had been in the Army for ten, fifteen, even twenty years. Most had only high school educations, but they were *expert* soldiers with multiple combat tours. If Hill didn't have the moral backbone to underwrite their decisions, especially when they displayed textbook judgment and execution, what other stock did he have to trade in? What other capital did he have besides his men's trust?

"Captain Hill!"

Hill was walking from the chow shack to his hooch when he heard Sammy calling him. He turned toward the FOB gate to see the terp walking up the dusty grade with a suitcase in his left hand and a package wrapped in brown paper in his right. Sammy had been on a five-day leave to Kabul. Hill walked down to meet him and the two embraced with the standard American-guy hug—handshake, pull in, a single, stern pat on the back, release. Over tours with three American units, Sammy had abandoned Afghanistan cheek kisses for social customs of the West. (Hill was grateful; in Iraq, "man kisses" multiplied the better you got to know a guy.)

He regarded the young interpreter warmly. Since Dog Company arrived in-country, he had rarely been away from Hill's side. A combat commander's terp is his eyes and ears. Hill was conducting a counterinsurgency in enemy badlands where he didn't speak the language. He relied on Sammy to navigate the province and its politics. Without Sammy, he could not communicate. Without Sammy, he could not gauge cultural nuances that meant the difference between a treacherous tribal elder and an ally. Without his terp, Hill was dead in the water.

On a personal level, Hill's relationship with Sammy lacked the weight of Army expectations. It was the only such relationship he had in Wardak. During quiet times on patrol, the two men talked about their families. Sammy adored his mother and shared about her often. Hill told Sammy about his wife, Lauren, how compassionate she was, how she'd changed him as a man. They also talked about the changes in the world, Sammy about his work with the 82nd Airborne and prior units, Hill about his tour in Iraq. Hill had succeeded in getting U.S. visas for his Iraqi interpreters, Fahmi and Jack, he told his terp. He planned to do the same for Sammy.

The terp held out the brown-paper package. "Sir, I got something for you... I mean, for your wife. My mother picked it out."

Hill was taken aback. Sammy made more money than the rest of the terps, but not enough to buy him gifts. Sammy pulled the string that bound the parcel and it unfolded, revealing a green faux velvet dress ornately embroidered in gold.

"Do you think she will like it?" he said a bit shyly.

Hill struggled with his emotions. In a bloody, violent land, this was as soft and warm a gesture as he had seen. "This is too much, Sammy. Too kind."

Hill took the dress and folded it back on itself to more closely examine the intricate embroidery at the neck and shoulders. He looked up at Sammy and put his hand on the young man's shoulder. "It's perfect. I hope one day you can see her wearing it yourself."

Sammy smiled. "I hope so, too, sir."

CHAPTER 21

DEEP IN THE Jalrez Valley, Shon Haskins held his rifle ready and eyed the lowering sun. LTC DeMartino, CPT Hill, and Major Faber were inside the Jalrez district center compound, powwowing with the local leadership in a "key leader engagement." Outside, SGM Judd was stalking among the battalion's trucks ensuring his gunners stayed alert.

Being here at all, Haskins thought, was a crappy idea from the beginning. He and 3rd had arrived in the district center as part of a twenty-vehicle convoy. A couple of D Co platoons, Battalion HQ and Scouts, and some Afghan National Army. The convoy had pushed in from Kowte Ashrow, where soldiers from D Co and battalion HQ continued to build out the new COP. The convoy was supposed to return to Airborne afterward. But at the last minute, Haskins had heard, LTC DeMartino changed the plan. They would proceed to the district center instead, twelve kilometers into Jalrez. Show the Taliban they didn't own the place or some cowboy shit like that.

Haskins didn't have a problem with pushing into the valley, but he knew the convoy had ventured beyond Bonecrusher's artillery bubble. He also noticed that their CAS had long since evaporated. So he kept an eye on his gunners, who were keeping an eye on the district center ANP, who were posted around the compound with AK-47s that looked suspiciously new.

Haskins and Donnie Carwile had been through the KLE drill, sometimes called a *shura*. First, you walked into a village and asked to speak to the tribal elder or cleric about how the Coalition could help their people. Then the cultural dance began. You couldn't talk business right away. First, you had to talk family, crops, the weather—anything but business, because that was considered impolite.

If you had kids, it was good to say, "Hey, I'm married and I've got three kids," to which the elder would usually say something like, "Ah, children are good! Why do you not have twelve?"

Haskins and his wife, Robyn, had two daughters, thirteen and nine, and a four-year-old son. The couple married in 1997, eight years before the Iraq deployment, Haskins's first combat tour. When he returned from Ramadi, Robyn noticed some changes. Always outgoing and funny before, her husband had become watchful and turned inward.

Haskins himself found that he couldn't tolerate crowds the way he had before. He caught himself checking people's hands, gauging whether that woman in the grocery store was carrying a baby or a bomb.

He had watched the Army's view on mental and emotional trauma evolve. When he first joined, PTSD (Post-Traumatic Stress Disorder) was just an excuse for being a pussy. But the Army had begun acknowledging the medical realities of the condition. After the 1-506th's Ramadi tour, every man in the unit proceeded straight to a series of briefs on topics from suicide prevention to what to do if you felt like hitting your wife. Then there was the Post Deployment Health Assessment, which included a psych eval in which a civil servant asked each soldier a series of questions:

Are you having trouble sleeping?

Do you feel you may harm yourself?

Do you feel like you may harm others?

It had been explained to Haskins that during World War I and World War II, soldiers returning stateside had a long ride on a ship with their brothers to decompress. But with modern troop transport now taking place via passenger jet, a soldier could be literally watching his battle buddy choke to death on his own blood one day and trying to decode the diaper aisle at a stateside Sav-On the next.

For Haskins, the clash of realities was surreal. In Ramadi, he had been standing watch at Observation Post Graveyard, just up from SFC Rogers and Andrew Doyle's position, when that female Marine got sniped.

That was the thing: The Army wanted you to endure that kind of shit, come back, answer a few questions, then train you up for a second, third, even fifth deployment. If a soldier goes to his leadership with an issue like PTSD, he buys a nonstop ticket to the shrink—no screwing around. But that's for young soldiers. For senior NCOs and above, now you were looking at a career decision, and every one of Haskins's peers knew it. The position of the Army is that its system of pre- and post-deployment checks and open-door policy on mental health issues creates the freedom for soldiers to admit when they're having a problem. But the unit-level reality is that a soldier who wants to make the Army a career would do better to keep his mouth shut. Though mental health issues are supposed to remain confidential, word gets out, and nobody wants to follow a twitchy leader into combat.

And so, when Haskins returned from Ramadi, he didn't talk to anyone about his struggles, not even Robyn. He just dealt with it quietly and resigned himself to a simple truth: Every tour, you lose a piece of yourself.

Now, at the Jalrez district center, Haskins figured the KLE had progressed from small talk about crops and kids to the ritual of tea. At every such meeting, the tribal elder always served tea, which tasted to Haskins like ass. The tea was served with a dish of hard candies that reminded him of Jolly Ranchers. The candy was supposed to make the tea taste better. Haskins wondered why they didn't just make better-tasting tea.

Khan, 3rd Platoon's terp, was always good at these meetings. After being shamed by the Taliban as a boy, he hated the sect and all its sympathizers. Sometimes, during a *shura*, the elders would try to make a buck—get what the Army calls a *solatia* payment—by saying the Americans had damaged a hut or killed a cow. When Khan thought an elder was lying, he would lean over to Haskins or Carwile and whisper, "Sir, he is full of sheet."

Occasionally, 3rd had gotten some good intel from an anti-Taliban elder or cleric. More often, though, *shuras* were useless tangos, with the Americans wanting information and the elders wanting goods or money, all doing their steps in the dance, waiting for the other to make good first.

Now Haskins watched the sky blush blood-orange behind the sinking sun. A Ghazni-based soldier from DeMartino's PSD walked over to Haskins.

"Well, this ain't shit," he said, his tone mocking the big, bad Jalrez Valley. "We came in here and nothing happened."

Haskins shot him down with a look. "We haven't left yet, dumbass."

In his mind's eye, Haskins could see the Taliban setting ambushes along the egress route. He had never doubted they'd get to the district center just fine. The problem would be getting out.

Roger Hill politely excused himself from the *shura* and walked outside. Once again, DeMartino had surprised him with an unplanned thrust into hostile territory. But this time, the convoy's CAS had long since flown back to Bagram, and Hill was concerned about the movement back to base. He didn't have time to work a CAS request through Airborne TOC, so he radioed Ghazni directly. Maybe they'd at least give him a drone to scout out any enemy ambushes.

As he waited for an answer, Hill's insides thrummed. Enemy contact was assured. There would probably be more than one fight, too. When Hill and a QRF had responded to Cadena and the Alpha Dawgs, they'd been hit three times—and that had been on Highway 1, where the Coalition arguably had the upper hand.

Hill's radio squelched. "Dog 6, Ghazni TOC."

"Ghazni, Dog 6, go ahead."

"Yeah, we sent that CAS request all the way up to Brigade. Request denied. Sorry. Ghazni out."

Shit. Hill knew the Taliban had been able to pin down the 82nd with an IED then pick them clean. How was he going to protect his guys out here in the badlands?

Hill turned to see Faber and DeMartino emerging from the KLE. "Hey Roger, we missed you in the meeting," DeMartino said. "No big deal, you didn't miss much."

Hill smiled, but his eyes transmitted urgency. "Sir, I couldn't get us any air for the trip back. Can you give Brigade a call? I really don't think we should get on the road without some eyes overhead." Hill thought higher might relent if DeMartino threw some rank behind the request.

"Roger, I'm not calling. That was your responsibility."

Around him, Humvee engines roared to life. Soldiers were climbing into trucks. Gunners appeared in their turrets. All at once Hill felt as if someone had switched on a treadmill underneath him. There had been a brief window in which to argue his case with DeMartino, but that had slammed shut. Now, Hill could either start running or fall on his face.

"Mount up!" Haskins called out.

He and SPC Joel Ochoa climbed into 3-3. Back at Kowte Ashrow, Donnie Carwile had given his seat in 3-2 to Faber, with SPC Paul Conlon on the gun.

Hill hopped into his truck and keyed up his mic. "Guidons, Guidons, Guidons, this is Dog 6, radio check in order of movement."

"Dog 6, this is Dog 3-6, got you loud and clear."

"Dog 6, Blacksheep, got you Lima Charlie." Loud and clear.

Blacksheep were the Battalion Scouts. As each of the convoy elements checked in over the net, Hill paused for a moment of regret. Maybe the better response to DeMartino's order to proceed to the district center without CAS would have been not "Yes, sir," but "Hell, no!"

Unfortunately, that wasn't who Hill was, though he sometimes wished it. Hill had always been one to give his CO the benefit of the doubt, and defer to his knowledge and experience. That was changing.

He collected himself and issued a series of orders to the convoy. "Guidons, this is Dog 6, we start patrol in five mikes. Break. Same order of movement. Break. Also, if you haven't noticed, the sun's going down so prep your NVGs"—night vision goggles. "And we don't have any eyes overhead for the trip back, so keep yours open. If we take contact, engage and push through. We aren't going to drag this trip out."

CHAPTER 22

ORCHARDS FLANKED THE road, and the convoy rumbled east between them. From the gun turret, SPC Joel Ochoa, twenty-five, of Deming, New Mexico, squinted into the trees, scanning for shapes that didn't fit. But field after field concealed only apples.

Ahead in 3-2, SPC Paul Conlon scanned his sector. On the gun, he felt he had finally found his place in the world. Not because he wanted to kill someone, but because he wanted to stop the Taliban from stepping on people. He'd spent a lot of time journaling about the opposite poles of the human heart. Altruism versus greed. Kindness versus violence.

Even at that, Afghanistan had been a culture shock. He had seen the way Afghan men treated women and children like chattel. He hoped Dog Company's mission here could change that, even if it was only in the tiniest way. That's one reason they were building the COP in Kowte Ashrow, so the kids could go back to school. Conlon especially wanted to see the girls be able to do that.

The convoy growled on, Jalrez's only road coughing dust in its wake. Below Conlon in the TC seat, Faber thought about an exchange he'd had with DeMartino when they arrived at the district center. The battalion commander had gotten out of his truck and stalked over.

"What are you doing here?" he asked Faber.

"The XO said to come on up," Faber replied, referring to Major John Karagosian, DeMartino's executive officer. Faber and Karagosian were friends. "I have to deal with the local leaders anyway. This was a good chance to meet them."

"I told you not to come out here," DeMartino said. "I didn't want anybody from Brigade out here."

Now, the long chain of trucks squeezed back through the villages that hugged the road. As Faber's truck passed into the next orchard, the trees exploded.

"*Contact, right!*" Haskins yelled.

Ochoa, Conlon, and the other gunners swung to the sound of guns and returned fire. The ANA soldiers dismounted, their squad leader positioning his men to meet the threat. Small arms fire sprayed in from the low side of the road. In 3-2, Faber heard through his earplugs the muffled *tink-tink-tink* of bullets bouncing off the truck's armor. Above him, Conlon hunkered behind his plate and unloaded his MK19.

Haskins directed his gunners. "Ten o'clock! Two hundred meters!"

Ochoa pounded the left side of the road with his .50-cal. Then, from the right, Haskins saw a black streak cut the air: a rocket on target to slice straight into Donnie Carwile's door.

No! Haskins thought, *Faber's door! Donnie gave his seat to Major Faber.*

The rocket's impact cut off Haskins's thought. In that microsecond, his heart seemed to stop. But the warhead's nose only cracked the ballistic glass, and Haskins saw the rest of the rocket burst into a thousand shards.

"I'm hit!" It was Conlon. Haskins saw him fall down through his cupola and disappear.

Inside 3-2, Faber turned to see Conlon drop to his knees, dazed. He uttered a small sound of pain, then jumped back up and reengaged.

For thirty seconds, Faber heard Conlon banging away up top. Then the specialist dropped into the truck again. He looked down at his arm, then at the major.

"Hey, I'm shot up," he said.

Faber saw blood blooming through Conlon's right sleeve, but the young soldier popped back up through the turret and started firing again. Faber and his driver began digging out the med kit. For another five minutes, Faber saw only Conlon's legs and boots, heard the MK19 hammering in five-round bursts. Soon the Coalition convoy had achieved fire superiority. The crackle of small arms tapered down, and Conlon sank back into the Humvee. His wound had started a steady bleed, and bright crimson drops mixed with the Afghan moondust on the truck's rear seat.

The ambush had led to an eight-hundred-meter break in contact between the first and second halves of the convoy. Faber could hear Hill over the radio requesting a status from each platoon. Haskins checked in. "Dog 6, this is 3-7, break. We have one WIA. We're working on him, more to follow, over."

"Dog 3-7, Dog 6, roger," Hill said. "I need you guys to catch up with the rest of the convoy so we can continue movement, over."

"Dog 3-6, roger that. Moving, time now."

Faber swung around to wrap Conlon's arm in gauze. Outside, sporadic AK fire plinked off the Humvee's skin. Then Conlon said something that the major would remember for the rest of his life:

"Sir, I didn't cry like a little bitch when I got hit, did I?"

Faber suppressed a laugh, not of derision but of astonishment. He shook his head and smiled. "Paul, you did fine."

Conlon's wound dressed, Faber took the driver's seat and the driver took the gun. Conlon sat in the TC seat as Faber double-timed to catch up with the other trucks. He glanced at the young man in the seat beside him.

Where do we get guys like this? he marveled. *Guys who want to make sure that when they get hit by a rocket, they take it like a man?*

The convoy was ambushed a total of three times before a pair of Apache Longbows responded to the element's "troops in contact" call for air support. Their Hellfire missiles and 30 mm cannons turned the rest of the trip into a quiet country drive. Inside multiple gun trucks, D Co and Scout platoon medics worked furiously on two more soldiers wounded in action.

Once back at the new COP, Haskins and the medics determined that Conlon's wound was serious enough to require a MedEvac. DeMartino stood on the steps of the new COP above the casualty collection point, where medics were staging the wounded for the MedEvac birds.

Sergeant Major Judd, DeMartino's senior enlisted advisor, trooped the line, checking on the wounded. Like Conlon, one scout had taken shrapnel in his arm. Another suffered a chest wound when shrapnel zinged through the crease between side plates in his body armor.

And for what? Judd thought. *So DeMartino could say we were the first ones that deep in the valley? So we could drink* chai *with the fucking Taliban?*

Back at Kowte Ashrow, just before the convoy pushed into Jalrez, Judd had confronted DeMartino. He wanted to tell him that he thought the mission was bullshit, that the last time anyone had gone this far into the valley, they got their asses handed to them twelve ways to Sunday.

But Judd kept his cool. "Sir, we don't have the coverage for this mission," he said. "We'll be out of artillery range and we don't have any air."

Now Judd posted himself on the edge of the casualty collection point next to Faber. "Sir, I sure hope Lieutenant Colonel DeMartino gets his Purple Heart soon," Judd said, "so he can stop putting our guys at risk."

Judd and Faber traded looks.

Over at the LZ, a Black Hawk MedEvac thumped to earth. Haskins was standing near the LZ with Carwile, who had rejoined his platoon at Kowte Ashrow. When it was Conlon's turn to climb aboard, he detoured over to Haskins.

"Sergeant, I don't want to lose my gunner slot," he said.

Haskins shook his head. "Bro, you did your part. Just shut up and get on the bird."

But Conlon wouldn't let it go. "Promise me, Sergeant! When I get back, I'll get back on the gun."

"Okay! You got it! *Jesus!* Now get on the fucking bird before I change my mind!"

Haskins not only wanted Conlon to go—he hoped he wouldn't come back. He was a bright kid who had done his duty. He'd gotten shot and lived to tell about it. Time for him to go home.

Conlon grinned, ducked under the Black Hawk's rotor wash, and was gone.

SPECIAL AGENT BRYAN McCOLLUM continued testifying, in substance, as follows:

Puckett: Agent McCollum?

McCollum: Yes.

Puckett: Sir, my name is Neal Puckett, I'm a civilian attorney, and I represent Captain Hill. I practice out of Alexandria, Virginia. How you doing?

McCollum: I'm doing good. Yourself?

Puckett: I'm doing great. I watch two of the three *CSI* shows. It sounds like your role was that of a CSI on that day, is that right?

McCollum: We do everything. We do all our own interviews, crime scene processing, we're a one-stop-shop type of organization.

Puckett: So in my understanding from what you said, you found traces of blood on the [coffee shop] walls. Is that right?

McCollum: That's correct.

Puckett: But there's no way at this point for you to determine which human beings that blood came from, right?

McCollum: That is correct.

Puckett: So one thing that could be speculated about that certain situation is that perhaps it was the blood of one of the detainees. Is that right?

McCollum: That is correct.

Puckett: That would only be speculation, right?

McCollum: That is correct.

Puckett: And also, is there any scientific way to make a determination as to how long those bloodstains had been there?

McCollum: Not to my knowledge. That would be a question for a laboratory.

Puckett: But you don't have any of those kinds of data available to you?

McCollum: Not here, no.

Puckett: So, it's conceivable that the blood came from a detainee, but it is also conceivable that one or more of those blood spots that you found could have been left earlier than that day, is that right?

McCollum: That is correct.

Puckett: And by someone other than the detainee, right?

McCollum: Yes, that's correct.

Puckett: Can you give me the total number of individual blood—I don't know what the right word would be—bloodstains, or blood spots?

McCollum: Seven.

Puckett: So you located seven areas after searching the whole wall, and you collected seven different ones?

McCollum: That's correct.

Puckett: Is there any evidence that the seven different bloodstains came from more than one person?

McCollum: Hold on. A single source on the south wall, from the west wall, from the north wall…and a mixture of DNA from at least three individuals from the gloves.

Puckett: You're talking about gloves. What gloves are we talking about?

McCollum: Those were gloves that we obtained from Specialist Moser and also from Sergeant First Class [Tim] Moriarty.

Puckett: Moser's gloves and Moriarty's gloves, both of those contained multiple sources of blood.

McCollum: From three unknown individuals.

Puckett: Now, other than the gloves themselves, is there anything about the bloodstains on any of the other walls that can tell you what the source of the blood was, or how an injury occurred?

McCollum: No.

Puckett: So there's no way for you to make a determination. We're really going into speculation here to say that a blood spot can give you any information other than DNA. In other words, it doesn't tell you how a wound was inflicted or who inflicted it or anything like that. It's just basically for identification information, right?

McCollum: Exactly.

Puckett: Although sometimes isn't it true that you can tell from the shape of the blood spatter as to velocity, its directionality and things like that?

McCollum: That's correct, but that was not done.

Puckett: Thank you.

Investigating Officer Byrd: This is Lieutenant Colonel Byrd.

McCollum: Hey sir, how are you?

Byrd: I need to cover something that you may have already covered. I understand that from Specialist Moser and Moriarty, is that his name?

McCollum: Yes.

Byrd: You got a pair of their gloves each and on their gloves were the blood of three different individuals that you cannot identify.

McCollum: That's correct.

Byrd: But was the blood on the gloves the same as some of the blood that you found on the walls?

McCollum: I need to look at the report here—it's a very long report, and I need to look at the different sections here. No, the report does not say.

CHAPTER 23

At the Army hospital in Landstuhl, Germany, Paul Conlon made friends with a female medic. He shared about the guys in his platoon, and how his platoon sergeant had promised he could get back on the gun when he returned to duty. He told her stories about growing up in the leafy charm of Cape Cod, and about his mom, Maria, whom he adored, and his dad, John Borges, who was a cop.

"He's not really my dad," Conlon told the medic, "but I love him like he is."

His mom had been single, he explained, raising him and his brother alone after their biological father evaporated from their lives following a contentious divorce. She'd been hanging in there but had confided in Borges about problems she was having with Paul. Not juvenile delinquency, just typical teenage stuff.

"John took me out to dinner," Conlon said. "He didn't have any kids of his own."

Dinner turned into regular trips to the movies, then bowling. Years ticked by, and Borges became Conlon's close friend and mentor.

"One night at a shopping mall on the Cape, I surprised him by introducing him to a friend as my dad," Conlon told the medic.

"Well, you should go home and see him," she said. The medic pointed out that Conlon's injuries were serious enough that he could go home.

But Conlon had already decided against that. Shortly after arriving at the hospital, he had called Borges, who picked up the phone in Taunton, Massachusetts.

"Hey, Paul! How are you doing?"

"Uh…I got in a firefight. An RPG hit my truck and I took some shrapnel in the arm, but I'm okay." Conlon said this all in a rush, as though hurrying to the *I'm okay* part. He explained that he was in the hospital in Germany.

"Yeah, your mom told me about it. How are you feeling?"

"I'm good," Conlon said. "Listen, you have to call Mom and convince her I should stay here. They said they would send me home to recover, but I don't want to come home. Mom will want me to come home, but I don't want to leave my platoon. I want to stay for my guys."

Borges heard passion in Conlon's voice. "Paul, I know what you're saying. If I was in the same spot, I wouldn't want to come home either."

"I want to stay for my guys. I *have* to stay for my guys!"

"Listen, you don't have to convince me. I would do the same thing."

"Will you talk to Mom?"

"Yes, I'll talk to her." Borges heard Marie's objections even as he said this. "You got a little shrapnel, no big deal. I'll try to convince her it's the right thing to do."

"Thanks," Conlon said. "I love you, Dad."

At the Jalrez COP in the village of Kowte Ashrow, conditions were increasingly Spartan. After building the COP under fire, Wilson, Mo, and the Shockers had been holding it for several weeks, fending off daily mortar and rocket fire from a fighting position atop the Afghan National Police station. Sometimes the ANP climbed up to join the fight. More often, though, they scrambled around behind the Shockers' guns, collecting spent brass they could trade at the markets. Chatter out of the valley predicted attacks on the COP, thirty to a hundred fighters strong. But the Taliban turnout was usually much smaller than advertised, and the Shockers were averaging five enemy KIAs per firefight while taking no casualties.

Ammunition shortages plagued the platoon. Standard procedure dictated that the COP perimeter be spiked with Claymores, the remote-detonated antipersonnel mines that shred enemy fighters with volleys of seven hundred steel balls traveling at nearly four thousand feet per second.

The first time Kris Wilson saw a Claymore, he chuckled at the idiot-proof directions stamped on each mine's green plastic case: FRONT TOWARD ENEMY. However, he had not seen any Claymores in Jalrez, though LT Kay had repeatedly requisitioned Battalion. The Shockers were also light on rounds for the M240B, a belt-fed, bipod-mounted medium machine gun—a key part of the COP's fire plan.

On top of ammo shortages, the Shockers were just thirteen guys fighting a valley full of Taliban. Had the enemy known that, Wilson and Mo had no doubt they would have amassed a large fighting force and attempted to overrun the outpost.

To keep Razak's crew guessing about 4th Platoon's numbers, Wilson and Mo improvised a bit of low-tech subterfuge: They stripped the foam lining from ammo cans and cut from them man-sized silhouettes. They then "armed" the silhouettes with lengths of scrap pipe meant to look like rifles, and propped them upright on frames built from pallet wood. These fake soldiers were deployed atop the ANP station at night, and taken down before dawn since, after sunrise, any eight-year-old shepherd boy with a pair of binos could have told the Taliban they were being held off by an army of crash-test dummies.

The Shockers were filthy, but it would have been worse if Davis hadn't rigged up a shower using a Gatorade bottle and some rubber IV tubing. The platoon cooked on a grill rigged from mortar ammo cans. Wilson made a mean barbecue sauce from ingredients collected from Airborne, and Colon had figured a way to cook rice on the grill. The men were crapping in a barrel and burning shit every day, but it was better than sharing a hole in the ground with the Afghan police.

The soldiers complained, but only to each other. The truth was, every man in Dog Company would have traded places with 4th in a millisecond. Holding down an outpost, shooting at the enemy from under camouflage nets, and shooting the shit with their brothers in between? Hell, that was why they'd joined the infantry.

In late June, LT Brett Erickson reported to Kowte Ashrow as 4th's new platoon leader. Erickson had grown up just outside of New Orleans, attended Louisiana State University, and completed the Army's Officer Candidate School after graduation. Like others in Dog Company, he had not completed Ranger school, and so, once in Afghanistan, he landed in the Battalion S-4 shop, jockeying supplies.

During his time in Ghazni, Erickson eavesdropped in the TOC and read the sitreps coming in from around the AO. Between firefights and WIAs, Kowte Ashrow was always in the news. As an infantry officer, Erickson wanted to go to combat. His performance at Battalion had apparently gotten someone's attention, because when 4th's PL slot opened up, he found himself next in the chute.

At his in-brief at Airborne, Hill gave his new lieutenant some advice for earning his stripes with the Shockers: "Stay out of the way, listen to Mo, and you'll be fine."

A day later, Erickson reported to the COP at Kowte Ashrow. It was late afternoon, but well before dusk. Wilson greeted him, showed him where to dump his ruck, and brought him up to speed.

"I'm sorry, sir, but I don't have time to train you," Wilson said. "We're too busy out here. We're getting shot at and mortared pretty much every day. Just sit back and watch what we do, assist where you can. You'll get into the rhythm of it pretty quick."

The Jalrez Taliban chose that moment to send a calling card. A pair of mortars crashed down just outside the COP perimeter, one short and one long. Erickson, who hadn't been on the ground for more than fifteen minutes, didn't have time to be afraid. Fourth Platoon swung into action, soldiers scrambling to their fighting positions. Erickson followed, flattening himself on the ANP rooftop, watching as Mo got comfortable, shedding his ACUs, and firing back at the Taliban wearing only body armor and a pair of boxer briefs. (Though that was not as creative as the thong Steinle had once made from a bullet bandolier.)

The fight lasted through sunset until sunup. Erickson stayed awake through the long watches of the night, ferrying ammo, water, and oil to the gunners. It was his first firefight, and from the dirty grunt perspective, his behavior was exemplary for a first-time PL: He kept his eyes and ears open, and his mouth shut.

CHAPTER 24

THROUGHOUT THE DEPLOYMENT, one mission kept popping up like an unwelcome guest: fishing transient units out of trouble in the notorious Tangi Valley. To a platoon leader unfamiliar with the area, it seemed to make sense to travel through Tangi; it was the shortest way to get from Khost Province to Kabul. The Taliban regularly ambushed Military Transition Teams and Police Mentorship Teams. Without escorts and miles from reinforcements, these small, three- or four-vehicle patrols made irresistible targets.

Historically speaking, Tangi fighters kept mainly to themselves. But ridding their valley of invaders was an art they had perfected over centuries, passing down generational knowledge of the terrain the way other families pass down heirlooms.

Prior to the Wardak deployment, Les Grau, an Afghanistan expert from the Foreign Military Studies Office, traveled to Fort Campbell to speak to Dog Company about the tactics used by the Tangi mujahideen during the Soviet-Afghanistan war. In May 1981, a tiny band of Tangi fighters, using a natural choke point formed by terrain, destroyed an entire Soviet column using a single RPG gunner, seven Kalashnikov machine guns, and two Enfield bolt-action rifles.

Dog Company had tried to put the word out: Take the long way around. If it was absolutely essential to transition through Tangi, at least give a heads-up so Dog Company could plan for the nearly inevitable QRF.

In July, a Police Mentorship Team passing through Tangi was ambushed at midday, leaving one of its gun trucks disabled. The team took several wounded, but the real danger was in every passing minute spent stranded on precipitous terrain owned by inhospitable hosts. RC East had a standing order to recover any stranded vehicle at nearly any cost. Hill understood the logic and agreed with it in most cases. But it did not make sending his men into Tangi again any more desirable.

Hill dispatched the Dirty First and 3rd Platoon from Airborne. Carwile and Haskins, with Allred, Hulburt, and Dudley, linked up with Hidalgo and the Alpha Dawgs out of Sayed Abad, along with a Route Clearance Package out of Logar. The recovery was successful, but both 2nd and 3rd Platoons were ambushed on the way out. After a brief firefight, 3rd Platoon captured two fighters during the sweep. One was carrying a mechanic's duffle bag full of what appeared to be materials used to build an IED. The other took several rounds to the body and would have expired from a collapsed lung had Doc Dunlap not inserted a chest tube before MedEvacing him to Bagram for surgery.

Back at Airborne, CPT Wade Barker dumped the contents of the duffle bag onto a table in the TOC. Barker knew exactly what he was dealing with: He had served as both the 101st's Counter-IED (CIED) Company Commander and its Asymmetric Warfare OIC during his last rotation to Iraq. At a general's request, he stood up a specialized counter-IED unit, recruiting only senior NCOs with two or more combat tours and deploying them in small kill teams with great success.

It didn't take long for Barker to build a pressure-wire IED initiation system from the duffle-bag parts. The only things missing were the blasting cap and the actual explosives. It did not surprise Barker that this fighter's kit did not include those items. They were precious commodities and normally retained by higher-level bad guys. Also, IED teams often worked in relay fashion, with one man dropping explosives at the target site and another connecting the initiation system.

Barker wrote up technical specifications on the device he had assembled using enemy parts. At Hill's request, he included in his sworn statement a few of his own résumé bullets to establish his bona fides. Finally, Barker photographed the device and included the pictures in the evidence packet, which was sent with the detainee to higher command.

Hill was excited about this capture. Dog Company had finally sent up a prisoner with enough evidence to keep him behind bars. He was sure Barker's credentials would put that evidence into a category that could not be ignored.

He was wrong.

A couple of days later, D Co received word that Duffle Bag Guy had been released. About two weeks later, the injured fighter whose life Doc Dunlap likely saved was returned to Airborne. Because of the rush to save his life, including a MedEvac to Bagram, the fighter had never been processed as a detainee. Now, he was outside the ninety-six-hour window. That meant the guy was olly olly oxen free. Battalion ordered Hill to return him to the point of capture—the heart of Tangi Valley.

Hill was livid. It made no sense: Shorthanded already, he was supposed to send his men into a known insurgent hotbed to give a lift home to an enemy captured during a firefight that occurred because Hill's men were *already* rescuing another American unit attacked in the same place, probably by this same guy. Was this Battalion's idea of winning hearts and minds? In the Afghan mind, which prizes resourcefulness and cunning, such a move would win only scorn.

Hill, Barker, Kay, and Scott discussed these latest catch-and-releases. Who decided such cases, and how, had never been disclosed to Dog Company. But it was becoming clear that even meeting the textbook requirements of enemy detention was not enough. At this point, Battalion was zero for ten on their handling of prisoners D Co took on the battlefield.

How the hell can you win a war, Hill wondered, without killing or capturing the enemy?

CHAPTER 25

ON JUNE 8, under a scorching sun, the Dirty First growled and bounced toward Badam Kalay, a medium-sized village about a click off Highway 1. Rocky and pocked, the road was lower than the village. There were no trees to conceal an approach, so the dust boiling in the platoon's wake announced its advance like smoke signals.

The mission had two purposes. First, hearts and minds—humanitarian assistance (HA) in the form of a food and radio drop. Second, 1st Platoon was in search of a potential source: an honest-to-God, regular American from Denver who was living in Badam Kalay, taking care of his mother. Taz, Dog Company's human intel sergeant, wanted to cultivate the guy, see if he might be willing to keep his eyes and ears open for the Coalition.

Back at the FOB, Dudley and Hulburt had talked it around. Drop the HA, Taz rounds up the person of interest, no big deal. It was Dudley's one-year wedding anniversary, a good day for a simple mission. He'd be back early enough to spend a little time on the computer with Rachel, his wife.

As 1st Platoon rolled toward the village, Hulburt, riding TC in 1-3, popped up on the net. "Dudley, I'm gonna take up overwatch on the south side. In case anything goes down."

"Roger that," Dudley said. "We'll stay with Taz."

Minutes later, Hulburt's section broke left and rumbled up the southern side of the hill. Dudley, in 1-1, followed LT Allred's truck to the right. Dudley took in the hard-packed mud, rocks, and scrub, and thought for the hundredth time that the whole country looked like the set of a Mad Max movie.

When D Co returned to Fort Campbell in 2007, Dudley realized that the furnace of Ramadi had gouged deep holes in his humanity. Not that he had done anything illegal or immoral. But he had fallen into the trap that armed conflict can set for a man whose job it is to kill. His viewpoint of the Iraqis as a people changed. The more aggressive insurgents became, the better a killer Dudley became. More agile, more lethal, harder of heart.

The Iraqis—whether fathers, brothers, husbands, or sons—became to him *haji*, just as the Vietnamese had been *gooks* and the Germans *Krauts* in previous wars. It was a useful psychological defense mechanism, Dudley knew from his college studies: Objectifying the enemy, making them "other" or "less than," makes it easier to kill them.

But philosophizing about it didn't make it sit well in Dudley's gut. In the same way pornography objectifies women, he felt that war objectified people across the board. Ramadi had constructed in Dudley the crude forms for this evil, even poured a foundation. He wanted to bring in a wrecking crew before the concrete hardened around his soul.

He found her on eHarmony.

A few months after Ramadi, Dudley found himself single again. Three days later, he logged on to the dating site. Yes, he could've tried the bar scene, but since returning from battle, he found that his usual gregariousness was held a bit in check. When other guys went out to clubs, he stayed back, preferring the company of his battle brothers. Besides, he'd always thought trying to meet girls in bars was tedious, all about posturing and chest thumping and trying to outdo the next guy.

After Ramadi, he didn't want a surface anything, much less a surface relationship. He wanted a woman he could trust—someone he could open up to about the bloody mess he'd just been through. He'd seen what happened to guys who keep that kind of poison bottled up. They wound up angry and withdrawn, angry and manic, or angry and dead.

Surfing the dating site from his barracks room, Dudley clicked through several matches. Then Rachel popped up. Her profile showed her working as a youth counselor with kids in a church.

A Christian woman who likes kids, Dudley thought. *That's two for two.*

None of the photographs showed a serious side: Rachel was always goofing off, leaning in with a kid or a friend, mugging for the camera. Dudley thought she was beautiful.

A series of emails and a couple of calls led to a first date at a Mexican joint. Over dinner, Dudley learned that Rachel had moved out on her own at eighteen and within a couple of years bought her own house. He was impressed.

The waitress brought a couple of combination plates. Dudley blessed the food, then the conversation turned to hobbies.

"I like shooting," he said. "Not just at work. I really like going to the gun range."

"Really?" Rachel said. "I own a shotgun and a .38 Special." Then she started laughing.

"What?" Dudley said.

"Wouldn't it be funny if we went to the firing range on our first date? How redneck would that be?"

Or how awesome? Dudley thought.

An hour later, they had picked up Rachel's revolver and were firing downrange, using Dudley's phone to take videos of each other. On Rachel's first turn in the lane, the only thing she hit was the wire suspending the man-shaped silhouette target. Dudley coached her a little, and her next turn produced much better results: The silhouette now had a nice little grouping of five bullet holes—all around the groin.

Dudley laughed. "I've created a monster!"

They shot a couple more rounds, with Dudley consistently grouping his shots center mass while also angling for a second date. But Rachel laughed off each approach, avoiding the subject.

Finally, he decided on a direct assault: "What do I have to do to get you to go out with me again?"

Her eyes sparkled. "You know the movie *Lethal Weapon?*"

"Yeah...?"

"If you shoot me a smiley face, I'll go out with you again."

Dudley didn't hesitate. Using the keypad, he sent the silhouette zinging down the lane, loaded the .38, raised it, and fired six shots. He punched buttons on the box, and the silhouette came flying back.

Rachel leaned in to look. Dudley's smiley face wasn't as perfect as Mel Gibson's, but it was definitely there: two eyes (slightly diagonal to one another), an off-center nose, and a crooked smile.

"Shit," Rachel said, smiling.

On Monday morning, Dudley told his whole platoon about this amazing woman he'd met: beautiful, funny, open, mature, took *him* to the firing range on their first date. Not only that, the video on his phone revealed that when Rachel was filming his turns at the firing line, the viewfinder kept moving down to his butt.

First Platoon's reaction was immediate and unanimous: "Dude! If you don't marry this girl, we will!"

So he had. Now, on their first anniversary, Dudley hoped they could wrap up this HA drop quick so that he could get back to base and spend a little time chatting with the woman who had saved his soul from war.

"Up there," Hulburt said, pointing up a low dirt hill that had the makings of a good overwatch position. In the driver's seat, PFC Jason Phothisen— "Photo"—pointed 1-3 in the direction Hulburt indicated, the truck's engine roaring and dropping a gear as it crept up the incline.

Photo, nineteen, of Dumas, Texas, was the son of Laotian refugees and a first-generation American. He had officially designated 1-3 the Crappiest Truck in Afghanistan. Half the time it wouldn't start, and today, the air-conditioning was busted. Ninety degrees outside was a hundred in the truck. It was like driving around in an oven.

"Stop here," Hulburt said, and Photo pulled into position overlooking the village.

Hulburt ignored the humanitarian aid packages for the time being. "Let's set up the mortars," he said.

Hulburt never traveled light. His truck was packed with mortars, grenades, antitank rockets, and enough cans of spare ammo to take up every available space not absolutely required to accommodate someone's ass. He had learned in Ramadi that it always seemed to be the simplest missions that blew up in your face. Sometimes you were your own QRF.

While Photo and Hulburt planted the mortar tube, PFC Alex Fernandez, nineteen, of Rockland, New York, sat in the turret, scanning the terrain. Fernandez's mom had cried when she learned his unit was headed for Afghanistan.

"You're going to get hurt, *mijo*!" she had sobbed into the phone. "You're going to die!"

"Mama, don't worry about it," Fernandez said. "God is my body armor. He already knows what's coming, even what's going to happen after we hang up."

Her crying tapered. "I know, but—"

"God knows which day is my day to die. And even if I die, my spirit will live," Fernandez said. "My body's just a shell. You know that. You raised me to believe that."

"Yes..." she said quietly. But Fernandez could tell she was only reining in her terror.

So far so good, though, since they landed in-country. The Dirty First had been in some hairy firefights, but when he talked to his mom, he kept that to himself.

Fernandez saw a row of *qalats*, and an orchard seventy-five to a hundred meters ahead. It looked like Hulburt had picked a good overwatch position.

PFC Trevor Carlin was in Bielsky's truck, along with SPC Richard Jacobs and two other soldiers, about twenty-five meters from Hulburt's team. Afghanistan's rugged ore-filled mountains often jacked up the FM radio signal, so Bielsky jumped out to reposition the TacSat antenna for better connectivity with the Airborne TOC. It was Carlin's first time on the gun. The sun baked his head in his helmet, but he felt good, ready for the trust Bielsky had placed in him. The .50 felt like chained thunder in his hands. He didn't want a firefight, but part of him hoped....

From his right, Carlin saw a man walk out of the nearest *qalat*. Light blue shirt, white *dishdasha*, scruffy brown beard. He crossed the road below Carlin's position and ducked behind a tall pile of rubble that might once have been a rock wall.

"Sergeant!" Carlin called out. He told Bielsky what he saw.

"Did he have a weapon?" Bielsky shouted back.

"Not that I could see."

Just to be safe, Carlin swung the .50's massive bore toward the rock pile. Then the man stood up from behind the rock and walked back to the *qalat*. Carlin shook his head. *What the—*

Machine-gun fire burst from the rocks. Rounds clinked and pinged off Carlin's turret.

"Incoming!" he yelled and returned fire. The big gun's recoil jarred his shoulders forward and back.

Twenty-five meters away, Photo hit the ground. On his side of 1-3, there was no cover. Rounds from the hidden machine-gun nest banged into the dirt inches from his face.

Lower in the village, Dudley heard the distinctive *tink-tink-tink* of AK fire. Hulburt popped up on the net. "Hey, we got fire coming in."

"Roger that," Dudley said.

Dudley had lost track of the number of firefights he and Hulburt had been in together. In Ramadi, he had discovered a secret to keeping his head together in combat. In the first three to five seconds of enemy contact, a soldier's reaction is basically, *What the hell just happened?* In the sixth second, he discovers that there is an insane, jabbering monkey latched to his back, trying to get him to do something stupid.

The trick, Dudley had learned, is not to let the monkey fuck you.

Get past those first five seconds, let your training and adrenaline kick in, take stock of your assets, and make a plan. Over countless firefights, he had been impressed by the amount of information an American soldier can process in the ensuing seconds: the primary threat, its distance and direction, and the resources required to destroy it.

No more calls came over the radio. *Hulburt's got this*, Dudley thought. *If he needs us, he'll call.*

Face against the dirt, Photo peered under the truck. Just seventy-five meters away, he saw the orchard sparkling with muzzle-flash. *Jesus!* he thought. *There must be thirty or forty guns!*

A wall of lead sailed into 1-3, centered on the turret. Photo heard it, looked up, and saw the turret around Fernandez actually caving in. From the ground, Photo could see that Fernandez was firing back with *both* his crew-served weapons. He had one hand on the 240, one on the .50-cal, and was fighting for his life.

Fernandez had tucked his head down in the turret and had both weapons on cyclic, arcing left, right, left, right, dumping literal kilos of ordnance into the orchard and nearby *qalats*. Brass casings flew up like confetti, and he could hear them jingling back down on the turret.

Suddenly, he thought maybe his mother had been right. *This is it. I'm going to die*, he thought. *But before that happens I'm giving these motherfuckers all I've got.*

Photo glanced at the nearest *qalat*, where Fernandez's one-man assault was chewing away chunks of mud and plaster. Then he saw a smoking black blur burst from the building and tear toward 1-3.

"RPG!" Photo yelled.

Head still in the turret, Fernandez felt the rocket sear across the back of his neck.

The rocket sheared off 1-3's rear antenna, and detonated in the ground between 1-3 and 1-4. An array of shrapnel knifed into Jacobs's leg.

"I'm hit!" he yelled, and dragged himself closer to the truck. Bielsky took an AK round to the foot.

In 1-1, Dudley heard sporadic fire explode into the thunder of many guns. Hulburt's voice erupted from the radio as he screamed to be heard above the roar: "We've got heavy contact! I say again, heavy contact! At least two wounded!"

Dudley turned to his driver, PFC Adrian Smith. "We're going up."

"Roger that," Smith said.

For Dudley, the most unnerving thing was hearing Hulburt scream. No matter what kind of sling his ass was in, Hulburt *never* screamed. As they drove toward the fight, Dudley knew this Taliban assault was the largest they'd faced. From the sound of it, 1st Platoon was outgunned by maybe four to one.

Two thoughts shot through his mind: *I'm probably going to die up there* and *When my wife finds out about this, she's really gonna be pissed.*

The instant the RPG exploded behind him, Fernandez popped his head up. "Holy shit!" He saw Hulburt staring straight at him. "Did you see that RPG?" Fernandez yelled. "That was *so fast!*"

Hulburt grinned—*Glad you didn't die just now*—and resumed firing into the orchard. Fernandez felt a tingle down his arms, something almost telepathic. He swung his 240 toward the nearest *qalat*. The fighter in the blue shirt was standing in the balcony door with an AK aimed at 1-3. Fernandez opened fire.

Stop-frame thoughts as he squeezed the 240 trigger:

He's so close.

I can see this dude's face.

Auto recoil jolted Fernandez's arms and shoulders. A gust of lead caught the Taliban fighter on his right side and spun him like a bullet. He fell back into the doorway, and all Fernandez could see were the soles of his shoes.

Dudley's section swung west around the base of the hill and drove up just far enough to see the space that had become the battlefield. Dudley could see Fernandez firing at the *qalat*, the Taliban machine-gun position, and an orchard so alive with muzzle flash that he couldn't count the enemy.

He yelled up to SPC Bruce Pickett on the .50-cal. "Put everything you've got into that orchard!"

Instantly, Pickett flipped the gun to cyclic and chewed into the tree line.

Dudley radioed his other truck. "Tell Rogers to put the MK19 into the back of the orchard! I don't want these assholes to get away!"

A moment later, Dudley could see trees falling and black smoke boiling up from the orchard. His section's arrival should've changed the dynamics of the fight, but Hulburt radioed again: The Taliban was still advancing. Considering the firepower his section had just brought to bear, Dudley was astonished. Maybe Allah was running a happy-hour special on virgins.

"Gimme the 203!" Hulburt yelled.

He meant the M203, a single-shot, under-barrel grenade launcher that hurls 40-millimeter projectiles about the size of eight-ounce Red Bull cans.

The M203 is especially effective against an enemy concealed from direct fire. The dark tube looked like a sawed-off shotgun barrel on steroids. Photo pulled the weapon out of 1-3 and tossed it to Hulburt, and the two men transformed into a bucket brigade of destruction.

Photo passed grenades to Hulburt, who launched them into the trees where they landed with a deep *thumpph*. No pyrotechnics, just a series of shattering concussions that pancaked sections of the orchard.

Hulburt did not take cover. Eyes slit, legs planted wide, he stood in front of 1-3's bumper and fired the 203 again and again as though it were a pump-action shotgun. Reload-fire-reload-fire-reload-fire. Rounds rainbowed into the orchard like long bombs at the Super Bowl, turbo-boosted by the cheerful stream of profanities Hulburt growled around his cigarette. For him, a good gunfight was the only thing better than sex.

Photo ran through his vest grenades, then yanked an ammo can full of spares from the truck and began passing those. Except for the pounding of their assault, the orchard fell silent. But the quiet lasted only as long as the 203 rounds. Almost as soon as the last grenade matchsticked a clump of trees, Photo saw survivors picking themselves up, regrouping. Within minutes, the tree line glittered again with muzzle flash.

Hulburt glared at the tree line. "All right, motherfuckers! Wanna play?" He shouted back over his shoulder, "Photo! Get the AT4!"

Whoa! Photo thought as he scrambled to comply. *He's not fucking around.*

Photo ran to the truck and unhooked the straps securing a vicious anti-tank weapon, an olive-drab tube half the length of a man. He checked the weapon, pulled the transport safety pin, and low-crawled it out to Hulburt, who still stood out in the open. Photo crawled back behind the driver-side rear door and watched as Hulburt shouldered the AT4. He cocked and unsafed the launcher and then pointed the rocket at the orchard. Checked his back-blast area to avoid incinerating any of his men. Raised his thumb, pressed the red firing button.

The roar was cataclysmic. In the same second, a ball of flame nearly as big as Hulburt erupted from the rear of the tube. Before him, half the orchard disappeared in a swirling mass of dust and debris. Carlin would later swear he could see blue sky concuss above the trees.

Hulburt turned to Photo. "Hey! I fired it!" he said, grinning like a kid with a cool new toy.

The AT4 was the great equalizer. Nothing but silence from the orchard for at least a minute. It was as if any Taliban fighters left alive had uttered a collective *Holy shit* and were considering their options.

While the orchard sat silent, Photo scrambled into the truck.

"Let's get the fuck out of here!" Fernandez yelled.

But 1-3 performed as usual: Photo cranked and cranked the engine but it wouldn't turn over. He slammed his hand against the steering wheel. "Shit, shit, shit!"

Outside, the Taliban assault roared to life again. AK rounds pinged off the skin of the truck.

"Let's go! Let's go!" Fernandez yelled.

Hulburt jumped into the TC seat.

Photo: "It won't start!"

Fernandez: "What the—?"

"I'm hit! I'm hit!" It was Photo. An AK bullet had zinged through a crease in 1-3's armor, grazed Fernandez's ACU's at the knee, slammed into the radio on the dash, and burst into fragments, one of which sliced open Photo's ear. If he'd been leaning an inch to the right, he'd have caught the lead with his eye.

Hulburt radioed Dudley that his truck was dead. Dudley ordered Smith to pull forward. Dudley then jumped out of his truck with a tow cable. AK and PKM fire streaked in, but he did not hear it. He did not hear anything. He just took the cable and ran. It was as though his brain had activated a pull-down menu—Attach Tow Cable—and his body was executing the commands. As he closed the distance to 1-3, a bullet crashed into the radio hanging from his vest and sent it skittering across the ground.

And then he was there.

Dudley and Hulburt exchanged grins. It was one of those weird war moments: *Hey, brother, they're trying to kill us, but we're still having a pretty good time out here, aren't we?*

Dudley attached the cable and dashed back to his truck, collecting his radio on the way.

Once on Highway 1, Photo was able to get 1-3 to start, and the four trucks rolled back to Airborne. Fernandez sat in the rear seat, his mouth in over-drive: "I can't stop shaking, man, did you see that shit? Oh my God, if I'd have stuck my hand up, I coulda grabbed that fucking RPG, I can't stop shaking, can you *believe—*"

"Ferny."

"Did you see that motherfucker on the balcony?"

"Ferny." It was Hulburt.

"I can't stop shaking, oh my God, I think I'm hit—"

"Fernandez..." Hulburt never raised his voice.

Fernandez's nervous babble stopped.

"You're okay, man," Hulburt said paternally. "It's okay."

"*OKAY*? What the fuck do you mean, it's *okay*? Did you not see that shit? Oh my God, I thought that round was gonna take my nuts off, and that rocket definitely almost took my head off. *It's NOT OKAY!*"

Hulburt smiled. "Ferny, calm down..."

"I *can't* calm down!"

The sergeant pulled a pack of smokes and a lighter from his breast pocket, lipped out a cigarette, and lit it. Held it out to Fernandez who was still bug-eyed and shivering.

"Here," Hulburt said mildly. "Smoke this."

Fernandez stared at Hulburt, eyes wild. "*I don't smoke!*"

"Smoke it anyway. It'll make you feel better.".

Fernandez took the cigarette. In three drags, it was gone.

CHAPTER 26

INTEL REVEALED WHAT the Dirty First had interrupted in Badam Kalay: an insurgent *jirga*, or council meeting of Taliban leaders, fifty to seventy-five men strong. Dog Company ███████████████████████ that a second *jirga* would soon take place in a nearby village. This one would host at least a hundred fighters. It appeared that the size of Taliban forces in Wardak was growing. Hill planned a mission to hit and disrupt the *jirga*. ████████
██
██
██ But with no CAS, going up against so large an insurgent force was out of the question.

Meanwhile, insurgent attacks on Highway 1 spiked in a wave that swept north from Helmand Province toward Kabul. Rebel fighters were blowing up bridges, overpasses, and culverts, and attacking Coalition logistics convoys—targeting one type of vehicle in particular: oil trucks. If oil stopped moving, so would Afghanistan's security and governance. ████████
██

Hill focused some resources on working with the Afghan National Army (ANA) to reinforce fighting positions along Highway 1, some of which were so old and entrenched that they seemed to Hill to date back to Alexander the Great. Hill, Sammy, and the HQ element rolled off FOB Airborne on a mission to check in with the ANA at several of these locations, with Westerhaus driving and Doyle on the gun. Tommy Scott and Larry Kay were farther back in the patrol.

At a guard tower in a river basin near an overpass, Hill told Westerhaus to stop the truck. Hill dismounted and went to speak with the ANA engineer in charge of improving the guard tower. Sammy was usually on his hip, but when Hill looked back, he saw that the terp was slow getting out of the truck.

Since the engineer spoke little English, Hill waited for Sammy to catch up. "Where do you plan to put your heavy machine guns?" he then said to the Afghan officer.

The engineer smiled expectantly at Sammy, who was peering across the wadis at a nearby hillside.

Hill looked at his terp. "Sammy, did you not hear what I just said?"

Sammy snapped back into the moment. "I'm sorry, sir. What did you say?"

"Ask the major where he plans to put his heavy weapons systems so they can best shoot over Highway 1."

"Yes, sir," Sammy said then translated into Pashto.

Hill wrapped up with the major, and HQ platoon proceeded south on Highway 1 toward a bazaar set up outside the village of Haft Asiab. D Co had visited this bazaar before, Humvees rolling through escorted by "dismounts"—soldiers on foot—in what is known as a presence patrol.

This particular bazaar spread for about a kilometer, one row of stalls on each side of a long aisle. Vendors and villagers dickered over cloth for *keffiyeh* (the head covering worn by Afghan men), packaged cookies and drinks, and loose produce—apricots, almonds, beans, and persimmons. Older Afghan men wore *dishdasha*, vests, and sandals, while younger ones wore a mix of traditional and Western clothes. All the women wore *abaya*, long dresses that covered them from neck to ankles.

Hill told Westerhaus to pull over at an Afghan National Police checkpoint about a half click shy of the bazaar. The plan was to proceed the rest of the way on foot. At the ANP shack, Hill got out and exchanged greetings with the officer there in Pashto. He was about to coordinate with the officer for further movement into the bazaar when he noticed that, once again, Sammy was still in the truck.

Irritated, Hill keyed up his radio mic. "Westerhaus, where is Sammy? I need him."

"Roger that, sir. He's coming."

Staring back at his Humvee, Hill saw Sammy climb out. The terp looked Hill's way, but hesitated beside the truck for a moment.

Hill threw his hands in the air, and put a *What the fuck?* look on his face.

He had never had to correct Sammy, who had always been nearly perfect at his job. Now, the terp jogged up looking preoccupied. Though his general appearance hadn't changed, he reminded Hill of someone showing up late to a meeting, with hair disheveled and glasses on crooked.

"I'm sorry, sir," Sammy said. "I'm sorry."

Hill glared at him. "Well, let's get our shit together, okay?"

"Yes, sir. I'm sorry, sir."

HQ Platoon made it back to the FOB just before 2130 that night. After the bazaar, there had been an IED attack on an ANA station about half a click up the road. Before turning in, Kay called the Battalion Forward Support Company (FSC). He wanted to see what items the Combat Logistics Patrol would be bringing out to Airborne on their next run.

"How are you doing?" he said when a Ghazni soldier picked up the line. "This is Lieutenant Kay from FOB Airborne. May I please speak with the support platoon leader?"

Three seconds later, a woman's voice cut across the line: "Why are you calling this late? I thought I told you not to call this late."

Astonished, Kay said quietly, "It's 2130." Nine thirty p.m. local. "I just got back from patrol."

"Well, don't call this late anymore."

"Okay, but I'm just calling to verify what's going to be on the CLP, and if you guys are going to be taking some of the soldiers here at Airborne back with you." Some Dog Company soldiers were due for midtour leave.

"It'll happen if it happens. Do you have anything else?"

"No, I guess not, but I just want to make sure that these soldiers are prepared for your arrival. Make sure they have their bags packed and everything."

"Yeah, I got it. Is there anything else?"

"No. Have a good night."

Kay disconnected the call and stood silently at his desk, staring at the phone. Larry Kay was rarely speechless. But now he couldn't pinpoint his emotion. Was it anger? Disappointment? Shock? He crossed the hall, found Tommy Scott, and relayed the phone conversation. "Am I crazy or was that fucked up?"

Scott, too, had no words. He could not even comprehend such an attitude from a person whose job it is to support frontline soldiers.

Kay returned to his desk. Maybe a round of deleting irrelevant emails would throw the world back on kilter. But instead of deleting, he clicked on a Bagram-related email with a bizarre subject line:

SUBJECT: New procedures for correcting deficiencies along Disney Drive

IMPORTANCE: High

Please be advised that there is now a zero tolerance policy in effect for deficiencies while walking down Disney Drive. Beginning tomorrow, personnel found to be in violation of publicized BAF standards, i.e. no reflective belt, no saluting, will be "secured." Personnel will be detained by the Military Police, placed on the bus, and taken to Division HQ. The detained Soldier will not be released until their Chain of Command comes to pick them up. Consider yourselves warned.

Instead of retrieving a little of his sanity, Kay nearly lost it. He found himself praying that he could jump a flight to Bagram Airfield and flagrantly walk down Disney Drive without a reflective belt. He yearned to be arrested and imagined the ensuing conversation with the Military Police.

"Well, what do you have to say for yourself?" an MP would say, his own belt reflecting proudly.

Kay imagined his reply: "Well, what I need more than a belt are showers, because my soldiers cannot bathe for weeks at a time. I need reefer vans because my perishable foods spoil before we can eat them. I need latrines, because my soldiers are sick and tired of pissing in a PVC pipe and burning their own shit with diesel. I need HESCO barriers, so that if a rocket does hit its target, my men might actually survive. I need batteries, so that my soldiers can see at night. I need ammunition for my M240B, so I can kill the enemy. I need Claymores so that my undermanned outposts don't get overrun. I need my Battalion to be at least *a little* empathetic, so that when I request artillery, they actually authorize it. Finally, I need soldiers, so that my wounded, injured, and exhausted ones can rest for a minute. Oh, and I did not have a reflective belt because they were sold out of them at the PX."

After his conversation with FSC, Kay stalked the FOB visibly angry for at least three days. Since when was it wrong for an infantryman to ask for support? The entire purpose of the Department of Defense is to support the tip of the spear. Everything else was secondary.

The United States of America
v.
CPT Roger T. Hill and 1SG Tommy L. Scott
2 December 2008

MAJOR ROBERT SMITH, Headquarters and Headquarters Company, 1st Battalion, 506th Infantry Regiment, Combined Task Force Currahee, was called telephonically as a witness and testified, in substance, as follows:

Latino: Your name is Major Robert Smith?

Smith: Yes.

Latino: Sir, do you remember being sent up to FOB Airborne to conduct an investigation?

Smith: Yes.

Latino: What did that investigation entail?

Smith: Alleged detainee abuse.

Latino: Did you take statements?

Smith: Yes.

Latino: Did you take a statement from Captain Hill?

Smith: Yes.

Latino: Do you remember what that statement said?

Smith: No, not without it being in front of me, no. I can give you some generalities.

Latino: Sir, can you go ahead and give us those generalities?

Smith: I believe I started by asking Captain Hill if he understood why I was questioning him. He understood and as I recall, he understood that there were allegations of detainees being abused at FOB Airborne. I know I asked him directly if he was involved with any of the detainee abuse, and I believe his response was no. That's about all I can really recall specifically, without having the sworn statement in front of me.

Latino: When you interviewed Captain Hill, did he give you any reasons to believe any detainee abuse had occurred?

Smith: No, except for the lieutenant who called me and said that they were aware of allegations of detainee abuse. During my investigation, I did not find any signs of physical abuse of the detainees.

CHAPTER 27

At Sayed Abad Base, Hill climbed to the compound rooftop with 2LT Miles Hidalgo, PL for A Co's Alpha Dawgs.[10] In response to increased Taliban attacks along Highway 1, Hill planned to relocate some of the Alpha Dawgs' mortar tubes so that Hidalgo and his men could provide indirect fire coverage to suspected hot spots along the route.

Because Hill considered Hidalgo a near peerless platoon leader, he had given him charge of Sayed Abad, one of the toughest AOs in Wardak. If anyone could lock down the area, it would be Miles, Hill thought.

Atop the roof, the two men looked south toward the proposed new site, and saw black smoke billowing in the distance. Hill pulled binos from his vest and glassed the horizon. "Can't tell what it is, but something is going down," he said. "See if the ANP can find out."

Five minutes later, the Afghan National Police chief partnered with Hidalgo came back with news: The Taliban had set up a roadblock and attacked an Afghan-contractor-secured U.S. logistics convoy with a force of more than a hundred men.

It was the largest attacking force since Dog Company had arrived, Hill realized. And they were getting bolder.

Minutes later, Hill, with HQ and 3rd Platoon, was rolling toward the scene. Ahead, he could see dozens of oily plumes corkscrewing into the

---

10. Hidalgo was platoon leader for an Alpha Company line platoon sent to cover Sayed Abad base in Wardak Province. In exchange, Dog Company's 2nd Platoon, the Jolly Rogers, was operating in Kapisa Province at this time.

sky. As the highway uncoiled, flames came into view, along with a chain of burning destruction at least a half a mile long.

Hill's driver slowed. A blackened boneyard of trucks was scattered across the road at panicked angles. They were "jingle trucks," vehicles decorated in the Afghan style with colorful flags, tassels, beads, and pennants. For a bizarre instant, Hill thought it looked as if a band of crazed clowns had torched a circus. Some trucks smoldered while others actively burned, the bright tassels forming giant candlewicks. Shell-shocked Afghan security contractors wandered through the smoking wreckage, crying "Taliban! Taliban!" Cargo spilled from the truck beds—U.S. mail, water, chow-hall-sized cartons of food, and cases of water. Letters from home fluttered in the wind.

Hill's mind had to stretch to embrace the scope of destruction, which resembled a scene from some postapocalyptic film.

From 3-3's turret, SPC Joel Ochoa could see the bodies of Afghan contractors slumped through truck cab windows, stitched with bullet holes. One corpse had a wide, through-and-through hole in his torso, ragged but cauterized.

RPG, Ochoa thought. He smelled cooking flesh.

Passing another dead man flung faceup on the asphalt, Ochoa saw that a large chunk of the face was missing. It was gruesome, but not the worst Ochoa had seen. That had been in Iraq, when his element found the decapitated corpses of a family of four, but only two heads. The children's heads were later found sewn up inside their parents' bodies.

This scene, too, had beheadings. As D Co rolled through, Hill counted six headless men beside the road, each head separated from its owner by the swing of some heavy blade.

That's some Mexican drug cartel shit, he thought. Then he applied a mental tourniquet, cut off the nightmare images, and put them away. It was the only way to deal with it, the only way not to come undone.

A few meters farther on, Hill saw an empty cargo pallet labeled ▮▮▮▮▮▮▮▮▮ ▮▮▮▮▮▮▮▮▮▮▮▮▮▮▮▮▮▮▮▮▮▮▮▮▮—and thought about how much more effective Taliban snipers would now be with American sights on their weapons.

In all, the Taliban had destroyed forty-four jingle trucks and driven another two into the mountains, kidnapping their drivers. Every intelligence report Hill received that day confirmed that the ambushing party was at least one hundred strong; most reports pegged it at closer to 150. Hill remembered the intel he'd received on the second Taliban *jirga*, the one he'd planned to disrupt before canceled CAS required him to scrub the mission. It now appeared the *jirga* had had a specific—and significant—target in mind.

Hill considered the escalating insurgency in Wardak. Attacks were increasing in frequency and the size of attacking forces growing geometrically. The first ambushing party they'd faced at Esh-ma-keyl had been fifty to seventy-five men. At Badam Kalay, the Dirty First fought seventy or more men. Now this. Dog Company's number two pencils mission was officially over.

Though already spread thin, some D Co soldiers would have to be detailed to clear the jingle truck wreckage from Highway 1. At Hill's suggestion, Battalion set up a temporary COP in an elementary school compound two clicks east of the highway, overlooking the annihilated convoy. Battalion sent units to help with the recovery op, including its mortars platoon, as well as a couple of platoons from Charlie Company and Echo, Battalion's Forward Support Company. Major Rob Smith, the new Battalion XO, was in charge of the operation.

The company spent the next week and a half helping Afghan heavy-equipment operators load the remains of each jingle truck onto lowboys, which then hauled them up to Kabul. The recovery was slow, grueling work. Some trucks burned for days, melting large swaths of gravel and asphalt right off the highway berm, leaving gaping gashes across the already patchwork pavement. Dog Company soldiers worked with the ANA and ANP, wrapping their faces in bandanas to filter the choking fumes.

On an Omigod-why-are-we-doing-this? scale of one to ten, the operation was for Donnie Carwile and Shon Haskins about a twelve. Of all Hill's platoon leaders, Carwile was the quietly rebellious one. An effective platoon leader walks a fine line between pleasing his company commander and taking care of his men. Commanders motivate their platoon leaders by pushing them until they push back. But Carwile didn't give a rat's ass how hard Hill pushed, because he already knew where all the buttons were. His men adored him for it.

The enemy had, at will, seized vital American supplies. Now, to avoid a Taliban PR victory in the form of news images of the smoldering skeleton of a large, U.S.-funded logistics convoy, Carwile's men were risking their lives—forced to distinguish between Taliban fighters planting booby traps and garden-variety looters, then shoot the former and not the latter, though they all looked about the same.

Carwile was pissed—and relieved when Hill tasked 3rd with several days of patrols in nearby Haft Asiab. He wasn't thrilled to be saddled with Paul Avallone, a reporter who was along for the trip. As embedded journalists went, though, Avallone, fifty-six, of Clarksville, Tennessee, was a good one to draw. A former Green Beret, he knew his way around a gun truck.

After accompanying 3rd in Haft Asiab for a couple of days, Hill joined 1st

Platoon in running patrols surrounding the jingle truck recovery. A few days in, Hulburt, Dudley, and some French Coalition soldiers apprehended two men leaving a *madrassa*, an Afghan schoolhouse that had been converted to a Taliban meeting house. The men had been following the patrol from a distance for several hours before dipping into the Talib safe house.

Inside, the Dirty First found notebooks detailing ambush plans, music with lyrics chanting "Death to America," and several belts of ammo. A quick biometrics scan revealed that one of the men was a known Taliban weapons smuggler. It was a valuable find.

LT Sean Allred, 1st's PL, relayed the news to Hill, then the Dirty First split out a detail to transport both prisoners back to the temporary COP near the jingle truck massacre. There, both a Battalion intel officer and CPT Wade Barker questioned the men, then worked through the night putting together an evidence packet strong enough to force the suspected smuggler to the next-higher level of detention.

The following day, a Black Hawk touched down at the COP, scooped up the suspect, and flew him to Brigade. As the prisoner was being loaded aboard, he boasted about being a Taliban fighter, and spit on and struck at the military policeman guarding him. The helo buttoned up and flew the prisoner to the brigade detention facility.

When 1st Platoon returned to the COP, Allred went to find Barker to congratulate him on transferring the captured smuggler to Brigade.

For Hill, the release of this prisoner was a kind of last straw. After more than a week of demoralizing recovery work, the capture had been for Dog Company a morale boost and also, they had hoped, a small measure of justice for their Afghan allies so brutally killed on Highway 1. After this, though, what else could Dog Company do? They had captured numerous EPWs in different environments, caught them actively engaged in espionage and firefights. This man was a known weapons smuggler, confessed to being Taliban, and physically assaulted his guards. How much lower could Dog Company's expectations fall? How much more demoralized could they be?

For those reasons, Hill never shared news of the smuggler's release with the rest of the men. They had worked too hard to hear how badly their command had let them down.

CHAPTER 28

A COUPLE OF days into the jingle truck recovery, Hill was waiting for the last of the lowboy trailers to show up when MAJ Smith called him into the temporary TOC. There had been a distress message, Smith indicated, from American vehicles sixty kilometers away, deep in the treacherous Tangi Valley.

The message was simple: S.O.S.

Hill's heart sank.

He rallied a QRF and briefed a short concept of operations: He and HQ Platoon would roll out with 3rd Platoon and a counter-IED RCP[11] unit that had been helping with the jingle truck recovery. They would connect with Hidalgo and the Alpha Dawgs at the Tangi turnoff and do a face-to-face over a map. Hill included some enemy analysis and two warnings: One, the narrow road into Tangi wound along the edge of a deep gorge, and maneuverability was severely limited. Two, the QRF would travel near Salar, a village in Sayed Abad where an Echo Company resupply mission had fallen under heavy fire a few weeks before.

From the COP, the QRF moved north on Highway 1 for about twenty-five clicks. Heat shimmered off the pavement; the outside air temperature was in the midnineties. SGT Eric Pierce drove for Hill with Sammy in the left rear seat and SGT Andrew Doyle on the gun. Most of 1st Platoon was back at Airborne resetting, but Dudley rode ahead with 3rd, in Carwile's truck.

The RCP was a unit from the 206th Combat Engineers. They had

---

11. RCP: Route Clearance Package.

just returned from Nawa in support of Charlie Company where they had faced significant enemy action alongside Charlie Company. ██████████

██

██ Hill admired the bravery of men who served in an RCP. They were cowboys at heart, triggering bombs on purpose, taking the hit so that others didn't have to.[12]

Moving down the highway, Hill could smell a cocktail of dust, motor oil, and sweat. He grew more watchful north of Salar, where the road was peppered with IED potholes that had been filled and refilled with earth and gravel. The truck commanders scanned for suspicious, newly disturbed patches, but the element cruised through Sayed Abad unscathed.

Minutes later, an IED erupted beneath an RCP MRAP traveling just behind Hill's truck. The MRAP's M240B was blown off its turret, but the vehicle itself sustained only minimal damage.

Hill paused and breathed a prayer of thanks. Had his Humvee been hit instead of the heavily armored MRAP, he and his crew might be dead. ████

██

██

██████████████████████ The lost patrol could simply be waiting for the cavalry to arrive, but something in Hill's gut told him it was worse. Urgency fluttered in his chest.

Hill's patrol made the mouth of Tangi. From the gun, Doyle saw a checkerboard of fields and orchards, brilliantly green. As per Hill's brief, the road into the valley skirted the edge of a steep gorge. It was almost impossibly narrow, barely wide enough for a Humvee to keep its outboard tires from slipping over the edge. As each truck rounded the first turn, its gunner let loose stones of fire. The big guns boomed at least a dozen times, echoing back as each round shattered against the mountainside.

Hill intended the ordnance as calling cards for the Taliban: *We're here. You've got our guys. Step aside.*

Dog Company had learned early on that the iron ore in Tangi's cliffs sucked up any radio transmissions from inside the valley. During the CONOP brief, Hill had assigned 3rd Platoon to establish a "retrans"

---

12. Michael Conn, "Route Georgia, 'Tangi Valley,' Wardak Province, Afghanistan," *Journal of Military Experience* 1, no. 1 (2011), Article 7. Available at http://encompass.eku.edu/jme /vol1/iss1/7/.

(retransmission) site to relay radio traffic back and forth to higher. As the patrol advanced, 3rd peeled off and crunched up the side of a foothill near the valley entrance. The rest of the element moved on, the gunners knocking more warning shots into the mountains.

The patrol passed through a string of tiny villages, each ghost-town still. Hill was calculating the odds of a vintage Tangi bottleneck ambush when a swirling tower of oily smoke came into view. At its base sat a gnarled and blackened mass of metal, a burning American gun truck.

CHAPTER 29

A DEEP IED crater encircled the truck, which belched gun smoke; a can of MK19 rounds had cooked off inside. Dog Company's dismounts fell out and formed a perimeter. Hill and some RCP soldiers carefully advanced, Sammy in trail. Hill could see the disabled truck's rear passenger, strapped into his seat, head resting on the seat in front of him. If he hadn't been charred completely black, he might have been only sleeping. Hill ducked to look inside the vehicle. The charcoaled head retained vague suggestions of facial features. A scorching fire had burned the hands and feet down to nubs.

Emotion welled up inside Hill. Sadness and empathy as he flashed to the moment of this man's death. Had he been knocked unconscious by the IED blast, only to wake up cloaked in flames, in terrified agony but unable to escape the inferno? As quickly as the image entered his mind, Hill shut it down. Compartmentalized it. Now was the time to focus on his job. The manner of the man's death could be examined later.

Using only his aviator gloves, Hill began to sift around the body for ID. The remains were still very hot and pieces of charred flesh fell off as Hill carefully tipped the man from side to side, searching. Between the body and the nearly fire-consumed seat, he spotted a wallet and carefully extracted it. It contained a few Afghani, the paper currency of Afghanistan, oddly intact, and a few bits of charred paper with handwritten notes clearly not in English. This was likely the team's interpreter, Hill realized. He was sitting where Sammy always sat, behind the driver and diagonal to the right front seat so that he could maintain eye contact with the TC.

Sammy was unable to make out the scribble other than to say an Afghan

had written it. Hill saw worry lines crease his translator's brow, sensed his
fear. The incinerated Afghan had awakened this morning doing the same
job Sammy did. He had chosen to risk the Taliban's wrath by working with
the Coalition and had paid the ultimate price. Now, if a strong wind came,
he would be scattered across the Tangi like winter leaves. Sammy turned
away.

Other than the terp's wallet, there was no way to ID this truck or its
occupants. Hill marshaled what little info he had and sent it up to higher
via Carwile and Dudley at the retrans site.

Carwile came back over the net. "There's another disabled gun truck a
little over a click to the east. Battalion says we're missing soldiers. We have
at least two if not more MIAs."

What the hell? Hill thought. *How did two trucks get separated by nearly
a mile in these badlands? How do multiple soldiers in gun trucks go missing?*

Soon after, a Special Forces team from Logar Province, ▮▮▮▮▮▮▮▮▮▮
▮▮▮▮▮▮▮▮▮▮ brought Hill a set of color printouts showing the possible
identities of the missing crew members. There were three names.

Hill looked again at the truck, which contained only the terp. That
meant at least three men were missing. His stomach rolled.

Hill remembered his early enthusiasm for combat, for leading an infantry unit. The latter was still there, soldiery as a calling. In a violent world,
violence is necessary work. But thinking of the missing men, who were his
brothers, Hill could form only one thought: *Waste. Waste on every side.*

The last vestiges of the *hooah* mentality instilled at West Point and
Ranger school drained completely away. He did not let go of big ideas like
freedom and democracy. But when he thought about these men's families,
their worlds colliding and crumbling under such loss, he wondered if this
particular war was worth the cost. If his commanders weren't even going
to take prisoners but instead allow the same zealots—armed with increasing intel and experience after each catch-and-release—to target American
soldiers over and over again, how did guys like these have a fair chance of
getting home?

He watched for a moment as the RCP crew gently, very gently, removed
the remains of the charred Humvee passenger and laid him in a body bag.
Amid a sacred hush, they covered his face. Today, they weren't cowboys,
just young men struck speechless by a gruesome and very personal war.

CHAPTER 30

AT THE RETRANS site, a pair of 3rd Platoon trucks monitored the relay. In one, Donnie Carwile kicked back with Sergeant Brandon Vega. In the other, Dudley sat in the TC seat with SPC Trent Crane on the gun, his red crew cut bright behind dark Oakley shades.

Back at Fort Campbell and through the Wardak deployment, Dudley and Crane had grown close. Dudley had come to think of the younger man as a guy he could trust not just with his life, but with his wife—a rare thing among soldiers.

An experienced mechanic, Crane, twenty-two, of Wilmington, Ohio, could repair nearly anything. Once, a Dirty First .50-cal went belly-up. A pin in the gun's feeder arm—the mechanism that moves the ammo belt through the weapon—broke, causing the gun to jam. The platoon was already down by one heavy weapon and couldn't afford to wait and see if the sludgy supply system would cough up a spare pin. So Crane and Carlin machined a homemade pin to get the .50-cal working again. The custom part actually improved the gun's performance, prompting the Special Forces guys to ask Crane and Carlin to make them some pins, too.

Among his platoon brothers, Crane was famous for making some fantastically bad decisions about tattoos. Back in the States, he'd commissioned an artist to ink a *Lord of the Rings* mural on his back. The artist had barely begun when the shop owner fired her for being a no-talent hack. That left Crane with only an Elven sword tattooed down his spine, and a red Eye of Sauron on his shoulder blade that the entire platoon regularly assured him looked exactly like the world's angriest vagina.

Inside the truck, Dudley could see into the lower reaches of the gorge.

It was Pleasant Valley–ish and picturesque, yet so full of death. It reminded him of those clichéd news reports from home, the ones where onlookers say they never thought so grotesque a murder could happen in their neighborhood.

Home, Dudley thought.

Rachel had given birth to their first child, a boy, just before the deployment. Dudley could have been with them both right now. His official tour of duty would have been up this very month, but the Army "stop-lossed" him—forcibly extended his enlistment in order to staff the war. He probably could have gotten out of it; a lot of guys did. But the truth was, he wanted to return to war. He loved his brand-new son, but he also loved his platoon brothers, and he didn't want them to face the enemy without him.

Still, Dudley was looking forward to stepping into the role of father when he finally got home. He glanced over at Carwile's truck in time to see the lieutenant throw his head back and laugh at something Vega said. Carwile had a knack for taking his soldiers' minds off the brutality of war. Dudley liked to listen to him talk about his daughters.

"Did I ever tell you about the time Reese was playing soccer and scored in the wrong goal?" Carwile had said one day when the two men were checking email in the computer shack on Airborne. Reese was his oldest daughter.

"No," Dudley said. "What did you do?"

"It was at Fort Benning, her first game. Jen and I were jumping up and down hollering, 'Go the other way! Go the other way!' But when she scored, she was so dang happy that we didn't have the heart to tell her she scored a goal for the other team."

Dudley laughed. "I can't wait to go home and be a dad."

Carwile leaned back and grinned. "It's the best, man. Nothing better."

███ According to the local Afghan gossip chain, the missing soldiers were not alive. Carwile relayed the info to Hill.

As it had Hill, it angered Dudley that these soldiers were not only missing but *separated.* Did they fall back? Did they freak out and run? Throughout both the Wardak and Ramadi deployments, Hulburt had pounded a single message into his soldiers' heads: "We will never leave each other. Either everyone's coming home, or nobody is."

For Dudley, there was a principle at work: He didn't give a damn what happened, you did not leave your battle buddies. He flashed back to an ambush on Highway 1 when LT Hidalgo's guys out of Sayed Abad were attacked during a security patrol. First Platoon was QRF, and they sped down Highway 1 to help repel the bad guys.

Assisted by an Afghan crane driver, the Dirty First then recovered an Alpha Dawgs Humvee that was disabled during the firefight. On the way back to base, they were ambushed just south of Maidan Shar. The crane driver panicked and careened off the road into a culvert, where the crane crushed him to death.

After a fierce firefight, Hulburt insisted on retrieving the crane operator and returning his body to his family. He had been an ally, helping the Americans. He deserved that, Hulburt believed.

Extracting the dead crane operator was hideous work. Hulburt had to stomp on his leg and break his femur to pull him free of the wreckage. Meanwhile, the falling crane had powderized the rest of his bones.

It was dark, and they worked by the eerie green light of their NODs. The man's collapsed skull stretched his features so that his face seemed to be sliding off his head. Handling him was like handling a beanbag. His limbs folded and flopped in unnatural directions as his pulverized bones shooshed inside his skin like sand.

Hulburt and Dudley got the crane driver into a body bag. But as they dragged it up toward the highway, the remains, without benefit of a skeletal frame, rolled themselves into a ball about the size of backpack at the bottom of the bag.

For Dudley, the experience was gorier and more haunting than any of the other bloody messes he'd seen. To get the job done, he dissociated himself, pushing the visual and tactile creep show away from his mind. He knew he would revisit it later, that he was taking out a line of credit on his own soul. He would pay it back another day, with interest.

But at least we didn't leave him, Dudley thought, comparing the situation to the soldiers now separated and missing across the Tangi. *We didn't leave that guy in the crane, and he wasn't even an American.*

The sun had already dipped below the rim of the Tangi gorge when two trucks from 1st Platoon rolled up to the temporary command post Hill had set up on a low hillside. Hulburt, Carlin, and others piled out. Hill had not wanted to set up in that particular location: The hillside was a local cemetery crowned with a stone crypt. He knew the locals would consider it a desecration for his men to conduct military operations there. But the PMT gun truck had been ambushed in an S curve just below the cemetery. Beyond that, the terrain fell away to irrigated fields, with a series of berms spoking out between raised cultivation rows.

There was no other place to safely overwatch the smoldering Humvee, as well as the soldiers who would have to patrol the lower fields in search of the missing Americans. Reluctantly, Hill had had his driver, Pierce, pull his Humvee up the hill and park it next to the crypt.

Hill's radio went hot. "Dog 6, this is Blacksheep 6, over."

"This is Dog 6. Send it, over."

"I think we've got one of the missing guys. It isn't pretty."

Hulburt and Carlin put together a small patrol and waded into an apricot orchard to assist men from Blacksheep and the Alpha Dawgs in recovering the body. The patrol walked for twenty minutes. As night fell in full, Carlin switched on his NODs, and tapped the infrared illuminator at intervals, turning the terrain Day-Glo green.

Finally, they caught up to the missing soldier. Carlin saw a man naked except for some tattered ACU scraps that still clung to his skin. His arm lay beside him unattached, the severed end ragged as if the limb had been hacked off. Carlin couldn't tell whether the soldier had been blown up, burned, tortured, or all three.

An ache crept into his chest. It wasn't the gore; Hulburt had dragged him along on so many missions that he'd seen a lot by then. This was the ache of anger. That this man, his Army brother, had been left alone in this God-forsaken field.

"Carlin, help me get him in the bag," Hulburt said.

The scene grew still and quiet. Hulburt unfurled a body bag and laid it flat. The Alpha Dawgs and Blacksheep looked on as Carlin and others lifted in the soldier's remains. Carlin zipped the bag closed.

"His arm," someone said in a near whisper. "Don't forget his arm."

Carlin picked up the severed limb and laid it on top of the bag. An hour later, the patrol reached the command post, set the bag at Hill's feet, and unzipped it.

"One of his arms is still missing," a soldier said. This matched intelligence reports Hill had received earlier in the day that the fingers of an American soldier were being sold at a local bazaar as souvenirs. "And we think his heart is missing. I don't know . . . he's pretty torn up."

They took his heart as a trophy? Hill thought. Outrage flushed through his veins.

He and the other soldiers stared down at their desecrated countryman. No one spoke. There was nothing that could be said. This soldier had been one of them and that was enough.

Hill processed this atrocity then radioed details to higher via the retrans.

The news sliced Dudley like a blade. He had heard plenty of stories. Of the Taliban blowing up children, mutilating women's genitals, horrible things. He understood that barbaric acts happened in every war, but this was his first encounter and it pissed him off. Dudley thought of the savages who had mutilated that American soldier, and his long, spiritual struggle over his own war ethic ended there and then.

Whatever I am, he thought, *I'm not that.*

The Tangi MIAs had occurred on the tail of the grueling jingle truck recovery operations on Highway 1, with both those evolutions punctuated by a bout of dysentery that coursed through Hill and his men like a poison river. Now, at the cemetery command post, Hill was exhausted, as were the men in his truck, Pierce, Doyle, and Sammy. Hill drew up a quick guard roster: thirty-minute shifts in a standing position only. He knew that any human being as tired as they were would fall asleep the instant they sat down.

Hill grabbed a poncho liner from his kit, found a stretch of dirt near the crypt, and lay down. It seemed only a minute later that he felt a hand on his shoulder.

"Sir? Captain Hill?"

Hill awoke facedown in the dirt, the poncho liner covering only his lower half.

"Sir?" It was Sammy shaking him gently awake for his guard shift. Normally a CO doesn't pull guard duty, but Hill knew his men were just as spent as he was.

Hill wiped his hands down his face, scraping away grit. "Hey, bud. Thanks."

The terp squatted in front of Hill, balancing Doyle's spare M4 across his thighs. "No problem, sir. Do you want to sleep longer?"

"No, no, I'm good. Thank you. Just give me a minute to change my socks."

Sammy took a walk around the hilltop as Hill made the switch, and was standing at the hood of the Humvee looking down into the valley when Hill rejoined him. "All right, Sammy, you can go rest a bit," Hill said. "Use my blanket if you want to."

"Thank you, sir." Sammy started away then turned back. "Sir, I am sorry for this." He tipped his chin toward the horrors in the valley. "This is bad. It is not right that this happens."

"Thanks, Sammy," Hill said. "One day...well, maybe soon, you won't have to deal with all this anymore. I really hope I can get you approved for that visa."

Sammy smiled, and Hill thought he saw a wistful hope. Visas had probably been promised him before. Hill remembered his two terps in Iraq,
Fahmi and Jack. They had been skeptical, but Hill was able to push their
visas through, giving their families a go at the American dream. He would
make it happen for Sammy, too.

CHAPTER 31

Brigadier General Mark Milley peered around the perimeter of Dog Company's Jalrez COP, taking in a sweep of buff-colored plains and olive-green scrub flanked by low, tawny hills that marched off into the valley. Then Milley asked Mo for his assessment of the outpost.

Mo looked at the general. "You want the edited version or my version, sir?"

"Call it like you see it," Milley said.

Mo thought of Milley as a hard-ass in the best sense of the term. An old-school general who hadn't let his years as a senior officer separate him too far from the men on the battlefield, Milley seemed to Mo the kind of guy ready to grab a pickaxe and dig a foxhole or get behind a weapon. And he wouldn't look like a pretty boy doing either job. For that reason, it was Mo's pleasure to escort Milley on a tour of the COP in Kowte Ashrow.

The general had graduated from Princeton University in 1980 with a degree in political science before accepting an Army commission through the school's ROTC program. An infantryman to the core, he climbed the Army's ranks through the 82nd Airborne, 10th Mountain Division, and the 1-506th. By the time he arrived to inspect the Jalrez COP, Milley was serving as the 101st's deputy commanding general, and as deputy commanding general for operations for Regional Command East Afghanistan.

Milley had flown directly to the COP in a Black Hawk flanked by a pair of Apache gunships. Hill and his HQ Platoon convoyed out to Kowte Ashrow to meet him, along with a delegation from Battalion and Brigade, which included COL Pete Johnson and LTC DeMartino.

It wasn't Hill's style to tag along on these sorts of tours, but it was expected for high-end official visits. Hill was confident in his NCOs and wasn't worried about them giving the "right" answers. In fact, he preferred that General Milley get the lowdown on the Jalrez COP, warts and all. Hill selected Mo as Milley's tour guide. If anyone would give it to a general straight, it was Mo.

A Taliban attack weeks before had triggered Milley's visit. Conditions were deteriorating at Bella,[13] a tiny OP near the Pakistani border, where LT Jonathan Brostrom, twenty-four, and Chosen Company held a small valley that was an historic infiltration route for foreign fighters. Chosen was augmented by a small ASG contingent—Afghan Security Guards.

Bella came under attack two to three times a day. In May 2008, while home on leave in Hawaii, LT Brostrom showed his father, retired Army Colonel David Brostrom, a video of a typical daily engagement. Late in the clip, an Afghan security guard could be seen deserting Bella's perimeter during a firefight.

"Boy, the enemy is inside your wire," COL Brostrom said.[14]

"Yup. They are," Jonathan replied.

When the younger Brostrom returned to Afghanistan, Battalion commander LTC William Ostlund ordered Chosen to build a second outpost about five miles south of Bella. As with the Jalrez and Sayed Abad COPs in Wardak, U.S. counterinsurgency strategy at the time called for Coalition Forces to extend their footprint, projecting the promise of security and order for Afghans who did not cotton to Taliban rule. On July 8, just under fifty soldiers from Chosen Company began construction on the new OP located next to the small village of Wanat.

From the beginning, LT Brostrom and others worried that the OP would be vulnerable to attack. First, it was to be built in a stark natural bowl, immediately ceding the high ground to even the most amateur enemy. Second, the site was surrounded by "dead space," areas that couldn't be seen from within the proposed perimeter. Third, just outside the perimeter, the terrain dipped down and away. Finally, the ground to the northeast led uphill to the village, where a mosque, a bazaar, and a cluster of other structures gazed directly down into the American position.

The Afghan heavy-equipment crew hired to do most of the construction was delayed, leaving Chosen to start building while also providing its own

---

13. "The Battle of Wanat," *Washington Post*, photo essay, http://www.washingtonpost.com /wp-srv/special/world/battle-of-wanat/. Accessed September 2013.
14. Mark Bowden, "Echoes from a Distant Battlefield," *Vanity Fair*, December 2011, http:// www.vanityfair.com/news/2011/12/battle-of-wanat-201112. Accessed September 2012.

security. ███████████████████████████████████████

██

██████████████████████████████████████ Chosen's intel
officer, CPT David Pry, objected so strenuously ███████████████
██████████████████████ that he would later tell an Army historian that he
breached professional etiquette in the process. Still, ███████████████████

Amid porous security, construction was brutal: The OP's initial defensive positions were formed only by trucks and Humvees.[15] Skeleton crews manned these makeshift guard towers so that the rest of the soldiers could begin digging into Wanat's reluctant soil. Armed only with picks, shovels, and a temperamental Bobcat, Chosen began filling HESCO barriers to build a more secure perimeter. But the Bobcat could not reach high enough to fill the barriers to the requisite six feet, so they had to make do with four-foot walls. After just a couple of days, construction slowed to a crawl as the men went nearly black on water, down to just less than a liter per soldier.

By day four, the perimeter had begun to take shape, but the fighting positions remained makeshift. Worse, Chosen did not control any high ground. Nor could it man a remote high observation post, as was standard procedure for all other OPs in Afghanistan.

Without enough men for both construction and security, Brostrom opted to concentrate on construction, placing an early-warning position, dubbed Topside, midway up the slope between the main perimeter and the village edge. The men were worried about this—it wasn't high enough for real, actionable early warning—but it was the best they could do until the Afghan contractors arrived.

There were other reasons to worry: From the first days, the men of Chosen noticed small groups of men who seemed to be tracking developments from the village bazaar. One night, a group of five men was seen moving across the mountains. Oddly, given the proximity of the bazaar to the OP, there were no women and children anywhere in sight. Then on July 12, a pair of staunchly pro-American villagers asked soldiers from Chosen whether they had drone surveillance and warned them to shoot anyone they saw in the mountains.

The warnings proved prescient. At 4 a.m. on July 13, a volley of RPGs seared into the Topside OP, immediately wounding or stunning all nine men manning the post. Then an attacking force later estimated at two

---

15. Douglas R. Cubbison, "They Fought Like Warriors: The Battle for COP Kahler, Wanat, Afghanistan," Combat Studies Institute. Revised Final Draft, 25 September 2009.

hundred strong aimed a barrage at Chosen's crew-served weapons. Early on, a devastating RPG attack took out the unit's TOW-equipped Humvee, trapping nine unused missiles inside the burning truck.

Brostrom's high-ground fears proved out: The attackers fought from the rim of the OP's little bowl, firing fish-in-a-barrel style down into the pit.

Chosen fought back with small arms and mortar fire. Chosen Company commander CPT Matthew Myer tried to guide in artillery fire from nearby Camp Blessing, but it was risky in a fight at such close quarters that the Americans could see the enemy's masks and fatigues. The fight was so tight that Chosen's MK19s were rendered ineffective, because the enemy was within the arming distance required by the weapon's grenades.

Minutes in, all nine men at Topside were either dead or wounded, their weapons overheated and jammed, or out of ammo. Several soldiers became battlefield heroes, providing covering fire to the wounded, saving others from bleeding out, or in Brostrom's case, charging into the fight to give up his own life for his friends.

At the main outpost, the fight raged on. With its crew-served weapons destroyed or disabled, Chosen battled back with M4s, RPGs, mortars, and grenades hurled by hand into the trough outside the perimeter. Finally, a B-1 poured its load on attackers to the north, then Apache gunships ripped into the hillsides, scattering the rest. Still, by sunrise, three-quarters of Chosen was either dead or wounded. Attackers had wounded twenty-seven U.S. soldiers and five allied Afghans. Nine Americans were killed, the highest death toll to that point in Afghanistan.

Military historian Douglas Cubbison would later study the Battle of Wanat for the Army Combat Studies Institute, interviewing soldiers who spoke with him candidly "at risk of professional censure." When Cubbison wrote that Brigade and Battalion support was poor and sometimes nearly absent, the Army replaced him as the study's author and had his findings revised.[16]

Long before that, though, Roger Hill and other RC East commanders were briefing their men on lessons learned at Wanat, while commanders like Milley inspected their small outposts for viability.

The Jalrez COP was even smaller than Chosen Company's OP. Since establishing the COP in May, 4th Platoon had manned it almost exclusively. Despite near-daily attacks, Wilson and his men were holding their own. So much so that Afghan children near the COP had been able to return to school.

---

16. Per authors' interview with Mr. Cubbison, June 2014.

Once the Airborne and Battalion delegations rendezvoused with Milley at Kowte Ashrow, Mo gave Milley the ten-minute grand tour, with Hill, COL Johnson, LTC DeMartino, and LT Brett Erickson, the Shockers' new PL, walking in trail.

The COP had been built with the understanding that either Battalion or Brigade would send more combat power to keep it manned, Mo told the general. That had not happened. As a result, the position was badly undermanned, with a baker's-dozen soldiers at the most. In order to keep the Taliban guessing, Mo said, 4th had to cut out those soldier silhouettes. The Shockers hoped the appearance that the COP had more soldiers might ward off an overrun attempt like the one at Wanat.

Resupply was a problem, Mo continued, especially 240B ammo. Living conditions were fairly Spartan, but they were getting by.

Milley nodded toward the lands rolling toward the ridgelines away from the COP. "Do you have Claymores out there?"

Mo looked at the general. "Do you *want* me to have Claymores out there, sir?"

"Yes."

"Then yes," Mo said. "Yes I do."

Milley laughed and shook his head. In that gesture, Mo saw that the general understood that 4th Platoon was holding this valley with duct tape, chicken wire, and not much else.

"Sergeant, what do you think is going to end up happening out here eventually?" Milley said.

"Well, sir, we have all these outposts getting overrun. I don't think it's going to be that easy for the Taliban to overrun us here, but if we keep going the way we're going, I think it could happen eventually. My men don't feel sorry for themselves, though. They'll throw rocks if they have to."

Milley laughed again, but more grimly this time.

Hill, who had hung back during the tour, now followed Milley, Johnson, and DeMartino as they walked up a berm in front of a vehicle fighting position. Johnson looked out toward the roof of the ANP station, where a handful of 4th Platoon manned machine guns under camouflage netting.

Johnson spoke over his shoulder to DeMartino. "Tony, you only have thirteen guys out here?"

"Sir, I had no idea we only had thirteen men out here," DeMartino said.

Hill looked at his CO, shocked, then glanced at Milley and Johnson. Both senior officers appeared floored by DeMartino's response.

CHAPTER 32

A BRIGADIER GENERAL visiting a dirty and remote little COP is not without some informal customs. After Milley's look around, he selected a couple of 4th Platoon soldiers and gave them "challenge coins" struck with the insignia of the 101st Airborne. Such coins originated during World War I and had sparked rich traditions, from proving unit membership to winning the right to have fellow warriors pay for a round of drinks.

Afterward, Milley caught Hill's eye and pulled him aside. "What do you need most out here, Captain?" the general said.

Hill, ready, pulled out a paper list and rattled off the most pressing items, those that Kay and Scott had been requesting from Battalion for months: Claymores, razor wire, HESCO barriers, sandbags. Hill wanted the general to understand that the lack of defenses around this COP weren't due to a lack of effort but a lack of resources.

"Your sergeant over there says you're having trouble getting 240B ammo," Milley said. "Is that true?"

"Sir, it is."

"You know, Battalion isn't some lifeless, limbless entity that can't get you resources."

"I know that, sir, and we've been making requests on a regular basis."

Milley held out his hand. "Give me that list."

"Sir?"

"The list you've got there. Give it to me."

If a man's heart can simultaneously sink and soar, Hill's did. He suddenly saw a ray of light, a lifeline for his men. After months of asking and not receiving, here was someone with clout offering a helping hand. But jumping the chain of command, whether intended or not, was risky. It is a simple matter for a general to enact an open-door policy, but the blowback on a junior officer who appears to circumvent his immediate superiors can be severe.

"Is it true you only have thirteen men out here?" Milley said, pocketing the list.

"Yes, sir. That's all I can spare."

Milley looked skeptical. "How is that?"

"I'm fixed out here, sir," Hill said.

Fixed is a doctrinal term used when a unit has no freedom to maneuver because its existing positions require certain manning levels. Hill pulled out his map: "I have three outposts and a full FOB. I'm manning all four locations with a heavy weapons company that's been winnowed down by WIAs and transfer requests by higher. You know about this COP and Sayed Abad Base. I have another outpost south of there with even fewer men."

"How many?"

"Eleven, sir. That's my 3rd Platoon at the schoolhouse. We were tasked with manning that COP after the jingle truck massacre on Highway 1."

"I see," Milley said, and sighed. "Where is this outpost located?"

Hill pointed to Haft Asiab on his map; Milley marked it on his own. Hill mentally crunched the sum of data the general had just received and hoped the look he saw in Milley's eyes was a dawning understanding of the tenuous nature of Dog Company's situation.

Milley put his hand on Hill's shoulder. "Captain, you know we can't afford another Wanat. If Wanat has taught us anything, it's that the American public doesn't have the stomach for that kind of loss. Do you understand what I'm getting at?"

"I do, sir," Hill said. And just like that, he knew that the Jalrez COP, Dog Company's only real progress in bettering life for the people of Wardak, was gone.

After Milley said his good-byes to Johnson and DeMartino, LT Erickson escorted him back to his Black Hawk, whose rotors had commenced a lazy turning. As the two men trudged toward the waiting bird, the general first glanced at the junior officer, then looked at him more carefully, as though truly noticing him for the first time.

"Did I give you a coin back there?" Milley said amiably.

Erickson shook his head. "No, sir."

"Well, if you're alive the next time I see you, I'll give you one."

Erickson glanced quickly at Milley's face to see whether he was joking, but the general just kept walking.

That night, Milley issued the order to close the Jalrez COP. Back at Airborne, DeMartino accused Hill of planning to give Milley his list of needed resources in a deliberate effort to make Battalion and Brigade look incompetent. The accusation confirmed at least one thing for Hill: The general had taken their talk seriously and followed up with Hill's chain of command.

"Just so you're aware," DeMartino said, "Colonel Johnson thinks you're disloyal to the team."

The comment saddened Hill, but did not surprise him. It was another indicator that advancing the mission in Wardak took a backseat to apple-polishing Army politics.

A day or two later, General Milley visited Sayed Abad Base. Milley was at the base primarily to interview the Alpha Dawgs' PL, 2LT Miles Hidalgo, for a job as his aide, and Hill gave the lieutenant a much-deserved rave review. Milley toured the base, where he ran into Erickson—still alive—and gave him the promised challenge coin. After the tour, Hill asked to speak to the general in private.

"May I speak freely, sir?"

"Of course, Captain Hill," Milley said.

Hill explained that he'd already taken heat for giving Milley his supply list at Kowte Ashrow. "How did you take our discussion that day, sir?"

"I took what you had to say only as a commander who had in mind the best interests of his men."

Hill detailed for Milley the discussion with DeMartino regarding Johnson.

"What about your command climate?" Milley asked.

"Tense, sir. The mission is stressful for everyone up and down the chain. I've had my job threatened a couple of times. I feel like I'm walking on eggshells."

"You've had your job threatened?"

"Yes, sir."

"All because of the discussion at Kowte Ashrow?"

"No, only partially," Hill said. "There have been other incidents."

In May, a Reuters reporter had quoted an unnamed soldier from somewhere in the Division as saying that the acronym ISAF stood for "I Suck at

Fighting." The reporter placed the quote—an aspersion on the abilities of non-U.S. Coalition soldiers—near an unrelated on-the-record quote from Hill. At Brigade, the immediate conclusion was that it was Hill who made the "I Suck at Fighting" comment. Outraged emails burned down from the Division to Battalion, with one senior officer calling for Hill's "head on a platter."

Another incident involved LT Justin Napolitano, who worked for DeMartino. Napolitano had been the officer in charge of the fratricide investigation that DeMartino initiated after Kris Wilson fired on the men who shot off his NODs with automatic weapons in Maidan Shar. Napolitano found Wilson to have acted properly.

Later, Napolitano lay shot and bleeding out after a firefight with Taliban insurgents in Hill's battlespace. When Hill responded with a QRF, DeMartino passed infuriated orders via radio: If Hill did not stand down and return to Airborne, DeMartino would relieve him of command. DeMartino then responded with his own QRF.

Milley listened. Then he assured Hill that his job would not be in jeopardy over Kowte Ashrow or any other situation. "And if you think something is really wrong, contact me directly."

"I will, sir," Hill said, relieved. "Thank you."

The conversation with Milley gave Hill the courage to finally confront DeMartino. He meant to address several issues. Hill was tired of executing what he thought were ill-advised orders despite the sick feeling in his gut and the potential danger to his men. He was tired of his job being threatened. And he was tired of trying to build proverbial bricks without straw: running a combat outpost without basic combat supplies; running missions with broken trucks; holding a Taliban-infested valley with too few men.

With Milley's assurance, Hill felt some renewed job security. Still, he knew what he had to say to DeMartino was inflammatory enough to be politically dangerous. The general's delegation had already departed Sayed Abad, and DeMartino was preparing to leave as well. Hill pulled him aside.

Hill plunged in. "Sir, you're probably not going to like what I have to say, but I feel it's important to be honest here. I feel like you're throwing my company away. Discarding us, throwing us under the bus."

To Hill, DeMartino looked mildly surprised, but at the same time—Hill couldn't put his finger on it—bemused? Indulgent?

Hill plunged on, detailing the violent, ad hoc trips into Jalrez, the manpower shortage, the demands of setting up the Haft Asiab COP after failing to man and supply Kowte Ashrow. He didn't mention nonoperational issues like the "I Suck at Fighting" story, but focused on combat and resource issues.

From the look on his face, Hill half-expected DeMartino to pat him on the back and say something conciliatory. Something like, "Everything's okay. It's been a tough mission. I've got your back."

But he did not say that, or anything of the sort.

Instead, DeMartino smiled paternally. "Roger, let me ask you something. You want the battalion at Airborne, don't you?"

Battalion headquarters, of which DeMartino was in charge, was scheduled to move from Ghazni to Paktia Province. But Hill had seen signs that DeMartino didn't want to move to Paktia. Instead, he wanted to move to Hill's province, Wardak. That was where the fight was, and everyone knew it.

Unsure where the conversation was leading, Hill said, "Yes. Of course."

"Well, in order to convince the boss, we need more SIGACTs in Wardak."

More SIGACTS? Hill thought. *DeMartino wants more firefights here? More troops in contact?*

The implications for his men took Hill's breath away. Objections sprang to his lips, but he couldn't find his voice. Hill was stunned into silence, utterly without response. At that moment, his focus changed from advancing the mission to surviving it.

The United States of America

v.

CPT Roger T. Hill and 1SG Tommy L. Scott

2 December 2008

MAJOR ROBERT SMITH, Headquarters and Headquarters Company, 1st
Battalion, 506th Infantry Regiment, Combined Task Force Currahee,
continued testifying, in substance, as follows:

Puckett: Sir, this is Neal Puckett, I am a civilian attorney and I
represent Captain Hill.

Smith: Okay...

Puckett: Sir, subsequent to your investigative report being filed,
do you know why Brigade sent Lieutenant Colonel Gunther and
Captain Scragg and Captain Latino to do yet another investigation?

Smith: Yes. Mine was a commander inquiry for the Battalion
commander, and the purpose of mine was going down there to
see if there should be a formal investigation conducted. At the
completion of my investigation I recommended that someone from
Brigade or from the Battalion come down and investigate further.

Puckett: Sir, tell me again what your recommendations were at the
end of your report.

Smith: I found that I had two soldiers...who at the time I felt had not
lied and whose integrity was great. So I knew one of them had to
be lying...I recommended that a formal investigation be conducted
outside of the Battalion either by Brigade or Division.

Puckett: Sir, I've got your Paragraph 5 recommendations in front
of me here, and I don't see that, sir. I see you recommended
command climate be conducted within Delta Company, and then
you recommend (B) that Lieutenant Morris be removed from the
company for his own well-being, and then (C) you recommend that
Lieutenant Morris and yourself be informed of the final results of
the investigation. Nowhere here do I read that you recommend a
formal investigation. Am I missing something, sir?

Smith: It may not be in the written, but that's what I recommended to the Battalion commander.

Puckett: Verbally?

Smith: That's part of that written statement, yes.

Puckett: No, sir, it's not here. We've gone over it, sir, and it's not here.

Smith: Okay, then for sure I recommended it verbally to the Battalion commander.

Puckett: Did you change your mind, sir? Is there some reason why you deny the written report?

Smith: I cannot give you an answer to why, but I do know that I did make it verbally known that there should be a formal investigation outside of Battalion.

Puckett: Sir, did the boss tell you what recommendations to put in there or not put in there, or what recommendations to make verbally?

Smith: No.

Puckett: Sir, do you know Captain Hill very well?

Smith: Yes, I do.

Puckett: In what capacity have you known him?

Smith: He worked for me in the S-3 [operations] shop at Fort Campbell.

Puckett: And after you took command, did you have interaction with him?

Smith: Yes.

Puckett: Tell me this, sir. Prior to this incident occurring out at FOB Airborne, give us your evaluation of Captain Hill as an Army captain, both in the S-3 shop and as a company commander.

Smith: Prior to deployment I made the comment to the Battalion commander that I felt that Captain Hill would be our best company commander. I thought he was a good officer, and I trusted him…

Puckett: And after he became a company commander and was there for several months, did you monitor the progress of the company and the engagements they had, and the casualty rate and all the mission accomplishments that they racked up?

Smith: Yes.

Puckett: It was pretty impressive, wasn't it?

Smith: Yes, especially under the circumstances. He was the only company commander who was securing a province by himself.

Puckett: A huge responsibility, almost one level higher, like Battalion level, is that correct, sir?

Smith: Correct.

CHAPTER 33

████████████████████████████████████
████████████████████████████████████
████████████████████████████████████
████████████████████████████████████
████████████████████████████████████
███████████████████

On August 5, one of CPT B's Special Forces NCOs called Hill to the Special Forces TOC and pointed at a monitor. "Check it out."

Hill focused on the black-and-white feed. It showed ten to twelve men moving between a *qalat* in Razak's Jalrez compound and a small six-passenger van. The resolution wasn't sharp enough to see facial features, but plenty clear enough to identify the AK-47s, PKMs, and RPG launchers slung across the men's backs. Hill could also identify what the men carried: mortars and rockets. In turns, the men disappeared into the rear of the van carrying the ordnance. They remained inside for a couple of minutes, then reappeared empty-handed.

Are we really seeing this? Hill thought.

"It looks like they're building a VBIED," he said. A vehicle-borne IED, pronounced "VEE-BID."

"That's exactly what they're doing," the NCO said. ███████████████
███████████████

Under orders from COL Johnson via General Milley, Hill had pulled 4th Platoon out of Kowte Ashrow and turned the little outpost over to the Afghans. Since then, CPT B's SF team had stepped up their surveillance of Razak and his men. ████████████████████████████████████

██████████████ on the Jalrez crew, bearded men in bootleg Ray-Bans buzzing around their rock-star boss. The problem now was that Razak was playing it safe. The current Taliban ground commander in Jalrez was only a lieutenant, likely one of Razak's primaries. CPT B was intent on bagging the main man before they rotated out. After the warm-tea incident in which the previous SF team missed Razak by minutes, CPT B was determined not to miss him again.

██████████████ there are multiple VBIEDs about to go on the move and that at least one is headed for Maidan Shar, maybe Kabul," CPT B said. "If we wait too long, they might split up, and we only have one set of eyes."

Hill and CPT B talked it around. The options came down to this: They could bide their time, continue to watch the camera feeds, and wait for a chance to grab Razak. Or they could show their hand, move on Jalrez now, and control the outcome of the VBIEDS, potentially saving lives. In the end, it wasn't even a choice.

The first VBIED van was on the move, headed east out of the valley toward Airborne. The Montana PMT, Caveman, had just come in from a patrol of the hotly contested Nerkh subvalley just south of Jalrez. Hill asked them to intercept this VBIED, and had the Shockers mount up to intercept VBIEDs 2 and 3. Minutes later, they rolled out of Airborne's gate, followed by Hulburt, Dudley, and the Dirty First.

Davis rode TC in 4-1, followed by Wilson in 4-2, and Mo in 4-3. LT Brett Erickson rode with Mo in 4-3, with Hill in HQ-6 in between 4th and 1st.

Within moments, the convoy ran into the PMT, already engaged in a standoff with VBIED 1. Via radio traffic, Hill learned that the van's occupants were not complying with Caveman's orders to exit the vehicle. He watched the van driver hit the gas and barrel toward the PMT. A Caveman gunner lit up the cab with a .50-cal, stopping the van for good.

One down, two to go, Hill thought, as Davis and 4-1 led the way around the standoff and the rest of the convoy rumbled into Jalrez behind him. They were headed west toward Kowte Ashrow and the COP they'd been forced to abandon. The convoy hugged a bank of barren rock that lined the right side of the road, opposite orchards and thick stands of marijuana on the left.

Farther on, *qalats* built into terraces appeared on the right, Kowte Ashrow. Above Mo in 4-3, SPC Justin Fox, the gunner, gripped his .50-cal a little tighter. In 4-2, PFC Ryan Haffner drove, with Wilson in the TC seat in front of PFC Michael Peake. PFC Bitting, aka McLovin, also rode in 4-2 as the platoon forward observer.

Beyond the village, the road widened and was smooth enough that the convoy could move at a serious clip, around 55 miles per hour. Four-one crested a low hill and Davis spotted an oncoming black GMC Jimmy SUV.

On contested thoroughfares, Dog Company's tactic was to "own the road." To that end, Davis had a PA system mounted on 4-1. He sounded a horn blast—like a fire truck or ambulance—warning the Jimmy to give way. At the same time, 4-1's gunner swung his .50-cal up and aimed it at the advancing SUV. This combination had proven persuasive in the past, but the Jimmy kept coming.

As it neared, Davis peered intently through its windshield. He could see two men, a driver and a passenger. VBIEDs typically carried a single operator, the driver only. Who was this, then? Davis wondered.

The Jimmy closed rapidly on 4-1. There was not enough room on the road for both vehicles. Suddenly, the SUV driver pulled his wheel hard right. Davis screamed into his mic, ordering the vehicle to halt. The Jimmy bounced off the pavement onto the dirt shoulder. Four-one's gunner arced his weapon, following the SUV's path as it sped past in a veil of dust. Davis caught a flash of black in his rearview mirror—the Jimmy careening left, back onto the road, headed straight for Wilson's Humvee.

Wilson saw 4-1 crest the hill then saw the Jimmy arrowing in. Haffner jerked 4-2's wheel hard right, but it was too late. The Jimmy slammed into the Humvee, an angled T-bone crash. The impact thrust the rear edge of 4-2's engine into its cab, jamming Haffner's legs as the SUV's forward momentum threw him straight back. Bitting's face smashed the rear of Haffner's seat. Wilson's seat back broke and pancaked into Peake's lap, crashing down on his knees.

Mo's voice pierced the net: "VBIED! VBIED! VBIED!"

As Wilson and his injured crew piled out of the truck, small arms fire bloomed up from both sides of the road.

It had taken Mo a second to put it together: two guys in an SUV. Usually suicide bombers rode solo. But the instant he saw the driver deliberately pull his wheel left, Mo knew the two-man setup was camouflage. He also knew the SUV would not explode, though later he would not be able to explain it. Just a battlefield sixth sense about Wilson and his men: *They're going to make it.*

At the moment of impact, Mo saw the VBIED driver and his pax pitch forward into the SUV's dash then slam back into their seats—the driver and his wingman knocked senseless from the impact but still alive.

Mo's driver, PFC Stuart Jaworski, braked 4-3 to a tire-peeling stop. Mo keyed his mic again: "VBIED! VBIED! Get the fuck out and *run!*"

He leapt from his truck, but did not run. Instead, he raised his rifle and advanced on the Jimmy, which sat still and smoking, accordioned against Wilson's truck less than twenty meters away.

One truck back, Hill radioed Wardak TOC to report the contact and call in a fire mission. AK fire pelted the convoy. Hill dismounted and rushed toward 4-2 as its stunned crew tumbled from the truck, crawling off the road through smoke.

Bullets snapped like bubble wrap past Mo's ears. He continued his advance toward the Jimmy. The Shockers and the Dirty First, now dismounted, laid down suppressing fire, covering Wilson and his banged-up crew as they bellied to take cover in the ditch beside the road.

Mo closed the distance to the SUV. He could now see the bombers, still alive, moving, coming to. Mo raised his M4 and fired. Controlled pairs into the passenger-side window. The wingman's right shoulder bloomed red.

Shit! he thought. *Too low.*

He had not compensated for his gunsight. At five meters out, Mo saw the bleary passenger look his way and slowly raise his left arm.

A wire dangled from his wrist.

The words *secondary switch* flashed through Mo's mind as the passenger raised his right hand. It shook as he fumbled toward the wire.

Time slowed for Mo. Now at near-point-blank range, data points sped past his rifle into his eyes: Propane tank wedged between the front seats. Daisy-chained rockets piled in the back. Enough to wipe out the entire convoy. Passenger still reaching, reaching for the detonator—

Mo squeezed his trigger and put a bullet in his head. The passenger slumped forward. Mo took two more steps, speared his gun through the window, and fired again. The driver died with his eyes open.

Small arms fire popped around Hill as he caught up to Mo. "Four-two is about to catch fire," he said. "We've got to get everyone through this choke point now. I'll start pushing the convoy around the high side of the VBIED."

"Roger, sir, I'll get our trucks moving."

The convoy's gunners returned fire until the ambush died away to scattered potshots. Dirty First dismounts moved house to house, clearing a hodgepodge of *qalats* on the low side of the road while the rest of 1st Platoon collected the Shockers' wounded. Caveman arrived on scene and made themselves the ground evac for Wilson's injured crew.

Wilson knew his ribs were cracked, but he wasn't about to leave the fight. He ordered Haffner, Peake, and Bitting to return to base with the PMT, and stayed with his trucks.

Once Dog Company was through the choke point, CPT B's SF team rolled up, their MRAPs towering over the fiery scene. They circled wagons with D Co about seventy-five meters west of the VBIED SUV.

Mo went back to his truck and climbed into the TC seat. Hill and CPT B joined him there, standing outside the Humvee. LT Erickson, still in training, sat in the rear seat behind Mo.

"We can't afford to lose 4-2, sir," Mo said to Hill, who reluctantly agreed.

The Humvee was locked in a death embrace with a live VBIED, and locked onto its turret was one of only two operational ████████ ████████████████████████ missile systems, a weapon so feared by the Taliban that they called it "the Finger of God." Dog Company had lost its other two in previous firefights.

"The CLU is in the truck, too," Mo said. The Shockers had used both systems in Jalrez constantly to spot the enemy before they could approach the COP. The thermal optic could pick up heat signatures at night, and point out a threat a great distance away.

"What are you going to do?" Erickson asked Mo.

"We need to go get that truck," Mo said.

"Mo, you're gonna get yourself killed."

"If we don't get that equipment, we're all gonna get killed."

CPT B stepped in. "We'll use my MRAP."

Hill agreed. The MRAP had the most protective armor and towing power. "All right, let's back it up to 4-2 and tow it out of there," he said. "We have to hurry. There's not much time."

The VBIED could explode at any second, especially if jarred during a recovery attempt. But if they could pull 4-2 free and clear the blast radius quickly, it would be worth the risk to retain the weapons systems for the six-month fight that still lay ahead. They sure as hell wouldn't be getting replacements. Not for any of it.

Mo stared at 4-2, entwined with the deadly SUV. "Give me some water," he said.

Jaworski passed him a bottle. Mo screwed off the cap and took a gulp. Then he poured the rest of the bottle over his head, climbed down from his truck, and handed his rifle to Davis. He wasn't going to need it anyway, he thought; he was pretty sure he was about to die.

What happened next happened quickly:

Mo and Hill sprinted to a D Co truck, grabbed a tow strap, and ran toward 4-2.

CPT B ground-guided the MRAP as one of his guys backed it up to the disabled gun truck.

All three men worked to hook up the tow. Just as they finished, the smoking Jimmy burst into flames. CPT B banged on the side of the MRAP. "Go! Go! Go!"

The driver hit the gas, wrenching 4-2 free with a bone-chilling screech of twisting steel.

The VBIED's payload began to cook off, banging and popping inside the Jimmy's skin. The MRAP dragged 4-2 west, its crippled chassis digging furrows in the asphalt.

The tow operation had created only the slimmest buffer when the VBIED went high order. Three successive explosions rocked the road, sending walls of shrapnel in a lethal bloom. The blast sprayed molten stars of steel over D Co and the SF team. Metal shards clipped Mo as he rounded the front of the MRAP. Five pieces of steel seared into Wilson's left arm. He yelled, "Hot! Hot! Hot!" and flung his rifle at Mo as he shook shrapnel from his sleeve.

When Hill reached a safe distance, he turned to watch the SUV burn. *No one died*, he thought, saying a silent prayer of thanks. *All that, and no one died.*

After the operation was mopped up, Dog Company and the SF team regrouped at Kowte Ashrow for a quick debrief. Yes, they'd been bloodied. But any day they all lived was a good day.

To celebrate, Mo and Davis improvised a little dance and a song with a three-word lyric: "Hot! Hot! Hot!" They knew about Wilson's cracked ribs and were making him laugh on purpose.

Later, Mo thought a lot about the two men in the SUV, especially the passenger. Mo had been in some pretty close firefights in Ramadi, but this was different. The passenger had definitely been reaching for that secondary ignition switch and therefore deserved to die. Still, somehow, it felt like an execution.

At home, between combat tours, Mo had sometimes found himself in a crowd, wondering whether anyone else there had ever killed someone. And though he knew it was irrational, he felt the fact that he had was tattooed on his forehead, and that people were judging him for it. A shrink might call that "projection"—that Mo was really judging himself. But hanging a technical term on it didn't help. In fact, no amount of therapy, of "processing" the difference between wartime killing and ordinary murder, could grow green grass over the graves in his conscience.

Because he had killed, he would always feel separated from the rest of the world. Once you kill, Mo felt, you never get clean.

CHAPTER 34

14 August 2008

Mo SAT IN Hill's desk chair, computer monitor lighting his face, eyes moving left and right across the screen. Hill stood behind him, waiting to hear Mo's take on the letter he'd written to Brigadier General Mark Milley.

"If you think something is really wrong, contact me directly," Milley had said at Sayed Abad. Hill had decided to take the man up on his offer.

Both Mo and Hulburt had told Hill that they had never seen a unit spread so thin in their entire careers. Mo had twenty years in the Army, Hulburt fifteen. They'd been fighting in this war since it kicked off in 2001, and had been true believers. Increasingly, though, both felt in their guts that what Dog Company was being asked to do was just not right.

It wasn't that Mo and Hulburt didn't support the war in principle. It was the way it was being prosecuted, in Wardak at least. The lack of support from Battalion was not spotty nor sporadic, but consistent, glaring, and epic. The platoon sergeants understood that front-line infantry was austere work. In fact, that was part of what they loved about it. But they were calling for artillery support and being told they weren't being shot at. They were asking for things like barriers to close gaps in the FOB's perimeter wall and being denied. Instead of asking their wives to send cookies, they asked them to send batteries to run their equipment. There were shortages of ammo, food, and even water. Not all the time, but at critical times.

▆▆▆▆▆▆▆▆▆▆▆▆▆▆▆▆▆▆▆▆▆▆▆▆▆▆▆▆

▆▆▆▆▆▆▆▆▆▆▆▆▆▆▆▆▆▆▆▆▆▆▆▆▆▆▆▆

▆▆▆▆▆▆▆▆ Meanwhile, out-of-company transfers, and the province's four outposts in combination with more than two dozen wounded, had effectively fixed Hill's men in the sprawling province. Battalion had not sent a single replacement soldier. And the company had dodged so many close calls that every trip outside the wire that did not result in a man killed began to defy statistics.

Hill's private conversations with Mo and Hulburt reminded him of *Twelve O'Clock High*, a movie cadets were assigned to watch at West Point. The film starred Gregory Peck as Brigadier General Savage, an executive officer tasked to lead a bomber group during World War II, and Gary Merrill as Colonel Davenport, the commander of the outfit. Davenport's commanding general relieved him for overidentifying with his men, for being too close to them. The general believed that Davenport's caring too much for his men would ultimately place his group at a greater risk of not accomplishing the mission.

Hill sympathized with the Davenport character. He understood what it meant to love his men. His own soldiers had been asked to return year after year to some of the most undesirable locations on the planet, to fight a war that had been highly unpopular throughout the world. They had seen suffering and death. They had given their fair share, and more besides. Even beyond this, the families of these men suffered more than any family should be asked to suffer with multiple twelve- and fifteen-month deployments. In American history, no generation of soldiers had ever been asked to face the same enemy again and again, year after year, this many times. Some fathers among them had missed more than half their kids' lives.

Given the lack of resources and support, Hill had come to believe that the idea of "winning" in Wardak by any metric was a physical impossibility. It had become difficult to ask his soldiers to treat every trip outside the wire with the same intensity when he knew, and they knew, that their higher headquarters was politically driven, out of touch, and easily distracted. Meanwhile, the complex op tempo and short manning had begun grinding the men down. Though they continued to suit up daily and move to the sound of guns, Hill knew they were unraveling. Little by little, day by day. And deep down, he knew that his own priorities were beginning to shift—from accomplishing the mission to getting his brothers home alive.

Now, Hill waited quietly as Mo scrolled down through the letter to General Milley.

Sir,

    I apologize for not getting this to you sooner. The last couple of days have been busy. What I am about to tell you was a family decision that a very close group of my leaders and I have made. My leaders and I want nothing more in life than to accomplish our mission, take care of our Soldiers and get home to our families. They understand the risk assumed with contacting you over the issues I am about to discuss.

We also understand that you are extremely busy and don't see everything that goes on, especially in this decentralized operating environment. We want to fill in some gaps because the Soldiers of this company and battalion deserve better.

You hit the nail on the head when you said that a battalion is not some limbless and lifeless entity that is unable to support its companies or platoons. With that being said, I want to be clear that I do not believe in circumventing the chain of command unless a legitimate correction needs to be made. A lot of what I have to say will not adequately capture many of the intangibles that should be discussed. You'd have to talk to the Soldiers one-on-one to get that perspective, but the climate in this battalion does not honor its lineage. I'm not an extremely articulate person, and would do better in face-to-face conversation, but I'll give it my best shot.

With this situation, I've really had to think about who, in fact, is charged with holding others accountable for their actions, especially if the "others" are one's supervisors. I've had to remind myself that all leaders are responsible for holding any and all persons in their sector (up, down, left, right) responsible for doing what is right. That is where I am at right now. I first want to preface what I have to say with a few lines.

1. Our BN CSM (Battalion Command Sergeant Major Judd) is awesome. He is a man of integrity and really cares about Soldiers. He is in a difficult position due to the command climate that exists.
2. For the most part, our [Battalion] staff is stellar, but their efforts are driven by the priorities of the commander. My men have not been a priority. This was obvious to see on your visits. The BN CDR has told me to my face that he knew what he was doing to my company, and I think this is a crime.
3. The men in my company (all of them) are beyond praise. I have men in this company that people should be writing books and movies about. You've met a couple of them. Pound for pound, they are easily the best company in this Division. With that being said, I know for a fact that this company could operate without me (or any CDR)

at any time and still reach the same high level of success they have always had. They need someone to be their advocate so that they can continue to complete their mission.

4. My men do not complain about tasks they are given and they will do anything that I, or their 1SG, ask of them. They are...starting to question the mission more and I cannot cover up for some of the unreasonable requests that have been made of my men.

5. D Co also has the highest retention percentages per capita in the BN (I'm pretty sure in all of the Brigade, but I haven't seen those numbers to be sure.) This is changing because morale is dropping. The situation has surpassed my 1SG's and my ability to shield them any longer.

Lack of Foresight:

These men have sweated and bled for this province for 6 months now. At this moment, my 1SG and I are processing 20 Purple Hearts out of an 89-man Delta Company. My men have worked extremely hard to learn the human and physical terrain in this province. They have an extremely good understanding of the enemy in this area and his TTP's (Tactics, Techniques & Procedures)...We have just begun to build the intel picture to a point where we are starting to turn some important targets. In just the last 10 days, we've interdicted 4 SVBIED's and found 5 different munitions and IED making caches...

Mo read down through the next section of the letter. Here, Hill had listed the facts surrounding the two surprise movements DeMartino had ordered into the Jalrez Valley. The letter continued:

Command Climate:

When I first took over this company; the BN CDR painted a very poor picture of the outgoing CO CDR to me. As it turns out, CPT Eric Tapp (the outgoing CDR) is one of the most honorable and combat proven leaders I know. He just was not a "yes man."

...As I was taking command, the BN CDR also made several negative remarks about my 1SG and XO, and stated early on that if I wanted to have them removed that he could make that happen. The funny thing is that 1SG Scott is the best NCO I have ever worked with in my 8 years in the Army. He is easily the best 1SG in your Division. I do not exaggerate. The BN CDR also stated that my XO was "dumb" and probably would not be able to handle a company XO job. You've met my XO, speaks four different languages, graduated from the University of Florida in only 2 years, while joining the military as a Marine all while in school. He is twice the XO that I was, and he is also not a "yes man."

The reason I bring these things up is to give you a small glimpse into the day-to-day rumor mill, gossip, and command climate poisoning that goes on in this Battalion... We live in an environment of mistrust and deception. Some of the things I mentioned may seem trivial, but my 1SG and I believe that command climate is the most important combat multiplier in our organization. We attribute most of our success to a strong company climate.

The climate in this Battalion is cliquish, cutthroat, and has a single source...

My men and I appreciate your consideration. My men and I have nothing to hide, and we welcome any further dialogue. Take Care.

Respectfully,
CPT Roger Hill
Dog 6
FOB Airborne

Mo finished reading the letter and swiveled around to face Hill. "You could get in a lot of trouble, sir."

Hill regarded the sergeant, who had been a steady source of rock-solid advice. He was right. It was a drastic move, writing to the general. Political suicide. Maybe even a career ender. But there was much more at stake than his career.

Since midsummer, Hill's wife, Lauren, had been passing along information from other Dog Company wives back home. Lauren was head of the company's FRG (Family Readiness Group), which meant she was the point of contact for the families, as well as one of the first people called when a soldier was wounded or worse. Fortunately, "worse" hadn't happened, and Hill thanked God for that. But several squad-level and junior enlisted had confided in their wives that it was only a matter of time before the unit lost someone.

Reading over Mo's shoulder, Hill scanned the letter to General Milley a final time. His eye caught on the date: August 14, 2008.

"We've got six months left in-country," he said. "If we could get the shit we need, it would be worth it."

He leaned over the keyboard and pressed Send.

CHAPTER 35

15 August 2008

THE LAST THING SPC Joseph Coe remembered for sure was downing his blue Gatorade and…something?…something to do with LT Carwile. Now, lying on a litter in a MedEvac bird, Coe's memories flickered through his mind like an old flipbook movie, leached of color and slightly out of focus.

They had been on a mission to Sayed Abad, something about food and water. Yes. That was it: food and water because the Battalion CLP had forgotten to deliver any to Sayed Abad…

He remembered rolling down Highway 1…

LT Carwile in the TC seat…

Conlon up top on the gun…

"Hey, anybody got a spit bottle?" Carwile had said…

Coe's head ached. He remembered driving with his left hand, downing his Gatorade with his right and passing the empty to Carwile, who had said, "Thanks, brother…"

The next thing he remembered was waking on the side of the road in a dust storm. A blur of legs speeding past his head. Sergeant Haskins yelling and running back and forth between Humvees. Ochoa wrapping his head, telling him everything was going to be okay…

Dudley and Carlin had carried him to the helo. Dudley had picked up a loaf of bread that had blown off the supply trailer and tucked it under Coe's head as a pillow. He also remembered Dudley carrying LT Carwile, and putting him on the same bird.

Now, on the helo, Coe lifted his head off the litter, straining to see his

PL. But he couldn't see, because a couple of medics sat between them, blocking his view.

At Fort Campbell, Kentucky, Lauren Hill was snuggled down in bed sleeping lightly when her cell phone rang. The distinctive ringtone told her it was Roger. She smiled as she reached for the phone: She always had a good day when he called in the morning. That meant her husband had survived another day in Afghanistan, and she could enjoy her day teaching without the white noise of constant worry.

She breathed into the phone, "Hey, baby, is that you?"

"Hey, honey, I need you to wake up. Can you do that for me? Wake up, baby."

"Okay..." Lauren said. "Everything okay?"

The sound of her, warm and alive, clashed in Hill's brain with the whirling smoke, the bloody pavement, the policing up from the earlier ambush. The bomb-trigger device and more than a kilometer of wire had been left behind. Those items would have some intelligence value. But the enemy was long gone, their exfil well planned.

Larry Kay and remnants of the Shockers and the Dirty First appeared as ants in the distance as they searched surrounding *qalats* for traces of the IED trigger team. Nearby, other soldiers picked through a bizarre mix of blackened bomb debris and undamaged bags of hot dog buns and breakfast sausages. Contrasting worlds warred in Hill's chest, making it hard to breathe.

He focused. "Yeah, I'm okay, but I don't have much time. Remember our deal about you taking time off if something happened?"

"Yeah...?" Hill heard her voice shed its drowsy warmth, come fully alert: "Yes."

"I need you to call into work today. You are going to need to stay home today, okay?"

"Wha—why? Is someone hurt?"

"Baby, just call in and stay home so that you're ready. Some of our ladies are going to need you today. Do you understand?"

Shock and dread coalesced in Lauren's mind. She struggled to absorb her husband's words. As the Family Readiness Group leader, she had fielded dozens of calls about wounded men, but Roger had never asked her to stay home. That could only mean one thing: The worst had happened. And it wasn't just happening *there*; it was about to happen here, too.

She found her voice. "Yes...yes, I understand."

"I gotta go."

"Okay...I love you, Roger."

"I love you, too, baby."

The line clicked shut. Lauren managed to dial the principal of her school and stammer out that she wouldn't be in because she was sick. It was only half a lie: She sprang from the bed, ran to the bathroom, thrust her face over the toilet, and retched.

In Cape Cod, Massachusetts, Maria Conlon awoke in a panic. She sat up in bed, her heart tattooing against her ribs. Something was wrong with one of her sons.

Maria threw off her covers and went straight to her computer. She and Paul had a system: He couldn't share specifics on his whereabouts, but if he logged in to his MySpace page, she'd be able to see the time stamp and know he was okay. She'd talked to him on the phone just the day before. The arm that had taken the shrapnel was still painful enough that Paul couldn't even lift a case of soda. There was a mission coming up and he was supposed to stay on the FOB, keep on recuperating. Instead, he'd talked his way onto one of the trucks.

Maria tapped her keyboard and the computer came to life. She scrolled down to Paul's latest MySpace entry. She gazed at the numbers, did a quick mental calculation. Today was August 15. Paul had last logged in early that morning, Wardak time. Eastern Afghanistan was eight and a half hours ahead of Cape Cod. So as of about six hours ago, he was safe.

Okay, that was one son accounted for—sort of. Maria picked up her phone and called her oldest, Daniel, at work. No answer. Not unusual for a workday, though.

Maybe it's nothing, she thought. But intuition told her otherwise. She couldn't count the number of times she'd felt something was wrong with one of her boys and had been right. Maria picked up the phone again, this time dialing her boss to say she wasn't coming in.

At midday, Lauren Hill stared at her ringing cell phone. The caller ID said: JENNIFER CARWILE. Word was out in the company that something terrible had happened. Jennifer, her best friend, would ask her point-blank what it was. Tears welled in Lauren's eyes. The rules were clear: She couldn't tell anyone what she knew.

The cell trilled half a dozen times then rolled to voice mail.

She remembered a conversation with Jennifer just before Roger and

Donnie deployed. Jennifer had been on the verge of tears. "I don't want to be the only one crying when we say good-bye," she said.

"Don't worry," Lauren said, "I'll bring the Kleenex and we can cry together."

Jennifer had laughed with relief.

The memory made Lauren catch her breath and at the exact same moment, her cell renewed its ringing. It was Jennifer again.

Lauren eyed the phone as if it were a live thing. Finally, it went silent.

The third time her cell rang, Lauren couldn't stand it anymore. She picked up the phone. "Hey, Jennifer."

"Lauren, I've been trying to call you! I heard something happened. What's going on?"

"Jennifer, I'm sorry. I don't know anything. I wish I could tell you more, but I don't know anything."

It was her second lie of the day.

Jennifer Carwile stood at her front door scanning the street, cell phone clutched in her hand. In the early morning, another Dog Company wife had called her. "Something bad has happened," she said, "but my husband wouldn't tell me what it is."

Lauren had said she didn't know and Simone DeMartino, the Battalion commander's wife, wasn't answering her phones. Whatever had happened, Simone was probably busy dealing with it, Jennifer thought. But an unwelcome intuition rippled in her gut. She'd dropped her oldest daughter, Reece, off at kindergarten at 8 a.m. Now it was after noon, Avery Claire was down for a nap, and Jennifer was pacing her entryway, peering through the screen door at the street like a sea captain's wife on a widow's walk.

Since Donnie shipped out with Delta Company in March, Jennifer had checked the news constantly, even though Robyn Haskins, Shon's wife, had advised her to stop obsessing. As a registered nurse, Jennifer was used to research, and she'd found that non-U.S. news sources were more forthcoming. That morning, she'd read on a foreign site that two ISAF soldiers had been killed in eastern Afghanistan.

It's nothing, she'd told herself. *There are thousands of soldiers there.* But now as she stared out the screen door, she couldn't get the report out of her mind.

When the Black Hawk touched down, medics hustled Joseph Coe into a tent. A flurry of faces, hands, and questions came at him.

"Where do you hurt?"

"Everywhere. My head, my arms, my back, my legs. I just freakin' hurt."

"Do you know where you are?"

"Yes, in Afghanistan, at the aid station." Coe saw a tangle of IV lines, heard orders barked out. "My L.T. Do you know what happened to my L.T.?"

Hands scissored off his ACUs and they fell away.

"Do you know your name?"

"Yes. Coe. Joseph Coe. How's my L.T.? He was sitting in the right seat of my truck. And my gunner, Paul Conlon. I haven't seen him. Is he hurt?"

It seemed to Coe there was a beat of silence. He tried to hike himself up on his elbows, make eye contact with someone. Hands pressed him back onto the gurney. More questions flew about the pain in his head, the pain in his back, what day it was.

Coe shot back questions about Conlon and Carwile—Where were they? Had anyone seen them?—but it was as though he were trapped in a glass bubble with his words bouncing off the inside. Anger swelled in his chest. He thrashed on the gurney, tried to throw off restraining hands.

"I'm looking for Lieutenant Donald Carwile! He's a little bit taller than me! Heavier than me! He was sitting in the TC seat of my truck! *Is he hurt?"*

A woman in scrubs appeared before him. "Take it easy, Coe," she said gently. "Take it—"

"Conlon! Specialist Paul Conlon! Shorter than me! Dark hair, buzz cut! He was my gunner! I haven't seen either of them! *Does anyone know who I'm talking about?!"*

Coe's anger melted down to seething rage. He wanted to scream, *Don't anyone fucking touch me until someone tells me something! Tell me they're fine, tell me they're hurt, tell me they're dead, but tell me something!*

He didn't scream, though. Instead, he went graveyard still. Because suddenly, he knew.

A warm summer rain pattered on the Carwiles' driveway, whispering in the grass that sloped down to the street. From the screen door, Jennifer could see it was time to mow again. She'd never cut grass in her life until May, when she got a nastygram from the post housing office warning her about her knee-high lawn. She would've been mortified if Donnie got word in Afghanistan that she was letting the house go to pot. That afternoon, she had plunked the girls in front of a Disney video and wrestled the lawnmower out of the garage. She muscled it up the overgrown slope, fighting it on the downhill to keep it from getting away and roaring out into the street. Determined to quash all future housing-office notices, Jennifer mowed down everything in sight, including the yellow-budded ornamental bushes in the flower beds. By June, she figured out that going sideways across the slope with the mower was easier. In her newfound confidence, she also let the flowers live.

Jennifer glanced at the clock on her cell. It was nearly 2 p.m. Something had happened. "Something bad," the other wife had said.

She sighed and let her shoulders relax. If it was Donnie, she thought, they would've come by now, wouldn't they?

Robyn was right. She *had* to stop obsessing. She was about to turn away from the front door when a car turned into her driveway. It was a black sedan.

At the Conlon home, morning and early afternoon ticked by like a metronome. The day was nearing an end. In the afternoons, Maria and her sister, Victoria, usually went to the gym together. Victoria was twenty years younger than Maria, more like a sister to Paul than an aunt. She arrived and tried to talk Maria into going, but Maria couldn't. She didn't say so, but she wasn't leaving the house until she heard from both her boys.

"Okay, are you sure?" Victoria said.

"Yes, I'm sure. You go, though."

Dressed for a workout, Victoria left, shutting the door behind her.

A moment later, the door burst open again. "*Maria!*" Victoria's face was white with panic. "There are two soldiers coming!"

Maria did not look outside. She knew who the soldiers were. Somehow, she had known all day that they were coming.

She put her hands on Victoria's shoulders and smiled. "It's okay," she said. "You should go, though."

Maria had gotten her baby sister all the way to the door, but it was too late. When she opened the door, two officers in dress uniforms stood on her porch. One wore the insignia of a chaplain.

"Are you Maria Conlon?" said the other one, the casualty officer.

"Yes."

"I have an important message to deliver from the Secretary of the Army. May we come in?"

Beside her, Victoria began to shake and cry. A preternatural calm enveloped Maria, though. A strength from somewhere else. Strength for her sister. She escorted the officers into her living room, where they sat next to each other stiffly, backs erect.

Maria thought they both looked like they'd prefer to be somewhere else, even in combat, anywhere other than where they were now. She didn't want them there, either. She didn't want them to say the words, didn't want this moment burned into her sister's memory.

Maria sat calm and dry-eyed. "Would you like something to drink?"

"No thank you," the casualty officer said. He took a deep breath and began, "The Secretary of the Army has asked me to express his deep regret that your son, Paul Edward Conlon, was killed in action in Wardak, Afghanistan, on August 15. The Secretary extends his deepest sympathy to you and your family in your tragic loss..."

Maria listened to the entire recitation. The chaplain gazed at her sympathetically. The casualty assistance officer looked prepared for a blow. She could imagine what they encountered in this grim job: shock, anger, hysteria. But she wasn't going to make it any harder for them than it was already.

"Do you have any additional details?" she asked in an even tone.

"No, ma'am," the casualty officer said. "I'm sorry."

"Thank you very much, gentlemen," Maria said, and stood.

The visitors took her cue and walked with her to the front door. She shook each of their hands, shut the door behind them, and locked the dead bolt. Then Maria Conlon fell to her foyer floor and started screaming.

BOOK 3

Inquest

Is it possible to succeed without any act of betrayal?

Jean Renoir

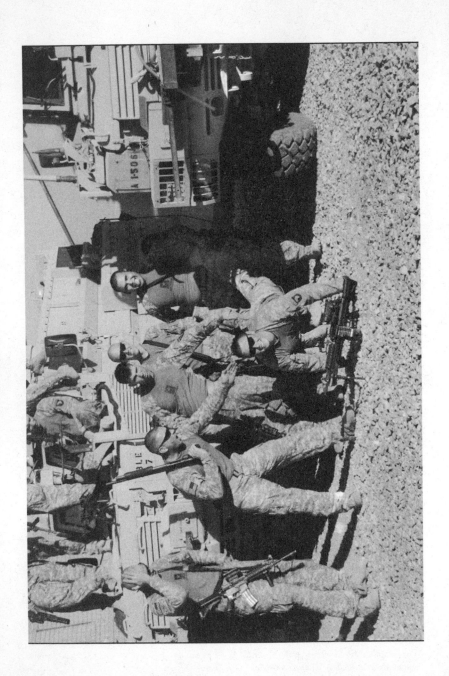

CHAPTER I

27 AUGUST 2008
FOB Airborne Coffeehouse

THE GUNSHOT ECHO died away, and all eyes locked on Roger Hill as his six-foot-three frame filled the coffeehouse door, Beretta 9 mm still in his hand. "Who's ready to talk?"

The ninety-six-hour clock was almost out on Kassiss and the Dalmar brothers and Hill was on a single-minded quest: confessions. D Co's options were limited. The only way Hill could legitimately increase the amount of time their prisoners stayed off the streets was if he could convince the National Directorate of Security to take them again, all of them this time. When NDS took custody before, they did so primarily on Hill's word that the prisoners were dirty. Upon returning the detainees to Airborne, the NDS deputy said his commander had chastised him because D Co had not provided evidence. But that was because Hill was not allowed to: The evidence of espionage compiled by Dave and the counterintel team was classified Secret NOFORN—Hill could not share it with foreign nationals, even if they were considered allies.

Now, the only way to persuade NDS that these guys really were spies was to get them to confess. That would be unclassified. It was the only way to keep from letting them go, the only way to shield his base and his men from retaliatory attack.

Hill scanned the room. Sammy still stood flex-cuffed in the center. Hill looked past him to other prisoners of lesser intel value. He pointed at a pair of men against the wall. "Those two," he said.

As Peake, Doyle, and Moser moved to follow the order, a couple of prisoners started to speak up in Pashto. Hill ignored them. The clock was ticking down, and he wanted to drive the threat home.

Peake and Doyle double-teamed one prisoner; Moser handled the other on his own. Both resisted being pulled to their feet, then fought every step. Peake and Doyle had just hustled their man through the coffeehouse door when Moser's prisoner dropped prone to the floor in defiance. Deftly, Moser flipped him to his back, bear-hugged him from behind and dragged him backward out the door.

The detainee already outside lay on his side, hands zip-tied behind his back. Hill realized immediately that he had a problem. He wasn't sure why the first detainee hadn't cried out. But for the detainees inside to think the ones outside were dead, they all had to be kept quiet.

"I need to gag them so they don't talk to each other," he said to the guards.

One of the guards dashed back into the coffeehouse and returned with a handful of rags. One by one, the guards wrapped the prisoners' mouths, knotting the rags behind their necks.

But when Moser tried to gag his detainee, the prisoner dipped his head and sank his teeth into Moser's hand.

"Fuck!" Moser screamed. He clocked the prisoner with a closed fist, but the man's jaws remained locked on Moser's hand. "Mother*fucker*!"

Moser punched the prisoner again, and then again until he knocked him loose.

Hill grabbed Moser's shoulder. "Hey! Hey! Stop it! Come on, man!"

"But sir, this fucker *bit* me!"

"I know, but look—now his lip's bleeding. What did I say about hurting these guys? We just want to scare them, okay?"

His face still flushed with pain, Moser clasped his injured hand with the other.

"We're good out here, brother," Hill said. "Run in and give the other guys a hand. I'll finish up out here."

Moser hung his head. "Roger, sir," he said, and trudged back inside.

"All right, that's all I need from you guys," Hill said, nodding to the other guards.

Once everyone was inside, Hill moved toward a wall of HESCO barriers running down the backside of the coffeehouse. He walked off about six paces from the prisoners. He stopped and, for a moment, gazed off into the distance, wondering again how he had arrived at this moment. He had already colored far outside the lines on detainee handling. Openhanded slapping, the shot he'd fired. He hadn't endangered anyone, but all that was against the rules.

The "rules," he thought. The fucking rules.

Wouldn't want to scare these poor Taliban spies, would we? Wouldn't want to play hardball in a war.

Battalion had made it painfully clear: They weren't coming. Now, Hill stood at the intersection of bad policy and poor leadership, his career and his livelihood in the path of a head-on crash. He could have chosen differently. He could have let the clock run out, had his guys escort Sammy and the rest to the gate. But that would have saved only himself. His ass would be covered, but his men's lives would be on the line. That was not an acceptable risk.

Hill raised the Beretta and fired two shots toward the barriers, into the dirt, at intervals he hoped sounded long enough for a man to fall dead in between.

Hill safed his weapon and turned around. All three prisoners lay on the ground, caked in moondust and sweat. He walked back toward the coffeehouse, narrowly missing MAJ Jack Cheasty, a physician's assistant who had come to Airborne to fill in for the FOB physician's assistant, who had gone on leave. Hill hadn't noticed him there before. Had he seen Hill fire the shots? No time to worry about that now.

Hill glanced at his watch and wondered if the ruse had been played well enough to get someone to talk. Any confessions would help move the detainees into Afghan custody. The Dalmars would be a home run.

He stepped back through the door, slamming it closed for emphasis.

"Well? Anyone?" he yelled.

Silence. Scott had returned from the ECP. He traded glances with Hill.

"Okay, two more!" Hill said. As if he had flipped a switch, several prisoners piped up at once. Hill glared at Sammy. Voice shaking, the terp translated and gestured with his chin. "He wants to talk...and this one, this one wants to say something."

Hill and Scott separated the remaining prisoners. The guards brought water.

Once the dam broke, information flowed freely. Hill pulled a notepad from his pocket and began to jot notes. The prisoners had been calling both enemy handlers and intermediaries, passing on devastating data: times of troop movements, number of vehicles, number of soldiers, direction of travel. These details were then being passed up to higher Taliban commanders who alerted regional commanders based on where a convoy was traveling.

Hill learned no high-level names, but gleaned more than enough unclassified enemy tactical and procedural data to plus up the evidence packets. Now the NDS could take them without risk to their careers.

Hill's spirits lifted. "All right, get these guys cleaned up," he told the guards. "I've got what I need."

That night at 1845, Larry Kay settled in for the FOB synch meeting. Tommy Scott sat to Kay's left. On his right sat CPT B and Taz, the ████████ team leader. Facing Kay on the other side of the table was his roommate, 2LT Pat Curran, along with Hulburt and the platoon leaders, including Zachary Morris, the young lieutenant DeMartino had sent to replace Donnie Carwile.

Hill was about to take his seat when the Airborne operations officer, Major Robert Fulmer, pulled him aside. Fulmer had just replaced Major Chris Faber, who had been promoted to a staff position in Logar Province.

Fulmer spoke quietly. "The governor called and said he had heard reports of detainee abuse on our FOB. I just wanted to let you guys know."

"Hey, sir, thanks. I appreciate it."

Hill took his seat. Kay led the meeting, with the usual rundowns on maintenance, weapons, intel, and missions.

Then Hill spoke up. "Hey guys, there have been some reports of detainee abuse circulating. In fact, the governor has called to inquire. As you know, we've been up to our necks in rooting out some insider threats. A lot has been going on in the way of questioning and detaining these guys. Let's try and keep any rumors to a minimum. If it comes up, just squash it until we get this whole thing sorted out."

The accusation, however, rankled Tommy Scott. "You know what? That's a bunch of bullshit. They're not here. They don't know what's going on. Fuck 'em."

The Dog Company platoon leaders smiled and Hulburt chuckled out loud. He knew his commander and his first sergeant well enough to know that neither of them would abuse prisoners.

Then the meeting was over. A half hour later, Able Company's leaders filed in. Able had arrived in Wardak a couple of weeks prior to relieve D Co in place. The company was still acclimating to operations in the province, a task made even more difficult since their new commander, CPT Al LeMaire, had been blown up by the IED that killed Carwile and Conlon.

Hill had purposely limited A Co's involvement in rooting out Airborne's spies. Now, at the start of their nightly meeting, he reiterated what he'd said to his own team: If you hear a rumor of detainee abuse, just squash it until all the insider threats have been sorted out and removed.

Back at his desk, Kay looked at the clock on his computer. In less than eight hours, they would have to release the prisoners. He picked up his Roshan cell and dialed Battalion. It was the sixth time on this particular issue. Frustrating.

"Ghazni TOC, Sergeant First Class Hammonds speaking."

"Hey, Sergeant, this is Lieutenant Kay. What do you guys want us to do with these detainees? We're running out of time to hold them. We need to get them sent up to Battalion or something so we don't have to let them go."

"We're working on a solution, sir. Trying to help you guys out."

Kay sighed. Battalion was in the process of relocating to its headquarters. Was that why no one could spare the time to process D Co's prisoners? He wasn't sure, but he was tired of being strung along. "Look, we're gonna have to hand these guys over to NDS in the morning."

"All right, that's fine," the sergeant said. "You do what you have to do."

2LT Zachary Morris was troubled. The talk at the FOB synch meeting about detainee abuse was, well…disturbing. CPT Hill had seemed to say that if anyone heard something about detainee abuse, they should lie about it. One of Hill's sergeants had actually laughed. And 1SG Scott seemed not to care what anyone thought.

Morris's reception at Dog Company hadn't been exactly welcoming. The XO, Larry Kay, had dressed him down within five minutes of reporting. Sergeant Haskins had stiff-armed him. Meanwhile, CPT Hill didn't have the best reputation at Battalion. The conflict between him and LTC DeMartino was well known. Morris had worked in the Ghazni TOC for several weeks and had seen the battle captains running interference.

Morris hadn't been at Airborne a week and he could already see that Dog Company was lazy about details. Soldiers on the FOB running around out of uniform, wearing T-shirts or flip-flops. Could the lack of discipline extend to freelancing with detainees?

Morris wasn't sure.

He thought about calling Battalion and reporting what he'd heard at the synch meeting. He'd already earned a reprimand from LT Kay, though, and he didn't want to make things worse. But if the detainees at the coffeehouse really had been abused, shouldn't he say something?

Morris talked it over with two other soldiers, LT Anthony Dey and SGT Jared Allen, both of Alpha Company. Then he thought it over some more. Finally, Zachary Morris found a quiet spot, pulled out his cell phone, and dialed Battalion.

CHAPTER 2

28 August 2008

WRAPPED TACO STYLE in his blanket, Larry Kay was dreaming. An ancient eastern warrior was prodding him toward a cliff's edge, forcing him along at the point of a sword.

Lieutenant! the dream-warrior whispered, jabbing him in the back.

Kay rolled over and opened his eyes. His tormenter dissolved into the darkness, replaced by Tommy Scott.

"Lieutenant! Time to hit the gym!"

Kay groaned and scrubbed a hand through his crew cut. "What time is it?"

"Oh four hundred. Rise and shine!"

"Are you kidding me right now? Wake me up when *you* get done working out. I'm going back to sleep."

Scott walked away laughing.

An hour later, Kay was up and in the TOC. The Combat Logistics Patrol was inbound that day with, Kay fervently hoped, some vehicle parts he had ordered over two months before. On the TOC Blue Force Tracker, Kay monitored their progress from Ghazni toward Airborne.

The NDS was slated to come pick up the detainees, so by 0600, MAJ Cheasty and Doc Brincefield, a medic, were busy examining prisoners at the coffeehouse. Hill had asked them to make a detailed record of the prisoners' physical condition prior to their transfer to NDS. Hill wanted to be sure D Co had written records of the detainees' condition before turning them over. When the exams were complete, each prisoner was given a change of clothes and an opportunity to wash up.

When Kay checked the BFT again, the CLP was just a click away, the lone icon on the screen. He went out to meet the trucks near the flagpole. Kay was mentally composing the nastygram he would fire off to Ghazni if his parts didn't come when an unexpected face startled him: Major Rob Smith, the Battalion XO. He had replaced John Karagosian in the slot weeks earlier.

Smith returned Kay's salute.

"Hi, sir," Kay said. "Did you come up with the CLP?"

"No, I came with the mortars. Where's Captain Hill? I need to see Captain Hill or Major Fulmer," Smith said.

"Roger that, sir. Let me go get Captain Hill."

Kay walked away, puzzling. An unannounced visit by a higher-up? It had literally never happened.

Flash. A burst of light bloomed in front of Sammy, who had raised his shirt to expose his torso.

"Turn him around," MAJ Smith said to a guard. He held up a small digital camera and snapped a picture of Sammy's back. The flash fired again.

Summoned by Kay, Hill had met Smith at the TOC. The major said he wanted to see the detainees. Immediately. A little hope had blossomed inside Hill: Maybe Battalion was coming through after all. He'd had Scott escort Smith to the coffeehouse. Scott then stood by as D Co's guards brought the prisoners to the XO, one by one. Smith snapped multiple pictures of each detainee, capturing the condition of each man's face, chest, belly, and back. He also had each man drop his pants.

With the prisoners examined, Smith exited the coffeehouse. Hill met him outside and the two headed down the hill. "I don't see anything wrong with those guys," Smith said casually.

"That's because there's nothing wrong with them, sir," Hill said. The two men laughed softly.

Back at the TOC, Smith sat down and made a list of people he wanted to interview. Later he disclosed that he was at Airborne to conduct a "15-6," a commander's inquiry into allegations of detainee abuse.

CHAPTER 3

29 August 2008

SMITH HAD BEEN running down his list, questioning numerous men. Then he called in Larry Kay. Having never been questioned in connection with a criminal act before, Kay found it an interesting academic exercise. In fact, after being shot at on a regular basis, he thought it might have been the least nerve-racking thing he'd done since landing in Afghanistan.

Kay was certain that Captain Hill and 1SG Scott had handled the detainees appropriately. In the TOC conference room, Smith had a standard 15-6 form waiting for him, a single sheet of paper lying on the long table. Kay sat down.

After dispensing with preliminary formalities, Smith got to the money questions:

"Have you seen any detainees being abused?"

"Have you heard rumors of detainee abuse?"

"Have you heard of a cover-up of detainee abuse?"

Kay's answers were no, no, and no.

"Thank you, Lieutenant. That's all I have," Smith said.

Kay exited the room as comfortably as he'd entered it.

Later that day, a Black Hawk touched down at the Airborne LZ. The bird carried four people in its belly: LTC Dixon Gunther, the deputy commanding officer of the Brigade; JAG[17] officer CPT Stephen Latino, a lawyer for the Brigade; Captain Victoria Scragg, the Brigade provost; and a law enforcement professional, or LEP, consulting with the Army. That afternoon, a convoy arrived, picked up Major Smith, and ferried him away. A new investigation was about to begin.

---

17. JAG: Judge Advocate General.

CHAPTER 4

30 August 2008

GUNTHER, LATINO, AND Scragg set up in Major Faber's old office and began interviewing soldiers. A former special operations planner and combat training battalion commander, Gunther did not like what he saw when he walked in Airborne's front gate: the charred, mangled carcass of a Humvee. It was clearly the truck involved in the IED incident, the one that had claimed two soldiers' lives. The wreck should've been hauled off the FOB already, not sitting there as a constant reminder of Dog Company's loss.

As the investigators combed the base, soldiers began to verbally and openly protest their presence. Some began to hunker in their quarters, fearful that if an investigator spotted them they'd be dragged in for another round of questions.

Scragg called in 4th Platoon to give their statements as a group. She was able to corral 1st Platoon on one of its rare stops inside the wire. All twelve men filled out their statements at the chow hall.

Afterward, Hulburt grabbed his guys and held a come-to-Jesus meeting.

"Look, one thing about the Army is, when you're in trouble, you don't have any friends. The higher-ups, they'll try to screw us. We weren't even here for this shit, but that doesn't matter. I'm telling you all right now, they're going to try to turn this into a fucking war crimes tribunal. The point is not to find out what really happened. The point is to make somebody else pay for making the higher-ups look bad."

Hulburt pulled a fresh cigarette from his blouse pocket, lit it, took a drag. "The most important thing for us is to stay together as a platoon when this is all over. The way we're gonna do that is to stay out of this shit. We're gonna stay outside the wire as much as possible."

Hill found Kay in their hooch and gave him the play-by-play on what had happened at the coffeehouse. "I'm sorry I didn't tell you, Larry. I was trying to keep you out of it. I figured the less you knew, the less you'd be accountable for."

Hill excused himself and went back to his office. Kay felt angry and disappointed. He skipped dinner, his stomach too upset for food, and roamed the FOB in a daze. He didn't even want to do the one thing that always made him feel better: talk to Jill, his wife.

Kay remembered reviewing detention procedures in ROTC and later in Officer Basic, where Abu Ghraib was Exhibit A on how not to treat prisoners. The whole topic had seemed academic and faraway then, one of those "never in a million years" things.

That night, Kay couldn't sleep. He lay on his bunk and stared at the ceiling. He knew he hadn't done anything illegal, but he still felt like a suspect.

MAJ Jack Cheasty walked into Hill's office, closed the door, and said without preface, "You need to get a lawyer."

Hill drew back, surprised. "For what?"

"Listen, I've seen this before. When there's an investigation like this, everyone wears the same patch and works for the same boss, including the investigators."

Cheasty had already served thirty years in the Army, first as a combat photographer in Vietnam. He'd been in his most recent firefight just a few weeks earlier, in Kapisa, at the age of sixty-two. Hill had met him only briefly when he first reported to Airborne.

A phrase the major used jumped out at Hill: *the same patch.* He flashed to watching the helo land that had deposited Gunther, Latino, and Scragg on the FOB. Behind it, there had been a second helo. As if reviewing a slow-motion film clip, Hill saw several soldiers stepping off that bird, one at a time. The first thing that had struck him then was how *clean* their uniforms were in comparison with those of his front-line soldiers—as if these new arrivals were about to appear in a Tide commercial instead of serve in a war zone. Second, Hill had noticed patches Velcroed to their shoulders emblazoned with the letters CID.

Criminal Investigation Division.

"These guys get fitness reports just like you do, Roger," Cheasty was saying. "In my experience, they will look for the answers they think their boss wants them to find."

Since the memorial service for Donnie and Paul, Hill had been trying desperately to get back to a normal schedule of operations. Despite manning shortages, he was still sending his platoons on missions. The investigators were keeping him largely in the dark, and that was fine. He was confident that when the truth came out, this whole thing would blow over.

That was why Hill had tried to leave a door open with his mentor, MAJ Robert Smith. While Smith was still at Airborne, he had asked Hill to fill out the same statement that Larry Kay and the other guys filled out. Hill answered no to all the questions but he did not sign the statement. When he returned the form to Smith, he left the unsigned signature page on top.

It was a tacit request for help. He hoped that MAJ Smith, being so familiar with his past performance and ethics, would see that this incident was being blown out of proportion. The major was now second in command under DeMartino. Hill hoped he would step in as a voice of reason, especially after having seen the condition of the prisoners.

Hill didn't like the fact that CID was crawling all over his base. The effect was like a poison, with rumors worming across the FOB—Scott beating detainees to a pulp, prisoners with broken bones, even water-boarding. It reminded him of the Salem witch trials, where rumors assumed the outlines of truth and inquisitors filled in the rest.

Still, Hill had work to do. Because some of the detainees had confessed to working for the Taliban, NDS had taken the lot of them. Now, he and CPT B were working hard to get the prisoners moved to a NATO facility in Bagram so that the prisoners could remain in custody and off the battlefield. Meanwhile, Hill resolved to pursue business as usual until the witch hunt burned itself out.

Doc Cheasty was still standing in front of his desk. "Your guys are already spooked, and there are rumors that this is going to get ugly," he said. "I come from a family of lawyers. You need to get one, and I would advise you not to talk to anyone but him."

"Thanks, Jack," Hill said. And he meant it. But in his heart, he really didn't think it would come to that.

CHAPTER 5

1 September 2008

IN THE TOC, Scott hunched over his desk working his numbers. Who was where right now? Where could he thin his lines to put more guys on the perimeter? He penciled through a couple of manning roster scenarios. Nothing added up.

He was already doing all kinds of gymnastics to keep missions running. He'd moved SPC John Paul Castro from HQ to 3rd Platoon. Castro was combat tested and had earned a Purple Heart in Ramadi after being blown up by an IED. Moving him would boost Haskins's numbers.

Still, Scott felt like he was shoveling sand into a holey bucket. The LEP who'd landed with the investigators had taken more of his men to go over to NDS and interview the detainees.

Scott threw down his pencil and picked up his stress ball. Nobody gave a damn about the prisoners when D Co was trying to get someone to take custody. Now Battalion and Brigade seemed to have all kinds of manpower to throw at them. A couple of doors away, Gunther and Scragg were still questioning soldiers. As far as Scott knew, the only people who hadn't been questioned yet were him and Captain Hill. Scott expected to be called in any minute and the truth was, he couldn't wait. He *wanted* to be interviewed. He wanted everyone to know exactly what had happened at the coffeehouse and why.

Scott was confident that when higher learned the limits of his and Captain Hill's actions—and the intel that motivated them both—Battalion and Brigade would lay the matter to rest. In twenty-four years of active duty,

Scott never had gotten within a mile of any disciplinary infraction. Never even so much as an adverse counseling statement. If he had to accept an Article 15 because he had slapped those guys, so be it. It might keep him from his dream of making sergeant major and retiring at the top of the enlisted rank structure, but it would be worth it.

With no help from Battalion, it had come down to a choice: either get confessions, or release those assholes and wait for them to strike back.

Scott had chosen to protect his boys, just as he felt their moms and dads back home would expect him to do.

Now his stomach rumbled. He headed up to the chow hut, grabbed a plate of grub, and sat down to eat. Behind him, two soldiers were talking.

"Did you see that picture of Sammy with blood all over him?" one was saying.

A scarlet flush descended over Scott. He spun full around and addressed the speaker. "What are you talking about?"

"The investigators showed us pictures of Sammy. His face was all busted up and he had blood all over the front of his shirt."

Scott abandoned his food and walked straight back to his office to find out what was going on. Sammy wasn't even one of the guys Scott had slapped. Did Captain Hill know about this? Where were the photographs that MAJ Smith took before Dog Company turned the prisoners over to NDS? The ones that showed the detainees in perfect condition?

He had just made it back to his desk when LTC Gunther appeared at the door of his office. "All right, First Sergeant, we're ready to interview you now."

The next moments became surreal.

...Scott following Gunther to the conference room...Gunther picking up a sheet of paper...reading Scott his rights...

He had the right to remain silent, the right to consult a lawyer. If he made a statement, it could be used as evidence against him...

Scott listened to UCMJ Article 31, the military version of Miranda rights he'd heard read to bad guys on a thousand cop shows, and he couldn't believe they were being read to him.

Impatiently, he waited for Gunther to finish. Scott was still ready to tell him everything that happened. He had yelled at those men, yes. He had slapped a couple of them with an open hand, yes. But that was it. And he hadn't laid a hand on Sammy. He'd been trying to scare those guys into confessing. He had been trying to keep them in custody so they couldn't come back and do what they'd done to Conlon and Carwile.

He had been doing what every first sergeant had taught him since he joined the Army: protecting his men.

Surely, Gunther would see that. Surely he would understand. If it were his men, he'd want the same thing.

Gunther finished his recitation and said, "Do you understand your rights, First Sergeant Scott?"

"Yes, sir."

"What would you like to do?"

Scott looked into Gunther's eyes and measured what he saw there.

"I want a lawyer," Scott said.

CHAPTER 6

3 *September* 2008

WHEN LTC GUNTHER summoned him to the TOC conference room for
an interview, Hill braced himself for an inquisition. Instead, he got a warm
and welcoming smile.

"Hi, Roger," Gunther said genially.

"You wanted to see me, sir?"

Hill had seen Gunther's name on a parking spot back at Campbell, but
he'd never met him. Now he took a seat opposite Gunther at the long conference table, but the senior officer moved to a chair on the same side.

"Roger, you guys have a tough mission out here," Gunther began.

"Yes, sir, we do."

"I was able to collect some stats on some of what you all have gone
through since you got here six months ago." He then recited perfectly the
dimensions of Dog Company's enormous battlespace; the number of outposts Hill was responsible for; the number of firefights, IEDs, enemy KIAs,
wounded friendlies. He ended with the deaths of Carwile and Conlon.

To hear the accumulation of events spoken aloud was oddly comforting
to Hill. It seemed someone had finally taken notice, that maybe all Dog
Company had endured had not been under the radar after all.

Gunther smiled. "You guys are doing a lot of good stuff out here, Roger."

"Thank you, sir."

"I know you've seen a lot out here. When I was in combat, back in Desert
Shield and Desert Storm, I saw some pretty bad stuff. I understand."

"Yes, sir." Gunther had seen carnage, it was clear, and there is no one who can understand what that's like except another combat commander.

Hill began to relax a little. "Sir, it *has* been tough," he said. "I really have not felt that I could trust my commander. I've tried and he's left me hanging on several occasions. When confronted, he's gone as far as to tell me outright that we needed more SIGACTs in this province. And as the busiest company in the Battalion, we've seen the least amount of resources..."

Hill continued for a few minutes and Gunther listened intently, nodding, encouraging. For Hill, it was good to let it out, to feel that he was genuinely being heard.

Gunther then slid a sheet of paper over to Hill.

"Listen," he said. "I have some statements I'd like to ask you to sign here before we continue our conversation further."

"Okay," Hill said, picking up the paper to read it.

"I'll have to read you your rights and then you'd have to sign here, noting that you agree to speak to me and waive your rights, or that you don't desire to speak to me at this time and that you'd like to seek out an attorney."

Gunther held out a pen.

Hill's eyes hardened. Major Cheasty's advice about getting a lawyer clanged in his brain, and he felt like a fool for having opened up to Gunther.

Gently, Hill placed the sheet of paper back on the conference table, unconsciously squaring it with the table's edge.

"Sir, thank you," Hill said, "but I don't wish to speak to you any further." He took the proffered pen and signed the line indicating that he wished to remain silent.

"Well," Gunther said, "I guess that settles that."

He seemed to Hill rather surprised.

CHAPTER 7

4 September 2008

AT 2000 HOURS, or 8 p.m., Hill and Scott reported back to the TOC conference room, where LTC Gunther and CPT Victoria Scragg were waiting. Gunther had asked Kay, along with Shockers Platoon Sergeant Kris Wilson, to wait outside, so they did, Kay sitting on a case of MREs, Wilson beside him.

In the conference room, Hill and Scott stood at attention. Neither man expected to walk away without a reprimand, even a formal reprimand, the kind that remains in your service record. They'd talked about it and were prepared for that.

A voice came over the speakerphone. It was COL Pete Johnson, the Brigade commander, calling from his HQ at FOB Salerno out on the Pakistan border. Hill and Scott had last seen Johnson at the memorial service, where he was head of the official party.

"Captain Hill? First Sergeant Scott?"

"Yes, sir," both men replied.

"Captain Hill and First Sergeant Scott, I am greatly disturbed by what Lieutenant Colonel Gunther and the investigators have brought to my attention. It is at this time that I suspend your duties as commander and first sergeant. Captain Hill, you are to hand over authority to Lieutenant Kay, who is temporarily assigned as commander of Dog Company, with Sergeant First Class Kris Wilson as his acting first sergeant."

For Hill, something very like shock set in. He felt confused, light-headed. Johnson's voice suddenly faded to a murmur.

Scott stood stiff, eyes fixed straight ahead.

Johnson continued. "In addition, you are no longer allowed to speak with anyone from the company. You are also not allowed to talk to each other. I am placing a gag order on both of you. You are to immediately hand over your weapons to Lieutenant Colonel Gunther and Captain Scragg."

On the other side of the door, Kay and Wilson could hear every word. They locked eyes and shook their heads. Kay propped his elbows on his knees and lowered his face into his hands.

Inside the conference room, Hill heard Johnson say something about packing a rucksack, that there were helicopters inbound to remove him and Scott from Airborne.

Is this really happening? he thought. *What on earth do they think they've uncovered? The new Abu Ghraib?*

Scott thought of his boys, his soldiers. About his stressing to them that a good man makes a good soldier. Whatever story the command was cooking up, Scott feared it would trickle down to his men in the worst way possible: that he couldn't walk his own talk.

Gunther called Kay and Wilson into the room. Hill stood and very slowly handed his Beretta M9 to Kay. Neither man had words.

Scott put his hand on Wilson's shoulder. "Take care of the boys. Do what you have to do and don't worry about me."

Wilson could not speak. For the second time in just over two years, he was receiving an unwanted promotion, replacing a man he loved and respected so much he would have followed him into hell.

BOOK 4

Crucible

I have no spur
To prick the sides of my intent, but only
Vaulting ambition, which o'erleaps itself,
And falls on th'other.

William Shakespeare, *Macbeth*

CHAPTER 1

WITHIN FORTY-FIVE MINUTES of their relief, Brigade sent two Black Hawks to extract Hill and Scott from Airborne and place them in detention at FOB Salerno in the eastern province of Khost. The flight was a blur, their in-processing unceremonious. By evening, he found himself in Spartan quarters and, like Scott, on a kind of house arrest. Looking out over the base, Hill could see the mountains of Pakistan. At last, though, he was alone. For the first time since the day Carwile and Conlon died, he called home.

When Lauren answered, he tiptoed to the edge of his bad news, then made the leap: "I've been relieved of command and I'm really in trouble."

"What? What happened, Roger? Tell me exactly what happened."

It took him about fifteen minutes. He told her about the twelve spies and how he and the CI guys suspected they were responsible for killing Donnie and Paul. He told her about Sammy, the 96-Hour Rule, how Battalion had ignored all their requests to transfer the prisoners. The narrowing options, the ticking clock, the fact that the detainees weren't just nickel-and-dime informants but very highly connected. His certainty that if he let them walk free, his FOB—and his men—would be overrun. Hill told his wife about his plan to scare the spies into confessing so that he could turn them over to the Afghans with unclassified proof of espionage. About how Tommy had straddled some of the detainees and slapped them in the face.

"And then I took three of the detainees outside and fired my pistol into a berm."

Hill heard Lauren gasp. Then there were a few beats of silence.

"And?" she said.

"And...that's it."

"That's it? You didn't kill anyone?"

"Yes, that's it. No, I didn't kill anyone. Just scared them."

"You're kidding. Roger, are you sure that's all that happened?"

"Yes, baby. I'm telling you everything."

"And they *relieved* you for that? Aren't you guys all on the same team? What the *hell*?"

Hill grinned in spite of himself. Lauren never cursed. She seemed dumbfounded by this turn of events. It was his first time feeling any sort of relief since the beginning of the investigation. His wife's response was worth a thousand *It's gonna be okay*s.

But that was the limit of Hill's comfort. For the next two or three days on Salerno, it was as if a cone of silence had descended around him and Scott. Although the FOB was as large as a good-sized village, it seemed the word was out: *The guys from D Co are pariahs. Shun them.* Brigade had assigned Hill and Scott to the same barracks, where they slept in rooms a hallway apart. They woke up, ate sandwiches at the Subway on post. They worked out at the gym and waited for guidance, which did not come. They were simply waiting, and they did not know what for.

CHAPTER 2

AT 1040 ON September 5, LTC Anthony DeMartino authorized CID to conduct a crime scene investigation of the FOB Airborne coffee shop. At noon, under a low, gray sky, Special Agents Bryan McCollum and Aaron Van Tassel of the Afghanistan Criminal Investigation Division trudged up the hill. Entering through the south-side door, they found the shop nearly empty, the air close and sticky.

McCollum and Van Tassel took note of the bare plywood floor. No laminate, no carpet, its only covering a patina of moondust. It appeared that the flooring had been removed.

While Van Tassel sketched the alleged crime scene, McCollum used a Nikon D70 digital camera to snap photos: a plywood table, desk, and shelving unit. *Click, flash.*

In the kitchen area, a metal sink, a large wooden table, and chairs. *Click, flash.*

Against the west wall, a flat-screen TV. On the north wall, a dry-erase board. On the south, north, and west walls, green-curtained windows. *Click, flash, click, flash, click, flash.*

Van Tassel stepped outside and fired up a metal detector. HESCO barriers flanked a dirt and gravel yard that formed an L shape around the building. Methodically, working a grid pattern, Van Tassel let the machine's search-head sniff the earth. Left, right, left, right, the agent swept the area. The machine remained silent.

About eight meters east of the building was a small green generator. Van Tassel moved toward it, sweeping as he went. About three feet separated the generator and the HESCOs. The area between was slender ground, but witnesses interviewed by Scragg and Latino said Captain Hill had fired his pistol in that vicinity. Scragg had already confiscated the gun, a 9 mm Beretta.

Van Tassel slowed his pace. Left, right. Left, right. The metal detector's control-box speaker emitted an audible alarm. The agent stopped and eyed the ground. Nothing on the surface. He squatted and used a tool to remove the top layer of dirt, then another. A bullet fragment emerged.

About a half-inch long, copper and gray in color. Nine-mil by the look of it. Van Tassel plucked the fragment from the earth, dropped it in an evidence bag, and labeled it. The time was 1545 local.

Hours passed as the agents combed the inside of the coffeehouse. On three walls, they spotted several reddish-brown stains. McCollum extracted a bottle of reagent from his kit and spritzed one stain. As he watched, the atoms on the wall rearranged themselves. Energized electrons then settled, their residual energy forming light photons. Within seconds, the stain glowed a faint blue-green. The substance was blood.

McCollum removed a swab from his kit, collected a sample, and labeled it. He then moved from wall to wall, repeating the process six times. The job took him a little over forty minutes, and he sealed the last swab at 1940 local. Outside, it began to rain.

CHAPTER 3

IT WAS ONLY by providence that Lieutenant Colonel Heather Masten was manning the phones in the Trial Defense Service office at Bagram Airfield over Labor Day weekend, 2008. Masten's jurisdiction was huge—all of Afghanistan—and she supervised a staff of military trial defense attorneys. As the head honcho, she could've tapped a junior lawyer for holiday phone duty, but she'd let them all off to enjoy a little downtime. On Masten's watch as head of the region's Trial Defense Service, however, the phones were never down.

That's because calls from soldiers needing legal defense were highly likely to come in at odd hours. Military justice is supposed to be swift and fair, effecting good order and discipline. And maybe it looked that way to government prosecutors. But for the accused and their defense counsel, military justice was sludgy, clogged, and freighted with politics.

It wasn't as if a soldier charged with a crime was handed an instruction manual on how to defend himself. Heather Masten knew firsthand. She had started her military career in 1983 as an E-2 in the Army military police corps and ended it just over a year later, demoted to E-1.

From the tiny farming community of Grand Island, Nebraska, Masten was hardly the model recruit. She was the smart-ass private you see in the movies, the one who brings three suitcases to boot camp (with curling iron) and argues with the drill sergeant that "hospital corners" are a form of architecture, not something she should have to learn in order to make a proper Army bunk.

For her misconduct, Masten received NJP—nonjudicial punishment—administered in the form of her first sergeant screaming in her face while ripping her stripe off her collar then ordering her several weeks of after-hours duty—specifically, mowing a large lawn that consisted mainly of rocks.

Still, Masten mouthed off. This resulted in more screaming and, since she had no stripes left to rip from her collar, more extra duty.

Just after completing her first year in the military, Masten became pregnant. During a field exercise, she was checked into a hospital with severe bleeding. In 1984, the Army discharged Masten for being pregnant, even though she had clearly miscarried.

Shortly after her discharge, Masten joined the Air Force Reserve, which generously paid for her bachelor's degree and kept her employed while she went to law school. In 1994, she returned to the Army as a military lawyer. During her JAG officer basic course, she was shocked to learn that while enlisted, she'd had rights. That there was a legal process. That the Army's disciplinary system consisted of something more than her first sergeant screaming at her and ripping things off her uniform. She realized that she'd been subjected to NJP, not just once but three times.

Since then, she'd learned she was not the only enlisted soldier to operate in a legal vacuum. In case after case, Masten found that soldiers' superior officers rarely explained due process to kids in trouble. And because she could actually relate to her clients' deer-in-headlights panic, Masten's desire to educate young soldiers turned into a passion for defending them in a system that seemed to regard "innocent until proven guilty" as a gooey sentiment reserved for civilians.

In February 2008, Masten was mobilized as a senior defense counsel and deployed first to Kosovo, then to Afghanistan. She quickly found that while commanders bringing charges couldn't actually *decline* a soldier legal counsel, putting up roadblocks wasn't uncommon. A soldier facing a court-martial or Article 32 hearing—a kind of military grand jury—might be told he couldn't use a phone during regular business hours. Or he might be assigned some kind of work detail to make sure it was well after dark by the time he could make a call, when surely all the lawyers had gone to bed.

Many commanders didn't want any disgruntled squeaky wheels rolling around polluting the command climate, so they tended to isolate the accused. Make them wait. Worry. Sweat. Which is exactly what Hill had been doing by the time Masten answered her office phone on September 6.

"Lieutenant Colonel Heather Masten."

"Ma'am?"

"Yes?"

"This is Captain Roger Hill. I'm in need of defense counsel." Hill couldn't believe the words coming out of his mouth. He felt in the grip of some nightmare.

Masten picked up a pen, pulled a legal pad over to jot some notes. "Okay, why don't you tell me a little bit about what's going on."

"All right, I'm not sure how much detail you want."

"Let's shoot for a condensed version. If I have questions where I need detail, then I'll stop you. How's that sound?"

Hill told the story again. It took about twenty minutes, with Masten occasionally circling back to clarify key points. Hill finished his account, ending with "and now I'm here."

A beat of silence on Masten's end, then: "And...?"

"And that's it."

"You didn't shoot anyone?"

"No, I did not."

Then Hill broke. The weight of the entire deployment. Donnie and Paul dead. His men now under fire because of his actions. His future in jeopardy. Tears gushed from his eyes. He felt ashamed for crying and yet powerless to stop the flood.

Masten waited. Hill's story did not surprise her. At first blush, he sounded like so many others she'd defended in Army cases. Young men in the heat of battle, making decisions, good ones and bad ones, in the teeth of onerous and conflicting regulations and restraints. Then being offered up, sacrifices on the altar of "justice" in a lawyered-up war. Thus were the gods of Army politics appeased, senior officers' careers preserved, and shitty policies left to fester on.

Hill collected himself. Sensing an ally in Masten, he uttered thoughts he hadn't dared to admit, even to himself. "Colonel, I am scared. I am *so* scared. I'm afraid I'm going to prison when all I was ever trying to do was take care of my men."

"Roger, it's going to be okay," Heather Masten said. "I'm going to help you."

CHAPTER 4

NEAL PUCKETT STRODE up the jetway into the humming international terminal at LAX, checking email with his right hand, pulling a carry-on with his left. He had just stepped into the gate area when his phone chimed in his hand. He recognized the caller: Bill Chatfield, a Bush appointee who headed the U.S. Selective Service.

"Bill!" Puckett answered the phone with customary good cheer. "Just getting in from Okinawa. What can I do for you?"

Puckett, a trim man with a goatee, kept walking as he and Chatfield exchanged pleasantries. Then Chatfield told him about a young captain being charged with alleged detainee abuse in Afghanistan. The case bore striking parallels to that of another officer Puckett had defended in 2003.

"The Hills are looking for an attorney to represent them," Chatfield said.

A former Marine Corps intelligence officer, Puckett had crossed over to military law in 1981. He served as a military defense counsel, chief prosecutor, staff judge advocate, then as a general court-martial and military trial judge. In 1997, Puckett retired at the rank of lieutenant colonel and entered private practice.

Four years later, President George W. Bush ordered a military response to the Al Qaeda attack on the American homeland, and the Global War on Terror began. At the same time, so did a new chapter in military law. Increasingly, Puckett found himself defending soldiers and Marines accused of breaking the rules of armed conflict in a war in which the enemy didn't play by the rules.

Over decades of practice, Puckett had developed a belief that when dealing with allegations of misconduct in combat, troops should be afforded

what he termed a "super-benefit of the doubt." That when junior commanders in particular were faced with making decisions in the crucible of war,
those decisions should first be evaluated in the most favorable light. But
since the terror war began, what he had found was an unfair opposite: An
allegation was made and there was a presumption of guilt. Then investigators
hunted—seemingly with relish—for anything that had been done incorrectly
so that someone other than a senior commander could be held accountable.

The result was that troops had to protect themselves from an armed
enemy and the threat of imminent death—*and* protect themselves and their
livelihoods from their superiors as well. That had led to a bunker mentality:
Instead of junior ground commanders having confidence in their leaders
and feeling as if they were on the same team, they were forced to look over
their shoulders, waiting to be ambushed for any small breach by senior officers concerned about preserving their own careers.

By the time he reached baggage claim, Puckett was on the phone with
Lauren Hill. After the call with her husband, her world had turned upside
down. That morning, she'd been an elementary school teacher, praying her
husband would come home safe. By nightfall, she was scrambling to keep
her husband out of prison. A phone call to a family friend, Ken Walters, a
retired Marine Corps officer, had led her to Chatfield, who had told her he
"knew just the person" to defend Roger.

"Lauren, this is exactly the type of case my firm has successfully
defended," Puckett told her from Los Angeles as he watched the baggage
carousel swirl with a hundred identical suitcases. "From what I know, Roger
has the moral high ground here. You don't have to worry about anything.
I'll take it from here."

Back at FOB Salerno, Tommy Scott was assigned a defense attorney, but the
guy was slammed with cases. Also, he was in Iraq. Scott didn't have a cell
phone, so he borrowed a landline at someone's desk on the FOB, called the
attorney in Baghdad, and explained the basics of his case. He and CPT Hill
hadn't been officially charged yet, he told the attorney, but the word from
Airborne was that Battalion was lawyered up, and the FOB was crawling
with investigators.

The attorney's first words shocked Scott. "You could always go ahead and
plead guilty," he said. "I've known a lot of people who've gone to prison then
got out and led productive lives."

Plead guilty to what? For slapping a couple of guys and yelling at them?
Scott was astonished. "No, I'm not going to do that. What else you got?"

The attorney advised Scott to write down his recollection of events step by step, and they agreed to connect again by phone. But when Scott tried to reach him again, the attorney was unavailable. Or he was in court. Or he was in transit. Scott called once a day for over a week, until the supervisor of the person whose phone he was borrowing heard that Scott was an accused war criminal on lockdown. And just like that Scott lost his phone privileges.

Scott reviewed his situation: COL Johnson had barred him from talking to the only person he knew on Salerno, CPT Hill. His lawyer in Iraq thought he was guilty and couldn't be reached. Even if he could, now he was banned from using all phones. It was then that Tommy Scott began to feel truly alone.

CHAPTER 5

It was Heather Masten who recommended to Hill that he hire a civilian attorney, someone who specialized in military trial defense. She explained that a nonmilitary lawyer had much greater latitude to capture the media and public attention in a case like his—and it was already plain to Masten that Hill needed that kind of support. Now, Hill sat, phone to his ear, the line ringing in Alexandria, Virginia.

"Neal Puckett here."

"Hello, sir, this is Roger Hill. I think you've been expecting my call."

"Roger, yes! How are you?"

"Well, things have been pretty tough here as of late. I think you might be able to help out with that."

"I sure hope so. Let's get right to it, I know this call is probably costing you."

Hill reprised the fifteen-minute version of events that had led to his relief, finishing with "And then I took three of the detainees outside and fired my pistol into a berm."

"And that's it?" Puckett said.

"Yes, sir. That's it."

"Roger, first of all, I'm so sorry that this is all happening. It's obvious that you care deeply for your men and wanted to accomplish your mission and ensure their well-being."

"Yes, sir."

"I'd like to tell you a quick story, if I may."

Puckett began: On August 8, 2003, in the town of Saba al Boor, near Tikrit, Iraq, the commander of an artillery battalion learned of a plot to assassinate him and his soldiers. The commander didn't believe the story until a convoy in which he was supposed to be riding was ambushed.

Intelligence developed the name of an Iraqi policeman who was known to have information about the plot. The commander had the policeman taken into custody. A trained but inexperienced female interrogator worked with the policeman for many hours, but he wouldn't talk.

The interrogator then called the commander, who walked into the room, drew his pistol, and told the police officer, "If you don't give us this information, I'm going to kill you."

The policeman looked at the commander and smiled. "I love you," he said.

At this point, the commander placed his pistol behind the policeman's head but pointed it away. He counted to three, then fired.

"The outpouring of information was instant," Puckett told Hill. "The Iraqi told the commander everything he wanted to know. The commander's name was Lieutenant Colonel Allen West. I represented Allen back in 2003 and 2004. After the incident, he was given a choice. He could resign from the Army just shy of his twenty-year mark and forfeit all his retirement. Or he could face court-martial and potentially eight to ten years in prison. We went public with his case. We received hundreds of emails and letters of support from the American people. Congress circulated a letter of support and ninety-five Congress members signed it. The Army backed down, and West was allowed to retire with full benefits."

At Salerno, Hill sat, phone to his ear and speechless. He had never heard of Allen West and was dumbfounded by that fact alone. If he had, he might have made different decisions back at the coffeehouse, maybe would never have taken it even as far as he did. And the parallels between West's story and his own were, well . . . astonishing.

Puckett continued. By going public with West's case, they had been able to raise money for a defense fund. "One thing we may have to do or consider soon is issuing a press release at Fort Campbell through the local media there with your wife as your spokesperson," he said. "In your case, it's public awareness that will help keep the command in check."

This idea hit Hill like a gut punch. His whole command thought he was a criminal; now the whole country would. He wanted to throw up. Or crawl under a rock.

But Puckett's confidence inspired trust and he kept his voice calm. "Okay, my wife and I will need to talk this over. And one more thing—my first sergeant. I want to know if by hiring you, his case will benefit as well.

Whatever we do, I want it to maximize his standing in all this. And I want to pay for it."

"Of course. I believe that given the similarities of your case, that they might actually pursue the two of you together. Regardless, though, your case and how I represent you does stand to have a direct impact on your first sergeant's case. And if we can achieve any synergies, we'll certainly do that and with no additional charge. How's that sound?"

"I really appreciate that. We'll get back to you soon."

"Sure thing, Roger. Keep your chin up. It is ludicrous that we punish our men and women for doing their jobs over there, and again, I'm sorry this is happening to you and your family."

Hill hung up and dialed Lauren back, sharing the good news. For the first time, they both felt a glimmer of hope.

Within days of Hill and Scott's relief, FOB Airborne, the remote and desolate base that stank of diesel and human waste, became a bustling hub. Black Hawks bearing investigators buzzed in circuits between Ghazni, Bagram, and Wardak like an inexhaustible supply of carrier pigeons. The phenomenon triggered disgust in Dog Company's new leaders: Just two of those flights could have moved the spies to Ghazni or Bagram for further processing.

They were discouraged, too, at the waste of Operation Nomad. The op had been a success, disrupting the Jalrez cell in both intelligence and matériel. For a moment, the fate of the province had seemed balanced on a fulcrum, perhaps even ready to tip toward the Coalition. But the moment vanished, plowed under in the churn of the investigation.

When the investigation was two weeks old, CID expanded its inquiry to FOB Salerno. On September 11, Special Agents Steven Geniuk and Christopher Moon spoke with the law enforcement professional (LEP) who landed at FOB Airborne with Captains Latino and Scragg on August 29. Geniuk and Moon were very interested in obtaining some evidence the LEP obtained when he and the captains visited the detainees at NDS.

At NDS, the three had interviewed Aziz Dalmar, the owner of the coffeehouse. Dalmar claimed that Hill and Scott had questioned him and struck him repeatedly. They also interviewed Sammy, who said he was beaten by Hill and Scott. Smith took a picture of Sammy. The terp's nose appeared "swollen but not bruised," the LEP reported, and more than a dozen splotches of bright red blood covered Sammy's gray ARMY T-shirt. Dalmar, meanwhile, had a black eye and an abrasion on his lip.

The LEP photographed both men and provided copies of his shots to Geniuk and Moon. He also provided copies of statements obtained from the two Afghans, written in Pashto along with English translations, as well as the statement of the head interpreter, K.J.

K.J.'s statement was of particular interest. He said Sammy told him he was hit by "ten soldiers and warrant officers...from night until morning," and claimed these assailants were Hulburt and Mo. K.J. also stated that one soldier "smothered the suspect [by] the name of Morcos and his mouth and nose have been closed for almost 25 through 30 seconds which was very dangerous."

"I saw First Sergeant Scott...hit the detainees with a baseball stick the whole day" on August 26, K.J. said. Another detainee, Farid, was thrown in a muddy ditch and "kicked seriously." The Dalmar brothers told K.J. that Dog Company soldiers tore from the coffeehouse's accounting books IOUs in the amount of $1,400 U.S.

"This is what I have seen and heard by myself and I am truthful in my confession," K.J.'s statement said. He later told investigators that he was applying for entry into the United States, and that he feared his visa would be in jeopardy because he had provided a statement.

Just before 4 p.m. on September 11, Special Agent Moon located Tommy Scott on FOB Salerno and advised him of his rights. Ten minutes later, Moon and Geniuk searched Scott's quarters—possibly for a baseball stick— and found nothing.

CHAPTER 6

SPECIALIST ALLAN MOSER'S promotion board for advancement to sergeant was scheduled for a late afternoon in mid-September. The day of, Moser sat in the TOC conference room at Airborne reviewing his study guide. He was confident he knew the information cold and would sail through the board. As a squad leader, he'd been working in a sergeant's job for months. A few short weeks after the board, he'd have the stripes and the pay that went with it.

As Moser turned a page in the study guide, Shon Haskins appeared at the door. "Moser?"

"Yes, Sergeant?"

"You're not going to the board."

Moser shook his head. "What? Yes, I am. It's this afternoon."

"Not anymore. You're flagged." It was vintage Haskins: less blood when you rip the bandage off quick.

Flagged is shorthand for "suspension of favorable personnel actions." When a soldier is flagged, a whole litany of privileges—including awards, regular leave, and promotions—are put on hold. The flag remains until the soldier is retrained and the offense is rectified or corrected.

"For what?" Moser said. "Why am I flagged?"

"Hitting that detainee."

"*What?* That was in self-defense!" Moser's mind reeled. They were going to stop his promotion because of that fucker who bit him?

"Sorry, man," Haskins said, looking genuinely sad.

Haskins left and Moser bolted through the door and out of the TOC. He tracked down one of the Jolly Rogers NCOs, who told him to check his Enlisted Record Brief. The ERB is a condensed summary of a soldier's career, including his occupational specialty, awards, assignments, and training.

Moser jogged to the tiny hut where soldiers checked their email and logged in. Sure enough, his record had been flagged for administrative action. His mind spun. When investigators asked him what happened, he had told the truth. He was helping Captain Hill with the detainees when one guy bit him and wouldn't let go. Moser hit the detainee, he told investigators. And yes, he hit him more than once.

That was probably what this was about, Moser thought—the fact that he'd let his anger get the best of him.

A few days later, Dog Company received a message: Moser, PFC Michael Peake, and SGT Andrew Doyle should pack for three or four days. Battalion was sending a patrol from Ghazni to pick them up.

Moser spoke again with his NCOs. Based on the message about a three- or four-day trip, they suspected Moser would receive an Article 15. An Article 15 is a form of nonjudicial punishment that includes a negative service-record entry and some form of discipline such as extra duty or forfeiture of pay. But when Moser arrived at Ghazni, the news was much more grim. He was charged with failure to report detainee abuse, lying to a commissioned officer about detainee abuse, and assault on a detainee with a closed fist.

Moser was incredulous. He hadn't thought the treatment of the detainees had amounted to abuse, so why would he report it or lie about it?

A week before, Moser had been on top of his game, doing his job the best he knew how, taking care of his men, making his NCOs proud, on his way to making sergeant in just two years. Now, he was not only *not* getting promoted, he wasn't even going back to his company. Instead, he was being kicked out of the Army.

Not even that was the worst of it for Moser, though. The worst part was that his platoon had five months left in-country. They were still getting shot at and taking rocket and mortar fire every day.

Fine, he thought. *Punish me for hitting the guy. Kick me out. But wait until* after *the deployment, after I help my guys get home.*

At FOB Airborne, CPT B was still working the insider threat angle and was *this close* to exploiting the intel gained from the coffeehouse confessions, and possibly cracking the Jalrez Taliban cell wide open.

By mid-September, the NDS was still holding Sammy, the Dalmars, and the others, but only at CPT B's passionate insistence. The NDS did not feel the spies' confessions were sufficient to detain them, but the counterintel team's link analyses and other hard evidence against the prisoners was classified. Sharing it was still a no-go. CPT B knew the NDS were about to release the spies. If that happened, they'd be in the wind, and months of painstaking undercover work with them.

CPT B could hardly believe the lack of contingency planning involved here. How could the Army have in place a detention procedure that required American forces to turn over detainees to the Afghan NDS at the ninety-six-hour mark, yet not have in place a provision that enabled U.S. forces to question those prisoners? This gaping procedural hole meant that the intel value of captured enemy fighters evaporated the instant U.S. commanders followed the rules.

Possibly the most infuriating part, though, was this: While warfighters were not allowed to question the prisoners about their spying, Brigade's investigators *were* allowed to question them—in connection with allegations of detainee abuse.

After engaging Neal Puckett, Hill and Heather Masten settled in to work on his case. Hill had not yet been authorized to travel and meet his counsel in person, so the two began preparing his defense by phone, Hill from his room at Salerno and Masten from Bagram, in the Trial Defense Service offices, a space built from CONEX shipping containers, two high and two across.

"Let me tell you what's going on here," Masten told Hill. "Right now, CID is interviewing your men."

"That's fine," Hill said. "I don't have anything to hide. And my men would never say anything to hurt me anyway."

"No, you don't understand. CID will grill your guys again and again. They will specifically and very intentionally wear them down to get answers, whether or not those guys did anything wrong or even know anything."

"Okay..." Hill said. He'd seen a little of this already.

"It's called the Reid Technique, and trained investigators use it all the time. Every time one of your guys starts to say he didn't do anything wrong, they'll interrupt him. If he has a logical explanation for why CID should believe him, they will shoot it down. Pretty soon, some of your guys will begin to doubt their own memories. CID will also play 'good cop, bad cop.'"

Hill's mind flashed to Mo and Hulburt, when he'd asked them to interview Sammy. Ironic.

"One agent will pretend to be on your guy's side while the other agent is antagonistic. Then they'll start throwing out possible motives. Things like, 'Maybe Captain Hill thought he was doing the right thing. We get that.' Or, regarding that young soldier that punched the detainee for biting him, CID might say something like, 'You know, if somebody bit my hand, I'd beat the shit out of him, too. Now would you say he hit the detainee or beat him?'"

And all this time, Masten said, the investigators would be watching. What is the suspect's body language saying? Is he holding his head in his hands? Fidgeting? Looking toward the door, for a way out?

"The agents are looking for signs of surrender," she explained, "and to escape the mind games, some of your guys will begin to give CID the answers they want."

CHAPTER 7

Mo was in his hooch when the word came down that CID wanted to see him. He had already signed a statement when 4th Platoon was interviewed as a group. He'd had to finish his after returning from a QRF mission.

That Scragg woman hadn't liked it, Mo thought, *but tough shit.*

He crossed the FOB to the company area. CID had set up in a back room. Mo walked in, sized up the investigators. One was an older gentleman, seemed kind of laid-back. He greeted Mo with a pleasant nod. The other agent was younger, stocky, and immediately more serious.

"Sergeant First Class Moriarty?"

"Yes."

"Thanks for coming in. We just have a few follow-up questions for you. Have a seat."

The questions were pretty routine.

Had Mo seen Captain Hill fire his weapon near the detainees?

"No. I wasn't there," Mo said.

Did you see Specialist Moser hit a detainee?

"No, I wasn't there."

"Look," said the younger agent, "we have other witnesses who say they saw Specialist Moser beating a detainee."

Mo looked the agent head-on. "From what I understand, Moser got bit, the guy wouldn't let go with his teeth, so Moser had to hit the guy to get him to let go. It was self-defense."

"Really? Was it self-defense for you to carry around an enemy's skull in your rucksack?"

Mo scowled. "What the fuck are you talking about?"

The young agent picked up a sheet of paper and read from it, sum-marizing. On his first tour in Iraq, Moriarty was dispatched to look for the remains of an enemy KIA. "We have information that you found the remains, including a skull with the skin burned off, and that you kept that skull as a souvenir."

Where do they get this shit? Mo thought. He looked at the agent and shook his head. "You guys are nuts, man."

The older agent now spoke. "Look, we really respect you guys. We know you're infantry and we really respect you. We heard about an incident where you were put in for a medal."

The VBIED incident, Mo thought. After he neutralized that VBIED by shooting the two insurgents, CPT Hill put him in for a Silver Star.

"Yes," he said.

The young agent now smiled at Mo. "What I'd like to know is, what does it take for a person to shoot two guys up close?"

Blood rushed hot to Mo's temples. The agent's implication was clear: If Mo could shoot two men in the head at point-blank range, beating up detainees would be no problem at all.

Lying on a pristine weight bench, Tommy Scott heaved a loaded barbell off the rack behind his head, lowered the bar to his chest, and pressed. Exhale. Press. Exhale. This routine had become a main rhythm of life. Sleep. Chow hall. Gym. Repeat. The workouts were therapeutic, reminded him of Larry Kay. Back on Airborne, Scott would be in the gym sweating hard and Kay would pop in.

"Time for my workout," he'd say, then pick up a pair of dumbbells, curl them three or four times, slam them down. "There. Done. Whew, that was rough!" Grin at Scott and walk out.

Scott smiled at the memory, pushed out eight more reps, and let the bar rock back into the rack. Sat up, swiped a towel across his head. Pain flared in his lower back then subsided to a dull throb. He'd felt it before, at Airborne, but only in twinges. He'd been too busy to think about it. Lately, though, it felt like his sacrum was grinding itself into dust.

Scott peered around the gym. It was the nicest he'd ever seen, and today he had it to himself. The room had been a refuge from stares and whispers at the DFAC (Dining Facility, pronounced "dee-fac"). He had even made a friend here, a soldier who worked in the FOB mailroom. The guy knew who Scott was, but offered to let him come to his office and use his com-puter anyway. Scott was grateful; it was his one line to the outside world.

Scott had a source who kept him up-to-date on what was happening with D Co. This guy worked at the Brigade TOC on Salerno and had access to the sitreps out of Wardak. In this way, Scott was able to keep daily tabs on whether his boys returned from missions in one piece.

D Co was doing okay, he learned, but *just* okay. The soldiers were pissed off at CID's repetitive questioning. It seemed like the agents were convinced that anyone who didn't spill dirt on someone else was hiding something. Why couldn't it just be that they didn't know anything because they weren't there?

The worst news was that Brigade was breaking Dog Company up, even at the platoon level. That meant that soldiers who had been fighting together, who knew each other's battle rhythms, who depended on each other for friendship and support, were being separated and farmed out to other units. A senior officer had told Scott's source that the plan was to "make the problem go away."

A couple of weeks passed. Then one day a FOB chaplain surprised Scott by pulling him into her office.

"This is messed up, how they're doing you, First Sergeant," she said from across her desk. "I see that white captain up there at Brigade using the phones, talking to people. Who's helping *you*?"

The very idea shocked Scott. That young officers like this woman were tallying issues in terms of black versus white. A couple of senior NCOs had approached him earlier about the same thing. Maybe he'd been naïve, but for his entire infantry career he had been color-blind. Dog Company itself was a melting pot. CPT Hill was half Korean. Photo was Laotian. Colon and Fernandez were Puerto Rican. Scott couldn't count the number of black soldiers. For him, there was no black, white, brown, or any other color but OD green.

Scott thanked the chaplain for her concern and her time—"I'll keep my ears open," she had assured him—and carried on. Though he and CPT Hill had not talked, he felt confident that his CO not only would never cross him, but that he also had his back.

All of this was temporary anyway. Once the investigators got everybody's statements, they'd iron this thing out, Scott thought. Then he and CPT Hill would go back to Airborne and resume the mission.

Meanwhile, having acquired a couple of allies, Scott set about recruiting good soldiers for Dog Company. When he and the captain went back to Airborne, he told his new friends, maybe they'd like to put in for a transfer, see what the real war was like. A couple of guys said they'd like that. Staying inside the wire at Salerno was not what they'd signed up for.

CHAPTER 8

██
██
██

At Bagram Airfield, near the offices of Trial Defense Services, stood an unusual structure: a wooden gazebo known as the "Amnesty Hut." Heather Masten and a friend, COL Christine Stark, a National Guard commander, had envisioned some type of modest sanctuary for TDS clients who were often banished and isolated from their peers. Masten and Stark scared up the raw materials and TDS clients executed the build. The Amnesty Hut quickly became a place to breathe, to find camaraderie and just enjoy a moment of refuge from the madness of war.

That night, Hill, Masten, and the rest of the defense team—Captains Kevin Cox and Jason Easterly—gathered in the gazebo.

"Roger, in here there's only one rule," Masten said. "Whatever words are spoken in the Amnesty Hut stay in the Amnesty Hut. Understood?"

"Yes, ma'am," Hill said.

Someone had lined the interior of the Amnesty Hut with plush pillows in Middle Eastern prints. After everyone had arranged themselves among the pillows, Masten produced a box of cigars. It was the Army's fault that she loved them. ██ ████████████████████████████████████ The Army issued cigars and alcohol (referred to officially as "Class Six supplies") for the purpose. Masten became part fan, part aficionado, developing a special affinity for Drew Estate brand and their ACID cigars from Nicaragua.

She passed the cigar box around the gazebo, and the defense team lit up. Then Hill and the three lawyers talked his case around, their cigars spinning sweet smoke up into the chamber. Over the course of the evening, Hill became a member of, rather than the object of, his own defense team.

For the next several weeks, the team waited for LTC Gunther's official 15-6 report, the findings of his investigation. In the interim, Hill took orders from Masten, and worked closely with Neal Puckett preparing a strategy. He began by researching cases similar to his own, cases like LTC Allen West's.

Hill had remained confident that when the evidence shook out, the prosecution against him and Tommy would collapse. So when Gunther's report came in, it hit Hill like a train.

The report was, in a word, scathing. It seemed to interpret every piece of data in the worst possible light, without regard for any other possible explanation. Hill sat in a TDS office and flipped through the pages.

"Once the detainee went through a mock execution, soldiers would beat the detainee outside the coffee shop," Gunther had written.

What? Hill thought. *That didn't happen.*

"While the beatings took place, MAJ Cheasty…monitored the abuse, and when a detainee was so badly hurt that he would not stop bleeding, MAJ Cheasty gave that detainee medical care."

What? Hill hadn't even known Cheasty was there until just before the confessions.

As he continued reading, the next line shocked him: "During this time, the interpreter also saw SFC Moriarty striking a detainee."

Mo wasn't even there, Hill thought. *He cooked that Cell Tower Mountain guy some ramen and left the coffeehouse just after Tommy and I came in.*

Other allegations in Gunther's report made it appear that he had concluded that Dog Company had been running what amounted to a torture camp:

"Detainees were slapped with an open palm to reduce risk of leaving marks."

No, Hill thought. *Detainees were slapped with an open palm to avoid actually hurting them.*

CID agents had found blood on the coffee shop walls, the report said. And the LEP had interviewed Sammy and one of the Dalmar brothers at NDS. Dalmar had a black eye, and Sammy's shirt was covered with blood.

But the detainees were in perfect condition when they were released to NDS, Hill thought. MAJ Smith had said so himself.

*   *   *

Weeks ticked by as Masten and Hill waited for the charge sheet to come in, the document that would list which parts of military law Hill and Scott had allegedly violated. The sheet, Masten said, would reveal whether Brigade intended to come after them full-bore or was merely executing due diligence before closing the books on this incident.

The sheer volume of resources being poured out on Airborne was a bad sign. Also, the political climate was ripe for a hanging. Abu Ghraib, and then the CIA water-boarding scandal, had focused international attention on detainee operations, and the United States had just dropped a bomb on a wedding party in eastern Afghanistan, killing innocent civilians, including the bride. That incident spurred President Karzai to call for more accountability of U.S. forces in his country.

If Brigade decided to come after Hill and Scott, the next likely step would be a military legal proceeding called an Article 32. An Article 32 investigation is a cross between a grand jury inquiry and an actual trial. The Army assigns an investigative officer who presides over a hearing. During the hearing, both prosecutors and defense attorneys put on evidence and cross-examine witnesses. After the hearing concludes, the investigating officer recommends action in the case, which can range from dismissal of all charges to general court-martial.

When the charge sheet arrived, Hill's defense team had their answer: Brigade was mounting a legal full-court press. The sheet listed six separate violations of the Uniform Code of Military Justice (UCMJ), some with multiple specifications.

Masten wasn't surprised. She called it "racking and stacking," a term Hill recalled hearing while watching *Law and Order* with Lauren in what he had begun to regard as his former life.

"The technical term is 'multiplicitous,'" Masten said. "It means throwing every possible charge at a defendant just to see what sticks. It's not unusual. I'm sure we'll be able to get some of those dismissed."

One violation floored Hill: Prosecutors charged that he failed to report the holding of detainees to his higher headquarters. After all those calls and emails from Kay to Battalion, Hill wondered how the government intended to prove that.

Another charge read, "CPT Roger T. Hill did . . . commit an assault upon a detained person by pointing and firing within his vicinity a dangerous weapon, to wit: a loaded firearm."

Hill believed this was patently untrue. He had placed himself between the detainees and his gun, firing away from them into a berm.

A third count charged Hill with making false statements. There was no doubt about that; he had the day MAJ Rob Smith arrived at Airborne to launch the 15-6 investigation. Smith had asked Hill whether he knew ▉ ▆▆ Hill had answered no.

There had been no way to admit that he'd fired his pistol near the detainees without getting his men in trouble. Also, Hill had been hoping to talk to Smith about his entire statement, but he hadn't gotten the chance.

Some charges alleged that Hill had engaged in cruel or inhumane treatment of detainees; others said he allowed his soldiers to assault prisoners. Not the words he would've used, but he wasn't surprised. What did surprise him was that there were so *many* charges.

The sheet also listed the charges against Tommy Scott: Dereliction of duty in failing to safeguard detainees. Encouraging the pointing and firing of a dangerous weapons near the detainees. And cruel and inhumane treatment of detainees, including three separate specifications of unlawfully striking detainees with his hand.

Hill and Scott had observed strict radio silence—an awkward arrangement since they passed in each other's orbits several times a day. From a distance, his first sergeant looked okay, but Hill wondered how he was really doing.

Tommy Scott was dreaming about his wife, Cassandra, when his door burst open in the middle of the night. He bolted awake as the overhead light switched on, glaring in his face. "What the—?"

An armed MP, a young sergeant, towered over Scott's bunk. "First Sergeant Scott, we need you to step outside. We have orders to search your room."

Bewildered, Scott sprang out of bed. Over the MP's shoulder, he saw a young private, also an MP. His rifle was unslung.

"Just stand at the door, First Sergeant," the private said.

Seeing no alternative, Scott gave way to the invasion. He crossed to the door in his T-shirt and briefs, pivoted, and stood helpless as two junior soldiers trashed his room.

The sergeant pawed through Scott's locker, turning out the pockets of his uniforms. Drawers opened, socks and underwear spilled onto the floor. The private stood by, eying Scott.

Scott shook his head. *Am I the enemy now? That this punk is going to need his weapon?*

"What are you looking for?" Scott said. "I didn't bring anything from Airborne but a few clothes."

The sergeant did not pause his search. "Sorry, First Sergeant. We're not authorized to tell you that."

In the hallway where Scott stood, a couple of doors opened a crack. He saw eyes. One guy, a fellow E-8, poked his crew cut out his door. "Scott. What's going on?"

Scott telegraphed him a look—*I can't even talk about it*—and cast his eyes at the floor. When he raised his gaze, his belongings covered the floor of his room. The private slung his rifle over his shoulder. The two MPs stepped over Scott's gear and walked past him empty-handed.

Scott entered his room. Closed the door behind him and stared at the wreckage. He sat down on the edge of his bunk, ears ringing with a hollow sound. He later decided that was the sound a man's pride makes when it is systematically crushed.

CHAPTER 9

FIVE DAYS AFTER the charge sheet came in, more bad news landed in Heather Masten's email in-box. It was a memo from LTC Robert Byrd, the man COL Johnson had assigned as investigating officer, or IO, for the Article 32. With a couple of keystrokes, Masten looked Byrd up. He was battalion commander for Task Force Ripcord, a military police battalion.

Masten uttered a curse and rocked back in her chair. An MP officer *and* a battalion commander. From the defense standpoint, drawing Byrd as IO was the worst-case scenario. First, as a battalion commander, he would likely see the case from the Battalion's point of view. Second, military police officers were famously hard-nosed. Black-and-white, letter-of-the-law types who wouldn't know an extenuating circumstance if one bit them in the ass.

Masten had already looked into the bios of the prosecuting attorneys, Captains Stephen Latino and Devon Runyan. Latino had earned his JD at the University of Dayton in 2004, and by 2005 was working as a detainee operations attorney with the 101st Airborne in Iraq. He did that for a year then transferred to Afghanistan as a JAG. So, three, four years experience, max.

CPT Devon Runyan had been practicing law for less than two years after earning her JD at the State University of Buffalo, New York. She had landed in Afghanistan the very month that Hill received his charge sheet. There was a very good chance, Masten thought, that she'd never been outside the wire.

Masten finished reading the email from LTC Byrd then clicked through a couple of links until she found a photograph of the man.

STRAC, she thought when she saw one.

It was old military shorthand that meant Skilled, Tough, and Ready Around the Clock. Byrd looked the part. His close-clipped haircut prompted her to look for a Ranger tab.

Yep, there it is.

Masten read deeper into Byrd's bio. He'd served with a couple of psychological ops units and as a deputy brigade commander. Had his master jump wings, a Bronze Star, a Meritorious Service Medal, and a Legion of Merit, the military's highest peacetime award. And—*oh, great*—he wasn't an MP because he couldn't find anything better to do in the Army. He held a bachelor's degree in criminal justice and a master's degree in international relations. Not exactly the kind of guy you'd expect to have a nuanced view of a case that Brigade was painting as criminal international relations.

Also, Byrd had received his regular Army commission in 1986 and was a very senior MP who had served more than once as a provost marshal. In layman's terms, that's the head rule enforcer/skull cracker. The Army had abolished the provost marshal post in the 1970s and had only resurrected it five years before, in 2003.

Masten clicked Byrd's bio shut. *Lucky us*, she thought.

LTC Robert Byrd sat in a cramped office at FOB Lightning in Gardez, Afghanistan. A sheet of Plexiglas pressed a map of the Middle East onto the desk before him. On the wall behind him, a corkboard framed schedules and rosters, along with a black bumper sticker with yellow lettering: DRIVER CARRIES ONLY $20 IN AMMUNITION.

When COL Johnson assigned him as the IO for the case involving CPT Roger Hill and 1SG Tommy Scott, Byrd thought it was probably the last thing he needed on his plate. He had already been in command for three years, a third longer than the standard length of a command tour. His battalion had been one of the last extended to a fifteen-month tour under Defense Secretary Robert Gates, a way to make up for the shortfall of soldiers.

It was a long time to be separated from his wife and their nine-year-old twins. Plus, his dad had just been diagnosed with cancer. At this point, Byrd felt he was in extra innings.

He understood why COL Johnson had picked him. With a case a little less serious, the colonel would likely have selected from a roster of company grade officers. But with the allegations here, he needed at least a battalion commander, and Byrd knew he was probably the senior battalion commander in the brigade. Neither did it escape him that military police had a law-and-order reputation. Truth be told, the Brigade probably viewed him as favorable to their case.

Byrd sighed. *I probably would've picked me, too.*

Since receiving the case, he'd been reviewing documents as they came in, ghosting key facts with a yellow highlighter, jotting notes in the margins. CID's procedural work looked solid. Witness statements concerning detainee abuse were numerous and corroborative. Both soldiers and local nationals had seen the accused strike detainees. Several also witnessed or heard gunshots fired near the prisoners. CID found blood on the walls of the FOB coffee shop, the alleged crime scene. Particularly striking was a photograph of an interpreter with what appeared to be a broken nose and blood all over his shirt.

Byrd thought about Hill and Scott's battalion commander, Anthony DeMartino. They'd flown to conferences together, made small talk in the air terminal, that sort of thing. Byrd wouldn't say he knew DeMartino, but the man also wasn't a stranger. In any case, Byrd felt for him. He would've hated to have something like this thrown in his own lap. Battalion commanders had enough on their shoulders without this kind of nonsense at outlying FOBs and COPs.

Byrd clicked open his email, lamenting for the thousandth time about what a huge portion of his time he spent glued to his computer. He'd much rather have been out talking to his soldiers. The contents of his in-box did not make his day. Patrick Huston, COL Johnson's Staff Judge Advocate, or lead attorney, had emailed him to say that the Article 32 hearing was to be held on FOB Salerno instead of Bagram Airfield.

Byrd sat back in his chair. That made no sense. ████████████

He clicked open a fresh screen, hit Reply, and began typing his objections. Over half his administrative staff was located on Bagram, he told Huston, along with plenty of huts to sleep witnesses. Transportation would also be easier, since most flights originated there. Byrd made his case, signed his name, and clicked Send.

Sometimes it paid to fall in line, and sometimes it paid to bitch a little.

CHAPTER 10

In the shipping containers that comprised Masten's Trial Defense Service headquarters was a tiny "jump" office, a cramped storage space packed with files, office supplies, lightbulbs, and miscellaneous junk. This had become Hill's work space, and he was sitting in it when Masten poked her head in the door. From the look on her face, it appeared to Hill that maybe the sun had traded places with the moon.

"The Division is holding the 32 at Salerno," she said.

"What? Why?"

"The only reason I can think of is to keep the media away."

Masten was livid. In a recent case, she had lost witnesses for a court-martial when the vehicle they were riding in was hit by an IED. In Hill's case, CID was already questioning nearly every Dog Company soldier *on Bagram*. It didn't make sense.

Masten withdrew and Hill absorbed the news. It surprised him, but no more than some of the reading he'd been doing. In the jump office, he'd been poring over file after file, statement after statement. *Seven* blood samples from *three* different walls in the coffeehouse? Hill had thought a lot about this. A couple of the detainees had bloody noses from being slapped. Also, some prisoners' wrists had been rubbed raw by their flex-cuffs. Maybe blood had transferred from their wrists to the walls...? Hill wasn't sure. Out of context, it probably looked like Dog Company had been running a torture chamber. Especially given K.J.'s strange testimony that a soldier had "manually suffocated" a detainee.

Then again, K.J. had also said Scott hit detainees "all day long with a baseball stick." It was an insane allegation, completely unsupported by the

detainee's physical condition when MAJ Smith examined them. Hill began
to wonder whether K.J., who had passed his security screening, may have
been an honest man before the coffeehouse incident who saw an opportunity afterward. He had applied for a U.S. visa; maybe he thought if he gave
investigators lots of juicy stories, they would help him get to America.

In any case, it infuriated Hill that investigators lapped up and cataloged
every detail of K.J.'s account then accused his soldiers of "obstructing justice" when they did not provide details to corroborate him.

Hill was also taken aback by Gunther's assertion that the same soldier
held a prisoner's head under murky water in a ditch outside the coffeehouse.
Over and again, Hill combed through the witness statements looking for
such an assertion. He couldn't find one, yet there it was in Gunther's report.
K.J., SGT Jared Allen of A Co, and a Dog Company soldier all said in their
statements that several detainees were bloody, had blood "all over themselves," or on their faces. Again, out of context, he could see why investigators might draw the conclusion that some kind of out-of-control slugfest had
occurred, but that just wasn't the case.

███

███████████████████████████████ He also learned how important "mitigating and extenuating" circumstances would be to a panel of senior officers
should his case go to a court-martial. █████████████

███

While in command, he had thought Dog Company was poorly supported. But even with the crush of missions, enemy contact, wounded, and
supply shortages, he'd simply marched forward. Now Hill began to think
more like his attorneys. He built witness lists. MAJ Chris Faber, who was
now serving as a battalion XO in Logar Province, was on it, as were Larry
Kay and MAJ Jack Cheasty, the physician's assistant. ███████████

███

███

███

Hill spent hours in the storage room, his penchant for order flowering
in full. He cataloged every document the prosecution sent, and created
spreadsheets of evidence. He analyzed witnesses for and against himself and
Tommy Scott. Because TDS was short staffed, Hill became his own law
clerk, running down precedents, statutory regs, and case law.

He was aware that he was technically guilty, as the soldiers in other cases
had been. And, like them, like LTC Allen West, he found himself in the
teeth of a question that pitted what is legal against what is moral:

What happens when the rule of military law clashes with a commander's duty to protect his men?

On October 23, the U.S. Criminal Investigative Laboratory at Forest Park, Georgia, issued its ballistics report, and LTC Robert Byrd received a copy.

Exhibit 1 was the 9 mm Beretta confiscated from CPT Hill by CPT Victoria Scragg. Exhibit 14 was the bullet fragment recovered by Special Agent Van Tassell at the alleged crime scene. The forensics report was short and sweet: Microscopic examination of Exhibit 14 revealed that it was fired through Exhibit 1.

Byrd printed the report and filed it with the rest of the case documents. As the evidence streamed in, this was looking more and more like an open-and-shut case.

CHAPTER 11

As the mountain of legal documents in the jump office grew, so did Hill's dread over the gravity of his situation. Some days it seemed guilt had replaced blood in his veins. Guilt over Donnie and Paul. Over not protecting his men from the insider threats. Over committing an act that worsened Dog Company's situation in Wardak. Now, the company was not only running missions in enemy badlands, but he could see from the volume of statements and interviews that the investigation was compounding their misery. Since Hill left Airborne, violence in the province had spiraled upward, including a suicide attack. A VBIED truck leveled Sayed Abad Base, wounding several of Hidalgo's men.

Hill regretted not standing up to DeMartino more and sooner. He regretted having been so indiscreet about his actions in the coffee shop and so naïve about the potential ramifications. He regretted that his men were now facing combat without him.

Hill also felt guilty for what his actions were doing to Lauren. Word had come down that the Dog Company wives were not to associate with her, or with Tommy's wife, Cassandra Scott. It was an informal, nonbinding order. But the other women in the company were terrified that if they violated it, their own husbands might wind up on the chopping block.

Captain Brett Blaylock, the "rear D" (rear detachment) commander and Lauren's military point of contact, told Lauren that he could not to talk to her either. Thus Hill's wife, who hadn't done anything wrong, was completely cut off from all information and support. After being on call twenty-four hours a day, delivering the horrific news of injuries and deaths, being the shoulder the other wives cried on in their husbands' absence, Lauren Hill felt abandoned.

In phone calls, she tried to remain upbeat. One consolation was knowing that Hill was safe on FOB Salerno. "At least they aren't shooting at you right now," she said one morning.

"I wish they were," Hill said sadly. "Then I wouldn't be here."

Like Scott, Hill had spent weeks in what Lauren called "the fairy tale land of We're-All-on-the-Same-Team." Now his illusions were crumbling and he was seeing with fresh eyes. He had been cut off from his men and his wife from her friends. He had also been cut off from Tommy. It seemed perverse that Brigade intended to prosecute the two of them as a single entity and yet forbade them from talking to each other about their case.

One day in October, Hill saw Scott walking across a common area. He intersected Scott's path and brazenly walked a dozen or so steps with his brother in broad daylight. The two looked down as they walked.

"We need to talk," Hill said.

"Okay."

"Let's meet at that building at our twelve o'clock. At 0200 hours."

"Roger that."

Hill peeled off and moved away.

The third week of October, ███████████████████████████ ███████████████████████████ During the insertion, Taliban fighters fired rockets, nearly scorching the paint off the helos. ██████████

Dog Company's 1st and 4th Platoons got the call: Mount a patrol to resupply the Scouts with ammo.

With Mo on midtour leave and Wilson serving as acting first sergeant, SSG Ray Davis was acting platoon sergeant. ████████████████ ███████████████████████████ The consensus among both leaders and regular Joes was that this mission was crazy dangerous. There was a reason no one had been that far into Jalrez since the war began.

The two platoons loaded their trucks to the frames with ammo: ██████

██████ Going that far into Jalrez, it wasn't whether they were going to get in contact, but when.

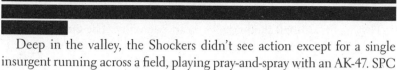

Deep in the valley, the Shockers didn't see action except for a single insurgent running across a field, playing pray-and-spray with an AK-47. SPC Graydon Kamp watched the fighter sprint across the open savannah.

How dumb is this guy? Kamp thought. *Why doesn't he stay in the wood line?*

Brett Erickson leveled his M4 and fired back. Then Carlos Colonruiz— "Colon"—now a sergeant, ▮▮▮▮▮▮▮▮▮▮▮▮▮▮▮▮▮▮▮▮▮▮▮▮▮▮▮▮▮▮▮ and blew the man in half. Davis, Erickson, and another soldier tromped across the field to do BDA, or "battle damage assessment." It was a blanket term that encompassed everything from surveying blast craters to policing up individual KIAs.

It always struck Davis as a little bizarre, this Coalition commitment to returning the enemy's body parts to their families, even if they had to scrape them together with a shovel. He wasn't sure how that helped Afghan/Coalition relations.

Now, the team approached the wood line where Colon had blown the guy up, dragging a blue tarp to put the body on.

But there was no body.

"There's blood all over the trees," Davis said to Erickson. "Where is this guy? There's got to be something out here to confirm we killed him."

Then Davis's foot hit something slick and he slipped banana-peel style, wheeling his arms to stay upright. Davis looked down. He had stepped on a severed penis.

Davis had seen some gnarly shit in the Army. In Ramadi, he watched a suicide bomber's face float to earth after the bomber detonated himself. No bones, just his face, drifting down like scrap paper caught in a breeze. That hadn't really bothered him. But slipping on a dead man's penis reached Davis on an elemental level and caused him to dry-heave.

The BDA team found the rest of the guy a couple of meters away, entrails splashed across the field, one leg severed, the other shattered and twisted up behind his back. They moved the body onto the tarp, a sloppy job steeped in the coppery smell of blood. Dragged it back across the field to the convoy, the disembodied leg falling off a couple of times along the way. They left the fighter's manhood on the field of battle.

*   *   *

The building where Hill asked Tommy Scott to meet him was in the middle of FOB Salerno. That was a risk. But the place was empty and under construction. It would have to do.

That night, Hill left the barracks, heart pounding. The air outside was still warm. There was no moon and a light overcast blanketed the stars. Illumination was practically zero, which was good.

Hill arrived fifteen minutes early. The construction was concrete with cutouts for windows. He pulled a couple of paint cans to the middle of the room for seating.

"Hey, sir, you there?" Scott had entered silently and stood just inside the door.

Hill crossed the room and embraced him. It felt to both men as if years had passed since the last time they had truly spoken.

"Sir, let's just stand a minute," Scott whispered. Early in his Army career, he had served on a Long Range Surveillance team. He knew how to move silently, without detection. He signaled Hill. Each took a window, backs to the walls and listened. Five minutes passed without a sound, then the two men moved to the paint cans and sat.

██

██

████████████████████████████████████

"How's Lauren?" Tommy asked.

"She's a trooper," Hill said. "Brave, like a Spartan's wife. The toughest thing is the gag order and everybody shutting her out. How's Cassandra?"

"Same. I'm glad they have each other."

"What do you hear about the guys?"

"Still running missions. Larry's doing a good job. Kris, too. Dudley's wife is starting to come around." Rachel Dudley had fallen deathly ill, and Jason Dudley was sent home on emergency leave to be with her.

Hill switched to business. "So Tommy, do you have a lawyer?"

"Yeah, but I'm not real happy with him."

"No? What's up?"

"Well, first of all he's in Iraq."

Scott spent a couple of minutes bringing Hill up to speed on the weeks since the no-contact order. Being ostracized, banned from using phones to line up a defense, the early-morning search, senior personnel raising the specter of racism. "And the whole time, my lawyer keeps telling me to plead guilty. Says he can get me down to ten years and I'm thinking, Are you *crazy*? I'm not pleading guilty to something I didn't do!"

Scott whispered this last fiercely, and for a moment both men went quick-quiet and listened intently to the night. The low hum of generators was the only sound.

Hill spoke next. "I hear you, brother. As far as pleading guilty, I'm being told the exact opposite. Let me talk to my lawyers for you. We need to get you a second opinion."

Scott agreed, then said, "Sir, this will pass. Tough times make tough men."

For the next couple of minutes he switched into first sergeant mode, uttering rapid-fire encouragement. Scott wasn't trying to make himself feel better, Hill realized. It was just his way to put others first, and it humbled Hill. He was the one with the high-powered attorneys, the one with the plan. Scott's guy had offered him nothing but jail. Still, here he was taking on the role of encourager. At that moment, Hill realized he had been feeling sorry for himself, and he was ashamed. Instantly, he resolved to knock it off, step up his game. The power structure was systematically denying Tommy Scott the rights he had earned after twenty-four years and multiple combat tours. Hill wasn't going to lie down for that.

"Tommy, let me get in touch with my civilian lawyer and get back to you. He specializes in these kinds of cases."

"Really?"

"Yes, and he's going to support both of us. He has to. We're the same case. You know what I'm saying?"

"That's great, sir. Sounds expensive, though. How are we going to do all this?"

"Already taken care of. My family is working with the lawyer to set up a defense fund. It's been done before. Besides, I've been working like crazy helping put both of our cases together. You'll see," Hill said, smiling.

It was the first good news Scott had had since COL Johnson made him surrender his weapon, and he said so.

"Let's link up in a day or two," Hill said. "I'll let you know what my lawyer says. We'll get you squared away."

The two men stood and embraced. At 0300, they moved out under cover of darkness.

CHAPTER 12

Dog Company was still deep in Jalrez. The morning after policing up the KIA, Davis heard the sound of rotors reverberating through the valley, ███ █████████████████████████. He and Erickson gave orders for the convoy to mount up. In Colon's truck, PFC Ryan Haffner was about to climb into the gun when Colon stopped him.

"No, bro. I'm on the gun today," Colon said. "I had a weird dream last night. We were on our way back and something bad happened."

Haffner laughed it off. "Great, man, why don't you just jinx us now, before we even leave?"

Colon didn't laugh with him. "We've been in the valley too long, bro. We're gonna get hit on the way out. I'm on the gun."

Haffner was taken aback. Bitting was riding in their truck, too, but still recovering from his VBIED wounds, and this was Haffner's shot at gunner. It was kind of a promotion, moving from the driver's seat to the gun mount.

He started to object: "That's my responsibility—"

Colon cut him off. "Don't argue with me. Something bad is gonna happen. I'm taking the gun."

██
██

Kamp was on edge; they all were. Then word filtered back over the net: halt movement, pressure-plate IED. First Platoon had spotted a pile of dirt containing a hastily buried explosive device. Hulburt traced a set of wires away from the device to some concealment, where he found a battery, but no one to detonate the bomb.

Again, news trickled through the convoy. *Weird,* Kamp thought. *At least we found it, though.*

Hulburt chunked a block of C-4 on the dirt pile and blew the IED in place. The convoy rolled on.

High over the valley, icy winds cut into LT Larry Kay and his team through the open doors of the ███████████████████████████████████████
███
███████████████████████████████████████

Kay ignored the cold and scanned the terrain below, airspeed melting vegetation into a blur. He wasn't supposed to be on this op. Prior to it, DeMartino had ordered him back to Airborne. But Kay knew his men would almost certainly be hit, and hit hard, this deep in the valley. So he had asked permission to put together a team that would ride in trail of the C2 helo.

"Just in case anything crazy happens," Kay had told DeMartino. "We'd be a mobile QRF and, if needed, a MedEvac."

DeMartino had checked with the aviation commander; both pronounced it a good idea. Next, Kay carefully selected his team. He needed a medic who could perform under intense pressure. He picked SSG Wilkerson. Kay also tapped SSG Kevin Doyle, who had been one of his soldiers when Kay was platoon leader in Bravo Company, along with 2LT Michael Wilda and SPC Ryan Boiano, a former Marine.

Kay briefed them. "If something goes down, we cannot afford any hesitation. Pack light and prepare your gear for running."

Kay had promised himself that no matter what happened, he would run as hard and as fast as he could for as long as he could. There would be no hesitation, just pure aggression.

Now Kay's eyes scoured the battlefield. He watched the Taliban take pot-shots at the air-assault helos lifting the Scouts out of the valley. Next, he saw Dog Company's trucks consolidate on the lone dirt road leading home, trailed by a pair of Apaches. ███████████████████████████████
███████ The high pitch of their jet turbines was a reassuring sound.
███
███
███
███████████████████████████████████ Then the convoy
rolled forward again.

███████████████████████████████   ████████

███████████████

Kay scanned the terrain, surprised that he could not spot an ambush. The long chain of trucks covered ten, then fifteen kilometers, and was approaching the old COP at Kowte Ashrow. Dog Company called it COP Conlon now, after Paul, and the outpost in Haft Asiab at the old schoolhouse, COP Carwile. Orchards hugged the dirt road, and Kay saw what appeared to be a footbridge flanked by high ground.

As soon as he spotted the bend in the road beyond it, he knew. But it was too late.

From the gun, Kamp saw the footbridge, with high walls of mud on either side and a blind curve ahead. His heart thudded against his ribs as his Humvee passed between the walls and under the bridge. Hair rose on the back of his neck. Then the walls exploded. A chain of embedded IEDs blasted earth and rock against the convoy, knocking Kamp out cold.

"Contact! Contact!" Davis heard the call over the net, but a cloud of dirt and debris cut his visibility to zero. He heard the hiss and boom of RPGs detonating around his platoon and a barrage of close-range bullets pinging off his truck.

Kay saw ████████████ roar in and unleash hell on the high walls concealing Taliban fighters. Fighter jets banked and dove toward the gunfight. The number of friendlies prevented them from dropping bombs, but they fired flares into the orchards, a show of force. In his rage, Kay prayed the flares burned the enemy's skin off. Then something caught his eye: a cloud of black smoke spewing from the top of a Humvee.

Davis heard Bitting scream, "My gunner's down! My gunner's down!"

That meant Colon. Colon was down.

Davis leapt from his truck, ran through a hail of incoming. He didn't think, he just ran. He sensed rather than saw enemy fighters popping up from behind the high walls, shooting at him as he passed. The walls were so tall that D Co's turret gunners could not angle their weapons high enough to hit anything with return fire.

From both sides of the road and the footbridge, RPGs burned through the storm of AK fire. Still Davis ran. Rounded the bend. Saw oily smoke spewing from Colon's truck, near the hood and up through the turret.

Davis reached the truck and yanked open the rear driver-side door. When he saw Colon, he believed with all his soul that he was looking at a dead man.

CHAPTER 13

WHEN KAMP CAME to, he could hear the battle raging outside. He remembered the high walls on either side of his truck and stayed low, reaching up just high enough to grab his gun grips and angle off some shots at the tops of the berms, the nearest just five feet over his head. As the .50-cal rattled in his hands, he heard over the net that Colon was dead and his heart tore in half.

His friend, his brother. They'd come up together. Colon had a baby girl he hadn't even met.

The radio squawked again: The Apaches had torched a van full of insurgents fleeing the scene.

Die, motherfuckers, Kamp thought. He was only sorry he didn't get to kill them himself.

"Colon!" Davis reached out, trying to find an unmangled place to lay his hand.

Colon lay slumped on the gunner's seat. The left side of his face was crushed, folded in behind his nose. His right arm had been shredded into raw meat. His left hand was a stump of bloody Jell-O, just a palm with shiny slivers of bone where his fingers used to be. He was unresponsive.

Davis looked up. One of the Humvee's bulletproof glass inserts was missing except for its blackened edges, which had shriveled to the frame like the flesh around a necrotic wound. An RPG had hit it, boiling and fusing the glass, and blasting Colon with a spray of jagged shrapnel.

Quickly, Davis checked the other men in the truck. In the driver's seat, Haffner had taken a wave of shrapnel down his right side. He was hollering in pain but coherent. Blood dripped from Bitting's ear. The overpressure had busted his eardrum, but he would make it.

Davis turned back to focus on Colon, calling his name, shaking him. Nothing.

Small arms fire was still pouring in. With Haffner and Bitting down, Davis needed to take over the gun. He was about to yank the quick-release strap that would free Colon to fall back into the truck, but he called out one more time. "Colon! Are you with me?!"

Colon shot straight up in the truck, roaring in pain. Davis reeled back, shocked. He would never forget Colon's one good eye, rolling like a stampede stallion's, wild with fury.

Colon flailed his muscled form and grabbed for the gun. Davis looked up, could see the ropes of Colon's neck, his lips pulled back, his one-eyed stare as he strained toward the gun like a bloody Hulk. Davis knew Colon didn't have much time. He had to get him under control.

███
███
██████ Kay prepped his gear, checked his weapon, released his harness.

"Here," he said, handing Wilkerson his med bag. Kay took a deep, endless breath. ██
████████████████████████████████ Rotor wash kicked up dirt and gravel eddies. Kay jumped out, took ten steps to clear the rotor blades, and took a knee to wait for his team, but they were already there. Rifle at the high ready, Kay turned and shouted, "Follow me!"

███
███
██ Kamp saw 4-4's spiderwebbed turret windows coated in blood. Saw Colon flailing, screaming in pain. Davis had him in a bear hug and was trying to pull him down from the gun.

Clicking off his harness, Kamp leapt from his truck, roof to roof. The smell of blood washed over him. He retched a little then steeled himself. The thought flashed through his mind that you usually wanted to encourage the wounded with hope, boost their will to live. But what Colon needed was a shock, something to break through his blind rage.

Kamp got in his brother's face: "Carlos! It's Kamp, man! You're fucked up bad! We need to get you out of here!"

Davis jumped up top to help. Together they tried to pull Colon *up* through the turret, but he fought them to stay in the truck.

Kay was running as fast and as hard as he could. Amid the dust storm, he could not see the ground. Every step was a chance and he did not care. He and his team had run flat-out for four hundred meters when they ran up on Hulburt.

"I'm the MedEvac," Kay said. The words rushed out, breathless. "Where are the casualties?"

Hulburt pointed and they both took off. When they reached 4-4, it was a maelstrom. Blood everywhere. Haffner lying faceup on the ground, leg strafed with shrapnel, cringing in pain. Bitting bleeding, shrapnel in his head and shoulder. A knot of soldiers screaming into the vehicle, trying to grab someone.

Kay approached 4-4 and saw a fleshy stub resembling a hand, reaching, reaching. Blood spurted from the limb. Kay saw Colon and put his hand out, trying to grab his arm above the wound. But it was slick with gore and Kay couldn't get a grip.

He heard a helo. It was his Black Hawk looking for another landing site. He ran to the middle of the road and threw smoke, signaling the pilot.

The chopper touched down, soldiers hopped out with a litter, and Kay ran toward the crew chief. "Three casualties!" he yelled over the rotor noise. "One urgent surgical and two walking wounded!"

Behind him, Davis and Kamp had finally wrestled Colon from the truck, but the big man was still combative.

"Colon, get on the litter!" Davis yelled.

"No, bro! I'm walkin'!"

"You've done your part! Now get on the litter, let us take care of you!"

Finally, Colon allowed himself to be strapped to the litter and loaded onto the helo. Though stiff with pain, Haffner tried to stay back, stay in the fight. He argued for a moment until Davis issued a direct order: "Get on the fucking helicopter. Now. I need you to look after Colon."

Haffner submitted and climbed aboard, along with Bitting.

When the bird was airborne and flying toward Bagram, Kay got his first, life-shattering look at Colon's face: Half of it was missing. There was no cheek to contain his tongue or the viscous mix of blood and drool that dripped from that side of his skull.

A thick, corned-beefy chunk of flesh flapped down over his eye socket. Kay reached out and lifted that chunk. "Doc!" he called to Wilkerson, "I can't find his eye!"

Kay and Wilkerson were wrapping Colon's head in gauze when Kay pointed to Colon's second most serious wound. One of his lungs was protruding from his right armpit. Kay was a little surprised that it wasn't covered in blood, but was actually a clean bluish white, encased in viscera that reminded him of Saran wrap.

When he tried to gently wrap the wound, Colon exploded. "Knock me out!" he cried, fully lucid. "Knock me *out!*"

Kay realized the helo was flying fast. It would turn out to be a record MedEvac, making Bagram from Jalrez in only twenty-seven minutes. At the airfield, medics and nurses pulled the litter from the bird. When the sunlight hit Colon, he shrieked in pain and tried to leap off the litter. He thrust his torn face at the nurses. Some of his teeth fell out on the ground, carried in the stringy fluid that streamed from his cheek.

"Knock me out!" he screamed. "*KNOCK ME OUT!*"

Medical personnel managed to get him into the treatment area, and Kay noticed some going green from the gore. Colon continued to thrash.

Kay pulled his face close, kept his voice even. "Hey, Carlos. It's Larry, man. Hey man, can you hear me?"

Colon pulled his good eye into focus. "Oh, hey, Larry. What's goin' on? Could you get them to knock me out?... *KNOCK ME OUT!*"

Doctors tried to move Colon from the litter to an examining table, but he pushed them off and got on the table himself, causing the armpit with the lung sticking out of it to spurt blood like a supersoaker water gun.

There was a lull. Working quickly, medics cut off Colon's uniform while a nurse closed in with a needle and finally knocked him out, just like he had asked.

Kay told the nurses his soldiers' names, then he walked outside and reboarded the helo. On the flight back to Airborne, all he could think about was Colon's hand. Kay was positive it would have to be amputated—which pissed him off, because Colon's wife had just given birth.

He won't be able to hold his new baby. Kay thought of what it would be like not to be able to shake his father's hand or touch his wife's face. He gritted his teeth and focused on the rotor noise to keep it together.

CHAPTER 14

HILL SAT IN the cramped jump office at Bagram processing the news: Colon and his crew blown up in Jalrez. Colon was such a physical specimen that it was hard for Hill to imagine him hurt so badly. Hill had heard that he was in Walter Reed Army Medical Center in Maryland in a coma. Even at that, there had already been multiple surgeries to keep him alive.

Haffner had two Purple Hearts now. Bitting had four, probably more than anyone in-country.

I should have been there, Hill thought. *Maybe if I had . . .*

His cell phone chimed, diverting him from the many shades of grief that seemed to have taken up permanent shelf space in his brain. The caller was Neal Puckett, on the line from Virginia.

Though Hill had yet to meet his attorney, he'd researched him and also gotten to know the man through several weeks of phone calls. He seemed to be the perfect mix of pit bull and golden retriever: friendly and reasonable at all times, except for those times when it was necessary to be ruthless.

After exchanging pleasantries, the two picked up the thread of a topic on which they did not agree. "Look, Roger, the last thing you want is for your case to go to a court-martial," Puckett said.

Hill flipped through a file folder plucked from the growing stack on his desk. "Okay . . . why? If Byrd decides to send us to a court-martial, maybe the mitigating circumstances will get us a not-guilty verdict."

"Could a jury find you not guilty even in the face of sufficient evidence to find you guilty?" Puckett said. "Of course. They can always vote not guilty. But here's what you need to understand: The convening authority picks the jury."

"Seriously? So the convening authority picks the investigating officer, and if the case goes to court-martial, they pick the jury, too?"

"Absolutely. That's one of things we deal with as defense attorneys."

Hill put his file folder down and listened as Puckett explained the legal hoops. A commander sends a case to an Article 32, in part so they can test its durability. The Article 32 IO is chosen by the convening authority, which is in a sense like a prosecutor picking his own judge. If that IO sends the case to court-martial, the convening authority then selects the jurors, all active-duty military.

Although it is never spoken aloud, most of those people are aware that the senior commander has decided there's sufficient evidence that the accused is guilty. And the subtext of that—again, unspoken—is that no commander would send a case to court-martial if he or she thought the accused was innocent.

"So what you have when you walk into a military court-martial," Puckett said, "is the actual presumption of guilt. Everyone in the courtroom understands that there was a screening process and evaluation of evidence done in advance of making the decision to hold a court-martial at all. So they know that the person sitting at the defense table is probably guilty of some, if not all, of the charges."

Hill closed his eyes, rolled his neck left, then right, gathered his thoughts. "Okay, so what you're telling me is that the deck is stacked."

"You wouldn't be the first person to say that. Yes, the deck is stacked against a military accused more so than a civilian accused. It would be fair to say that every possible advantage has been provided to the government side of a court-martial."

"So how does anybody get a fair trial?"

"Well, we get to voir dire the jury and make challenges. We explore the relationship between the jurors and the command—for example, is the convening authority the one writing their fitness reports? Or are any jurors being rated by any of the other jurors? We're asking them all these questions before the jury is empaneled. Also, the instructions a military judge will give the jurors—and remember, this was my job for a long time—are aimed at insulating against some of those other factors.

"So could a jury find you not guilty? Sure. But it is more likely they would find you guilty then give you a lesser sentence due to mitigation and extenuation. Then you'd have a federal felony conviction on your record and probably prison time. Maybe not as long a sentence, but still federal prison. We don't even want to go there, Roger. What we want is for Byrd to recommend against a court-martial based on mitigation and extenuation. If he doesn't do that, what we want then is a deal."

In late November, Hill ███ ████████████████████████████ This would be his last trip from ████████ ████████ before the Article 32 hearing. When he flew back through here again, would he and Tommy be free men or prisoners?

Neal Puckett was due to land in Kabul in less than a week. As the clock ticked down, Hill's nerves ratcheted up. The logistics involved in transporting a single human being from America to Afghanistan were daunting. A million things could go wrong. Bad weather and flight delays, yes, but also bribed officials, a truck bomb at the airport, or a coup. Traveling here was not like traveling in the Western world.

The ticket Hill and his wife purchased for Puckett cost them $7,000, more than they both made in a month. To have forked over that kind of money then fall short of having Puckett in the courtroom . . . well, that was a scenario Hill didn't even want to contemplate. He trusted Heather Masten, but they had built their strategy on Puckett's style of defense. Hill's and Scott's futures depended on it.

A familiar voice cut into his reverie. "Captain Hill?"

Hill turned to see a guy dressed like an air conditioner repairman. "Dave! How *are* you?"

Hill stood and shook hands with ██ ████████████████████████

The two men settled into uncomfortable terminal chairs. "Man, it is so good to see you," Hill said with genuine pleasure. "So, how's it going? Still busting spies?"

"I'm on my way to Kunar now," Dave said. A threat similar to the Airborne scenario was unfolding on a U.S. base there, with lead terps and contractors possibly involved. ██████████████████████████████████████ ██ ████████████

Dave looked at the floor, then back at Hill. "Listen, I'm sorry we couldn't stay at Airborne longer. We got called back to Bagram to deal with another hot-button issue. I would've stayed longer if I could've, seen things through to the end."

"Dave, you don't have anything to apologize for," Hill said, meaning it. "You guys did what you came to do."

"Yeah, but I still feel like shit about it. Listen, I had to provide the findings of our Airborne operation to a Lieutenant Colonel Gunther, the 15-6 IO for your case."

Accusations in the case and the specter of prison remained unspoken but hung there like an unpleasant smell.

"I know," Hill said. "My first sergeant and I have the Article 32 in a couple of weeks."

"I heard you guys were down at Salerno. How's that going?"

"To be honest with you, it's been rough. But we've got good attorneys, and I feel confident we can prove that we were just trying to protect our men."

Dave had had his own trials related to the Airborne op. Gunther and the 15-6 investigation team had come close to naming him as a conspirator, at times implying he had been aware of and even contributed to the conditions leading to the coffeehouse incident. Dave had cooperated with CID, providing investigators with his operational log and photos of the CI team's activities on Airborne. In a subsequent interview, investigators claimed falsely that his photos showed pictures of bloody detainees. Dave later wondered if CID made an honest mistake or purposely tried to bait him.

Dave shared none of this with Hill, who he felt had enough to worry about. Instead he said, "Sir, you wouldn't believe how much we learned from working with you guys."

"You guys can detain threats now?" Hill said.

"Yes, sir."

"Under OEF authority?"

"Roger that."

Hill swallowed and looked away. If Dave's team had had OEF authority a few weeks back, he and Tommy would still be in command. The company would be operating as normal. All of it, *all* of it would—

Hill arrested his thoughts. "That's awesome, Dave," he said. "That's really awesome."

The terminal PA system blared, announcing a flight to Landstuhl. Dave waited until the speakers fell silent, then turned in his seat and held Hill's eyes. "Listen, there is no doubt the nine spies we busted were responsible for the death of Coalition troops. And I know the pressure you guys were under with all the friendlies in the valley during Nomad. If it helps, I think you guys saved lives."

Hill breathed deep. He felt the weight of his decisions falling like dominoes, one after the other, leading him to this moment. Since the coffeehouse, his relief, the excruciating investigation, his men suffering for his mistakes, Hill had doubted himself a thousand times. Ten thousand. Dave's words reminded him of why he'd taken the road he had. Why he'd risked it all.

Hill's heart swelled with a strange mix of gratitude and sadness. "It does help, Dave," Hill said. "You can't even imagine how much."

CHAPTER 15

TOMMY SCOTT SAT alone at a table in the corner of the DFAC, shoveling some kind of sinister chicken into his face. Only a few days remained until the Article 32. He and Hill had continued their predawn rendezvous, with the captain updating Scott on the legal push and pull as the clock wound down toward the hearing.

Scott had abandoned the notion of trust. After seeing a statement from a young man he had loved and mentored saying that he and Hill had colluded on their story, Scott realized there was no one he could trust except his CO.

This new reality saddened him. After Desert Storm, Scott had been hungry for a more elite level of soldiering. He had already completed the Army's Recondo school, but now there was a new echelon: Army Ranger. Based on his superior performance, Scott's first sergeant had promised him he could go, and Scott was willing to trade six more years of his life for the chance. But on the day he was to reenlist, the first sergeant reneged. Told Scott he could transfer to another unit and apply for Ranger school via some long-ass bureaucratic process that Scott knew—*knew*—would land him at a desk somewhere and not in Ranger school at Fort Benning.

So, being twenty-seven years old and knowing everything, as many arrogant twenty-seven-year-olds do, Scott gave the Army the mental finger and got out. It was a rash decision that he would miserably regret.

Scott went back to Florida and stayed out of the Army for about three years, becoming a tree trimmer at a golf resort. He was good at it. But he hated it. Hated that his life wasn't going anywhere. Hated that he was back where he started, that the only upward mobility in sight was the highest tree branch on the back nine.

Plus, the money reeked. Seemed like he was busting ass harder than he ever had and wasn't gaining any ground. He missed the Army badly: the camaraderie, the challenge, and yes, the pay. Scott needed money.

Scott's heart was still in the Army, in soldiering. He knew he was made to fight, to lead, to mentor. He decided to reenlist, and he called his uncle Joel to talk about it. Years before, Joel had moved to Philadelphia and quit the bottle. Cleaned himself up. Now in his fifties, he dressed sharp, kept his mustache razor-trimmed. Scott admired him all the more for having overcome his love affair with booze.

"Tarpon Springs ain't no place for you," Joel said. "You're doing what you need to do. Going back to the Army. But you have to do it right. You got to promise me, now. Promise me you'll work as hard as you can and be your very best."

Scott promised. Then he shipped out, landing in Korea. Six months later, Scott got a phone call: Uncle Joel had died of a heart attack. Scott took emergency leave. The family held a wake in Tarpon Springs. In ones and twos, tearful, black-clad mourners shuffled forward, peered into the casket, and whispered final good-byes.

Scott, crisp and creased in his dress uniform, stepped forward. He looked down at his uncle, who was sporting a fresh shave and a double-breasted suit like he was going out to dinner. Scott leaned down near the casket's white satin lining, put his mouth next to Uncle Joel's ear, and whispered, "I'm not going to let you down."

Now he felt maybe he had broken that promise. Already, he had begun to withdraw into himself. The stack of statements Scott had seen was as high as his boot tops. How was he ever going to overcome that? Word from the prosecution was that he and Captain Hill were looking at serious jail time. He thought back to Nick Kanus, his boss at the Chicken King in Tarpon Springs. How he, Scott, had joined the Army to get out and see the world. Now it looked like he was going to see the inside of Leavenworth.

Scott finished only half the chicken. He stood, bused his tray, and stepped outside just as air raid sirens cut across the sky. Scott heard an explosion and recognized it as a rocket crashing down somewhere near the FOB. Around him, he saw men and women scrambling for shelter.

Suddenly, it hit Scott that he was an infantryman on a base under attack and he didn't even have a weapon. To defend himself or anyone else. The thought galled him. Another explosion hit nearby, but to Scott it seemed miles away. Protocol said he was supposed to head to one of the bomb shelters. Instead, he adjusted his patrol cap and walked to his quarters. Stepped inside his room and lay down on his bunk.

If he got lucky, he thought, maybe the next rocket would land on him.

Larry Kay hoisted his pack to his shoulder and stepped off the Black Hawk that had spirited him to FOB Salerno. His visit was in response to an "Order to Appear" that he'd received earlier in the month. He'd been called as a witness in the Article 32 for Hill and Scott. Not sure where to report, Kay reasoned that he should go check in with some legal type, a JAG or something. He dropped his gear, asked around, and found a building where the lawyers were supposed to be.

Earlier that month, LTC DeMartino had called Kay in to explain the summons.

"You know why they called you to Salerno?" DeMartino said. "It's for an Article 32 for Captain Hill and First Sergeant Scott."

"What's an Article 32?" Kay said.

"It's a hearing where they ask you questions under oath and you tell them your version of what happened."

"Okay."

Then DeMartino began prodding softly, gauging just what that version might be. Finally, he came out with it: "You don't suspect me of any wrongdoing, do you?"

"No, sir. You weren't even on the FOB at the time."

Kay's answer was truthful, but only in the narrowest sense. Of course the colonel had not been involved in the events at the coffeehouse. But Kay doubted whether DeMartino would even entertain the idea that his leadership was an issue. Any words to that effect would've been wasted, so Kay said, "If I'm called as a witness, I am going to say my piece. But if you're asking me if I'm going to say that you ordered Captain Hill to beat detainees or whatever, then no. I know you didn't do that."

Now, at Salerno, Kay rapped on the lawyers' door and introduced himself to the woman who opened it. "Hey, I'm Lieutenant Kay. I'm here because I got a subpoena for something to do with Captain Roger Hill."

"Hi, Lieutenant," the woman said. She then asked another soldier to leave, escorted him to the door, and closed it.

"I'm Captain Devon Runyan. Do you know why you're here?"

"Not really," Kay said.

"You've been called to testify on behalf of the accused, Captain Hill."

"Okay…"

"Are you familiar with the Fifth Amendment?"

"Yes," Kay said. His copy of the Constitution was still in his shoulder pocket.

"Okay, so you know that you have the right not to incriminate yourself?"

Kay frowned. He wasn't sure where this conversation was going, but he didn't like the initial heading.

"You understand that if you lie under oath, you'll be guilty of perjury," Runyan continued. "If you and I are talking, and I suspect you're admitting to a crime, I'm obligated to report that. Do you understand?"

Admitting to a crime? Kay thought. *I haven't committed a crime.* But he nodded. "Yes, ma'am."

"So, do you want to tell me now if you've done anything wrong? Because it's better if you tell me now than if it comes out during testimony."

Kay looked carefully at the captain. Was she trying to intimidate him? He remained respectful, but steeled his voice. "I don't have anything to tell you, ma'am."

Runyan returned his gaze. "Are you sure?"

"Yes, ma'am. I didn't do anything wrong."

Suddenly, the conversation was over. Outside, Kay's ears went red. He'd knocked on the wrong door. At that moment, Lieutenant Larry Kay mentally placed Captain Devon Runyan on his personal list of people he would not trust.

CHAPTER 16

A VISA HICCUP stranded Neal Puckett overnight in the Delhi International Airport. He had visited more than twenty countries over his career, and it wasn't the first time he had spent the night in an airport. Still, all things considered, he'd have preferred a comfy hotel.

Puckett found a seat on the edge of the busy terminal, which teemed with colorful sari-wrapped women, men in business suits, Muslim women in *abaya* and *hijab*. The air smelled of espresso, curry, and naan. He couldn't sleep for ten hours sitting upright in a straight-back chair, so Puckett slipped a folder from his briefcase and reviewed the latest notes from Heather Masten.

For Puckett, Hill's case came down to a question of necessity and the exigencies of combat. Rather than let prisoners go who had not only helped kill his guys, but who had so much information that they would likely help kill more, Hill had chosen to err on the side of protecting his men. In Puckett's view it was the right thing to do. To do what you believe is morally right, regardless of consequences, regardless of castigation, loss of livelihood, or even criminal punishment—that is the definition of moral courage.

Of course, the Army didn't see it that way. The Army's view was that this really wasn't Hill's call. He should have adhered to the 96-Hour Rule, waited for prisoner transport—and, if it came to it, let the detainees go. From a purely legal standpoint, the Army was correct: Hill had violated the UCMJ. Technically speaking, he was guilty. And that, as Puckett saw it, had become a rampant problem in this particular war.

Over his years as a JAG, then as a military judge, Puckett had watched the military justice system evolve. In the old, old days, the system was designed mainly for good order and discipline. A soldier or Marine busted the rules, he stood tall in front of the commanding officer—the "Old Man." Over time, though, inequities in this way of doing business led away from a disciplinary approach to a more justice-oriented system. This, of course, required lawyers. Then more lawyers.

Having been first a JAG himself, Puckett didn't have anything against military lawyers per se. What he had a problem with was the hypertechnical application of military criminal laws by lawyers who did not take a full enough measure of the risks, split-second judgments, and mental fatigue associated with combat.

This was especially true in the terror war, which differed wildly from other American conflicts. Since 9/11, soldiers and Marines were regularly seeing three, four, even five combat tours in a six- or seven-year period, most of them compulsory. The result had been grief without time to heal. Exhaustion without respite. And a penetrating war weariness that was causing even the most seasoned warriors to flag in spirit.

On top of that, this enemy engaged exclusively in irregular warfare, which does not follow any of the Geneva Conventions or international rules of armed conflict. On the contrary, this enemy blended in with the civilian population, knowing that collateral damage inflicted by Americans is as useful as dead Americans themselves. Every civilian death was a propaganda victory, a chance to weaken popular and governmental support of the Coalition—as well as the battlefield boldness of Coalition commanders.

Puckett took a break, found a vendor, and bought a coffee. Returning to his seat, he extracted another folder, sipped his coffee, and scanned again the list of charges heaped on Hill and Tommy Scott. This was familiar territory. There was the old catchphrase about throwing as many charges as possible against the wall to see what would stick. But there was another angle to it: Prosecutors are trained to maximize the criminal exposure of the accused and, in doing so, maximize potential punishment. The military justice system is at its base adversarial in nature, designed to work best when each side is pulling as hard as it can until a judge or jury steps in to figure out where justice resides, somewhere between the poles.

Puckett believed that left to their own judgment, battle-tested commanders could have made better, more just decisions about cases like Hill's case, and Allen West's before him. Unfortunately, in this lawyered war, Puckett had watched politics increasingly color justice, as career officers sought to minimize their own exposure to the criticism of the media, their peers, their raters, even of foreign powers.

Following cases like Abu Ghraib and Haditha, American military policy had shifted toward placating host nations' concern with American war crimes. A legitimate concern on its face—except that the hyperfocus had drastically altered the definition of "war crime" and the pendulum had swung wildly toward the mere *perception* of war crimes, and overprosecution as a form of ass covering.

In the process, Puckett thought, a great deal of moral courage had slunk away into darkness.

Scott was walking past the base Laundromat when he saw across a gravel lot a familiar, stocky silhouette. Kay saw Scott at the same moment, and the two men grinned and walked toward each other.

"Hey, motherfucker, what's up?" Scott said, and the two friends embraced.

"Good to see you, brother," Kay said. "They got blueberry muffins here?"

Scott laughed. After the isolation, seeing his closest brother felt like a rare moment in the sun. The two men chatted for a moment, Scott asking about his boys at D Co, Kay filling him in on the latest.

Kay looked at his friend, and saw a haunting around his eyes. "You okay?"

"Yeah, I'm okay." It wasn't true, but Scott wasn't going to whine.

"I'm hungry," Kay said. "Let's go get something to eat."

Kay pivoted and started toward the DFAC, but Scott hung back. "Hey, Larry—"

"What?" Kay said.

"It's not exactly official, but unofficially nobody's really supposed to be talking to me."

Kay scowled and pulled in his chin. "What do you mean?"

"The Brigade has pretty much discouraged people from hanging out with me. Like I'm a bad seed or something. And guys have pretty much followed that because they don't want it to rub off on them, make them look bad with the command. It would probably be better for you if you kept your distance."

Kay shook his head and uttered a snort of pure contempt. "Fuck that. That's not happening." He slung his arm across Scott's shoulders. "Let's go eat. I'm buying."

Scott chuckled. "Oh, okay, moneybags."

For the next three days, Kay and Scott were inseparable. Kay as yet unstained by scandal, and Scott the pariah of Salerno. When they went to the gym, the room cleared. When they sat down in the DFAC, people got up and left the table.

What is this, Kay thought, *junior high?*

More than once, Scott pleaded with Kay: "Man, you're going to get me in trouble. You should just go off with the other D Co guys who are here for the hearing."

But Kay knew Scott was looking out for him, not for himself, just as he always had.

For three glorious days, Tommy Scott was not alone. Gone were the fantasies of being killed by a lucky rocket, as well as darker dreams in which he checked out of life on a voluntary basis. Sometimes, Scott forgot that Kay was only twenty-three years old. He would later say that in those three days, that young officer saved his life.

The next day, November 29, Neal Puckett landed at FOB Salerno, where he met Roger Hill for the first time. His initial impression was of a man with an easy laugh and a gentle spirit.

For his part, Hill was relieved. With Puckett finally on the ground, he felt another surge of hope. Maybe this would all turn out all right... or at least go away. The two men headed over to the DFAC for dinner. Johnson's staff had dawdled over the defense team's routine request to supply Puckett's meals while he visited the FOB. The approval had come through only the day before. Though it could've been an oversight, it had seemed to Masten and Hill like penny ante foot dragging, a way to make life difficult.

As they entered through the main door, Hill saw a tall frame trailed by an entourage on the other side of the wide hall. He hesitated.

"What's up, Roger?" Puckett said.

"Um... nothing. I just saw the boss over there, that's all."

"You mean your commander?" Puckett said this with surprised delight, as if he'd just discovered the chow line was stocked with his favorite entrée.

Just as an *uh-oh* sounded in Hill's head, Puckett said, "Let's go meet him."

Before Hill could answer, Puckett was on the move, crossing the DFAC with the confidence of a man on his own turf.

Hill sighed and followed. *Oka-a-ay. I wonder how this is going to go.*

He quickened his pace to execute his duty of introductions, but Puckett smiled, strode the last few feet, and stuck out his hand with gusto. "Hi, Colonel Johnson, I'm Neal Puckett, Roger Hill's attorney."

Johnson stumbled a bit over his greeting and Puckett understood why. In the hypertechnical new world of military justice, it is not customary for the convening authority to meet with defense counsel. Such meetings were usually brokered by formal request, requests that were often denied lest a crafty defense lawyer talk the convener out of something he didn't want to be talked out of. But Puckett had found it good practice to demonstrate that he was a collegial fellow, ready to sidebar should the time come.

"I'm here for the Article 32 that starts day after tomorrow. And, hey! Thanks for letting me get chow here."

Johnson remained silent a beat too long, and Puckett let the awkward moment marinate.

"Well, I just wanted to introduce myself," Puckett finally said. "I'm really looking forward to working with your legal team over the next few days."

More awkward pause, Johnson looking unsure what to say, his staff alert, listening, balanced on the moment's edge.

"Well...okay. Take care," Puckett said, then turned and walked away, Hill following.

"Good to meet you," Johnson called after him.

Good to meet you, too, Colonel, Puckett thought. *I'm going to make you famous.*

BOOK 5

Trials of War

It is the spirit and not the form of law that keeps justice alive.

Earl Warren

(Overleaf) *First Sergeant Tommy Scott (left) with Lieutenant Larry Kay at FOB Salerno. Kay had been called as a defense witness for the Article 32 hearing in the case of* The United States vs. CPT Roger T. Hill and ISG Tommy L. Scott.

CHAPTER 1

1 December 2008
Longhorn Conference Room, FOB Salerno
Khost Province, Afghanistan

THOUGH IT WAS already 0700, the sky was still dark when Paul Avallone walked into FOB Salerno's Longhorn Conference Room on the first day of December 2008.

Avallone was the journalist and former Special Forces soldier who had ridden along with 3rd Platoon after the jingle truck massacre. He gazed around the room, wondering where to sit. Someone had arranged six or seven long tables into a horseshoe with the open end nearest the door. Fluorescent lights cast a yellow pall, as though the space suffered from some kind of bureaucratic flu.

Avallone had brought with him another man, P. J. Tobia, a reporter for the *Nashville Scene*. Tobia had been planning to ride along as an embedded reporter with another unit, but when Avallone told him about the case involving Hill and Scott, he decided to stay at Salerno. He pitched the story to his editors at the *Nashville Scene*, and they weren't interested, so he took a chance with the big boys, the *New York Times* and the *Washington Post*. After a mini–bidding war, the *Post* won, and Tobia found himself with a national story.

Slowly, the players streamed into the room and settled into place. LTC Robert Byrd sat on the closed end of the horseshoe, opposite the door. The defense—Puckett and Masten, along with Captains Jason Easterly and Kevin Cox, sat with their clients in folding chairs on Byrd's right. The prosecutors, Captains Stephen Latino and Devon Runyan, sat to his left, up toward Byrd.

Avallone and Tobia took seats on the defense side directly across from an empty folding chair that sat in the center of the horseshoe. That was the witness chair.

Buoyed by his time with Larry Kay, Scott had regained his optimism. CPT Hill had told him about LTC Allen West's case. Also, he'd reread the stack of sworn statements, and most of them matched his own recollection of events. Scott felt that once the IO heard why he and the captain had done what they'd done, he would recommend that Scott and Hill be disciplined and returned to duty.

Sitting at the defense table, Hill organized his notes. In the four months since he'd been relieved, Hill had existed in a kind of military limbo. Preparing his case had meant, by default, a long period of waiting. One hundred sixty days toward an unknown future. It reminded him of his time on the boxing team at West Point. During his short time as an amateur in the sport, it was the waiting he hated most, the anxiety of days. Waiting to see whom he would fight and on which card. Then once in the ring, waiting for that first solid blow to his face.

Although he hated getting hit, Hill always welcomed that first taste of leather. Because once the punch landed, he could gauge his opponent, know his reach, and decide how to counter. Now, sitting at the horseshoe in the dim yellow light, he was ready to finally get into the ring.

At 0800, Byrd called the hearing to order. After some wrangling over whether verbatim transcripts of the proceeding would be available—COL Johnson had authorized only summary transcripts—the prosecution called its first witness, LT Zachary Morris, the young officer who had called Battalion to report suspected abuse.

CPT Latino questioned Morris first, establishing how he had come to learn about events at the coffeehouse (at the FOB synch meeting that same night) and with whom he had discussed these revelations (LT Anthony Dey and SGT Jared Allen, both of Alpha Company).

Puckett then cross-examined Morris, establishing that he was very new to the Army, even newer to combat, and possibly suffered from a measure of naïveté about how things worked on a forward outpost.

Puckett: So, based on no combat time with Captain Hill or really not understanding anything about what they had been through, or experienced it with them, you stood in judgment, didn't you?

Morris: Based on what I knew, I decided something bad had happened, and it needed to be investigated, sir.

Puckett: You didn't witness any detainee activities at all that they were talking about, did you?

Morris: No, sir.

Puckett: You heard rumors from men who may or may not have had personal knowledge of events themselves, right?

Morris: Yes, sir.

Puckett: So, based on rumors about things that might have gone wrong, you put your company commander on report.

Morris: I had a very, very strong feeling based on the things that I heard from a number of people, and I believed it based on the climate that I had seen, so yes, I did.

Puckett: What if, after all of this is over, you turn out to be wrong? How would that make you feel?

Morris: Bad, sir, if I was proven wrong, but I don't think I am.

Puckett: But you didn't see any of it, did you?

Morris: No, I didn't, sir.

Puckett: Did Captain Hill ever tell you to lie?

Morris: In the meeting? Yes, he told everybody, hey, if they come and investigate, tell them it didn't happen and you didn't see anything.

Puckett: Captain Hill told you to say that you didn't see anything?

Morris: In the meeting, yes, sir, he did.

Puckett: You didn't see anything, did you?

Morris: No, I didn't, sir.

Puckett: So, he didn't tell you to lie, did he?

Morris: No, sir. But he was telling people to lie and say they didn't see or do anything.

Puckett: Did you see anything or not?

Morris: No, sir.

Puckett: Okay, so he did tell you to lie to an investigator?

Morris: No, sir.

Puckett: He didn't, did he?

Morris: Not unless I had seen something.

Puckett: What I'm asking is about you personally. Did he tell you to lie to investigators if an investigator showed up?

Morris: He told me to lie if I had seen any abuse going on, yes.

Puckett: He looked at you, and personally and individually told you to lie?

Morris: He told the group to lie.

Puckett: That's what you heard?

Morris: Yes, sir.
Puckett: And that's your testimony today?
Morris: Yes, sir.
Puckett: You'll stand by that even if it turns out that that is not true?
Morris: Yes, sir.

From the defense table, Tommy Scott watched Zachary Morris. Despite the fact that Morris had set this whole train in motion, Scott found that he didn't dislike him. He was just a kid, tossed on seas much bigger than himself, clinging for life to a limited set of facts. He had come from Battalion where, no doubt, he'd heard the grumbling about Hill and Dog Company. Scott wouldn't have been at all surprised to learn that Morris's opinion of the company had been formed before he arrived. Once at Airborne, Morris had had no idea of the danger he was in as the result of a well-entrenched insider threat. Still, Scott could see in Morris's eyes that he was telling the truth as he saw it.

Puckett, meanwhile, hated to do what he had to do next. But it was necessary.

Puckett: Which is more important: serving the rules on detainee treatment or taking care of soldiers?
Morris: Serving the rules on detainee treatment...
Puckett: Really? Are your soldiers aware that you feel that way?
Morris: I don't know, sir.
Puckett: I want you to imagine yourself in combat, and I want you to imagine yourself faced with a choice in combat. If you had a choice between doing something that you knew would preserve the lives of your soldiers, or following Army doctrine, which would you choose?
Morris: Is it the legal Army doctrine or tactical armed doctrine? If it's legal, I'm going to follow Army doctrine.
Puckett: At the cost of your soldiers' lives?
Morris: If necessary.
Puckett: Thank you.

Paul Avallone also felt bad for the young lieutenant. Puckett had painted a blistering contrast: Hill, who would sacrifice himself to bring his men home, versus Morris, who would put the letter of the law above his men's lives. But how else could Morris have answered? Avallone thought.

Avallone, who had spent his entire Army career as a Green Beret, understood nuances, that every situation did not represent a true dichotomy. But presenting the question as a simple dichotomy was exactly what Puckett had done, and to devastating effect: If Morris had answered that he would do something other than follow Army doctrine … well, that would've been the wrong answer, too.

LTC Heather Masten, however, was not feeling as charitable. She gazed at Morris from under lidded eyes and thought of a quote made famous by the social critic and theologian Erasmus.

Dulce bellum inexpertis.

"War seems sweet to those who have never experienced it."

Captain Devon Runyan, the female prosecutor, spoke up and tried to salvage Morris's testimony.

Runyan: Were Delta Company and Able Company doing anything tactically to prepare FOB for imminent danger?

Morris: Other than removing local nationals from the FOB? No.

Runyan: Reinforcing the exterior? Were people in proper uniforms ready to take on a fight?

Morris: No.

Prosecutor Stephen Latino: Going back to questions about the XO, Lieutenant Kay, and the fact that you didn't go to Lieutenant Kay about what you heard Captain Hill say, what are your thoughts on Lieutenant Kay?

Morris: I don't trust him. I think he did a lot to help the company to set up property accountability. But he didn't use the system properly, and this created a lot of problems. He hates Afghans. I don't trust him.

Latino: There are issues of property accountability?

Morris: Yes, sir.

Latino: What was his relationship like with First Sergeant Scott and Captain Hill?

Morris: I don't know…

Latino: One last question: Regardless of the rumors, can rumors be based on truth?

Morris: Yes, sir.

CHAPTER 2

AFTER MORRIS'S TESTIMONY, LTC Byrd excused him from the room. Latino next called a number of soldiers, witnesses for the prosecution. These included SSG Justin Pizzoferrato, an Able Company soldier who testified that Hill in the FOB synch meeting "made a comment about mishandling, making a mistake with some detainees." Hill told soldiers that if they heard any rumors to, in Pizzoferrato's words, "keep it on the down-low."

On cross-examination, Pizzoferrato told Puckett, "I never witnessed anything. Everything I know about the incident was heard from someone else."

SPC Allan Moser testified along with Bryan McCollum, the CID agent.

At 1525, Latino called Brigadier General Mark Milley, deputy commanding general for operations for the 101st Airborne Division.

Milley testified by telephone, his voice emanating from a speaker into the Longhorn Conference Room. Neal Puckett asked the general about his visit to Kowte Ashrow. Milley said that Major General Jeffrey Schloesser, commander of U.S. forces in eastern Afghanistan, had asked him to assess the COP.

"I thought the post was tactically exposed and the soldiers were placed at high risk," he told Puckett, listing a range of concerns from inadequate defenses to insufficient combat power. "It would surprise me if Colonel Johnson and Lieutenant Colonel DeMartino didn't see any issues with the security of the COP...I was not happy with it. I didn't want to see them killed or overrun."

After his visit, Milley recommended that the COP be closed or turned over to Afghan control, he said.

Puckett asked Milley whether he was surprised to receive the letter from CPT Hill.

"It didn't shock me that he jumped his chain of command," Milley said. "It's ordinary for me."

He did not take from the letter that Hill "was in a state of crisis," the general added. "I took it as venting."

At the defense table, Hill scribbled a note: "Did not jump the chain." The general had given him an open door.

Puckett then asked for Milley's opinion on the pressure Hill was under, both from the tension with Battalion and having lost men in combat.

Milley's answer was unequivocal: "I'm a general officer in the United States Army. There are rules that we all have to live by. There is no amount of pressure that will justify or allow us to commit a war crime. I cannot underwrite the commission of a war crime, and I won't."

Hill wasn't surprised at Milley's forceful answer. What did surprise him was his use of the phrase "war crime." It was as though by charging him and Scott with war crimes, the prosecution had set in place a false lexicon that was now the accepted vernacular.

The last witness of the day was SGT Jared Allen, the Alpha Company sergeant who had burst into the coffeehouse during the interrogations and asked Tommy Scott to accompany him to the entry control point. In preparing for the case, Puckett felt the young sergeant would be the strongest witness for the prosecution. As CPT Latino began his questioning, Puckett picked up a folder containing a set of diagrams and placed it on the table before him.

Latino: Why were you going to the coffee shop?

Allen: I originally went to the coffee shop to meet with First Sergeant Scott.

Latino: Why did you need to meet with First Sergeant Scott?

Allen: I don't remember, something about a SOG, I had some business with him.

Latino: What does SOG stand for?

Allen: Sergeant of the Guard, sir.

Latino: So what did you see when you came upon the coffee shop?

Allen: A number of U.S. Coalition [soldiers] outside, and detainees on the ground. The door was closed.

Latino: The detainees on the ground, were they flex-cuffed, do you remember?

Allen: They were restrained, sir. I don't really recall that well.

Latino: Were they either blindfolded or gagged or in any way being held down or anything like that?

Allen: They weren't being held down, sir. They were blindfolded, restrained.

Latino: And what did you do next after you saw that?

Allen: I entered the coffee shop and sat down to wait to talk to First Sergeant Scott, sir.

Latino: What was going on in the coffee shop?

Allen: There were a number of things. Mostly First Sergeant Scott was interviewing one of the detainees. There were other guys who were kind of walking around, detainees sitting down.

Latino: How was he interviewing the detainees?

Allen: At the time, I saw First Sergeant Scott was on top of one of the detainees. Two other soldiers were holding his arms and he was yelling at him.

Latino: What was he yelling?

Allen: At that time, I don't remember, sir.

Latino: So there were two soldiers holding down the arms?

Allen: I believe so.

Latino: Now, what happened to the detainee when First Sergeant was done asking questions?

Allen: I believe he was taken outside the coffee shop with the others, sir.

Latino: And what happened when that detainee went outside the coffee shop?

Allen: I honestly don't know.

Prosecutor Runyan: Did you follow the detainee out, or did you stay in the coffee shop?

Allen: I did at one time, ma'am. I don't remember which time that was. The first one that was taken outside, I believe I stayed inside.

Runyan: From your recollection, what happened next?

Allen: I recall, I stood and walked around. I saw Staff Sergeant [Ron] Rideaux, who was behind the bar. I don't remember if First Sergeant Scott left or not, but I know eventually they moved on to the next detainee.

Runyan: When you say "moved on to the next detainee," then what happened?

Allen: They grabbed a different one in the same manner, firing questions. The interpreter was translating. First Sergeant Scott was on that one, kind of the same manner of interrogation.

Runyan: Did he strike that detainee?

Allen: He did.

Runyan: With an open hand?

Allen: Right.

Runyan: Was there anything with food going on that you remember?

Allen: I recall either that detainee...I recall one that had said something positive, and he was rewarded by giving him food. They gave him an MRE.

Runyan: So he didn't go outside.

Allen: He did not.

Runyan: After the second one, so that was number two that you saw, correct?

Allen: Yes, ma'am.

Runyan: Then what happened after number two?

Allen: There was another detainee, same process. At this point everybody in the room was kind of upset that another one wasn't cooperating, I guess. This detainee got led outside by Captain Hill, and then I remember First Sergeant Scott was there. I had followed Captain Hill and the detainee out of the building.

Runyan: Did First Sergeant Scott say anything to these detainees that you can recall before they went outside?

Allen: Not that I remember.

Runyan: You eventually followed Captain Hill out with a detainee.

Allen: Yes, ma'am.

Runyan: Can you tell me what happened then?

Allen: He led the detainee out to the back where the others were lying down. After that, the detainee kneeled and Captain Hill fired a shot by his head.

Not true, Hill thought. He glanced at Puckett, who looked unperturbed. Puckett picked up a sheet of paper and began.

Puckett: Sergeant Allen, you've been questioned several times about what you saw that day, is that right?

Allen: Yes, sir.

Puckett: You even did a diagram a couple of times, right?

Allen: Yes.

Puckett: I'm going to hand you one now and I want to see if you recognize that. Does that look familiar?

Allen: It does.

Puckett: Did you draw that diagram?

Allen: I did.

Puckett: When did you draw that diagram? Is it dated?

Allen: On the 4th of September.

Puckett: Who did you draw it for?

Allen: CID.

Puckett: Did they ask you to draw a diagram?

Allen: They did.

Puckett: In drawing the diagram, what were you asked to portray? What were you asked to draw about?

Allen: In this one, sir, they wanted to know where the detainee was, where I was, and where Captain Hill was when the shot was fired.

Puckett: You've indicated on that diagram by writing your name next to a triangle where you were, is that right?

Allen: That's correct.

Puckett: And I think from the legend that you drew, that the triangles mean where U.S. soldiers were, right?

Allen: Yes, sir.

Puckett: And the *X*'s are where you remember the detainees being placed on the ground, is that right?

Allen: Yes, sir.

Puckett: Isn't there also—and I highlighted it there—there's something called "point of impact." Explain that to me.

Allen: They wanted me to find a way to demonstrate where the bullet would have struck the ground...

Puckett: That place where you said point of impact was, did you actually see a round strike the ground?

Allen: Yes, sir...

Puckett: If you look at that diagram, and you look at labels from top to bottom on the diagram, the significant labels, you've got a point of impact, and down from that you have Captain Hill, and down from that you've got the detainee?

Allen: Correct.

Puckett: So from your diagram it appears as though Captain Hill is standing between the detainee and the point of impact, is that correct?

Allen: Um, yes, sir.

Puckett: So, from geometry and physics and the fact that someone can't be in two places at once, it appears from that diagram that if Captain Hill fired to that point of impact—bullets travel very quickly in a straight line in a short distance, don't they?

Allen: Very rapidly.

Puckett: From that diagram, isn't it fair to say that what you have represented is that Captain Hill had a detainee on one side of him, could have been behind him. Well, let me ask you this, which way was he facing when he fired the shot? Was he looking at the place where the impact was going to be?

Allen: He was, sir, he was facing the HESCO wall.

Puckett: So, he was facing the HESCO wall? Right?

Allen: That's where he was looking.

Puckett: By that diagram, that would have put his back to the detainees, am I right?

Allen: No, sir.

Puckett: That's what your diagram says; do you want to change your diagram today?

Allen: My diagram says his back is to the detainee?

Puckett: No, it doesn't say that, but you just told me that. You told me he was facing the HESCO barrier.

Allen: No, I said he was looking at HESCO. His body was still oriented in the direction that I indicated.

Puckett: Okay, let me see this. Okay, you say his body was facing to the right, but he was looking over at the HESCO barrier where he was firing?

Allen: Yes, sir.

Puckett: So he was looking where he was shooting, right?

Allen: Absolutely.

Puckett: Okay. By that diagram he's standing between the point of impact and the detainees, is that right?

Allen: That is correct.

Puckett: The direction that he is firing—follow me—the direction he is firing is away from the detainee, isn't that correct?

Allen: Yes, sir.

Puckett: Didn't fire at them, did he?

Allen: No.

Puckett: Now tell me, from the position from where Captain Hill was standing, how many feet away from his own feet did the round impact, from your recollection? In other words, how close to his own feet did he shoot?

Allen: I'd say about two meters' worth, four or five feet.

Puckett: Two meters is about seven feet or six and a half feet.

Allen: Five or six feet.

Puckett: Five or six feet away from his own feet? How far were his feet from the detainee?

Allen: Two or three feet, sir.

Puckett: So now what you're telling me is that the round impacted about ten feet away from the detainee, isn't that correct?

Allen: That is correct.

Puckett: So, you've had some weapons training, haven't you?

Allen: I'd say so.

Puckett: They talk about weapon safety?

Allen: Yes, sir.

Puckett: And you know which end is the business end of a rifle or pistol?

Allen: Yes, sir...

Puckett: So it's pretty clear from that diagram that the detainee in actuality was never in danger of getting hit by that bullet? It was never fired at him?

Allen: It was perfectly clear that he wasn't intending to shoot a detainee.

Puckett: He didn't fire it right down next to his head, where he could have missed and hit the detainee. There's no way that detainee was in any danger from that weapon, is that correct?

Allen: That is correct.

Puckett had been right about Allen: His testimony had been sure-footed and detailed. Still, Puckett had been able to impeach his most damning testimony—that Hill had fired his pistol near the prisoners' heads. After his cross, Puckett was confident no one would be able to conclude that Hill had endangered the detainees when he fired his weapon.

CHAPTER 3

2 December 2008
Longhorn Conference Room

THE ARTICLE 32 hearing reconvened the next morning at 0800. Hill felt optimistic. Puckett called Larry Kay as the first witness for the defense.

Puckett: What is the role of the battalion itself with respect to the company?

Kay: The role of the battalion itself with respect to the company is to provide resources that allow a company to accomplish its mission. Similarly, the company accomplishes its mission in order for the battalion to accomplish its mission, and it's sort of like a symbiotic relationship.

Puckett: Okay, and how well do you think your company was doing its part in this operation?

Kay: Best we could, I think, for what we had.

Puckett: How well was your battalion doing in its operation?

Kay: As far as supporting us, not too well.

Puckett: Why not? Why do you say that?

Kay: Because your battalion exists for a reason; your S4 exists for a reason; your [Forward Support Company] exists for a reason; your battalion XO exists for a reason. When we make resource requests, supply requests, enabler requests, it's not necessarily our jobs to secure it ourselves. It's the battalion's job to secure it for us, and understandably there are limitations, based on resources...but for the most part, we were not afforded many of the things we requested.

Puckett: How diligent were you in requesting the things you needed?

Kay: I was working every day to secure resources and assets. I would say daily diligence, twice daily diligence.

Puckett: And what sort of responses did you get from your requests?

Kay: They ranged from slightly humorous to slightly insulting, I would say the worst response I ever got was asking for a fuel pump, and the response was, do you have a weed whacker?

Puckett: Have you ever run short of essential, life-sustaining things?

Kay: We went red-black on water.

Puckett: What is red-black? Can you explain that system?...

Kay: It's more like a formula where it's based on how many soldiers you have [in relation] to what they needed, and based on consumption in certain aspects. You categorize your supplies in order of black, red, amber, green.

Puckett: So tell me what the colors mean.

Kay: Black means that you have less than 10 percent of what you need to have to conduct a mission. Red means you pretty much have 40 percent of what you need to conduct a mission. Amber is about 60 percent. Bronze, 70 percent. Green is 70 percent and above to conduct the mission.

Puckett: So, explain within the context of that system, how you ran short on the supplies?

Kay: We ran short on Class One water when I arrived...I increased the consumption rate because it started to get hot and we increased our op tempo, and so for three months, there was a steady decline of water and there was no delivery whatsoever.

We were almost black on water, at which point I called my Battalion S-4 [supply officer] and noted that I had been doing what I was supposed to do and I had not received one delivery of water. At which point, they told me that you had to let the system fail in order for any flags to go off.

I replied, I can't let the system fail on water, because that will kill us and we will not be able to conduct missions.

Puckett: You were told that you have to let the system fail? In other words, deprive the soldiers of water in order to fix the system?

Kay: Correct, sir.

A palpable hush blanketed the room, and Puckett paused to let the revelation sink in. Then he turned to a forensic matter. In earlier testimony, Special Agent Bryan McCollum of the Criminal Investigation Division revealed that CID had confiscated the hard knuckle gloves of two soldiers, Mo and Moser. Those gloves, McCollum testified, had contained DNA from three separate individuals.

> **Puckett:** I want to briefly ask you something and then just leave it. What are tactical gloves?
>
> **Kay:** It's what you wear outside of the wire. You have your standard-issue Nomex gloves. That is the SOP [standard operating procedure] for going outside of the wire and conducting combat operations.
>
> **Puckett:** On the day of the fatalities that your guys were working on, did these guys have gloves?
>
> **Kay:** Yes.
>
> **Puckett:** And guys who assisted in casualty evacuation and treating the wounded would have all been wearing gloves? Would it be fair to say there would be blood on their gloves?
>
> **Kay:** Well, I have blood on my gloves. I'm sure that PFC Parsons has it there.
>
> **Puckett:** Is it possible even after it happens, that blood might still be on some of their gloves?
>
> **Kay:** You might not have the red. I still have brownish-reddish crap on my gloves.
>
> **Puckett:** And other soldiers would, too?
>
> **Kay:** Mm-hmm, yeah.

At the defense table, Hill's throat closed with unshed tears. He remembered driving up with the QRF after the IED blew up under Carwile's truck, seeing Mo take over chest compressions on Donnie.

Of course, there was blood on Mo's gloves. He could see why CID would try to tie the gloves to the detainee incident. But it was also an example of how investigators fixated on the most damning explanation for physical evidence when the truth was, in fact, heroic.

Next Puckett focused on the meeting at which LT Morris claimed Hill told soldiers to lie about detainee abuse. Kay said Hill had not told people to lie. Rather he emphasized "that just the presence of this rumor can be really, really bad. If soldiers were to go to the MWR (Morale, Welfare and Recreation) and be like, 'Oh my God, they're killing people,' or some craziness like that. So, the idea was to have the chain of command just not really talk about it. Not cover it up, but just don't propagate it."

When it was time for the prosecution's cross, CPT Runyan zeroed in on the vaunted rapport Hill and Scott had with their men.

Runyan: Lieutenant Kay, when you first started off, after the whole property spiel, you said Delta Company took care of their soldiers, and they revered Captain Hill and Sergeant Scott because they took care of soldiers, correct?

Kay: Yes.

Runyan: Now, do you think it's responsible of the company commander and first sergeant to put their soldiers in a situation where two of them are facing summary court-martials, and they're facing other-than-honorable discharges from the Army, three of them are facing Article 15s, and they've admitted to their wrongdoing. Do you think that's taking care of soldiers?

Kay: I don't think they put them in that position.

Runyan: You wouldn't put your soldiers in that position?

Kay: No, no, no. I don't think *they* put them in that position, so I can't answer the question.

Runyan: Okay. So you stayed away from the coffee shop.

Kay: It wasn't a matter of staying away. I had my headphones on in my office listening to LeAnn Rimes, while doing FLIPLs [equipment loss reports]...

Runyan: Is it okay to strike detainees?

Kay: If you are in harm's way, for self-defense it is.

Runyan: How about mounting them and slapping their faces multiple times with open hands?

Kay: I don't think you'd get anyone to say, yeah, that's okay.

Runyan: How about blindfolding them with duct tape?

Kay: If they were able to take off their blindfolds multiple times, and you have to find a way to secure it.

Runyan: What about if they were restrained?

Kay: If, once again, if their blindfold keeps on falling off. Because you don't need your hands to get a blindfold off.

Runyan: What about gags?

Kay: If they're making a lot of noise, and they are noncompliant—

Runyan: Do—

When Runyan cut Kay off, LTC Byrd, the investigating officer, cut in: "Would you let him answer the question please? Thank you."

Kay: Yes, gagging in order to silence the detainees or EPWs is authorized.

Runyan: Okay. How about having blindfolded, restrained detainees on their knees, taking out a 9-mil, and charging the handle two feet away from his head?

Kay: I would never do that.

Runyan: Would you put your soldiers in a position to see you doing that?

Kay: I would never do it, so I would never put them in a position to see me doing it.

Runyan: Would you put your soldiers in a situation where they observe you knocking a detainee down and slapping them with an open hand, repeated times?

Kay: It might be uncontrollable, if the detainee resists.

Runyan: How about three detainees?

Kay: If three detainees attacked a guard, and he had to mount them, and defend himself?

Runyan: What about to do it for tactical questioning?

Kay: Was he resistant?

Runyan: No.

Kay: What was the question again?

Runyan: Would you allow your soldiers to be put in a position to observe you doing that?

Kay: Since I wouldn't do it, I wouldn't put them in a position to see me doing it.

Runyan: Would it be taking care of soldiers if you did put them in that position?

Kay: What's the purpose of the tactical questioning?

Runyan: To take care of soldiers.

Kay: What's the question again?

Runyan: So the purpose of tactical questioning in that situation was to take care of his soldiers.

Kay: And what's the question?

Throughout this exchange, Kay grew more contentious. Runyan was trying to corner him, and it was not in Kay's repertoire to back down. Observing this, the journalist Paul Avallone thought Kay wasn't doing himself any favors with Byrd. Runyan was a prosecutor doing her job. Avallone thought Kay was showing a little too much disdain. On the other hand, he had to admire the lieutenant's courage. Kay had nothing to gain, but was arguably throwing away his own career for what he believed was right. During a subsequent portion of Kay's testimony, he and Runyan went at it again.

Runyan: Would you admit that other companies had supply issues?

Kay: Yeah, undeniably, but I don't think anyone else went black on water or red on fuel.

Runyan: I would encourage you to go to Brigade when they have those updates, and you will see FOBs that are black and red on water and fuel.

Kay: Where are they? Are they in Tarawa or Doa China? Those are away from main MSRs in austere conditions. I can understand those. But if you are on Route 1, all you have to do is be dropped.

It's dangerous, yeah, because security has gotten crazy out there. But you don't need to rally air support, you just need to have your system functioning, the system that automatically delivers me water, that automatically delivers me fuel. But if that system is not allowed to function, then I don't get water or fuel.

I can understand FOB Tillman going black, and sometimes I can understand Sayed Abad going black. But what I can't understand is if I have my COPs and FOBs on the main MSR, the Main Supply Routes, and I can't get supplies, it's a failure on someone's reporting mechanism. It's not mine, because I went out there daily, and I counted bottles because I thought it was nuts.

Runyan: Isn't there a whole other task force that deals with supplies in country? A logistics Task Force?

Kay: There's a Battalion S-4.

Runyan: But the contractor, not Battalion.

Kay: No, no, *no*. Contracts through Salerno, that's something completely different than the massive theater contract for the deliverance of water from point A to point B.

Runyan: But it's not necessarily the 1-506th that has complete control of supplies?

Kay: Correct, but do you want me to call the Task Force and tell them that I don't have fuel?

Runyan: No.

Kay: I want Battalion to call Brigade to call division to call the task force. Actually I don't want there to be a call. I want there to be the system existing and working.

Runyan: But it wasn't the 1-506th targeting D Co at Airborne in not delivering supplies.

Kay: I can't say that. I don't know.

Runyan: And even if they were?

Kay: That's pretty sad.

Runyan: Does that allow you to slap detainees?

Kay: In self-defense, yes.

Runyan: Does that allow you to blindfold them, flex-cuff them, charge a weapon two feet away from their head, and fire a shot into the ground?
Kay: No.

As Kay and Runyan hammered back and forth, Heather Masten grew frustrated listening to the female captain. Runyan's questioning was so rapid-fire that she cut in on Kay's answers, not allowing him to elaborate even when it was clearly appropriate. She could see Kay growing frustrated, too.

Masten knew one of LTC Byrd's tasks would be to determine the credibility of individual witnesses. Would Kay have improved his by patiently explaining to Runyan the realities of life outside the wire, and the danger-close nature of the insider threat? Probably. But Runyan seemed to Masten to be championing the detainees as victims, instead of recognizing that they had betrayed the trust of the men in this very room, and killed some of their closest friends. So for a heart-on-his-sleeve man like Kay, a patient explanation may have been a bridge too far.

Kay's testimony lasted a full six hours with only a single fifteen-minute recess. In that space, he asserted that Roger Hill was an effective leader and that loyalty in the company was "uncompromising, from the soldier at the gun mount to the commander and back"; that Dog Company's area of operations was impossibly large for a company of its size; that Battalion had not adequately supported D Co.

Then Neal Puckett zeroed in on the resupply mission to Sayed Abad:

Puckett: So, I want to be clear, the Battalion failed in its routine mission to deliver food to these people in Sayed Abad?
Kay: Yes, it wasn't the first time it happened.
Puckett: But they knew they were supposed to?
Kay: Mm-hmm.
Puckett: So then you prepared a patrol to go out and resupply with food these people?
Kay: Yes, I led 3rd Platoon out, as it's my job as the XO to conduct resupply missions within the company...We were driving south on Route Ohio and around the village of Durani in the district of Nerkh. We hit a command wire IED, which subsequently killed two soldiers and wounded three others.
Puckett: Has anyone told the Battalion commander that he killed those people?
Kay: No.

CHAPTER 4

AT 1400, LTC Byrd excused Kay from the room and recessed the hearing for fifteen minutes. At 1415, Byrd reconvened, and Puckett called his next witness, MAJ Christopher Faber, the former Wardak field grade who had transferred up to Logar Province, where he had taken over as a Battalion XO for 4th Brigade, 101st Airborne Division.

Puckett: Major Faber, let's cut right to it. What were your duties beginning on about April of 2008?

Faber: From April to about July 26th or so, I was the Wardak operations officer. I was assigned to 1-506th from Brigade headquarters to do key leader engagements, interface with the Wardak governor, and provide developmental assistance...

Puckett: What was the level of your interaction with Captain Hill?

Faber: I interacted with Captain Hill daily, hourly.

Puckett: Did you have an opportunity to observe his leadership style?

Faber: I did.

Puckett: Could you give your evaluation?

Faber: Captain Hill was a very caring, charismatic leader, cared about his soldiers, and was very tactically and technically proficient.

Puckett: Yet there is some evidence that perhaps his particular company was not well supported and sometimes came up short of supplies?

Faber: Wardak was the economy of force for the Currahee Brigade and Red Currahee Battalion. It was about the size of Connecticut, but had about 110 people maximum, so you could arguably say by just looking at numbers that it was at the lowest end of the totem pole. If you look at some of the interfaces and the kind of things that happened between the Battalion and the company, you could get that perception that they were at the short end of the stick. It was very obvious.

Puckett: So it wasn't just Captain Hill's perception?

Faber: No, from my interaction with the Battalion, I felt that Wardak was an afterthought.

Puckett: Who was your boss at the time?

Faber: Lieutenant Colonel DeMartino.

Puckett: Did you ever hear him speak ill of Captain Hill?

Faber: There were a couple of times where he was concerned with Captain Hill's performance of things that were arguably out of Captain Hill's control. Some with communication issues, or the ability to report back to Battalion. There was a reporter there who quoted CPT Hill out of context, and there was talk of relieving Roger for something that was, at best, a counseling session. From my first couple of weeks there, it was clear that Lieutenant Colonel DeMartino wasn't super supportive of Delta Company, and that relationship only went downhill...

Puckett: Earlier there was some testimony about whether or not there was a personality conflict between CPT Hill and LTC DeMartino. Do you know anything about that?

Faber: ...I know that LTC DeMartino has favorites and he has nonfavorites, and CPT Hill was outside that inner circle. Every mistake or anything that Roger ever did, the response was, "Oh well, we're going for a relief for cause."...That puts a subordinate commander on thin ice and feeling like he has less opportunity to make decisions.

Puckett: Did you say LTC DeMartino was always looking for a "relief for cause"?

Faber: He'd always use that set phrase: "If he keeps on going this way, I'm going to relieve him."

Puckett: We had testimony like yours that Captain Hill was a very fine leader. Can you give us an evaluation of Colonel DeMartino?

Faber: ...It's who he knows, and he'll let you know whether or not you're smoking cigars with him, or whatever. He's looking for the next step, and he's already talking about being the Brigade commander, things like that. So you can tell that's his focus. But a lot of folks are looking at stuff like that. Alone, that's probably not a huge indictment, but when you consider that on two occasions I've seen him openly lie to his XO about something he said to him—I've seen him do other things that I would call morally bankrupt.

Puckett: You know for sure he has lied to officers?
Faber: Yes, I'm sure of it.
Puckett: On more than one occasion?
Faber: Yes, absolutely. I was on both sides of the conversation by accident.
Puckett: So you would consider him morally bankrupt?
Faber: "Morally bankrupt" is the term that I would use.

Faber's raw assessment floored Tommy Scott. Over the years, most of the field grades and higher who had passed through his orbit had been about getting the next medal, making history, becoming the next Patton. But here was a major who was willing to be truthful, to put it all on the line no matter what anyone said about him afterward. Chris Faber had instantly and single-handedly recalibrated Scott's opinion of senior officers.

Faber's testimony had centered on DeMartino's personal ethics. Puckett now honed in on his military leadership.

"Major, earlier we heard testimony that Lieutenant Colonel DeMartino would seemingly, without military purpose, make the company perform certain missions."

"A couple of times," Faber replied.

The major then gave the details of two missions, first the zero-notice "movement to contact" order he'd given during the reconnaissance of Razak's house in Jalrez.

Faber: Lieutenant Colonel DeMartino says, we have a reconnaissance force with two platoons, I think we can do this. They moved about four or five kilometers and had an ambush, and at this ambush site—arguably this is where you think it's somewhat reckless—somewhere in the middle of the ambush site, they would quiet down for a little bit, then we started to get air cover and Lieutenant Colonel DeMartino is taking pictures with his staff.

The mission was to do a reconnaissance to establish a COP forward. That was the mission. That's what we rehearsed. That is what the resources in arms were to do. So in that sense, I would call that reckless, especially the attitude at the end.
Puckett: Was there a second time?
Faber: The second time we were in Jalrez, we were building the COP...We were there about two or three days and the COP was about 60 to 70 percent done. LTC DeMartino comes out for a visit to see how things are going and things were going pretty good. LTC

DeMartino decided that they're going to take a trip to the district center. Now, the only reason I know is that [one of DeMartino's officers] said that he [DeMartino] is going to be bored with this construction out here and he's going to be itching for a fight...

It was uncoordinated, unplanned, and after talking with [the officer] ahead of time, he said LTC DeMartino is itching for a fight, so he's probably going to go looking for one. That is what would lead a person to believe that this was somewhat reckless.

Puckett: Do you have any sense of how widespread this knowledge is?

Faber: The command sergeant major and I had a conversation at the end of June, and he said, "Sir, I sure hope the colonel gets a Purple Heart soon so that he can stop putting our guys at risk."

Puckett knew it was time to step aside: "No more questions, sir," he said. Prosecutor Stephen Latino then waded in.

Latino: Did you ever hear Colonel DeMartino say, "I need to get a Purple Heart"?

Faber: I never heard him say that, no. Only the sergeant major said that.

Latino: It's a rumor?

Faber: It's what his sergeant major said to me about the colonel. That's what he said to me.

Latino: Could it be that Colonel DeMartino wants to take the fight to the enemy?

Faber: Sure. That's one way to look at it.

Faber delivered that last answer in a dubious tone, and here, Runyan cut in. "Do you think a bad Battalion commander excuses decisions by a commander to violate the Law of Armed Conflict?"

Faber fixed Runyan with a knowing gaze. "How very loaded a question that is. I think it leads to those kinds of decisions being made, and I think it creates the atmosphere. We all want to be commanders, and we all accept some of those responsibilities, and so the atmosphere creates some sort of level of responsibility. Certainly no one is excused to go and be lawless and reckless. That's a slippery slope there that I think you're trying to reach for."

CHAPTER 5

PUCKETT'S VICTORIES WERE stacking up. Both his examinations and the prosecution's cross had landed firmly in Hill's and Scott's column. Faber's testimony corroborated others' claims that Battalion leadership failed on multiple occasions. As Puckett saw things, it also ensured that if Byrd recommended a court-martial, a repeat of this testimony in open court would have disastrous consequences for everyone up the chain of command.

Scott's new lawyer, CPT Jason Easterly, next called Major John Karagosian as witness. Karagosian, the 1-506th's former XO, had served directly under LTC DeMartino during the first half of Dog Company's Wardak deployment. Karagosian was to testify telephonically. Latino, the prosecutor, called the major and activated a speakerphone that piped his voice into the hearing room.

Easterly: Sir, this is Captain Easterly. You were the executive officer for Battalion, correct sir?

Karagosian: Yes, that is correct.

Easterly: We've had a couple of people testify here today sir, Major Faber and Lieutenant Kay, regarding some use of military assets by Colonel DeMartino that I think were termed "reckless"?

Karagosian: Okay.

Easterly: For instance, there was an operation in Wardak Province to open a COP. The operation was supposed to be reconnaissance and there ended up being an ambush, and my understanding from the prior witnesses is that their view of that operation is that it was reckless. Do you have any comment or insight into their views on Colonel DeMartino, sir?

Karagosian: I know that there were a few operations that I'm aware of. One involved movement of mounted elements in the Jalrez Valley which I was on and which Captain Hill was on. I can't comment on whether I think they were reckless or not. They were separate, and based upon the economics at the time, LTC DeMartino made the decision to move forces into Jalrez. Did any of those operations result in anyone killed in action? No. I believe during the first one, there were no casualties. The second, there were four or five wounded...Would somebody else say they were reckless? Sure, people will say they were reckless. In my professional opinion, they were not reckless.

Easterly: Sir, one last question. Would you say, though, that regardless of the success of the operations that we just talked about, that it might have contributed to a sense in Delta Company that Battalion was—how shall I say this?—perhaps not as concerned about risk as members of Delta thought it ought to be?

Karagosian: Sure, I would agree with that. There were some disagreements between the Delta chain of command and the Battalion chain of command about these operations. I would say that LTC DeMartino exercised prerogative as a commander and used assets as he saw fit, and the results varied.

Easterly: What I hear you saying is that you're satisfied that Colonel DeMartino used his assets as he saw fit and the results bear that out. That's what I hear you saying, sir, is that correct?

Karagosian: Yes, that's basically what I'm saying.

The defense next called Major Jack Cheasty, the physician's assistant who had been outside the coffeehouse when Hill fired his Beretta M9.

Puckett: You were present when detainees were brought to FOB Airborne?

Cheasty: I was. I didn't know that they were brought to FOB Airborne. I thought they were actually detained on FOB Airborne.

Puckett: Yes sir, some were brought to and some were detained on. Do your duties include making physical examinations of these detainees?

Cheasty: Technically in that setting I would not be required to do so, but the command asked me to do so, so I went ahead and performed a physical exam and history on each patient that was brought in... They came in with an interpreter.

Puckett: I am going to hand you a stack of documents which I know you've already reviewed, but can you just identify what that stack of documents is?

Cheasty: These are copies—some of this stuff is illegible here—of physical examinations that I performed in the company of SGT Brincefield on the 27th of August, when we were turning over these detainees to the NDS. I believe this is where they went and the executive officer of the Battalion had already examined these patients. He asked me to come down and do these physicals formally, physical exams specifically to determine if was there was any type of injuries or abuse.

Puckett: Sir, can you summarize the findings on those physicals that you did?

Cheasty: I can. There was no systemic evidence of abuse. There were a couple of marks that were not consistent with a beating. I will tell you how I did the exams. I examined starting with the head, looked at both ears to make sure there was no ruptured eardrums. I looked in the mouth and checked the nose to make sure there was no tenderness. I looked at the teeth, to make sure there were no teeth knocked out, or loose teeth. I examined the neck, both clavicles, looked at the chest, backs, and abdominals to make sure there was no tenderness in the abdomen.

I used a flashlight that I carry in my case. I didn't disrobe them, but I pulled their waistbands open and dropped the light and looked around, checked the back, and had them lift both of their pants legs. I saw no systemic evidence whatsoever that these individuals had been beaten or any way severely injured. There were some marks on these individuals here and there, and I so noted. I also asked those individuals if they were injured, and they said no. I indicated that they were not.

Puckett: Take a look at that one on top. That's the one I selected. That's the fellow called Sammy. I noticed at the bottom there—and it's kind of hard to read—something about reported injuries.

Cheasty: "Patient tearful, states he did nothing wrong." I asked if he was injured and he denied any injuries. This individual had a previously broken nose. Photographs taken of this detainee, of this interpreter, with the defendant in more favorable times clearly show that was the case.

Puckett: If I can interrupt here, sir, I'm going to show you those photographs and ask you about them with the caveat that I ask you to keep these close to your body because it shows the individual's face. Take a look at those two photographs and see if you can identify the individual in them.

Cheasty: That's Sammy.

Puckett: Sir, you've learned during the course of this investigation when this last series of photographs—other than these first two—were taken, is that correct?

Cheasty: I did.

Puckett: On what date were those pictures taken?

Cheasty: On or about the 30th or 31st of August.

Puckett: And on what date were the detainees released?

Cheasty: We released them, I last saw the detainees at 1630 hours on the 27th, and I can tell you that the individual in question sat in a chair as close to myself as to the captain behind me. We carried on a conversation. I was very upset that he was involved in this thing. I believed what he was saying. I really felt for the guy, and he was not injured, sir.

Puckett: I am going to show you another photograph.

Cheasty: This is a photograph depicting an individual, not showing the head, standing in a U.S. Army PT shirt, with fifteen or twenty splotches of bright red blood.

Puckett: ...Describe the significance of the red blood, and also the pattern, from a medical perspective.

Cheasty: Well sir, the pattern here appears to be not a flow pattern, but a blotch pattern as if somebody wiped his nose in various places.

Puckett: Like for a bloody nose?

Cheasty: On that shirt and for a bloody nose. One of the things significant about it is that it is red blood. I can show you a towel after I cut myself shaving and show you what that towel looks like twenty-four hours later; it's a dark brown stain. Red blood cells [become] crenate—they open up, the hemoglobin dries out, turns a dark brown and eventually may even turn black.

Puckett: So what does that tell you about the recent application of the blood on the T-shirt?

Cheasty: That it was fairly new. That it was not blood that was four days old.

Puckett: Meaning from the 28th?

Cheasty: The 27th or the 28th. That blood occurred probably within twenty-four hours of the injury.

Puckett: So what you're saying, sir, is that it's basically impossible to have the blood on that shirt from injuries that occurred on the 27th?

Cheasty: Photographs taken on the 31st showing red blood—it couldn't be from the 27th.

Scott sucked in his breath with relief. Here was Doc Cheasty saying clearly that the photos in evidence could not have been the photos taken by MAJ Rob Smith when he appeared suddenly at Airborne and went immediately to the coffeehouse. This showed that Scott, who had no contact with Sammy after the NDS took him into custody, could not have bloodied the terp's nose or his shirt.

Puckett turned his attention to events Cheasty witnessed outside the coffeehouse.

Puckett: I'm going to hand you a couple of exhibits. One has six photos of the coffee shop, and the other one is a diagram which one of the witnesses created. I would like you to take a look at those to see if those would assist in you telling us where you were standing.

Cheasty: Okay.

Puckett: Just show me.

Cheasty: *[The witness points to a spot on the diagram.]* I was standing here. At the time, there was a small ring of concertina wire from here to here.

Puckett: Okay, here is where he is talking about. From that position, what did you observe?

Cheasty: The detainees were sitting in a line parallel to a ditch on the far right, on a mound of dirt that was piled up there...

Puckett: If SGT Allen said these detainees were by these X's here, is that not what you recall?

Cheasty: I did not see all the detainees by those X's in SGT Allen's diagram.

Puckett: For the record, sir, I'm going to say this aloud and I'm also going to show you. He's indicated that he saw three native detainees sort of in a line along the berm to the right of the picture created by Sergeant Allen, parallel to the berm?

Cheasty: Parallel to the ditch.

Puckett: The ditch, I'm sorry. So, then what did you see?

Cheasty: I saw Captain Hill walking towards me, very purposefully, eyes fixed straight ahead, not looking at anybody. He had a 9-millimeter pistol in his right hand as he came parallel to the side of the building at a distance of maybe six feet, maybe seven feet. He discharged his weapon into the ground. Several shots, two or three shots.

Puckett: And into the ground in which direction? Straight down?

Cheasty: I believe so.

Puckett: Did you say the witness stood up and walked forward? He was walking forward, he moved his right hand ahead of his feet,

and he fired a pistol into the ground? Did he appear to make eye
contact with you?

Cheasty: Sir, I don't think he was aware I was even standing there.

Puckett: Describe his demeanor.

Cheasty: His face was tight, his eyes were straight ahead, he passed by
within a foot of me, didn't recognize me, didn't say anything to me.

Puckett: Right by you?

Cheasty: Right by me.

Puckett: Did you see him discharge his weapon?

Cheasty: I did.

Puckett: Looking directly at him?

Cheasty: I was looking directly at him.

Puckett: Okay, sir, can you tell us, when he began discharging his
weapon and also when he finished discharging his weapon, how far
from the nearest detainee was he?

Cheasty: I can speak to that issue because I paced it off, twenty yards,
from the place where he discharged the weapon, about maybe
twenty-three yards from the actual door of the coffee shop.

Puckett: Again, sir, the question is, that's to the nearest detainee?
Twenty yards?

Cheasty: From the nearest detainee, where they were sitting on that
berm, I shot a pace line and it was twenty yards.

Puckett: So he fired straight into the ground, twenty yards away from
the nearest detainee?

Cheasty: That is true.

Puckett: Did you verify that by any other means?

Cheasty: A day or so later, I asked someone from Delta Company to shoot
[a range finder] to give the distance, and it matched my pacing.

Hill noticed that LTC Byrd seemed particularly engaged with Doc Cheasty, whose testimony was detailed and credible. Scott was happy that Byrd was hearing from a witness who actually saw what happened outside the coffeehouse.

Now Captains Runyan and Latino launched their cross.

Latino: Why would you pace off the distance?

Cheasty: I was curious as to how far away he was from the detainees. If
this was an attempt to scare them, if this was to bring fear to them,
it crossed my mind, so I wanted to know how far away they were.

Latino: I'd like to talk a little bit more about not just immediately what
you saw on Captain Hill, but his demeanor throughout that entire
short period when he fired his weapon.

Cheasty: He wasn't responsive. He didn't look like he was responsive
to his surroundings. He was someplace else. I am not trying to put
a diagnosis on it.

Latino: Sir, I have no medical training whatsoever. I think, when I
hear your description, of people in shock, dazed. How would you
best characterize that? Anger? Frustration?

Cheasty: A daze. That would be the common term, was that he was in
a daze. That's the way it appeared.

Latino: Thank you, sir. I have no further questions.

Prosecutor Runyan: So you gave a soldier, a detainee, stitches?

Cheasty: Sutures, yes [for a half-centimeter laceration on the lip].

Runyan: You didn't see him on the last day?

Cheasty: I did not.

Runyan: So you don't know where he went?

Cheasty: I do not.

Runyan: So it's true that you may not have examined everyone who
was in the coffee shop?

Cheasty: I examined the individuals that they presented to me. The CI
guys that were there, they had a list of people. The first day when
I got there, before any of this ever started, they were rounding
people up. They had all kinds of people that were possible suspects.
As they cleared them, they released them.

Runyan: So, there were more than these twelve detainees in that
coffee shop?

Cheasty: On the first day.

Runyan: Sir, you said you paced out the distance to the detainees
because you sensed maybe there was something going wrong?
Did you have a feeling that something was going on in that coffee
shop?

Cheasty: I didn't know, but when shots were fired, I wanted to
know how far away he fired those shots from the detainees
outside.

Runyan: Were you uneasy about what was going on?

Cheasty: No, after I got there and realized they were uninjured, no.
Perhaps I should have been, but I can only tell you how I felt.

Major Cheasty's testimony both humbled and galvanized the defense
table. His testimony bolstered what they'd been saying about the health of
the detainees in contrast to the torture scenario the prosecution had tried to
paint. Hill was grateful to Cheasty, who'd had a long, distinguished military
career. Like Kay, he'd had nothing to gain.

CHAPTER 6

3 December 2008
Longhorn Conference Room

ON THE MORNING of the last day of the proceeding, Neal Puckett stood to deliver the closing statement for the defense. He turned toward the head of the horseshoe and spoke directly to the investigating officer, LTC Robert Byrd.

"Sir, it's been a long two and a half days, and I just want to thank you for your patience. You have been put in a very difficult position here. The Army is the only service that routinely uses non-lawyers for these hearings. It has some advantages and it has some disadvantages. One of the disadvantages is, of course, when we lawyers try to argue the law to you or read the law to you or try to argue the fine points of the law to you ... it does not make your job any easier. So I am not going to do that. It is just not helpful. What this all comes down to really, what the end product of this whole UCMJ process is, is what is to become of First Sergeant Scott and what is to become of Captain Hill? So, I would like to tell you a story."

Puckett related the story of LTC Allen West, the Battalion commander who fired his pistol near an Iraqi policeman's head in order to foil an attack on himself and his men. It was the case Puckett told Hill about the first time they spoke. After laying out the facts of the case, Puckett told LTC Byrd what happened next.

"I went to Iraq and went to an Article 32 investigation, which was somewhat similar to this. A unit commander, a lieutenant colonel, was assigned as the investigating officer. He heard all of the evidence and heard all of the circumstances that caused Lieutenant Colonel West to act the way he did.

As you know, your first task is to see if there is reasonable cause to believe that offenses were committed, and the IO did, in fact, find that there was reasonable cause to believe that offenses had been committed.

"But, it was his concluding paragraph that I think is what made the right outcome happen. He said that certainly Lieutenant Colonel West crossed a legal line, but he acted the way he did because it was in the best interest of his soldiers. He truly believed that there was an imminent threat, and intelligence could pretty much back that up. The investigating officer recommended that the disposition in Lieutenant Colonel West's case be determined at a commanding general's Article 15. General Ray Odierno adopted those recommendations and held an Article 15 on Lieutenant Colonel West. He took half a month's pay for two months and he wrote him a letter of reprimand. And he retired in grade as a lieutenant colonel."

Puckett spoke amiably, as if telling a story to an old friend. Byrd scribbled notes as the attorney continued.

"I tell you that story to put things in context," he continued. "Arguably, Lieutenant Colonel West, a far more senior and experienced officer in this same Army, and under the same overall command of General Odierno, did far worse than Captain Hill. He did much worse. But yet, General Odierno understood the circumstances. He understood the reasons why he acted the way he did."

Puckett paused, took a sip of water. When he resumed, his voice carried just the slightest hint of irony. Odierno's Staff Judge Advocate (SJA), he said, a lawyer newly arrived in-theater, thought West had behaved horribly. The SJA was certain West had committed a war crime and needed to answer to the American people.

"And you know what, sir?" Puckett said. "When the American public found out about West's case and thought that the Army was going to try to put Lieutenant Colonel West in jail, and perhaps deprive him of the pension that he had earned, they went ballistic. Congressmen signed petitions. Multiple congressmen signed petitions demanding that the Secretary of the Army explain why Lieutenant Colonel West was being put on trial when he was doing what he was trained to do by protecting his men. No one could believe it. All of the news networks and all of the conservative media could not believe that the Army could turn against a soldier like this. He certainly needed to be disciplined. He needed to be corrected. His behavior needed to be corrected and an example needed to be set, if you will, that no other Battalion commander should do this. There are consequences to stepping over the line. So, then you have to ask yourself if discipline is required in *this* case, and it clearly is, there is no question about that. What level of punishment does Captain Hill need to be exposed to?"

Puckett paused, letting the question hang in the air for a moment.

"If it goes to a general court-martial," he continued, "as my brother attorney mentioned before, he would be exposed to life in prison and a dismissal, which as you know is the officer equivalent of a dishonorable discharge. Has he acted dishonorably? Or did he exercise poor judgment as a result of everything he had experienced in that command at that location? Through all of the patrols, through all of the casualties, to later find out that his interpreter who went out on patrols with them became a spy or was always a spy, and put the lives of his men in jeopardy. Can you react to that information without emotion? Could any man react without emotion to that?

"Now, going back to what I told you before about General Odierno having it right with the Article 15. It's a funny thing when lawyers get involved. I have been doing this for twenty-four years. I have been a prosecutor. I have been a defense counsel. I spent five years as a military judge. I know military law. And what you will find, sir, if you spend any time in the system, is that young prosecutors get these CID investigations. Young prosecutors who have never been outside the wire on patrol feel it is their duty to find as many of the UCMJ articles as they possibly can that can even be remotely described by the conduct of the investigation and then they do what they've done here. They put on three or four charges that are supported by the same act. All in order to present to an investigating officer like you, to think, 'Hey, look! It fills up a whole page. And look! It goes on for a second page because we forgot to add a couple of assault charges, so we are going to add those, too.'

"Sir, all of this, if this charge sheet got in front of a military judge—I am just going to make it easy for you—four or five charges would be reduced to one. What did Captain Hill do? He lost control of the situation as a commander. A commander should never lose control of his soldiers or of a situation. How can we possibly justify calling that felony criminal misconduct and sending it to a general court-martial?

"Now that's the defense lawyer in me saying, 'Oh, please recommend Article 15 for CPT Hill,' and I can justify that for you because of General Odierno, who is still in command of us in this war. It's the same Army. That set the bar. That set the precedent. That worse scenario went to Article 15, but this less severe scenario should go to general court-martial? What does that say to America? That we eat our young? That senior guys get off and junior guys take all of the heat? Is that fair?

"Now sir, what you just heard is from the defense attorney. I am not a liberal. I am a retired Marine. I am not a guy who wants all of my clients to get off. Some of them deserve punishment. Captain Hill deserves punishment. He should not be acquitted or exonerated. Sir, I would suggest to you, and now I will even address First Sergeant Scott, that there is no way that justice is served by a court-martial for either of these men."

Here, Puckett paused. When he spoke again, his tone seemed to indicate that his next words were regrettable but necessary.

"If we are pushed into a corner, we will have to push back. Careers will suffer. Lieutenant Colonel DeMartino will never be a colonel, I can promise you that. I know where to go to make that happen. Colonel Johnson will never be a general. We can make that happen. Trust me, sir. None of those things would be a good thing. I am not threatening, sir. I am just saying what has to happen in a general court-martial.

"Sir, you can be the start of this or you can be the end of this by making a compelling argument that, yes, reasonable cause exists to believe that offenses have been committed. And, yes, he should be disciplined, but it should be done at a commanding general's Article 15. That's what's right. That's what's just. That's what common sense requires. And we trust that you will do that. Thank you very much."

BOOK 6

Last Stand

Never do anything against conscience, even if the state demands it.

Albert Einstein

CHAPTER I

4 December 2008

THE DAY AFTER the hearing, Neal Puckett flew up to Bagram, where he requested a meeting with LTC Patrick Huston, the command judge advocate for Combined Task Force Currahee. Huston greeted Puckett warmly.

Puckett took a seat in a guest chair opposite Huston's desk and led off. "Colonel, I think our mitigation and extenuation here is strong. There's a very good chance the IO will recommend against a court-martial. But if he does recommend court-martial, there's a lot that's going to come out in open court."

Then, like cards on a poker table, Puckett laid down his logic.

Evidence and testimony showed that the Battalion commander had not adequately supported Dog Company, even by the standards of an economy-of-force mission.

His own division commander, Brigadier General Milley, had said he would be surprised if LTC DeMartino had not been aware that the Jalrez COP was undermanned.

There had been damning testimony about DeMartino's character, how he played favorites, even how he put his men in harm's way. DeMartino had also continually, and seemingly without reason, looked for a reason to relieve CPT Hill.

All of these factors, it had been shown, had likely contributed to Battalion's slow response to the detaince situation, despite Dog Company's repeated calls for help.

Puckett leaned back, elbows on armrests, and tented his fingers before him. "I've been in your shoes before, Colonel," he said. "I've been on the government's side. I know it isn't going to play very well if all this becomes public about Lieutenant Colonel DeMartino, and, basically, his role in this whole sordid story. Wouldn't it be better if we just dealt with this here and now? Captain Hill is happy to accept the commanding general's Article 15 and submit his resignation from the Army. Then we don't have to have a court-martial and air all this dirty laundry. Give us an Article 15 and we can be done with this."

Huston sat at his desk and smiled a collegial smile. When he spoke, it sounded to Puckett as if Huston had genuinely listened to his offer, and genuinely thought it was, well...a little silly.

"Mr. Puckett, I hear what you're saying, but I think what the general is looking for is something more along the lines of an agreement by Captain Hill to plead guilty to the charges he would face in a general court-martial."

If Hill would do that, Huston said cordially, the general would agree to a limit on confinement of perhaps two years.

Puckett smiled. "I see," he said, then transitioned to closing pleasantries. Further legal discussions, he knew, would be a waste of both men's time.

Back at Bagram after the hearing, Hill sat alone in the Amnesty Hut, enjoying one of Masten's Drew Estate cigars. Relaxing against a pillow, he puffed the stogie, then held it out to inspect the tip. Masten had told him that a really fresh one could give you a four-inch ash.

It had been a good week, maybe the first good one since he and Tommy handed over their weapons on Airborne exactly four months earlier. In Hill's view, the vast weight of the Article 32 testimony seemed to show clearly that Dog Company had been at best grossly undersupported by Battalion. He wished fervently that Wade Barker and CPT B had been available to testify. He also wished that a couple of the other officers had told as much about what they knew as had Chris Faber and Larry Kay.

In the distance, Hill heard the airfield churning out Black Hawks and Chinooks. He hoped he'd soon be on one, rejoining some remnant of his company. Maybe he was imagining things, but a couple of times when he glanced up at LTC Byrd, Hill thought he saw a different aspect to his face than when he'd first opened the hearing.

It wasn't a softening—there was nothing soft about Robert Byrd. But something. Wheels turning, weights counterbalancing. Hill couldn't peg it, but something was different.

That and the strong case the defense put on gave Hill an inkling of hope that he and Scott might rejoin Dog Company, or at least transfer to staff positions somewhere in the Brigade and move on with their careers and their lives.

CHAPTER 2

5 *December* 2008

ROBERT BYRD HAD come to a decision on the Article 32 case: He hated it.

In his office at FOB Lightning, he spread his case notes across the Middle East map that covered his desk, and found himself at a crossroads. On the one hand, it still seemed open and shut: Hill and Scott should not have treated the detainees the way they did. On the other hand, the mitigating circumstances were playing hell with his decisions concerning consequences.

The evidence against the two soldiers was rock-solid. Even Hill did not deny what he had done. But he said he'd done it because he and his first sergeant felt backed into a corner, abandoned by their Battalion commander and his staff, and concerned for the lives of their men. Byrd felt that on those counts, Hill and his attorneys had proven their case.

It didn't seem right to let these men go without consequences; detainee abuse simply could not be tolerated. But while these soldiers had made poor decisions, they seemed to have been acting in the vise grip of impossible circumstances. So, it also didn't seem right to send them to prison.

During his time in the Army, Byrd had served under a long line of sterling leaders, but his career had also been pocked with officers who could have put on clinics in how *not* to lead. For years, Byrd observed a pattern among these leaders that he could both qualify and quantify—he just couldn't hang it with a label. Then, in 2004, he read an article in *Military Review* by Colonel George E. Reed. The article discussed military leaders who demoralized their subordinates, kept them walking on eggshells, short-circuited initiative, and destroyed organizations from the inside out.

Reed called the pattern "toxic leadership."

For Byrd, the article was a breakthrough. Finally, he could put a name to what he'd seen over the years, squash it when he saw it, and, as important, educate his own subordinates on how to lead effectively.

Was LTC DeMartino a toxic leader? Byrd couldn't say. He believed the soldiers who had testified to how undersupported they felt. But sometimes senior officers had legitimate reasons for what they did, and had neither the time nor the obligation to explain it to their juniors.

Then there was the issue of DeMartino allegedly putting his soldiers at unnecessary risk in his own pursuit of battlefield glory. Byrd found that disturbing. To ride around the battlefield looking for trouble was irresponsible. Yet again, there were two sides to that testimony. Major Faber had called it "somewhat reckless," while another witness, Major John Karagosian, DeMartino's former XO, had termed it a "calculated risk."

There was no question that a personality conflict raged between Hill and DeMartino. But how much of it was DeMartino, and how much of it was Hill? Again, Byrd didn't have sufficient information.

He didn't feel he could in good conscience recommend that Hill be set free without consequences. In the larger scheme, that would set a bad precedent: Americans are not supposed to treat prisoners that way.

For the next few days, Byrd racked his brain, trying to come up with some balance of justice for these men who felt backed in with no alternatives, who tried to do the right thing morally, but did the wrong thing legally in the end.

Byrd ran the case past two different sergeant majors. These were men who cared deeply for their soldiers but were law-and-order guys through and through. Byrd wasn't asking them for a solution or a recommendation; it was more of a sanity check—was he, Byrd, somehow missing something? In the end, both sergeant majors understood his dilemma completely and were as on the fence as he was.

CHAPTER 3

6 December 2008

THREE DAYS AFTER the hearing, Neal Puckett caught a Kam Air flight to Dubai, riding in a dubious Soviet-made plane that belched the stench of jet fuel all the way to the United Arab Emirates. From there, he endured a long but trouble-free flight back to the States. Puckett had been home less than twenty-four hours when he received an email from LTC Patrick Huston. Apparently, someone high in the food chain had had a change of heart.

Hill was walking toward the Trial Defense Service offices when his cell phone rang. The caller ID read HEATHER MASTEN.

"Hi, ma'am. What's up?"

"Hey, I've got great news. Huston emailed Neal. They're offering you and Tommy a deal."

Elation surged through Hill. "What? That's fantastic! What are they offering?"

"I'm in the office with Tommy and I've got Neal on speaker. Come back and we'll bring you up to speed."

Hill was seated in Masten's office in less than two minutes. CPT Easterly was also there, as was the voice of Neal Puckett, emanating from a cell phone lying faceup on the corner of Masten's desk.

Tommy sat in a side chair near the desk. Hill noticed that he was not smiling.

"Roger, this is a victory!" Puckett was saying. "Congratulations!"

Hill sat down in an empty chair. "Thanks, Neal. Give me the details."

Puckett read aloud the email from LTC Huston. The command was willing to give Hill an Article 15 if he would plead guilty to three charges: failure to control the situation surrounding the treatment of detainees; willfully discharging his firearm with the intent to frighten detainees; and encouraging his soldiers to assault detainees. In addition, Hill would be required to resign his commission and leave the Army. The character of his discharge had not been nailed down. It would not be honorable, but could be anything from "other than honorable" to a general discharge.

The command would also allow Tommy Scott to be disciplined by a summary court-martial rather than a general court-martial. In a summary court-martial, a single commissioned officer decides the fate of the accused, and certain harsh punishments are excluded, including dismissal, discharge, and confinement of more than a month.

Hill sat silent. Now he understood why Tommy looked grim. Masten watched them both from behind her desk.

Puckett continued. "Guys, in the world I live in, this is a major victory. This doesn't always happen. Remember where the command stood at the beginning of this thing? Remember how zealous they were to prosecute you to the limit of the law? Well, we really put the battalion command on trial at the 32. This reversal and this offer says a lot about how the command sees the case now."

Hill and Scott locked eyes across the room. The captain saw his first sergeant turn his head right then left. The movement had been almost imperceptible, but the message was clear: No.

"I hear you, Neal," Hill finally said. "But—"

"Listen, Roger. You guys don't have to take this plea. I know you and Tommy feel strongly about the actions you took. We all do. But listen to me. I want you to hear this very clearly. The Army will *never* pull the two of you aside and apologize. That will simply never happen. With all the sound and fury they put into prosecuting you, they are never going to say, 'Oops, our bad. We were wrong.' This really is a victory, and about as good as we could have hoped for, all things considered."

Hill looked up at Masten, who was gazing in him in a way that was firm and unyielding. He felt outnumbered.

"If you don't take the plea," Puckett went on, "you'll start this whole process over again, and the risks will be higher. Both your fates will be determined by a panel of field grade officers, many who have not led men in combat. I'm not saying they wouldn't side with you, because they very well might. But you yourself have pointed out the disconnect that many field grades have with their ground commanders because they don't realize what they're asking them to do day in and day out.

"If we did go to a general court-martial, we still have some aces up our sleeve," Puckett continued. "You two didn't testify at the 32, so the prosecution wouldn't be able to prep for that. But we did play a number of our cards, including the core of our defense strategy."

"What do you mean?" Hill said.

"The government now knows that our defense is going to be essentially one of necessity. Military exigencies. Now they will have months to build a counter to that. And more resources will be thrown at the case, because they won't want to lose on such a grand stage. If this moves to a general court-martial, it becomes very public. The government will do everything in its power to smear you and Tommy in order to set the conditions to win."

Hill sank into contemplation mode, left arm folded across his abdomen, right elbow resting on his left wrist. He covered his face with his right hand, fingers and thumbs combing his jet eyebrows toward the center.

As he thought, a new voice arrowed across the room. "But we didn't do anything wrong."

It was Scott, finally speaking up. "I will never, ever admit that what I did was wrong. They cannot punish us for protecting our men, for doing our jobs. I think we should fight."

Hill stopped rubbing his brow and raised his head. "The Army cannot be allowed to continue doing this. They have to be held accountable for scapegoating and hanging soldiers out to dry for the sake of their careers, or this insane policy that says it's better to let American soldiers die than... than to"—he searched for words—"than to do *anything* remotely scary to the poor, helpless bad guys.

"I mean, we capture them and higher lets them go, capture them and higher lets them go. If we shoot at them, we get investigated. If we *scare* them, our commanders want to try us for psychological 'torture' and *war crimes*? These fuckers wounded a third of my company. Donnie and Paul are *never* coming home because of these men. And where are the prisoners now, the ones we took *off* the battlefield? Probably on another FOB killing more American soldiers while collecting paychecks paid for by the American people. It's insane."

He glanced at Scott, who was nodding his head. Hill collected himself and continued.

"I don't like the idea of backing down now if for no other reason than that it will set another precedent that says there is no accountability up the chain. That when shit goes sideways, no matter how culpable they are, the field grades just need to lawyer up, paint the guys on the ground as rogues and criminals, and go on with their next promotion. Look at Allen West. All these guys getting brought up on charges for trying to do the right thing. I didn't even know about those guys when I did what I did. But now that I do, it looks like an epidemic."

Hill stopped. He needed more time to think. Most of all, he needed to talk to Lauren.

"Neal, I think Tommy and I need to think about this," he said. "We need to speak to our families and then get back with you."

Hill glanced at Masten. Her face was neutral and still, but he sensed she was willing herself to keep quiet.

"Okay, but you guys need to decide pretty soon," Puckett said. "There's a time limit on the offer. I think we only have a day, day and a half at most, to give Division an answer."

That evening, Hill called his wife. "I have news."

"Okay..." Lauren said.

"The command offered us a plea bargain. Neal says it's pretty good." He laid out the details, bullet-point style. "What do you think?"

A pause filled the line. Then Lauren said, "I think we should fight."

Hill sat quietly, awed by her strength, what she stood for. She had come to Fort Campbell as green as any freshly minted private in Dog Company. But she had taken learning the Army as seriously as she had her master's degree. And she was as dedicated to the soldiers' families as to the kids in her classroom. Her standing by him meant more to him than he would ever be able to explain.

And yet in the time since his big speech in Masten's office, the hard corners of reality had elbowed their way into Hill's mind. It was as though he had been existing in a fabled valley where good guys with right hearts rode perpetually off into the sunset. But then the sun rose, revealing the real world. A world of politics and backroom deals where a crappy compromise held more appeal than going to prison on principle.

Hill spoke softly into the phone. "If we fight, it could take months."

"Okay..." Lauren's voice weakened. Then there was silence.

At that moment, Hill's insides began a meltdown. Suddenly, all the separations that marked their marriage ran through his mind, like boxcars on a train to a hated country.

His heart screamed at him, *Go home! Go home to your wife and be done with this! Besides... what does it matter?*

Hill sighed. The problem was, it did matter. He, his men, and their families had given everything they had. And not for themselves, but for others.

Lauren's voice was gentle in his ear. "I'll support whatever you decide."

"Okay, baby. I'm going to talk it over with Tommy."

"Okay, I love you."

"I love you, too. And . . . thank you."

She knew what for. "You're welcome. I'm proud of you, Roger."

"Thank you. I'm sorry all this has happened."

"Roger, we're okay," she said. "We are okay."

Hill's conversation with Lauren broke something inside him. Suddenly, he was exhausted. Tired of wrestling Leviathan. What if Neal was right and he was on the expressway to legal disaster? What if he learned later that he had passed up his one chance to take an off-ramp that would save not only himself but Tommy?

CHAPTER 4

7 December 2008

HILL SAT WITH Scott in Masten's office. The two men were alone, the air between them thick with tension. Hill had just spent the better part of twenty minutes explaining to Scott what Neal had said about the probable outcome of a general court-martial. As he spoke, he had watched Scott's brow darken and his eyes turn to flint.

He knew Scott didn't like what he had to say, but he pressed on: "In the end, it might be you that gets the worst sentence, because you were the most physical with the prisoners. My career is over for sure. I can't do anything about that now. But if you accept this summary court-martial instead of escalating to a general court-martial, you could stay in the Army. You could retire with your pension and all your benefits. You can take care of your wife and son."

Hill saw Scott's jaw muscles clench. When he finally spoke it was as if he were restraining a great wave of pressure, his mouth a valve that he dared open only so much. "After all this, you want to *give up*?"

"Tommy, I don't want to give up. But I think this is the best we're going to do. Neal and Heather—"

"No! Fuck that! It's not their lives. It's not their reputation! We didn't do anything wrong!"

Scott boiled inside. He couldn't believe Hill was ready to cave. If Scott had it to do over again, he would do the same thing. God put him in those boys' lives to bring them home to their families. If he had to risk prison for that, he was willing to take that chance.

Hill spoke again, his voice low and gentle. "Tommy, I know what you're thinking. You're thinking we did the right thing. Yes, we did the right thing by our guys, but by law, some of what we did was wrong. The Army will never see it differently. Do you want Cassandra and Jaylen to be visiting you in prison? Because there's a good chance that might happen—for both of us."

Hill reprised what Puckett had told him about general court-martials. How they were set up. The actual presumption of guilt. "If we go down this road, it will be very public. Is that what you want?"

"No, that's not what I want—"

"The Army will go after us balls to the wall, and whatever happens will be the end of the line. We might be able to appeal, but that would be from behind bars."

Scott burst up from his chair like a drowning man desperate for air. "That's not going to happen! A jury is going to see *why* we did what we did! How could anyone outside Battalion or Brigade see it any other way?"

"Tommy, the jury will be *picked* by Brigade."

Scott fell silent. His shoulders sagged and he gazed at the floor. As much as his soul rebelled against the idea, he was beginning to see that Hill was right. A jury would have to find them guilty. And the Army would never deliver an apology or search its own soul. Down this legal road, there would be no justice, only consequences.

Well, Scott thought, *I did my best.*

Suddenly, he realized that he had not broken his promise to his uncle Joel: He *had* done his best. He'd protected his men and fought a system that wanted to convict him for it. Now, maybe the best thing he could do was finish his career and go home to his family. Keep his pension. That way, he wouldn't have poured half his life into the Army just to wind up broke and in jail. Hell, he could've stayed in Tarpon Springs and done that.

Scott drew a deep breath and exhaled it slowly. Finally he said, "What would I be charged with? I don't want my son to grow up thinking his father is a war criminal."

Once Hill and Scott decided to accept the plea bargain, events moved swiftly. First, there was wrangling over the charges to which Hill would agree to plead guilty. With coaching from Masten and Puckett, he went to work crafting the language of charges that he could plead guilty to in good conscience. Sitting in his little Bagram office, Hill keyed characters into Microsoft Word then deleted, revised, deleted some more.

One afternoon in the second week of December, Masten poked her head in the door. "We just found out that Division has you down to meet with General Schloesser at 2000 hours on 16 December."

Major General Jeffrey J. Schloesser, commanding general of the 101st Airborne Division.

"Okay, I think I can make that," Hill joked. "I don't think I have anything going on."

Heather cracked a half smile. She was relieved matters seemed to be working out for Hill, but she wasn't going to let her guard down until she saw this thing through. "Pat Huston tells me we have a choice. You can either meet the general with counsel, which means that I can be there, which means Huston would also be there. Or you can meet with the general alone."

Hill raised his eyebrows. His brain spun off for the millionth time on how entrenched lawyers had become in the military's decision-making cycle—

He stopped himself. His goal now was to get home to his family and move on.

Focus, he told himself. The word was becoming a mantra.

Hill looked at Masten. "I'll go it alone if you won't be offended."

"I think that would be wise. The fact that the command is offering a private meeting is a considerable gesture."

"I think it's the right thing to do. Maybe we'll have an opportunity to level with each other some."

"Maybe. Just be cautious."

Masten closed the door, and Hill returned to the proposed charges. He typed another sentence and a period, then sat back to review what he'd crafted. His original charge sheet had contained six charges. Hill was proposing to plead guilty to violating three articles of the UCMJ; he had added his amendments to the charges in bold:

Article 92

In that CPT Roger T. Hill, U.S. Army, who knew his duties as a commanding officer to control and process detainees between on or about 22 August 2008 and on or about 27 August 2008, and was derelict in the performance of those duties in that he willfully failed to control the situation as it was his duty to do so **in an attempt to elicit information from the detainees to prevent an attack on Forward Operating Base Airborne.**

Article 133

In that CPT Roger T. Hill, U.S. Army, did at or near Forward Operating Base Airborne, Afghanistan, between on or about 22 August

2008 and on or about 27 August 2008, allow and encourage Soldiers under his command to assault detainees **caught in the act of espionage in an attempt to elicit information from them to prevent an attack on Forward Operating Base Airborne,** to the disgrace of the armed forces.

Article 128

In that CPT Roger T. Hill, U.S. Army, did, at or near Forward Operating Base Airborne, Afghanistan, between on or about 22 August 2008 and on or about 27 August 2008, wrongfully and willfully discharge a firearm, to wit: firing a weapon in the proximity of military and civilian personnel, under circumstances such as to endanger human life which was to the prejudice of good order and discipline or was of a nature to bring discredit upon the armed forces.

Hill reread the amended charges and decided they were as much as he could do. As much as he could admit to and live with himself.

But as the proposed charges badmintoned between Masten and Huston, the expositional—and arguably exculpatory—phrases Hill prized were gradually shaved away. It was either that, Masten explained, or uncountable months of legal battles like the one they'd just been through, with a worse outcome virtually guaranteed.

Bottom line, Hill thought, *they've got me by the balls.*

But he had set a course for himself in agreement not only with Tommy, but also Tommy's wife, Cassandra.

"Focus," he said to himself.

CHAPTER 5

14 December 2008

An H-60 Black Hawk skated east over the thirsty ground between FOB Lightning and FOB Salerno at an altitude just out of missile range. LTC Robert Byrd sat belted in, a binder in his lap. He was carrying his final report on *The United States vs. CPT Roger T. Hill and 1SG Tommy L. Scott.* Indexes of reports and evidence, Byrd's own conclusions, and a summary transcript of all testimony in the Article 32 hearing.

Byrd felt the weight of the document. The responsibility had been huge. In 1SG Scott's case, Byrd had been given the authority to essentially wipe out with a signature the man's twenty-four–year career. Meanwhile, Hill had served eight years, plus his time at the Military Academy. Impeccably, as far as Byrd could tell, prior to this incident.

And yet, he could understand the Brigade's side of the equation. In a tight-knit unit with a high-profile reputation like the Currahees, this was the kind of thing that could become a media scandal. Empirically speaking, Hill and Scott had broken the law, and Brigade was right to exact consequences. But it also seemed to Byrd that Brigade was trying to distance itself from Dog Company, to label Hill's men "rogue" and their actions completely inconsistent with the leadership examples set by their highers. Better that than admit that the company was underresourced and overexposed.

As for Hill, or any company grade commander prosecuting the

economy-of-force mission (a sorry euphemism if Byrd ever heard one), which of them was *ever* going to admit he couldn't handle what he'd been assigned? In a culture in which checked blocks and glowing performance evaluations meant the difference between upward mobility and being shown the door, no one was going to challenge the prevailing orthodoxy. No one was going to hike back up the chain of command and say, "Hey, this 'economy of force' thing you've got going? It's really not working."

Byrd didn't think the Division or Brigade was necessarily wrong. The mission is handed down and you do the best you can with what you've got. But when you push men and materials farther than they can possibly go, you shouldn't crucify soldiers when things break down. The Hill-Scott case wasn't the My Lai massacre, for God's sake. It wasn't Haditha. Byrd was sensitive to the fact that fine, young Americans volunteered to come over to some pretty shitty places and do some pretty shitty jobs. It was wrong, he felt, to just throw them to the wolves.

The flight to Salerno took a little over forty minutes. As the helo approached the LZ, it flared then settled, a cloud of moondust brewing up past the windows. Byrd deplaned, and the Black Hawk was still taxiing away when he saw a soldier running toward the LZ.

"Sir! Lieutenant Colonel Byrd!" A soldier ran up and rendered a salute. "Sir, I need to get the Article 32 findings from you!" He was yelling to be heard over helo.

Byrd frowned and yelled back. "Why? I'm supposed to give my report to Colonel Johnson!"

"Sir, you can't give it to Colonel Johnson! I have to take it!"

Byrd stood in the fading wind of the Black Hawk's rotors and it hit him: Someone had cut a deal. But why hadn't anyone told him? Even if the deal had been made that morning, someone could have let him know, and he could have avoided this whole damn trip.

Ever since the Article 32 concluded, when he hadn't been discharging a task specifically related to running his battalion, this case had consumed him. He had lain awake nights pondering the moral questions at the center of the debate. Now, it was almost as if the entire proceeding, months of preparation, reams of memos, testimony, and reports, had been for nothing.

Byrd tracked down his return flight, boarded another Black Hawk, and headed back to FOB Lightning. On the way, he wondered why Brigade hadn't even wanted to *see* his report? He could only conclude that the nature of the Article 32 testimony had made its way back up the chain. That someone, somewhere, had decided it would be better if that testimony never saw the light of day.

They quash the 32 findings, they're never made public. This young captain goes away, senior officers move on, get their next ranks. From a practical standpoint, it was the safest thing. Morally, Byrd wasn't so sure.

CHAPTER 6

16 December 2008

CPT ROGER HILL swam awake, a thought already fully formed in his brain: *This is my last day in the Army.*

Each step of his morning routine seemed tinged with a strange finality. He ran a sink of steaming water, wiped fog from the mirror, and watched himself shave. He had only two uniforms with him and had saved the clean one for his meeting with General Schloesser. Hill laid both on his cot, and stripped three Velcro-backed patches from the worn uniform. One by one, he affixed them to his clean blouse. On the left shoulder, he placed his home-station unit patch, the Screaming Eagle of the 101st Airborne. On the right shoulder, he placed the 101st combat patch. Hill had fought with other units and could have chosen any of their patches, but the Screaming Eagle was the one he was proudest of.

On the ACU blouse, an officer's rank is worn down the center of his chest. Hill affixed a patch embroidered with captain's bars there. He had looked forward to someday exchanging the bars for the gold oak leaf of a major. That would never happen now.

He put on his camo pants, then the blouse, sat down on the cot, and pulled on his desert tan boots. Adjusted the dog tags that were tucked in behind the laces—his ID, in case he was killed in battle. He stared at the tags for a moment, at what he had been willing to give.

This morning was not the last time he would do these things, but somehow it *was* the last time in the only life he had known since he was a teenager. The only life he'd ever dreamed of. After today, he would step out onto a new path, unmarked and unknown.

Hill busied himself making lists, including a list of talking points. He'd been rehearsing these in his head, sort of a running tally of all the dominoes that had fallen during the deployment. Lunch passed, then dinner. As the time for his meeting with General Schloesser neared, Hill's emotions spun up. He wanted to tell the general so much. He decided he wouldn't volunteer anything, but if Schloesser wanted to hear what he had to say, he would be ready.

At 1800, Hill pocketed his talking points and began the long trek across Bagram to Division headquarters. Too nervous to stomach food, he skipped the DFAC and caught the shuttle. He had seen the Combined Joint Task Force building once when the sun was up, but all he could remember was that it was somewhere past the shoppette, the fast-food joints, and the massage parlor.

After the scarcity at Airborne, Hill felt resentment rising as the shuttle trundled past Bagram's city-esque amenities. He immediately squashed it.

Focus.

The bus stopped at the shoppette. Hill got off and walked until he found a maze-like entry control point fronting a formidable facade. Inside, the building's security was redundancy defined. He passed through layers of it until he reached still another security desk that served the command hallway. Another surreal moment hit him: It was as if he had entered a Stephen King dreamscape and a guillotine lay somewhere off this hall. If he tried to run in either direction, the corridor would stretch endlessly away, escape forever just out of reach.

At the security desk, an NCO checked him in and escorted him up flights of stairs that reversed on themselves. Hill noticed nameplates on doors and was startled to recognize some. One caused a flashback to an email thread Major Faber had shared with him, part of the "I Suck at Fighting" dustup, when Division blamed Hill for the off-color quote that a soldier from another unit gave to a reporter. The general whose door he was now climbing past had at the time called for Hill's head on a platter.

Maybe he's getting his wish, Hill thought. The ironic self talk didn't soothe his nerves in the least.

At the top of the stairwell, the NCO led him through a door and passed him off to the general's aide, another army officer who offered Hill a seat outside General Schloesser's door.

LTC Huston, file folder in hand, walked past Hill with a nod and disappeared into the general's office. Minutes ticked past. Hill's heart raced. He felt uncomfortably special, as though the reason he was here was being broadcast to the building on a loudspeaker loop. But really, there was only the hush of the room, empty except for the aide whose eyes remained on his work.

Huston reappeared, closing Schloesser's door behind him. "The general will see you now. His desk is about five paces from the door and to the right. So you'll have to walk in, right-face, and report, okay?"

"Thanks, sir. I appreciate it," Hill said. He stood, heart pounding, and knocked on the door.

"Come in."

Five paces. Pause. Right face. And there sat Major General Jeffrey J. Schloesser, ramrod straight in his ACU uniform, a row of stars Velcroed down the center of his chest.

Hill snapped a salute. "Sir, Captain Hill reports as ordered."

The general returned the salute. "Go ahead and have a seat."

A chair faced Schloesser's desk. Hill pulled it out and sat down, back erect, hands on thighs, just as he had learned his first summer at the military academy. He remained silent, watching the general flip through a stack of documents. Hill remembered reporting to Fort Campbell, COL Johnson paging through his record, his encouraging words at their first meeting: *Roger, we need to get you in line to take command.*

Deep sadness spread in Hill's chest. He had dreamed of standing shoulder to shoulder with men in combat since he was six years old, since that night in Germany watching his father's infantry battalion performing nighttime maneuvers. It seemed impossible, absurd even, that he would claw his way through West Point academics, follow every jot and tittle of every manual with pristine precision, watch his men bleeding, maimed, and dead, only to have what he thought was his life's calling shriek to a halt like a freeway crash.

Schloesser raised his eyes, which Hill could not read. Then the general dove in, reciting directly from Department of the Army Form 2627. "Captain Roger Hill, I am considering whether you should be punished under Article 15 for the following conduct..."

Schloesser then intoned the charges that Masten had brokered with Huston.

Dereliction of duty in failure to control the detainee situation...

Allowing soldiers to assault detainees to the disgrace of the armed forces...

Wrongfully and willfully discharging a firearm, endangering human life...

Hill winced inside. He had read and signed off on those charges in order to take the plea. But now, stripped of context and spoken aloud, they sounded brutal.

Ticking down the form with a pen, Schloesser finished reading aloud some pro forma verbiage in which the disciplining officer is supposed to say that he has not yet decided on a punishment.

Hill ignored the recitation. The lawyers had decided. The lawyers had decided everything.

In some ways, he felt that the soldiers at the heart of cases like his were simply casualties of an imperfect system. The mantra and expectation was that every soldier up and down the chain would uphold Army values, like courage and integrity, that make the American military such a professional force. In a perfect world, working with people who had in mind each other's best interests and not their own, it might've been easier to choose differently than he had.

There were many times when he wished he *had* chosen differently. In some ways, he felt like a spinning computer cursor, stuck in place on the last event in the queue. Hill had replayed decision points between August 15 and August 27 like an endless video loop. The IED blast that killed Carwile and Conlon, the revelation of spies, the intel of impending suicide bombers and a mass attack, learning the spies had ties to lethal anti–Coalition Forces, warnings from Dave of a potential retaliatory attack, the prisoners' resolute silence, and the ticking clock, the ticking clock, the ticking clock...

Of *course* he technically shouldn't have done what he did, but once in that position what else could he have done? There was only one answer: Release the prisoners. Would that have been the "right" thing? To put his men in harm's way to save his own ass?

But even that was part of Hill's endless loop: Though Dave and others believed his actions had saved lives, that was only a theory. It was indisputable, though, that his actions led to his men's suffering.

The general put down the form and peeled off his reading glasses. "Roger, these are serious offenses."

"Yes, sir, they are."

"Is there anything you want to say?"

Hill collected himself, then plunged in.

"Sir, I did break protocol. I did break Army regulations, there's no doubt about it. But First Sergeant Scott and I acted solely out of concern for our men and only after repeated failure in support, right up until the end when our command failed to secure a dozen spies after they had been proven an imminent threat to Coalition Forces. Sir, we undoubtedly lost men to those spies. And sir, there is so much more I could share in terms of—"

Hill paused and took stock of Schloesser's face. A slight grimace had formed around his mouth, and he had physically pulled away, ever so slightly. Hill knew he was turning him off.

And yet, he had rehearsed so much that he knew needed to be said. In Wardak, Taliban forces had mounted a surge of their own, he wanted to tell the general, growing exponentially in size from Esh-ma-keyl to Badam Kalay to Haft Asiab. The enemy was also emboldened: the frontal VBIED attack on the Shockers, the jingle truck massacre, the mutilated Americans at Tangi, the truck bombing at Sayed Abad. The attacking force on the jingle trucks alone was nearly double the size of Hill's entire company—*if* he had been able to rally all his men in one place. With the capture of the spies, D Co had for once had the advantage. They could've exploited the intel, executed missions, turned the tide.

But the moment had been lost. Victory was sacrificed to ass covering, and war fighting supplanted by infighting, like children scrabbling for pennies in the dirt.

But Hill didn't say any of that. They all—everyone in the Division—already knew what he would say.

Only two days before, the *Washington Post* had spelled it out in a head-line: A WAR'S IMPOSSIBLE MISSION. In the accompanying article, P. J. Tobia, the freelance reporter who had attended the Article 32 hearing with Paul Avallone, summed up Hill and Scott's dilemma perfectly:

> To me, their story encapsulates the impossible role we've asked U.S. soldiers to play in the reconstruction of this devastated country. They are part warrior, part general contractor, yet they are surrounded on all sides by a populace that wants nothing more than to kill or be rid of them... Watching the prosecution destroy the reputations of Scott and Hill was heartbreaking, tragic—and deeply conflicting. As an American who fiercely believes in the rule of law and due process, I understand that the actions of D Company are inexcusable. A mock execution, under almost any circumstance, is antithetical to the ideals and standards our nation aspires to.

And perhaps Hill's superiors had good reason not to take these particular men into custody. Maybe they were on the radar of U.S. intelligence and taking them out of circulation might have meant losing valuable information.

But the soldiers of D Company felt that they were out of options. I fear that this kind of story will repeat itself in other parts of Afghanistan again and again, if only because U.S. forces know that their enemy's mission is clearer than their own.

Hill had known enough people who had served closely with General Schloesser that he knew him to be an honorable man. But he was in an impossible situation. There was testimony about a "morally bankrupt" Battalion commander and a breakdown in Battalion support, now underscored by an article in a respected, internationally read newspaper. But several men under his command had undeniably broken the law. The whirl of clashing facts and the general's reputation all told Hill to stop.

Stop speaking. Stop justifying himself. Just stop.

This isn't about hearing me out. This is about moving on.

"Roger, you took matters into your own hands and that is unacceptable."

"Sir—" Hill's brain made a break toward rebuttal, but his mouth hemmed it in. "Sir…" he finally said. "Yes, sir."

"Roger…" the general began.

Silence ticked in the room. Schloesser placed his pen on top of the 2627, next to the signature blocks that he and Hill would sign. He began again.

"Roger, if you will admit that what you did was morally wrong, then I will transfer you within the Division. It would be a rehabilitative transfer. You would remain in the Army and continue with your career."

For a split second, Hill's throat and stomach traded places. Hope surged in him. He wouldn't be disgraced. He wouldn't lose his job. He could continue the career he'd dreamed of. He would be hobbled, yes. But he had always been a top performer. He would earn his way back.

Hill caught the general's eyes and searched them for ulterior motives. The face was stern, but the eyes were soft. Hill saw sincerity. His heart flashed to calling Lauren with the good news—

But his brain, hardened by experience, weighed his alternatives.

In an instant, Hill cycled through the pros and cons and when his mental wheel stopped, it landed on Tommy Scott. Michael Peake. Andrew Doyle. Allan Moser. The list went on. Tommy was still looking at a summary court-martial. Doyle, Peake, and Moser were being processed out of the Army. Peake had already served time, for God's sake.

Suddenly, shame engulfed Hill. How could he have been so selfish? How could he have even considered Schloesser's offer?

Focus, he thought, as he steeled himself to speak irrevocable words.

"Sir, I can't. What we did was not morally wrong. We just took care of our men."

"Okay," Schloesser said simply. He pointed to the 2627 and handed Hill his pen.

CHAPTER 7

August 2011
Clarksville, Tennessee

ROGER HILL STEERED his gray Toyota Tundra pickup to a stop on a shady street. He put the truck in Park and looked up at the house, a modest facade of redbrick, the home of Jill and Larry Kay. At least a dozen cars were parked up and down the street. As he watched, the men of Dog Company, some with wives he'd never met, streamed toward the house bearing pot-luck platters for the company's first-ever reunion.

Hill was nervous. He'd stayed in touch with many of the guys but hadn't seen most for a couple of years. About half the company had RSVP'd that they'd be here today. Hill had wrestled with his feelings over the event. He very much wanted to see his brothers, but he deeply regretted that he hadn't been able to fix anything for his men. Though the insider threat on Airborne had been removed and lives likely saved, the cost had been high. If things hadn't come down the way they did, Tommy would have been on his way to becoming a Brigade command sergeant major. Similar conse-quences for other men weighed heavy on Hill's heart.

Several soldiers had received Article 15s—nonjudicial punishment result-ing in forfeiture of some pay and a negative service record entry. Others were kicked out of the Army: SGT Andrew Doyle, PFC Michael Peake, SPC Allan Moser. Doyle's Purple Heart was "lost" by the Army multiple times on his way out. He never received it.

On December 17, 2008, 1SG Tommy Scott and his attorney, CPT Jason

Easterly, appeared for a summary court-martial before LTC Robert Byrd in his tiny office on FOB Lightning.

"First Sergeant," Byrd said, "if it were up to me, I wouldn't give you any punishment at all."

Easterly smiled and spoke up quickly: "Sir, can we get that in writing?" His question was only half in jest.

But it hadn't been up to Byrd. Army legal protocols tied his hands, and in the end his decisions were only recommendations. He opted for the lightest discipline he could, recommending dismissal of two of the charges against Scott, and as punishment for a third, a reduction in pay grade—but a suspended reduction. Schloesser accepted the dismissal of charges, but rejected the suspension and reduced Scott in grade from E-8 to E-7.

Hill himself had languished in Afghanistan while the Army processed him out. In early 2009, he arrived home still unable to learn the results of the four-month disciplinary proceeding that had upended his life. LTC Byrd's findings in the Article 32 hearing remained buried, effectively denying him and Tommy any direct knowledge of what he had recommended to Brigade. Defense attorney Neal Puckett submitted two requests for the findings under the Freedom of Information Act, but received no response. Eventually, Puckett obtained the findings from Byrd, who emailed him a copy because he thought it was the right thing to do.

It turned out that Byrd had recommended against a general court-martial, that instead Hill be separated from the Army.

All his life, Hill had traded on competence. Where he had no natural gifting, he had succeeded on sheer effort, a habit instilled by his parents. In this, though, this series of events that had wrecked his beloved company, he felt he had utterly failed.

Now, Hill got out of his truck. *Nobody needs to hear all that today,* he thought. He grabbed a beer-packed cooler from his truck bed and walked toward the Kays' house behind a determined smile.

Inside, Jill and Larry Kay rattled pots and pans in their kitchen. Kay was putting on his trademark cookout menu: Johnsonville Brats simmered in Bud Light and finished off on the grill. Their first child, Benjamin, who looked like a miniature Larry, toddled from room to room.

After his testimony at the Article 32 hearing, Larry Kay had become persona non grata at the 1-506th. Senior officers seemed intent on ushering him quickly out of Afghanistan, as if he were a stain on the unit. Then it seemed they wanted to usher him out of the Army. The infantry branch manager in charge of cutting Kay's next set of orders sent him an email: Was Kay aware that his unit was trying to send him to Fort Benning? If Kay didn't accept orders there, the branch manager said, he would have to leave the service.

The truth was, Kay and his wife hadn't been sure of Kay's next career move. On one hand, they wanted to start a family, and the Army did offer financial stability. On the other, Kay's recent experience had not been good. After Brigade broke up Dog Company and scattered her across Afghanistan, the Army claimed Kay had "lost" truckloads of government property. Brigade tried to stick him with the bill: $2 million. Kay fought the allegations and eventually prevailed. Or thought he had. In the end, the brigade prorated the bill and sent it to CPT Hill.

The "Fort Benning or you're out" orders prompted Kay to draw his line in the sand. He had not done anything wrong and would not be pushed out of the Army as though he had. He just needed time to figure out his next move.

Now, the guys and their wives trooped through the Kays' two-story foyer: Joseph Coe, Allan Moser, Trevor Carlin, Alex Fernandez, Michael Peake, Mike Anzalone, Jason Dudley, Graydon Kamp, they all came streaming in, laughing, calling out names, embracing. The air in the house seemed electric with their joy at seeing each other again.

By early afternoon, the Kays' big backyard had become the scene of a pickup football game and an ever-evolving series of reunion photos, beer bottles raised in endless toasts. Tommy Scott could hardly stand it.

During the party, he laughed and drank with everyone else. But at least five times during the day, he ducked into the Kays' downstairs guest bath, braced his hands against the wall, and cried.

After the deployment, he'd had back surgery to repair discs crushed during more than seventy parachute jumps. While lying in bed recovering, he had been heartsick. To reach the point where you tell another man "I love you" without shame, and mean it; to achieve that level of kinship, and then to have it all come to a screaming halt, had devastated Scott.

During his physical rehab, he found himself inexplicably isolated. What had happened while he was gone? He was still the same man, but somehow the *whole world* was fucked up. A man cut him off on the highway; Scott poured on the gas and tailgated him home, cursing the entire way. He found himself viscerally aware of mundane but somehow sinister objects— trash cans, bushes, parked cars—and tensed when he passed them. At the hospital, he screamed at the staff: They weren't helping him with his rehab, weren't even *trying* to help him. And they were all in it together.

His family drove him crazy. They cared about the stupidest shit, he thought. Didn't they know there were people in the world blowing each other up, using *children* to blow each other up? Scott loved his wife, Cassandra, but found her voice like nails on a chalkboard. Any innocuous question she asked—*How's your day going?*—sparked in him an incredulous outrage.

How the hell do you think *my day is going?* he wanted to scream. *Why would you even* ask *me that?*

Vaguely, Scott knew that these weren't normal reactions. But it wasn't until he threw a remote control through a fifty-inch flat-screen television and trashed his garage in a tornado of rage that Scott knew he needed help.

When facilitators first suggested Scott might be suffering from PTSD (Post-Traumatic Stress Disorder), he scoffed. He was a goddamn first sergeant in the United States Army. He'd been in combat in four countries. If it hadn't bothered him in twenty-four years, why should it bother him now? Wasn't the *P* in PTSD for "pussy"?

Reluctantly, he took a class on the subject, slouching in his chair, aggressively bored. In the third week, though, doubt began to wash up against the barricades he'd built. If he did have PTSD—and that was a big if—didn't that mean he was weak? That he couldn't handle what he'd signed up to do? That he was a flawed human being and a worse soldier?

In the fourth week, the emotional rucksack he'd been dragging around—trauma, heartbreak, gore, grief, bitterness, fear, fury—burst open. Tommy Scott realized that it wasn't his family, his wife, or the guy on the highway with the problem. It was him. He was sick. In Afghanistan, he'd been fighting ghosts. Now he was fighting demons.

For Allan Moser, the D Co reunion was like coming home. He didn't know which guy to hug first. The best part was that although he hadn't seen any of them in two years, it was as if they'd parted only the day before, picked up right where they left off.

The highlight for Moser was seeing Tommy Scott and Roger Hill in the same room. He missed them, especially his adopted "dad," Scott.

"God*damn*, Moser! It's good to see you!" Scott had greeted him. The two men embraced for a solid minute.

After Battalion spirited Moser, Doyle, Peake, and Frey to Ghazni, Moser was assigned a lawyer. He never met her because she was in Kuwait. During a brief series of phone conversations, the lawyer pointed out that Moser had already admitted to hitting the detainee.

"But it was in self-defense!" he objected. "He bit me and wouldn't let go!"

"They're saying *he* acted in self-defense," the lawyer said. "He bit you because he thought he was going to be shot."

Moser went to a summary court-martial, where a major read the charges against him, as well as Moser's statement and those of his character witnesses. Instead of an early promotion to sergeant, the major reduced his grade to PFC and his pay by two-thirds. Also, he was to be chaptered out of the Army.

After Moser returned to Fort Campbell in 2009, a captain named Eliason asked him whether he wanted to stay in.

"Absolutely!" Moser said, overjoyed. "I love the Army!"

"You're not going to make me look bad?"

"No, sir! You can talk to anybody! I've been Soldier of the Month a couple of times, promoted early to E-4 and squad leader, and I was going up for early promotion to sergeant when all this went down. I'm a good soldier."

Eliason promised to talk to DeMartino.

Later, the 1-506th held a ceremony in which DeMartino was conferring end-of-tour awards. When DeMartino got to Moser, he said, "I hear we're keeping you."

"Yes, sir," Moser said.

DeMartino smiled. "Good. I'm glad to hear it."

Many months later Moser was still awaiting his retention paperwork when he got the news: They were kicking him out after all.

He was separated from the Army on the day his regular enlistment was up. He was furious and felt betrayed all over again. Why would they lead him to believe he was staying in, that he didn't need to line up a job or any of that, then kick him out after all and take his veterans' benefits?

If anyone had asked Moser that day, he would've answered the way he had in the witness chair in Salerno:

Had Dog Company done the right thing? Yes.

Did they save American lives? Yes.

Should they have gone about it a little differently? Maybe. But they were men at war, imperfect human beings forced to act to save themselves from two enemies, *both* inside their wire. The local nationals in custody weren't some low-level schmucks selling a few scraps of information. They were highly connected insurgents who had already killed two men and had tried to kill dozens of others.

In Moser's opinion, if Battalion had simply taken the detainees, none of the rest would have happened. He believed the entire evolution illustrated the reason terror groups do not fear the American military: They can lie, steal, spy, and kill, and the Americans pat them on their heads and send them back onto the battlefield.

After the incident, Moser encountered many people who said Dog Company would've been better off to have killed the spies. Quietly, somewhere off the FOB. Make them disappear. What incentive did American soldiers have to take prisoners? Moser expected that future soldiers might be a little more ruthless: Stay alive and keep your job.

The sun-splashed day faded to afternoon gold. Some of the guys were returning from a trip to a nearby cemetery, where they visited the grave of SGT John Paul Castro, the soldier who had replaced Paul Conlon in 3rd Platoon. Castro was killed in Afghanistan on a subsequent deployment—his third combat tour in a career of less than seven years.

The temperature had dropped a few degrees, releasing from the Kays' lawn the loamy scents of summer. Hill sat on the back porch and pulled out a pipe made of marbled briarwood. He had bought it in Germany when he and Lauren traveled there to spend some time with CPT B and his wife.

Hill was new to pipe smoking. He had taken it up as a kind of homage to his grandfather, Pop Hill, to Heather Masten's cigars, and to Jack Cheasty, the pipe-smoking physician's assistant who had testified so courageously at the Article 32 hearing. For Hill, the pipe had become a ritual of remembrance. Most times, memories of the Wardak ordeal were unwelcome, pouring in like poorly timed rain. But when he pulled out his pipe, opened the tobacco pouch, inhaled its scent, and packed the bowl, he gave himself permission to relive the things that happened. To embrace responsibility, which he sometimes felt lay nowhere but at his feet.

He had not stopped trying to fix things. Working through friends still on active duty, he was trying to get Purple Hearts for soldiers like Doyle, along with Mo's Silver Star. He had also begun the process of pursuing a discharge appeal for some of his soldiers and himself. But mostly, he was just trying to start over.

Hill had begun a new career as a project manager and engineer at Georgia Tech Research Institute and was also studying for his MBA. As an engineer, he had learned to deconstruct events and eventualities to the base level, weighting each choice at every major decision point. The new skill was a double-edged sword: It was useful in his new profession, but he also applied the analysis to those twelve fateful days in Wardak in that never-ending loop that never quite left his mind.

What role had he played? At which points? How could he have altered the outcome?

Then a colleague shared with Hill "Reason's Model of Causation." Throughout the investigation and disciplinary process, he had been made to feel that he was the *only* one who could have altered the outcome. After the Article 32, COL Johnson, the Brigade commander, actually told him that the damage done to his soldiers' careers was on Hill's hands alone. It seemed that no one wanted to hit the Rewind button and look at *all* the latent failures, the players seen and unseen, their actions or lack thereof. No one wanted to look at the systemic priorities and policies that had set the conditions for the way things turned out.

Something Mo said helped Hill's perspective with that. Mo had been training troops in counter-IED, counterinsurgency, and urban combat at Camp Atterbury, Indiana, and Hill thought the soldiers there were lucky to have him. In a phone call one day, Mo told Hill, "All of our senior leaders, our battalion commanders and higher, none of them have grown up in combat like we have. They got to make all their mistakes in peacetime, where the stakes were low and everything was a training exercise."

That was true, Hill said, but he still didn't like the mistakes he'd made, the fact that he had not understood the politics of the modern military.

"Look, sir, you jumped on a grenade for us," Mo said, "but that doesn't mean that the rest of us weren't going to take some shrapnel."

Hill hadn't looked at it that way.

"I heard the command checked 'No' for all the 'Army values' on your outgoing fitness report," Mo said.

It was true. Instead of a narrative evaluation, his last fitness report had simply listed the charges to which he'd pleaded guilty. A series of blocks on the evaluation form listed Army core values such as loyalty, honor, selfless service, and personal courage. They all had been checked "No."

"Well, that's bullshit," Mo said. "You had to choose your loyalties, between policies and the careers of your commanders and the lives of your men."

In January 2010, CNN special investigative reporters Abbie Boudreau and Scott Zamost had stepped up to look at that piece of the puzzle: the ISAF ninety-six-hour detention rule that had forced Hill to choose between the letter of military law and protecting his soldiers. During the piece, Boudreau caught up to General David Petraeus, then commander of U.S. forces in Afghanistan. They confronted him about the detention policy, citing the Airborne case in particular.

Two months later, Petraeus rescinded the 96-Hour Rule. For Hill, it was a significant victory. But it didn't stop his decision-point loop, his walking backward through events again and again.

In the Kays' backyard, the sun was falling. In the dimming light, Hill let down the cheerful mask he had hidden behind all day. He repacked his pipe, tucked the stem in his mouth, and released a sweet-smelling stream of smoke.

"Sir?"

Hill turned to see Trevor Carlin and his wife, Ashleigh. Carlin had been with the Dirty First. He was one of the men who had recovered the mutilated American soldier in Tangi. Trevor and Ashleigh were newlyweds.

For him, this reunion had been so joyful an event that he would remember it as something worth reliving every day of his life. Carlin felt closer to the guys in this company than to his own blood. They understood him. They had lived together through things that others only read about. And though they had been broken apart, they had knit themselves back together again. Stronger than before, the way a snapped bone heals stronger at the break.

"Hey, Trevor. How're you doing?" Hill said.

Carlin pulled up a pair of lawn chairs. "Sir, you seem really quiet. Are you doing okay?"

Hill tried hard to turn his happy face back on, but it was too late. The Kays' backyard was empty but for the three of them, and Hill was tired.

"Thanks for asking, Trevor. It's just hard to see how some of you guys have struggled after everything that happened. I'm wrestling with not being able to make it right."

Carlin leaned in. "Sir, nobody did anything that day because they were following orders. They did it because they were brothers, taking care of each other."

When speaking of Wardak, Carlin had at times tried to draw comparisons civilians might understand: You're at home in the States. Someone has killed two members of your family, and is in a position to kill more. You can't run, and you know the police aren't going to help. Would you stand by and let more of your family be killed? Or would you take care of it yourself? Carlin didn't think there was a man in America who wouldn't act on his own to take care of the problem.

"You don't have any reason to feel guilty," Carlin said to Hill. "Anyone in the circumstances, with as tight a bond as we had, would've done the same thing."

Hill felt his soul lift and for a moment, he couldn't speak. For someone as intelligent and thoughtful as Carlin to understand him at the heart level, to grasp not only his actions but also his intent, was like a ray of light piercing the dark water of his self-condemnation.

Hill smiled. "Thanks, Trevor. You have no idea how much that means to me."

Conversations throughout the day lifted Larry Kay. Laughing and swapping stories with his platoon brothers wiped mud from his memories, setting the good ones back in place.

When the infantry branch manager offered Kay Fort Benning, he refused it. "Give me an assignment that puts me at Fort Campbell for eighteen months," he said.

"Well, there's an opening for an XO at WTU."

"I'll take it," Kay said instantly. After a pause, he added, "What's WTU?"

It was Fort Campbell's Warrior Transition Unit. WTUs support wounded, ill, and injured soldiers who require at least six months of rehabilitative and medical care. A WTU closely resembles a "line" unit, with a cadre of officers and NCOs whose mission is to help wounded soldiers transition back to active duty, or to civilian life.

Kay knew it was a perfect fit. Tommy was in the WTU at Fort Campbell. PFC Ryan Haffner was also there, recovering from injuries sustained in the Jalrez attack that nearly killed SGT Carlos Colonruiz.

Colon lost two fingers on his left hand, along with his left eye and the socket around it. He also lost all the hearing in his left ear and most in his right. He had undergone seventeen surgeries, not counting those performed while he was in the coma at Walter Reed. It was his three kids that motivated him to fight his way back to health—and into the gym. By 2011, he was looking like Schwarzenegger again, and was even upbeat about the scars that covered his arms, torso, head, and face, telling his friends, "Scarface don't have shit on me!"

Now, Kay's kitchen was a rowdy pub and his backyard a busy (if slightly wobbly) athletic field. Looking around in satisfaction, he remembered a comment made by a key officer during the Airborne investigation.

"Either this is the most loyal company on earth," the officer said, "or everyone in it is a fucking liar."

Clearly, the latter was not true. But the officer's first assessment was correct: Among these men was a tightly woven fabric of trust, camaraderie, and love—the tightest Kay had ever seen.

The Army had tried to make Dog Company disappear, he realized. *They separated us, silenced us, tried to make us go away.*

They might have broken up the company, but they could not break the brotherhood. That, Kay thought, is indestructible.

EPILOGUE

In the case of *The United States of America vs. CPT Roger T. Hill and 1SG Tommy L. Scott,* officers of the 101st Airborne determined that if LTC Byrd's Article 32 findings were never delivered to COL Johnson, the convening authority, then the findings would be technically incomplete and therefore shielded from the Freedom of Information Act. It was for that reason that a soldier was sent to retrieve Byrd's findings the moment he landed at FOB Salerno on December 14, 2008. The Brigade refused to disclose the results to Hill and Scott, and even their attorney, Neal Puckett, was unable to learn the Article 32 findings through official channels.

For the counterintelligence community, the techniques and experience gleaned from the Airborne op were a game changer, ███████████ ██ ████████████████████ A few months later in Afghanistan, █████ ███████ detained four individuals firmly connected to Al Qaeda and the Taliban. No shots were fired, no detention time lines busted. The Army conducted immediate interrogations at approved facilities, and the entire spy network was disbanded before the enemy knew what hit them.

Shortly afterward, ████████████ left behind on that base were hit with well-aimed indirect fire, and nearly killed. The CI team later learned that the bad guys had gotten their targeting intel from the spies the CI team had neutralized during the op. It was the same retaliatory scenario Hill had feared at Airborne.

In the year following the Airborne op, Dave and his OIC codified their findings in contributions to policy updates to ensure that the next generation of CI agents knew what was possible and how to get results—allowing combat commanders to focus on fighting the war outside the wire while saving American lives.

The 1-506th Battalion commander, Lieutenant Colonel Anthony DeMartino, declined to be interviewed for this book. DeMartino was the subject of a Department of the Army Inspector General (IG) investigation in connection with the Afghanistan deployment. He did not respond to requests for a copy of the IG findings, which the authors were unable to obtain through the Freedom of Information Act. In 2014, DeMartino retired from the Army as a lieutenant colonel.

Trial Defense Service attorney Heather Masten was morally outraged that the Army would so zealously prosecute soldiers whose actions, while definitely violating Army regulations, did not in her opinion merit discharge nor rise to the level of "war crimes." Because of this and similar Army prosecutions of soldiers fighting the terror war, Masten retired from active duty.

Tommy Scott has had three back fusions and a knee replacement since leaving the Army. At the invitation of his instructor, he returned to the class on PTSD and continues, slowly, to fight his way back. Scott has become an advocate for other soldiers suffering combat-related post-traumatic stress.

Major General Jeffrey Schloesser, who commanded all U.S. forces in Afghanistan, was cleared of wrongdoing in the Battle of Wanat, the incident in which LT Jonathan Brostrom and eight other men of Chosen Company died while repelling a massive Taliban attack. But rather than continue on active duty, he resigned from the Army, choosing instead to share responsibility with the officers under his command.

Soon after Dog Company was disbanded, an infantry unit of nearly 1,200 men took over FOB Airborne and Wardak, the violent province held by Hill's eighty-nine-man unit. During the Army's investigation and prosecution of Dog Company soldiers, the spies who conspired to kill LT Donnie Carwile and SPC Paul Conlon were released.

AUTHORS' NOTE ON SOURCES

This book is based on the following sources:

More than two hundred hours of interviews were conducted between 2009 and 2015 with the men of Dog Company and other soldiers on the ground in Afghanistan during the Wardak deployment.

Some senior Army sources agreed to provide information for this book with the agreement that no information be attributed to them because they feared Army reprisal.

LTC Anthony DeMartino declined to be interviewed. LTC Dixon Gunther, who headed the investigation at Airborne, agreed to be interviewed, then stopped answering follow-up requests and was not interviewed.

The authors attempted to contact MAJ Robert Smith (by then a lieutenant colonel) at his U.S. duty station, both directly and through the post public affairs officer, but were unable to reach him.

The portion of the book that covers the investigation at FOB Airborne and the events surrounding the Article 32 hearing at FOB Salerno is based on government documents, including but not limited to the following: sworn statements from MAJ Smith's 15-6 investigation; sworn statements from LTC Gunther's investigation at Airborne; Criminal Investigation Division (CID) reports and sworn statements; charge sheets; case-related emails, letters, and memos; forensic reports; Offers to Plead; LTC Byrd's Article 32 report; and summary and verbatim transcripts of the Article 32 hearing. Vincent also conducted numerous interviews with defense attorney Neal Puckett, defense attorney Heather Masten, and LTC Robert Byrd, the Article 32 investigating officer.

The narrative of the Battle of Wanat, in which LT Jonathan Brostrom and the men of Chosen Company heroically repelled an overwhelming Taliban attack, was based on the *Vanity Fair* article "Echoes from a Distant Battlefield," by Mark Bowden; a *Washington Post* photo essay on the battle (available at http://www.washingtonpost.com/wp-srv/special/world /battle-of-wanat/); military historian Douglas Cubbison's original report on the battle, written for the Army Combat Studies Institute; and interviews with Mr. Cubbison.

The Article 32 transcripts excerpted in this book were compiled from two sources: a "summary" transcript prepared by Army court reporters during the Article 32 hearing, and verbatim transcripts prepared by a private transcriptionist from audio recordings of the hearing. In the summary transcript, only the witnesses' answers and not the attorneys' questions were recorded by the court reporter. The audio recordings included the voices of all hearing participants, but because there was only a single microphone in the hearing room at FOB Salerno, audio quality was poor. The authors hired audio specialists to enhance the recordings in order to make possible a verbatim transcription.

Because the Army's summary transcript conveyed the sense of what a witness said and not his actual words, the authors used the verbatim transcripts whenever possible. Where the recording of witnesses' answers was inaudible, the authors included the answers recorded in the Army's summary transcripts. While the volume of hearing transcripts prevented including them all, the authors made every attempt to use a range of excerpts that fairly represented both the prosecution and the defense. Ellipses in the transcripts (...) indicate that text was omitted for brevity when it did not change the impact or meaning of a witness's testimony. The authors did not omit testimony where doing so would have favored either side of the case.

The authors enlisted the support of numerous military subject-matter experts to ensure the accuracy of a range of details, including equipment nomenclature, military protocols, tactics, and procedures. Wherever possible, though, military jargon was reduced or eliminated to make the story easier to read.

In the interest of national security, the authors submitted the manuscript to Army counterintelligence, to two attorneys who were prior military intelligence officers, and to the defense department Office of Security Review prior to publication.

ACKNOWLEDGMENTS

The authors would like to thank the men of Dog Company and their families. Your courage, professionalism, and loyalty have set an immeasurable standard. We would especially like to thank the Carwile, Conlon, Castro, and Crane families. We hope this story honors the memory of the heroes you have lost.

To all the soldiers of the 506th Band of Brothers Regiment and to all our nation's present-day warriors: This story is also your story. Day in and day out, you silently carry the banner of freedom and democracy on behalf of our great nation with the hope of sharing it with others. The burden you bear grows heavier as the wars we have fought slip further from the front page and the minds of an increasingly distracted nation and government. Still, you march on.

The authors also received support from scores of active duty and retired military personnel, along with journalists, academics, legal, intelligence, and other subject-matter experts. Special thanks to Robert Byrd for his integrity and his desire for fairness in a difficult case. To Heather Masten and her defense team, Jason Easterly, Kevin Cox, and Kevin Farmer: Thank you for your courage to repeatedly take on the impossible. To Neal and Marcy Puckett: Thank you for always fighting to give our troops more breathing room out on the battlefield. To David Bolgiano, Ed Soyster, Kevin Donaleski, Bob Weimann, Bill Donahue, Colby Vokey, John Maher, and the men and women of the United American Patriots Warrior Fund: Thank you for defending those who defend our country. Also, thanks to Paul Avallone, P. J. Tobia, Melissa Preen, Diana West, Andy O'Meara, Thomas McInerney, Paul and Muffin Vallely, Pat Carfagno, Tim Sumner,

Troy Steward, Jessi Joseph, Abbie Boudreau, Scott Zamost, James Zumwalt, Kimberly Bellissimo, Timothy Webster, and many others for your pursuit of transparency and justice in the court of public opinion. And to Ken Walters, Bill Chatfield, Ed Kennedy, Douglas Cubbison, Wulf Lindenau, Steve and Patty Shewmaker, Christine Stark, and Dave for contributions that are too numerous to list here. Transcriptionist Danielle Ardan, line editor Anita Palmer, research assistant Suzy Q. Haines, and our technical assistant, Damjan, you rock! Ben and Sara Huntley, you roll!

Grand bouquets of gratitude to our editor, Kate Hartson, and our publisher, Rolf Zettersten, for their faith in us through this marathon project. To Rick Christian, our literary agent, we are grateful for your steady hand of guidance, and we wish our rock-solid friend and *Dog Company* champion, Lee Hough, were still with us to see the project he believed in come to fruition. We know he is cheering from heaven.

Lynn extends a special thanks to:

The men and families of Dog Company. Thank you for opening up and letting me into your lives and memories. I know that telling me your story was like ripping open deep wounds again and again. Thank you for your time, patience, and generosity.

My husband, Danny, whose patience and loving guidance provided the space and wisdom to see this project through.

My sons, Christian and Jacob, who listened patiently to all my "you're not gonna believe *this*" Dog Company stories along the way, and to whom these men are American heroes.

Roger extends a special thanks to:

The men of Death Dealer Company: You are the epitome of courage under fire and selfless sacrifice, of honor and heroism. Your example made me into a better leader and a better man. Thank you for allowing me to serve as your C.O.

To those who were persecuted alongside Tommy and me: Thank you for enduring such hardship with an even greater measure of courage and dignity. I hope that this story will serve as some consolation for the emotional anguish, loss of benefits, and professional setbacks you and your families have endured in the line of such honorable service to our nation.

To those who were interviewed for this story: Thank you for the countless and often difficult hours so many of you spent revisiting the past to help perfect my and Lynn's writing. Not every man was mentioned by name, but I trust it was made clear that every man gave his all, day in and day out. As this project evolved, certain narratives self-selected for the scope and themes Lynn and I felt necessary to maintain. And in the end, there were just too many wonderful scenes of courage under fire, brotherhood, sacrifice, humor, and other anecdotes for us to fit it all in. I hope that you will find all that was shared to be representative and honoring of our collective sacrifice.

To those who served alongside us in Wardak: Wardak's Operational Detachment Alpha U.S. Army Special Forces, Montana Army National Guard Police Mentorship Team and other Embedded Training Teams, 2ème Régiment étranger d'infanterie (2nd Foreign Legion Infantry Regiment) and the 35e Régiment d'infanterie (35th Infantry Regiment) French Operational Mentor Liaison Teams, and Task Force 51 of the Norwegian Army Special Forces. It was a privilege to serve alongside you, and it is our honor to call you brothers and sisters.

To our families and to the ladies of the Dealer Family Readiness Group: Thank you for your courage and dedication. Year after year you sacrificed alongside us on a parallel battlefield. Coming home is not easy for anyone, especially from a war without an end state. Thank you for your continued grace and understanding. As with all military families, our country is indebted to you for your service and sacrifice.

To Lauren and to her family and friends: Thank you for your love, sacrifice, and support and standing with the men and me when the chips were down.

To my sweet Michael and Emma: "Yes, your Daddy was a soldier, and it was hard. But your love makes me better and better every day, thank you. I love you to the moon and back!"

To the Hill, Choi, Kim, and Lee families: Thank you for your love and support. There is so much I could say about my family, but my mother's lead-from-the-front example sums it up best. In the beginning, Yong spent many weekends reaching out and individually meeting with hundreds of complete strangers from around the country to raise awareness for our case. My mother and others whose help she enlisted were the media before the investigation gained any traction in the news. If there is a type of love that could be described as "fierce," my mother's example would have coined it. And a portrait of my family would be alongside hers.

Like many veterans, I really struggled to adjust to life after years of fighting and years of having been institutionalized by the military experience. Once back home, I especially struggled with being away from *my brothers.* Our common experiences forged a bond so strong that it created in me a lens through which I involuntarily viewed all other relationships. That lens leaves many of us feeling alone, even within our own families. And as for many veterans, it took a community to pull me out of my cave and help me realize that I ultimately had to choose each day to start living again.

Along with the men of Dealer Company, several close friends reached out and held me in those darkest of moments. They never walked away even when they did not understand my mood or attitude. They gave me community and encouraged me to carry on when I didn't think I could take another step. To those friends, I am forever grateful for your unconditional and steadfast love and support.

To Lynn: Thank you for being such an awesome friend and teammate. You came to know many of us better than we knew one another. Probably because men just can't talk to other men about so many things. You were one part investigative journalist and one part therapist to us all. (It probably didn't hurt that your previous life provided ample opportunities to, shall we say, "talk like a sailor.")

Finally, we both thank God, who sustained us through deep, shadowed valleys during this seven-year project. Lord, you get all the credit, every bit. You put every relationship together. We were in your hands all along.

GUIDE TO MILITARY WEAPONS AND TERMS

ACUs: Army Combat Uniform, the fabric is a universal camouflage pattern of tan, gray, and green.

ANA: Afghan National Army.

ANP: Afghan National Police.

ASAP: As soon as possible.

BAF: The aeronautical designation for Bagram Airfield (also known as Bagram Airbase), Afghanistan.

Blackhawk: The Sikorsky UH-60 Blackhawk helicopter is a four-bladed medium-lift utility helicopter. Two Blackhawks were used to infil the Dirty First into blocking positions during Dog Company's first attempt to bag Raʐ ːk in Jalrez.

CAS: Close Air Support; spoken as "cas." Air action by fixed or rotary-winged aircraft against hostile targets in close proximity to friendly forces. "CAS" is often used to reference the aircraft and crew providing the close air support.

Chinook: The Boeing CH-47 Chinook is a twin-engine, tandem rotor, heavy-lift helicopter. Its primary roles are troop, supply, and equipment movement.

CI: Counterintelligence, "spy catchers."

CID: Criminal Investigation Division, the organization in the U.S. Army tasked with investigating serious crime within the ranks.

Click: Slang for a kilometer.

CLP: Combat Logistics Patrol, pronounced "clip," a U.S. Army element that transports supplies to forward troops.

CONEX: A military shipping container, usually 40 feet x 8 feet x 8.5 feet.

COP: Combat Outpost. Dog Company manned and sustained up to three combat outposts and one forward operating base.

DFAC: Dining Facility.

ECP: Entry Control Point, as in the main entrance of a forward operating base. On FOB Airborne, the ECP was manned by both U.S. and Afghan Army soldiers.

ETA: Estimated time of arrival.

FOB: Forward Operating Base, Dog Company, was headquartered out of FOB Airborne.

FSC: Forward Support Company, responsible for supply distribution, maintenance, feeding, and administrative support to battlefield units.

HESCO®: Rapidly deployable earth-filled defensive barriers.

HLZ: Helicopter Landing Zone, often referred to as an "LZ."

Humvee: More properly HMMV or HMMWV, acronyms for High Mobility Multipurpose Wheeled Vehicle; a four-wheel-drive, diesel-powered truck seating four plus a gunner.

IED: Improvised explosive device.

Intel: Intelligence; the product of intelligence-collection operations.

IO: Investigating Officer; the officer presiding over the Article 32 hearing was known as the IO.

ISAF: International Security Assistance Force, the NATO-led security mission in Afghanistan established by the United Nations Security Council in December of 2001.

LCLA: Low Cost Low Altitude aerial resupply, supplies that are air-dropped by parachute.

LN: Local National, also known as host-country nationals. We referred to all Afghans as one of two terms.

Medevac: Medical Evacuation; often refers to the vehicle or aircraft and crew conducting the evacuation.

MIA: Missing In Action, a casualty classification assigned to troops who are reported missing during wartime or cease-fire.

MRAP vehicle: Mine Resistant Ambush Protected vehicle, kind of like a 1.5 story version of the Humvee with more armor and a hull designed to better withstand an explosive blast.

NATO: North Atlantic Treaty Organization, an intergovernmental military alliance based on the North Atlantic Treaty signed in 1949. Article 5 of the treaty requires member states to come to the aid of any member state subject to an armed attack. Article 5 was invoked for the first and only time after the September 11 attacks.

NCO: A Noncommissioned Officer in the pay grades E-4 (corporal) through E-9.

ODA: Operational Detachment Alpha, a U.S. Army Special Forces or Green Beret detachment.

OEF: Operation Enduring Freedom, the name used by the U.S. government to describe operations in Afghanistan from 2001 to 2014.

Op: Operation, as in military operation.

OPFOR: Opposing Force, the unit playing the role of the enemy during military training or war games.

PL: Platoon Leader, the officer (or NCO) in command of a platoon.

PMT: Police Mentorship Team. Wardak's PMT was from the Montana Army National Guard.

Qalat: A mud-walled compound common to Afghanistan.

QRF: Quick Reaction Force. In combat, a unit—typically platoon-sized—capable of rapid response to a developing situation.

RCP: Route Clearance Package, typically an engineer unit equipped as MRAPs, a variety of bomb detection and disposal technology and bomb disposal experts.

SF: Special Forces; the U.S. Army's SF are also known as Green Berets.

SITREP: Situation Report, a concise statement describing a unit's current location and tactical situation.

TC: Truck Commander. In a combat platoon, rides in the front passenger seat.

Terp: Short for Interpreter, not pejorative.

TOC: Tactical Operations Center, the command post or "nerve center" from which a small group of officers and expert NCOs maintain awareness of and guide tactical elements in the field.

UAV: Unmanned Aerial Vehicle, also known as an aerial drone.

VBIED: Vehicle Borne Improvised Explosive Device, a "car bomb."

XO: Executive Officer. At the company level, a first lieutenant or junior captain; at the battalion level, a major.

Guide to Dog Company Weapons

.50-cal: Dog Company platoons were equipped with the Browning M2 .50-caliber machine gun, recoil operated, air-cooled, fully automatic truck-mounted or crew-transportable machine gun.

60 mm mortar: A 60 millimeter mortar is a lightweight, high angle of fire, indirect fire weapon system. The "60s" were typically carried in the back of Dog Company gun trucks and used on the move because they were easy to set up for quick reaction ground engagements.

81 mm mortar: An 81 millimeter mortar is a medium-weight, high angle of fire, indirect fire weapon system. The "81s" were typically kept on FOB Airborne and Sayed Abad base to react to enemy rocket attacks.

105 mm artillery: The Bonecrusher artillery platoon used the M119A2 howitzer to fire 105 mm high explosive (HE) ammunition in support of Dog Company operations conducted within range of FOB Airborne.

A-10 Thunderbolt: The Fairchild Republic A-10 Thunderbolt is a single-seat twin turbofan engine close air support aircraft commonly referred to by its nickname, the "Warthog." The sound of the A-10's GAU-8/A Avenger 30 mm Gatling-type autocannon has been known to cause arousal among infantrymen, especially when multiple passes of this gun are made against enemy positions. The A-10's official name comes from the P-47 Thunderbolt, a WWII fighter effective at attacking ground targets.

AK-47: Taliban fighters were often armed with this Soviet-designed selective-fire (semiautomatic or automatic), gas-operated assault rifle.

Apache: The Apache Longbow attack helicopter is typically an infantryman's favorite form of close air support.

AT4: An 84 mm unguided, portable antitank weapon, effective in close spaces. SFC Grant Hulburt used the AT4 to suppress the Taliban assault at Badam Kalay.

B-1: The Rockwell B-1 Lancer is a heavy strategic bomber used by the U.S. Air Force.

B-52: The Boeing B-52 Stratofortress is a long-range strategic bomber used by the U.S. Air Force.

Beretta 9 mm: Captain Hill and other soldiers carried the Beretta M9 pistol, a 9 mm semiautomatic handgun.

Bradley Fighting Vehicle: The BFV is an American armored personnel carrier and fighting vehicle manufactured by BAE.

C-130: The Lockheed C-130 Hercules is a military transport aircraft used by the U.S. Air Force.

C-17: The Boeing C-17 Globemaster is a large military transport aircraft used by the U.S. Air Force.

C-4: Composition C-4 is a variety of the plastic explosive family. Dog Company used C-4 to demolition caches of enemy munitions, breach doors, and destroy IEDs.

CLU: The Command Launched Unit is the targeting component of the man-portable surface-to-air Javelin missile system.

F-15 Eagle: The McDonnell Douglas F-15 Eagle is an American twin-engine all-weather tactical fighter aircraft used by the U.S. Air Force.

IED: Improvised Explosive Device, today's weapon of choice by fighters engaged in unconventional warfare. In Iraq and Afghanistan, IEDs account for about two-thirds of Coalition casualties.

M4: Dog Company soldiers carried M4 carbines, a shorter and lighter variant rifle that is replacing the M16 in the U.S. infantry.

M-14 rifle: The last American "battle rifle" issued in quantity to U.S. military personnel. It fires a 7.62 mm round and is typically carried by an infantry squad's "designated marksman," a soldier with additional marksmanship training for longer range engagements.

M18 Claymore Mine: Directional antipersonnel mine named after a large Scottish medieval sword. The Claymore is command-detonated, directional, and fires about 700 3.2 mm steel balls using a layer of C-4 explosive.

M67 grenade: A spherical steel grenade that can be thrown about fifteen feet by the average male soldier. This is the type of grenade Mo threw when three armed men fired on Kris Wilson during the Shockers' counter rocket patrol.

M203: SFC Hulburt and PFC Jason "Photo" Phothisen used this single-shot 40 mm under-barrel grenade launcher at Badam Kalay.

M240: Dog Company platoons carried this general-purpose 7.62 mm medium machine gun that can be mounted on a bipod, tripod, aircraft, or vehicle.

M249: Dog Company platoons carried this general purpose 5.56 mm light machine gun that can be mounted on a bipod or vehicle.

MK-19: Dog Company platoons were equipped with the MK-19, a fully automatic truck-mounted or crew-transportable machine gun that can fire a variety of 40 mm grenades.

PKM: The PK is a 7.62 mm general-purpose Soviet-designed machine gun used by the Afghan security forces and Taliban alike. It is the Soviet-made equivalent to a U.S. military M240 medium machine gun.

RPG: Taliban fighters often attacked using the RPG, or rocket-propelled grenade. This shoulder-fired antitank weapon fires rockets equipped with explosive warheads, some of which can pierce armor.

RPK: The RPK is a 7.62 mm general-purpose Soviet-designed machine gun. It is very similar to the PKM but fires a slightly lighter round.

TOW, or TOW missile: Tube-Launched Optically Tracked Wire-Guided Missile. 3rd Platoon used this antitank weapon to engage enemy ground forces during a heavy rocket attack early in the Wardak deployment.

Unit Level (approx.)	Enlisted Leadership	Officer Leadership
Squad (5-10 Soldiers)	Staff Sergeant (SSG)	
Platoon (3-4 Squads) (16-40 Soldiers)	Sergeant First Class (SFC)	2nd or 1st Lieutenant (2LT or 1LT)
Company (3-4 Platoons) (90-200 Soldiers)	First Sergeant (1SG)	Captain (CPT)
Battalion (3-5 Companies) (500-600 Soldiers)	Command Sergeant Major (CSM)	Lieutenant Colonel (LTC)
Brigade (3 or more Battalions) (3,000-5,000 Soldiers)	Command Sergeant Major (CSM)	Colonel (COL)
Division (3 Brigades) (10,000-18,000 Soldiers)	Command Sergeant Major (CSM)	Major General (MG)

Guide to Army Command Structure

INDEX

ABOUT THE AUTHORS

Lynn Vincent is the *New York Times* bestselling writer of eleven nonfiction books with more than 14 million copies in print. She lives in the mountains east of San Diego with Danny, her husband of twenty-eight years, and their three Labrador retrievers. A U.S. Navy veteran, Lynn was on duty at Naval Air Station Sigonella, Sicily, when intelligence sources reported that Libyan dictator Muammar Gaddafi was launching a missile strike against U.S. bases there. Lynn was ordered to take cover under a desk, which she gladly did. Gaddafi missed.

Roger T. Hill left the U.S. Army to work at the Georgia Tech Research Institute, where he supported various security-focused research and development initiatives. Roger currently works for Utility, Inc., where his team provides the smartest police body-camera technology in the world. Roger lives in Atlanta with his two beautiful twins, Michael and Emma. Fly-fishing, hiking, and microbrews are a few of his favorite North Georgia pastimes. Roger is also active in his support for the following nonprofits: the Atlanta Dream Center, whose mission is to reach, rescue, and restore the homeless, those who are commercially sexually exploited, and at-risk underprivileged children; the King's Treasure Box Ministries, helping heal the victims of child abuse; CBN's Superbook, bringing the Bible to the children of the world; the Refuge Foundation, providing renewal, revitalization, and recalibration for leaders of churches and nonprofits; the Schenck School, building solid educational foundations for students with dyslexia; United American Patriots, providing troops accused of war crimes with legal defense services at no cost; Warrior 2 Citizen, helping veterans and their families heal from the unseen wounds of war; and Hire Heroes USA, empowering veterans and spouses to succeed in the in the civilian workforce.